THE
IMPOSSIBLE
DREAM

Circa 1966. Three haircuts and the truth.

THE
IMPOSSIBLE
DREAM

THE STORY OF SCOTT WALKER
AND THE WALKER BROTHERS

ANTHONY REYNOLDS

THE **IMPOSSIBLE DREAM**
THE STORY OF SCOTT WALKER AND THE WALKER BROTHERS
ANTHONY REYNOLDS

For Margaret

A GENUINE JAWBONE BOOK
First edition 2009
Published in the UK and the USA by
Jawbone Press
2a Union Court
20-22 Union Road
London SW4 6JP
England
www.jawbonepress.com

ISBN: 978-1-906002-25-1

EDITOR: Robert Webb
DESIGN: Paul Cooper Design

Origination and print by Regent Publishing Services Limited

09 10 11 12 13 5 4 3 2 1

CONTENTS

ABOVE Regents Park, 1965. "It all looked very strange to me," recalled John.
"Not at all like California! [There was] white stuff on the ground. Snow!"
ABOVE RIGHT John would work out James Brown-inspired routines for some of
the set – seen here frugging wildly to 'Land Of A Thousand Dances'.
RIGHT A rare shot of the group in original 'power trio' mode. With success,
John and Scott would both give up their guitars for live and television
performances, while Gary would be supplemented by another drummer.

ABOVE The young girls understood: John and the Walkers' touring band The Quotations, preaching to the converted, 1965.

ABOVE RIGHT Gary in full swing on one of the Walkers' first UK tours. He is flanked by two members of The Quotations: Jimmy Pritchard is on drums and Graham Alexander on bass.

RIGHT Gary: "There were so many television shows. Pop shows, where we came over as a very romantic, moody type of group."

LEFT The classic image of solo Scott.
RIGHT Scott as peroxide pop candy, Japan 1968.
BELOW A late-period television appearance.

ABOVE FAR LEFT Solo Gary on the eve of 'You Don't Love Me'. "You know, I'm always thinking I think too much."
ABOVE LEFT Solo John: "My pet bitch is that I'm compared to Engel."
LEFT Backstage, pre show. Scott and Gary deal with two equally important components: set-list and hair.
ABOVE Scott with sometime girlfriend, the model Irene Dunford, circa 1967.

BELOW LEFT "The horror, the horror..." Scott at the height of his fame, 1967.
LEFT Left to right: engineer Peter Grant, producer Johnny Franz (background), and Scott Engel. *Scott 4* sessions, Olympic studios, 1969.
RIGHT The drinking years. A lost Scott with the ever-present glass of Scotch, circa 1974.
BELOW Working through songs for the 'comeback' album, *No Regrets*, 517 New Kings Road, London, 1975.

LEFT Scott in healthy diet mode, circa 1975.
ABOVE "The Walkers were the drunkest group ever," admitted Scott. By the end of the 70s, both Gary and Scott had a hold on their drinking habits. John did not manage to do so until the 90s.

... Is A Cabaret

The Walker Brothers' very last tour was the last time that Scott Walker sang live on stage. But the setting hardly seemed to fit such a historic pop occasion. The final venues graced by the gold and honeyed fire of John and Scott Walker's combined voices were not symphonic halls, ornate theatres, or even art centres. One of the biggest groups of the 60s found themselves repaying dues they had surely long since settled. Due to bad timing, misguided judgment, and contractual obligation, The Walker Brothers, fronted by one of the most original singer-songwriters of the 20th century, were finally reduced, in the British summer of 1978, to playing cabaret gigs at regional supper clubs.

Since the mid 60s, The Walker Brothers had been responsible for some of the most beautiful, successful, perverse, accessible, obtuse, and plain weird pop music ever made. A year before this final tour, they had completed *Nite Flights*, an album that would in time be seen as harbouring some of the most seminal and influential songs of the 70s. The album drew on such diverse influences as cocaine psychosis, the occult, contemporary French philosophy, David Bowie and Brian Eno, a love of Dutch brothels, and Krzysztof Penderecki's seminal 'Threnody To The Victims Of Hiroshima'.

In the wake of *Nite Flights*, the Walkers' next step should have been at least silence – if only to be true to the law of evolution that states that once something has graduated from sea to land, it does not go back. Yet by the ragged arse-end of the 70s, due to some unnamable freakish fluke, they found themselves touring through a weird and profoundly inappropriate hinterland.

Such an aberration was especially painful for their lead singer, who had only now begun to find himself as a writer again after almost a decade of enforced limbo.

In 1978, at Birmingham's Night Out club, you got a complimentary portion of chicken and chips with your ticket to the show plus a flagon of beer that was refilled free throughout the act. The audience was made up of a nondescript conglomerate of hardcore fans and casual punters – regulars who came every week to such venues, no matter who was on the bill.

The Walkers' tour was poorly advertised. As a fan, you knew about tonight either because of the modest advert in the local rag, through simple word of mouth, or because you subscribed to one of the dwindling photocopied Walker newsletters that still circulated erratically throughout the worldwide network of fans. As such, you could purchase a ticket well in advance, and although you couldn't choose whom you'd share your table with, it was a good seat nonetheless: not too far from the stage, with a clear enough view through the banks of cigarette smoke and chatter.

There was little in the way of souvenirs on sale in the foyer as you'd come in: merely a copy of their *No Regrets* album – both vinyl and cassette formats, on display behind a glass cabinet by the cloakroom. That was it. As a veteran of previous Walker tours, it struck you that this was one of the first without a programme. And they had released another two albums since 1976's *No Regrets* – the more sophisticated and refined MOR of *Lines* and the patchy weirdness of the David Bowie-influenced *Nite Flights*. Yet there was no sign of either album on sale.

You got the feeling that this tour wasn't as well organised as it could have been. It even said "Live From America – The Fabulous Walker Brothers" on the board outside the club. What was that about? Even the most casual fan knew that Scott and Gary were long-time residents of London.

This was the kind of club at which the Walkers now played residencies, usually week-long stints where they employed the house band at each venue. Scott had always loathed the travelling that regular touring entailed. By playing live this way it meant that the Walkers were in one place long enough to provide the punters with ample enough opportunity to come to them. The mountain would go to Mohammed. There was also the added advantage that John, Gary, and Scott didn't have to ferry a road crew and musicians around.

Maintaining a regular band had always been an unholy hassle, and the Walkers themselves had long ago given up any idea of playing as a trio. They could keep costs to a minimum by playing residencies in budget venues such as Bunny's of Cleethorpes, Fagin's of Manchester, and Birmingham's Night Out, leaving enough profit to make the whole ordeal just about viable. For some, however, this was not necessarily bearable. The main thing was that Scott Walker did not have to endure the ridiculous amounts of driving that most tours entailed. Glasgow one night; Brighton the next. Scott had outgrown that life in the 60s.

The 60s. For one summer back then, The Walker Brothers had been even bigger than The Rolling Stones and The Beatles. True to this astonishing past, much of the audience at that Birmingham club in 1978 were anticipating the return of 'The Blond Beatles' and their full armada of hits: 'My Ship Is Coming In', 'Make It Easy On Yourself', 'The Sun Ain't Gonna Shine Anymore'. No one there could have known that Scott had vowed privately never to sing those songs again, and you had even less chance at guessing his reasons why.

Before the headliners apeared there were warm-up acts. Perhaps a comedian, or maybe some local lads playing a covers set. A few instrumentals by the ropey-sounding house band. All introduced by a cheesy MC through the barely adequate PA system. And then, before you knew, it there they were. The Walker Brothers! Close enough to touch if you reached out, although such a display of fanaticism seemed oddly inappropriate.

Still, the Walkers appeared just like they did on the cover of the album in the foyer. They hadn't changed that much – they were still American-looking. Fit and tanned with wavy, blow-dried hair. The dress was casual. Rangy Scott looked youthful in a Lacoste t-shirt and denim combo. Ever-eccentric Gary sported a houndstooth jacket over a skinny-ribbed Boy Scouts Of America shirt. John, always a tad more attentive of his appearance than the others, was dressed slightly more smartly. Denim combo, but with a neatly pressed shirt – dapper, but still casual, as befitted the show.

Gary had walked on first, smiling his lottery-winner's smile and waving to a psyched crowd before settling himself behind the drum kit. And then came John and Scott, entering stage left simultaneously, still looking so alike that they could pass for actual siblings. John grinned that movie-star grin, while Scott, in contrast, appeared almost to be grimacing beneath his aviator shades. Funnily, by the end of the week, Scott and John still came on together, but neither would be smiling, and they'd enter from opposite sides of the stage.

The band kicked in immediately, but it was apparent that something wasn't right. The sound balance was skewed and the band was out of tune, or something. The timing was off, too, a problem not helped by having two drummers up there – a precautionary measure for Gary's lack of chops. The first number was rubbish, frankly, and immediately afterward, John apologised to the audience, explaining that there hadn't been enough time to rehearse, or tune up, or somesuch. Scott appeared pained, while grinning Gary, looking left to right and back again in rapid succession, tried to laugh it off. This pretty much set a standard for the rest of the evening, but despite the technical hitches, there was a good buzz in the air. To the majority of the audience, this group stood for something far beyond a one-night stand.

By a few songs in, the atmosphere relaxed and women began shouting out requests. Then someone called for 'Joanna', one of Scott's biggest solo hits. His reaction was ... no acknowledgement whatsoever. He didn't even dignify the call with a response. He just blanked it. And then the awkward atmosphere was banished as the house band started up again.

The set was mostly made up of material from *No Regrets* and *Lines*. There were a few hits from the 60s, but nothing from John or Scott's solo records and not a whiff of 'The Sun Ain't Gonna Shine Anymore', not even as part of a medley. The vibe was loose; it was like they were busking it. Laidback and low-key, if not quite funky. There was none of the hysteria of the 60s – no riots, police escorts, hospitalisations ... none of the insane fervour of youth.

For Scott, at least, this must have been some cold comfort. But it was never enough.

As the seven-day residency ground on, the set got tighter, but Scott in particular appeared to become more pissed off and more tired. By mid-week, he and John were regularly disappearing backstage, mid-set, presumably for refreshments, leaving Gary to hold the fort.

One night, alone in the spotlight, Gary dug in bravely with a drum solo: 'Fanfare For The Common Man'. By the time he'd exhausted his chops, though, the singers still hadn't returned. Ever the pro, he grabbed a mic, left of the drumkit, and took a jaunty stroll through the audience. "Anyone got a birthday tonight?" he called in that distinctive, nasally Jerry Lewis-like voice. "It's great to be in Cleethorpes!" he wailed.

On one occasion, he gave the audience a detailed description of his day at the races from the afternoon before. Despite Gary's goofy, nerdish charm, the audience eventually broke into slow handclapping. Through the cigarette and cigar smoke, you could see Gary's smile freezing on his face as a panic slowly set in beneath his thinning perm. For a moment, he stood there in the pregnant air, smile spreading like shit on a windscreen, a rabbit boy frozen in the spotlights. After what seemed like an eternity, Scott bounded back on, gazelle-like, smiling merrily. Ignoring the audience and muttering into Gary's ear, he patted the hapless drummer on the back, the show loped back into gear, and John sloped on soon after. Gary was the only one who really connected with the audience, and by the end of the week, it seemed that John and Scott weren't even connecting with each other. The singing was always great and the band much tighter by then, but you got the feeling that their hearts weren't in it. Somewhere, alimony and rent had to be paid. By the week's end, John and Scott were going through the motions.

Some of the real hardcore fans thought it odd that nothing from the latest album was featured. Yet it's hard to see how the gorgeous nightmare modulations of 'The Electrician' or 'Den Haague' would have slotted in among affable fodder like 'Have You Seen My Baby' and 'Many Rivers To Cross' while the chain-smoking, Babycham and beer-guzzling audience chowed down on their chicken in a basket.

Some of these same fans were disappointed when, on the last night, after making ready with the autograph books and scuttling backstage, they were brutally informed by the club's bouncers: "No fucking way are you going backstage to see these fellas! They don't want to see you! It's not I'm telling you that you can't go back, *they're* telling us to tell you that you can't go back."

No one knew then that these would be the last live shows The Walker Brothers would ever perform. Such a finale seems sad and tawdry when compared to the massive artistic and commercial heights they had attained at their peak during the mid-to-late 60s, but in a perverse way it was apt.

The Walker Brothers were an anomaly. John, Scott, and Gary should not have existed together as a group in the first place, much less have been so massively successful. The Walker Brothers were a seductive and pretty paradox, a quixotic three-headed beast that was almost too exotic for the very climate it in which it briefly thrived.

CHAPTER 1

THE BIRTH OF THE BLUES

There are three sides to every story. My side, your side, and the truth.

Robert Evans, film producer (1994)

As a hit group, The Walker Brothers did not come together overnight. They assembled piecemeal, over time, through a series of casual decisions and freakish luck, both good and bad. As with so many bands, groups, movements, and schools of thought, there is no authentically exact moment of Immaculate Conception.

The processes of willpower, time, space, and luck that would eventually manifest in the all-conquering melancholic beauty of 'The Sun Ain't Gonna Shine Anymore' are liquid and indistinct. It is a misty, shifting history where the opening credits are missing frames, lacking in continuity and staggered by time-lapse. Everyone involved remembers things differently.

John Joseph Maus was born in New York on November 12 1943. He was the only Walker Brother to have a blood sibling: sister Judy, two years his senior. In the summer of 1948, the Maus clan moved to California, where young Johnny forged an immediate and lifelong rapport with the sun, sea, and the surfboard. Naturally athletic, he developed a parallel passion for baseball, becoming a junior star centrefield player. A violent knee injury shortly before his 12th year caused a premature retirement.

John: "At school, I was Mr Athlete. I took everything that made you move. I was what they called 'an end' when we played football. That's the position where you don't get hit. Only one day I did. The guy kicked me straight up into the air, and when I came down I had one tooth knocked behind the other, what felt like a broken back, and a permanent knee injury that still bugs me in the cold weather."

Immobilised by a plaster cast, John found his energy imploded. Confined to the indoors, the confident pre-pubescent applied his energies to music, learning acoustic guitar, saxophone, clarinet, and violin. Although he would abandon the violin first, he would credit this brief fling to a lifelong love of strings. "If Mantovani comes on TV or radio at home," Maus would josh, "no one moves!"

Every musician, no matter their level of 'talent' or point of focus, is said to have a 'first instrument' – the one apart from all others for which they feel the greatest affinity. For Elvis Presley, it was the piano. For John, newly enraptured by Chuck Berry's 'Maybellene', it would be the electric guitar.

Like so many nameless others, as Maus came into his teens, he took on various part-time jobs in order to buy his very own Fender Stratocaster, rescued from a local pawnshop. It was the beginning of a love affair that would endure throughout his entire life.

As if these activities were not enough, John had also begun a part-time career as a child actor, his thick, blond bowl-cut and sun-freckled complexion often casting him in the role of a Huckleberry Finn type. "I had a fringe right down to my nose and I learnt how to deal with the 'are you a boy or girl?' routine at a very early age," said Maus. "They always cast me as a country kid with freckles – I was revolting."

In a scenario straight out of Hollywood, both literally and figuratively, it was during this period as a child star that John first met the similarly blond Scotty Engel. Engel had accompanied best friend John Stewart to a television audition that the 14-year-old Maus was also attending. Stewart did not get the gig, but Maus and Engel did. Scott lucked into a walk-on part, while Maus attained the giddy heights of a speaking role in the production. It was a befitting omen that on this occasion the two did not particularly get on. Both were united in their passion for music, however, enthusiastically showing each other new chord shapes on the guitar while they waited in breaks between filming. After the show they drifted apart, with no knowledge of the mutual star-crossed destiny that awaited them.

The rich, southern California air of the mid-to-late 50s was ripe with musical talent. Moving up through the classes of Inglewood High, and one year ahead of John, were future Beach Boy legends Brian Wilson and Al Jardine, as well as sometime Beach Boy David Marks.

"Marks lived across the street from the Wilson brothers, and I was giving him guitar lessons," recalled Maus. "Mark said, 'I've got a friend across the street who wants to learn to play some more guitar. Can you help him out?' It was Carl Wilson. So I started to teach Carl to play. I didn't realise that Brian had been working on the thing for The Beach Boys, and it turns out that one of the things I taught Carl, Brian used to write his first song 'Surfer Girl'."

Carl Wilson confirmed the story. "The funny thing was that [John's] house was almost directly across the street from the studio. It was a real casual thing. He had a Fender Stratocaster that I thought was fantastic, and we used to sit and jam. ... My style was a combination of John Maus, Dick Dale, and Chuck Berry."

An early incarnation of The Beach Boys would also rehearse in that same humble garage, to the displeasure of Maus's parents. Mr and Mrs Maus put aside the occasional noisy disturbance from the garage and instead encouraged their little John'n'Judy to form an act of their own. Joined by a rhythm section and known variously as Judy & The Gents and The John & Judy Four, the act became a 'dance band' playing at low-key happenings at hotels, beach parties, and barbeques. This slightly bland, blond combo were popular with pretty much everyone who encountered them. Everyone that is apart from local hustler and self-proclaimed genius Kim Fowley.

"My first contact with any of the Brothers was with John when he was working with Judy – The John'n'Judy Duo or something – and I promoted them at some teenage nightclub," sneers Fowley. "They turned up and did their sister and brother act with some anonymous drummer. And that's when I first saw John.

"He had the personality of a dry wall, she talked too much, and the drummer was forgettable ... they were adequate. And that's the first time I ever saw them.

"Judy was a nice person in a pushy sort of way. They were a kind of band you'd see at a teenage fair or with people who weren't on 'the inside'. They were like the 'C' team.

"He was like a poor man's Jan and Dean, a blond guy who could play a stringed instrument. He looked good."

In 1960, the Maus family moved again, this time to LA where, despite the bitter indifference they aroused in hipsters like Fowley, Judy and John – with John now a strikingly handsome 16 – continued to perform at frat parties and dance halls, wedding receptions and balls. Beyond these transient one-night stands, they were also now beginning to make tentative inroads into the murky world of demo recording and budget studios.

It was while doggedly flogging their brother-and-sister act that John and Judy met the man who would become The Walker Brothers' first drummer, Albert Schneider.

Albert, aka Tiny Rogers, was a fellow student at El Camino High and already making a successful living as a drummer for hire, gigging solidly and appearing on local television shows. He was a burly, dark-haired figure in contrast to the wiry Maus, and the origins of his nickname were obvious while those of his adopted surname were more obtuse. "I stuttered worse then and could not say my regular last name," Schneider told author Steve McPartland. "So when they would hold a mic in front of us for interviews on television shows, I had to say something that was comfortable. My nickname was Tiny and I played Rogers drums, so instead of Tiny Schneider I said my name was Tiny Rogers, because it was much easier to say."

The group continued the rounds as before, a more solid proposition with the rock steady and propulsive Tiny in the engine room. Increasingly they were directing their energy and focus toward recording, resulting in further low-key short-term provincial record deals. This was nothing special, according to Fowley. "Everybody had a single. You could make a single for under $100 and press it up for another $100. It was like getting a pair of socks or something."

The results of these humble releases were negligible and they met with varying shades of indifference. But this would not have caused John particular grief. Noticeably good looking, tall, and athletic, he stood out even in a town overcrowded with such statistics. Teenagers were becoming a new world power, and John was thriving in a climate of deep sunshine, constant music, and romance. He had recently begun dating Kathy Young – who would soon have a hit with 'A Thousand Stars In The Sky'.

The only thing that really bugged Maus was his name. It was pronounced 'Moss', but even those without Tiny's unfortunate impediment had problems with it. By the time he was 19, professionally at least he was calling himself Walker.

It has never been convincingly established why he chose the name Walker, although in a 1970 interview Maus claimed it was an anglicisation of his mother's Austrian maiden name – something that Tiny now confirms. Whatever the reason, it was a choice that would profoundly affect another young American who, in all innocence during that summer of 1963, was never more than a few blocks away from a name-change that would signify a whole new destiny.

Scott Walker was born as Noel Scott Engel on January 9 1943, in the town of Hamilton, Ohio. His father, Noel Walter Engel, had enjoyed a successful career in the Navy and was now working as a geologist for the Superior Oil Company. It was a prestigious, well-paid job that took him all over the vast country, which meant constant relocating for the Engel trio. Scott and his mother, Elizabeth Marie, moved where Noel's job dictated, so the young boy was never at any one school for long enough to make steady friends. Like many an only child, Scott learned to entertain himself at an early age, developing a love of the outdoors, music, and cinema. "I just didn't associate with people," he would reminisce as a man, many years later. "I had this tremendous thing for seeing movies, then dashing home and trying to re-enact the hero's part in front of a mirror."

By the time Scott was seven, his parents had divorced and he and his mother relocated to Denver, Colorado. Within three years they would move again to New York. Such a nomadic childhood can play havoc with the psychology of a young mind. When asked years later what the idea of home meant to him, Scott replied: "I gave up on this desire years ago. It's impossible." Nonetheless, his early struggle would contribute much to his future muse. And by 1956, music was becoming Scott's main obsession.

"I did love people like Frankie Lymon, Johnny Ace, and Elvis," Scott recalled in the mid 90s, still sounding enthused. "Particularly Elvis. Like a lot of kids in the 50s I was just blown away by those Sun recordings and the whole Elvis thing at the time. It was the inspiration to get into rock'n'roll. I loved Johnny Ace ... mainly doo-wop records were what I liked in those days. The Flamingos – the greatest doo-wop band. The first record I ever bought was Frankie Lymon's 'Why Do Fools Fall In Love'. What a great singer!"

He was blessed and cursed with a voice that people loved to hear, with a sound and style but a few blocks away from Frankie Lymon's himself. Noel evolved from fan to performer, becoming 'Scotty Engel, Baritone from Denver'. In the process, he came temporarily under the wing of one of the peripheral members of the Rat Pack – the pejoratively-named association of drinking buddies that revolved around Frank Sinatra, Dean Martin, and Sammy Davis Jr. The one who looked out for Scotty was Eddie Fisher, movie star (and husband of Elizabeth Taylor).

"I sang at a luncheon in Palm Springs and Eddie Fisher was there," stated Scott, "and he kind of adopted me. He took me on a tour of 15, 16 TV shows with him, but then he got burned by Liz Taylor and my deal fell through."

American Fan Club Magazine, 1957: "In today's wide-open recording race, even the lollipop set has its own particular hero. He's Scott Engel, 13, who still likes his model airplanes but is just discovering girls. Scott, who gathered his own fan clubs while appearing as star of George Scheck's *Star Time* on ABC-TV, belts out his first recording in a big voice. Appropriately, his RKO-Unique platter is entitled 'When Is A Boy A Man'. Scott himself has been doing a man-sized job ever since he was five, when he simultaneously learned to ride a horse, sing a song, and act his first role in a Texas production of *Ten Nights In A Barroom*. He acquired a more dignified credit on Broadway. His first role was in *Plain And Fancy* followed by *Pipe Dream*.

"While still calling Denver his home, he shares a New York apartment with his mother. Scott's room is filled with model aircraft and cars he has assembled, and drawings he has made. He took to his first song-plugging tour heartily. It afforded him not only an opportunity to meet disc jockeys, but also to get out to visit friends in Ohio who had a big farm. Scott made the most of it. His one objection to Manhattan is: 'It's no place to own a dog, ride a horse, or shoot a gun. I'm the outdoor type.'"

Yet another gig that Scott fell into was that of demo singer. At inexpensive New York recording studios, Scotty would record demonstration versions of new songs, the publishers of whom would then submit the still warm acetate to managers and labels in the hope that an Elvis, a Lymon, or even a Fabian would record them properly. He had school to consider alongside his various showbiz endeavours, but as far as this particular gig went, the singing surrogate was under no pressure. He did it mostly for the craic.

"It was never really that I had to record those demos," confirmed Scott. "The point is that I went to various schools and would sing in various choirs, and when people would want to cut covers of standards, or whatever, they'd pick me. It wasn't anything I had to do, or anything serious. In fact, I didn't do any serious singing before I started The Walker Brothers. I was a musician before that. But I never did that kind of [early] stuff for money. It was just for kicks.

"I was singing for many years – I was no Sammy Davis Jr, but I'd sing ... Stop ... Drop it again... ."

"The New Singers Of 1958!" announced *TV/Radio Mirror*. "Among the interesting young singers who have made new records are Frankie Avalon and Scott Engel, two well-trained teenage veterans who have been in show business since childhood. In *TV/Radio Mirror*'s 1957 round-up of new recording stars, 13-year-old Scott Engel was entered as The Dreamboat For The Lollipop Set. In his first recording for a minor label, he belted out a ditty titled 'When Is A Boy A Man?'.

"Appropriately, this season he answered his own question by appearing on the *Eddie Fisher Show* to introduce his new Orbit platter, 'The Livin' End' and 'Good For Nothin''."

In a year, Scott had shot up faster than a blond rocket, growing four inches (but gaining only two pounds), and he was ready to pitch for full-scale popularity. At 16, Scott and mom relocated again, moving to California to be closer to Ms Engel's parents. By now sporting a thick James Dean hairdo, Scott enrolled at Hollywood High. As a member of the orchestra, he would discover his 'first instrument'.

Scott: "When I got to Hollywood and to high school, there I got kicked out of about five schools [for] vandalism and all kinds of things – with these weird friends of mine. We all ended up in the same schools. Then you do become outside, and I was outside constantly in that situation. You are like Holden Caulfield – this character in J.D. Salinger's *Catcher In The Rye* book. This famous American character that doesn't fit in. So I started then.

"Finally, another way I got into this business was that my mother had to start paying for me to go to school – because there were no other free schools that I could go to, because I ran out of schools. This one school I went to was a professional school. They had kids who were in movies ... or on television shows, and it was a paying school – one of the places left. So, I met a lot of guys who were starting to play then.

"I sort of fell into it. ... Everyone else started on guitars, so somebody needs a bass player. ... One of my great idols in those days was a bass player called Ray Brown – wonderful bass player. I took some lessons from ... Marty Budwood, who was a very famous West Coast jazz player. He played with Howard Rumsey and I played a little in high school."

Scott was a liquid presence within the local social scene, choosing his friends carefully, and never a boy uncomfortable in solitude. Playing music with others was a sublime way of interacting with people while bypassing the need for verbal intimacy. During this period, Scott would spread his talent enthusiastically, playing bass in a local instrumental surf combo called The Routers and forming a group with best friend John Stewart, The Dalton Brothers.

John: "The Dalton Brothers ... was Scott and another fellow named John Stewart. In those days the cool thing was to hang around in Hollywood, go drink coffee in all the cool places, and meet people who were making records. People used to hang out with, like, Jack Nitzsche and Phil Spector and Scott and John Stewart and myself and Dobie Gray. That was what we did – we hung out. Everybody had some kind of input with music but no vast success. It was just the early 60s and we were just hanging around. It was 1961 or 1962. All I know is that The Dalton Brothers made a couple of records in that period. They came and went like everybody else."

P.J. Proby: "I had known about Scott long before I ever met him. Years and years, cos he had been signed to Liberty records where my best friend Eddie Cochran was signed. But I didn't meet Scott until '63 when he came to the house for some music.

"John Stewart and Scott Engel came to my house in LA in 1963. They were looking for material, and they were called The Dalton Brothers. I played 'em about 15 songs, and 'I Only Came To Dance With You' is the one they took.

"When I first heard their recording of the song I loved it. I thought it was great. I always thought Scott had an excellent voice. He always sounded 15, 20 years older than he was."

With The Dalton Brothers on the back burner, Scott began to concentrate on his bass playing in The Routers. He wasn't the most gregarious kid on the block. Kim Fowley says: "As far as Scott Engel is concerned, I never ran into him in LA; I saw his pictures as a member of The Routers, and he had that curvature-of-the-spine/praying mantis look." Inevitably, Scott soon drifted once more into Maus's orbit.

John: "Scott and I played in different bands at the same period. There was a club called Pandora's Box [that] had different groups. ... I had the house band. Scott came to play with The Routers. The band I was in, the musicians weren't the greatest. I was progressing and they weren't. Scott called me up one day and said, 'You need a bass player!' I said, 'Boy, you've got that right!' He wanted to play with different people and so did I – that's how we started. We just got together, no plan. It was just something to do."

John and Scott would play together when it suited, when it was fun, as it was cool – but there was no firm commitment. Outside of their shared musical activities, the relationship had little context, and when they weren't playing together they would invariably lose touch. It would be a much older man who would be responsible for bringing the two young 'Brothers' together again.

Vocalist John Abohosh – aka Donnie Brooks, aka 'The World's Oldest Teenager', aka 'Mr Personality' – had scored a nationwide smash with 'Mission Bell' in late 1960. But despite almost ten follow-up singles he was failing to impregnate the charts again. Three years after what would be his only hit single, Donnie was doing OK, appearing in various teen-market bubblegum flicks, and finding himself fully booked on the live circuit. Keeping busy. As a professional entertainer and a name, Donnie rarely had need of a regular band, and an integral part of his contract with any venue that wanted him was that the booker provided the musicians.

So it was that one night during the Hollywood fall of 1963, John Walker and Scott Engel played together once more, as part of Donnie Brooks's backing band. The drummer was their old friend Tiny Rogers. "I was working with Donnie on and off, depending on the gigs that were available. I don't recall exactly how John and I ended up working behind Donnie. I think Donnie knew both John and Judy before he knew me. It was a time when everybody kinda knew everybody or heard about you from someone in the biz. It was a very small world of rock'n'roll musicians working this area."

John: "Donnie Brooks called up and said would I play guitar with him for an audition. I said 'Who's playing bass?' He said Scott. So, we got a lot more serious about being musicians. Scott had owned a Fender Showman amp and I had every gadget money could buy. We were both kinda flash. But when he rolled into the gig, he impressed me. He had the most basic bass amp you can get. I thought, 'Wow, he's gotten serious.' I had this '59 Twin Amp, with nothing on it, and we looked at each other and thought, 'Hmm, something's changed.'"

Following the gig with Donnie, Scott joined John & Judy for the usual circuit of frat nights and airport lounges. During a gig at a bowling alley, Scott stepped into what was then a rare role: a singing bass player. John had temporarily lost his voice, so Scott subbed for him. It made little impression, least of all on Engel, who confessed: "The club owner groaned at the idea – I was no knockout."

P.J. Proby thought that Scott as singer should have been the norm. "John was more the working musician. But none of 'em were any good on any instrument," he says. "The best thing they had was Scott's voice – which wasn't being used."

It was also during this period, at a show on November 30 1963 at The Trolley-Ho! Nitespot, that John & The Judy Four became The Walker Family. The 'Family' tag was almost certainly down to Judy, John, and Scott's shared Nordic appearance.

As to why they became the Walker Family as opposed to the Engel Family, John reasonably explained: "No one else's name fit as a name for the group, so we went with Walker." Tiny adds: "Yeah, I believe that's the first time they used the name. They all did look incredibly alike."

The Walker Family toured LA with Donnie Brooks, both as a support act and as his backing band. Tiny explains the improvisatory life of the jobbing musician. "Behind Donnie, we played some hotels in the heart of Hollywood. When we weren't working behind Donnie, we would get whatever gigs that we could. ... John and Judy worked as much as they could and Scott wasn't on all of them. There was a number of bass players – whoever was available."

While Scott did enjoy the John & Judy experience, he was not particularly enamoured of 'Mr Personality', aka Brooks. Scott's lack of enthusiasm for the Brooks gigs may explain, in part, how he acquired an underage taste for liquor at this time.

Jonathan Young, a regular on the scene, recalled: "They played the Whisky-A-Go-Go with Donnie Brooks. When I hung out at the Whisky, I noticed that Scott had a bit of fondness for booze."

Scott would spend as much time as he could on other projects, writing in collaboration with John Stewart for the vocalist Margie Day and taking session work when he could. (One of the singles Scott and Stewart were involved with around this time was Day's 'Have I Lost My Touch'/'Tell Me In The Sunlight', a very Spector-sounding record that credits Engel & Stuart [sic] as producers and writers.)

"I was working as a session musician at Gold Star, where Phil [Spector] made his records," recalled Scott. "I knew Larry Levine and all the guys in his team. I was just a kid at the time, and Larry knew that I loved the records Phil made.

"So at night he let me into the studio on the sly to play me the new songs before they were released. That's how I was the first to hear the Christmas album [*A Christmas Gift For You*]. But I never played on any of his records."

The time that he spent at the studios and Spector's work itself made a powerful impression on the young man. Spector's revolutionary methods would influence much of Walker's work throughout the next decade. At the same time, Scott was unaware that musicians in the UK – particularly drummers – were lifting chops from Spector's records. Hal Blaine, drummer of Spector's Wrecking Crew rhythm section, was rapidly becoming a major musical influence across the sea. Some of these besotted English musicians would come to play on some of the Walkers' greatest records. But this was all far off in some unknown future.

Back in the balmy LA winter of 1963, the Walker Family boys were about to lose their sister. "John and I went to do some other gigs and it was too expensive for them to hire Judy. They could only hire three people," explained Scott, unaware at the time that this would mark the next crucial step in Walker Brothers history. "They hired me, John, and the drummer. We became a trio."

Following Judy's departure, they called themselves The Walker Brothers Trio. John: "We wanted to sound like some hip nightclub act." They moved on, signing with Chuck Gringer at the Bob Leonard Artists Agency at the RCA building.

Such a prestigious contact ensured that the trio rarely had a night off. Tiny and John were happy to follow the musician's traditional lifestyle of working and sleeping late, but Scott added to his already exhausting schedule by enrolling at the Chouinard Art Institute, in December 1963.

Tiny: "John and I were just a couple of flaky musicians, hanging out in the day and playing at night. Scott was pretty laidback. It was like he didn't really care, but he was doing it, you know? I believe he was going to art school, but he never talked to me much about it, and John never talked about it a whole lot. I said once, 'What does Scott do during the day?' – or we were talking about rehearsals or something like that – and the response was, 'He's in school,' something about art school. It never really came up a whole lot."

Scott: "It was a very exciting time. I was up 'til four in the morning every night. I was doing these four or five-hour sets with fifteen-minute breaks in between. After a while I couldn't go to school in the daytime. It was killing me, so I chose music."

Scott's 20-hour days couldn't continue indefinitely. He quit art school, but the time he did spend there would set a pattern for the next few years of his life. He would involve himself in academic pursuits, both officially and auto-didactically, for the next few decades, even at the height of his success. It seems he would make occasional attempts to share these interests with his immediate colleagues of the time, eliciting varying degrees of indifference, which perhaps goes some way to explain his 'reticent' character.

During this period, Scott was also developing a passion for MOR singers such as Bobby Darin and Jack Jones. "He was quite affected when Bobby Darin came out," says Tiny. "Bobby started to do what I would call his Caucasian Sammy Davis Jr type of routine. He did everything ... he acted, he danced, and every move was choreographed and he really worked at it. ... I think, secretly, that's what Scott really wanted to do. He wanted to be that type of cabaret entertainer."

Meanwhile, on the opposite point of the compass, Scott had a parallel interest that, while infinitely cooler than his passion for prematurely middle-aged crooners, would probably have left Tiny and John just as nonplussed.

Scott: "I used to go and see a lot of movies – that escapism is a big thing if you're an only child. European filmmakers fascinated me. I liked all the directors from the 60s and 50s – European directors mainly. I used to go to these art cinemas on Wilshire Boulevard and watch Bergman or Fellini or Bresson. It was like it was in my blood, y'know? When I was 16, 17, I became obsessed by European directors and European music. ... I had an enormous desire for something that was not American, for something that nobody in my environment really understood.

"I was a kid from Southern California who from a very early age had just loved watching *Lola Montès* and films like that. I used to watch the movie *The Rocking Horse Winner*, an English film, and I was just fascinated. I must have been very young when I had seen this, and it had such a dream-like quality that the American things didn't have for me."

Following these private rituals of popcorn and subtitles in the dark, Scott would rejoin his buddies at the other end of the aesthetic spectrum. Gigging exhaustively around the golden miles between Doheny Drive in the East and Laurel Canyon in the West, the trio continued to pay their dues on Sunset Boulevard, backing 'Mr Personality' in some of the worst dives around.

Scott: "We had to do 20 minutes before this fool [Brooks] ... who used to come out and do what seemed like an eternity of a nightclub act, and we were backing him. We would do 20 minutes before he came on every evening, as a trio." Although The Walker Trio had a great agent and were working regularly, it could not sustain their interest forever. Scott and, to a lesser extent, John and Tiny would not be content to see out their days as mere guns for hire. Although they were doing good, they could always do better. The life of the bar band musician was ultimately unfulfilling.

P.J. Proby: "I wouldn't have sung for a living in the places that Scott and them were singing in. As far as I'm concerned, those places weren't good enough. I played nightclubs. They were playing bowling alleys and such, working every night of the week and hardly getting any money. Fuck that!"

CHAPTER 2

LA TANGO

Now the other clubs run only half-filled or empty while the walls of the Whisky-A-Go-Go shake and swell from five times their comfortable capacity. Is it nicer? Better? Cheaper? No man, it's in. Go. Go.

Peter Bogdanovich, director, actor, and writer (1975)

The downtown LA of 1963 finally saw the previous decade giving it up for the new. Three years in, and only now were the 50s submitting to the 60s. It was a time of powerful change. The exclusively adult clubs were dying off and in their place hipper, brighter, younger scenes were blooming and budding. Rock'n'roll demanded its due. The resulting riptide had the Walkers floundering.

As essentially hip, bright, and young as the individual Walkers were, this wasn't apparent from their act. As they went through the motions at the Beverly Cavern on Beverly Boulevard, it was obvious that they were not keeping up with the profound developments that were happening all around them. Musically, they were treading water, neither going forward, nor back, unable to locate the ladder to the next level, let alone climb it.

Tiny Rogers sets the scene. "It was east of Hollywood. It was just the three of us, and it was pretty bleak. It was the night we were to break up. We had just had it. We weren't really making any money at all. We knew we had some kind of good sound, but nobody was coming to the club ... and that night, somebody brought Bill Gazzarri ... and he immediately wanted us to play his club. When Gazzarri heard us, he said, 'Yeah!' So that turned everything around."

Bill Gazzarri was a first-generation Italian almost 25 years their senior, the self-proclaimed Godfather Of Rock. A tough and thriving survivor with a theatrical charisma that outshone many of the acts he worked with, 'Mr G' was a man at home in any era, and mere seismic shifts such as the coming of the 60s held little threat. Indeed, he capitalised on such upheaval.

"Bill was a no-nonsense guy," confirms Tiny. "He was a nice guy. He had a raspy voice with a New York accent. He was a very Italian-looking guy and looked like he had come up the hard way, but he had put a few manners on. He had put on a little bit of culture, as far as he knew how to dress. He knew how to sweet-talk people. He had a lot of connections." Gazzarri was as smitten as the Walkers were desperate. He immediately hired the trio to play at his club on La Cienega Boulevard.

This was Bill's first real club. Typically christened after its owner, Gazzarri's would become forever linked with the birth of local legends, a vortex for native bands that processed raw talent into world-class celebrity sausage. Situated at 319 North La Cienega and originally a jazz den – and as a punter, Scott had probably frequented it – this club was a forerunner to its more famously known incarnation on Sunset. Gazzarri's would midwife the birth of The Doors, The Byrds, Buffalo Springfield, and Van Halen among many others. All were patronised, happily or otherwise, by the Legend Of The Strip and the Dirty Old Man: Bill Gazzarri himself.

Not everything went the way of the jovial Italian, however. By late 1963, Mr G had lost his star act, Johnny Rivers, to entrepreneurial rival Elmer Valentine's Whisky-A-Go-Go club. The spunky Rivers had been a surprise hit at La Cienega's, and Gazzarri was not keen to lose him. As a last resort, extra-judicial pressure was brought to bear, and the newly-born Walker Brothers were witness to Rivers being 'leaned on' by local heavies.

Like some extra in a gangster flick, Tiny looked on mutely. "They threw Johnny Rivers to the floor – there were a couple of muscle men there. They put him in a chair and started slapping him around, and Bill [Gazzarri] said, 'No, no, no. Hold it. Don't hurt him. Let him go out and earn some money. We'll handle it.'"

Despite or because of this good cop, bad cop routine, Rivers flew the coop anyway. But it would not be the kind of clean break Johnny hoped for. Six months later, a Rivers tour was cancelled due to the singer suffering a sudden impediment in the walking department. The incident was assumed to be not unrelated to Gazzarri's wounded pride and sense of betrayal. Johnny Rivers had suffered a broken leg and now Mr G was looking for his hip replacement. In walked the Walkers. "We went in after Johnny Rivers because Bill needed something to keep up the business," states Tiny. "Johnny started his own following and Bill got the taste of doing good."

Sharing the stage time with another group, a Latin trio known with beautiful simplicity as Tony Vic & Manuel, the gum-chewing Walkers were too busy even to socialise with their fellow trio-in-arms, barely finding time to exchange wisecracks as one band passed the other en route to the stage and dressing room. The Walkers worked six nights a week, and were happy to do so. Their shift was between 8pm and 2am, alternating 20-minute sets with their Latin comrades. In respect of hard graft, Gazzarri's was to The Walker Brothers what The Star Club was to The Beatles. And as the group's popularity grew, so did their hair.

"I wondered how I would look in a Beatles haircut," mused Maus. "Then Scott did it. Nobody was doing it then. Everyone goes to this barber called Jay Sebring who turns everyone out looking like everyone else. We adopted the long hair because it was different. Some of the other groups would like to as well but they don't have the guts."

Tiny: "We were the first group in Hollywood to embrace the long hair style. Immediately after, we started seeing pictures of the groups from the UK – and, I might add, that's when it really took balls to walk down Hollywood Boulevard with long hair.

"Scott was a lot more vain than John and I. I think John came next, and then I learned from both of them and, I think, passed both of them up after they left! Scott was much more aware of his hair, flopping it over and making it look like that Hollywood problem-child type."

A photo from this period taken between sets at their residency shows two immaculately turned-out blond dudes staring moodily into the middle nothingness. Alarmingly cheek-boned, sharp-suited, and skinny-tied, the image is classic, and even today it does not appear dated. In contrast, Tiny towers over them somewhat incongruously with his relatively dark and clumsy bulk. Whatever the drummer's musical proficiency, he did not look the part. His awkward pose reveals that he knew as much.

"Tiny didn't really fit our image," reasoned John months later. "Not that he was bad-looking, but I mean, if you ever see a guy who weighs 280 pounds and looks better than Tiny, I'd like to see him." Other irregularities were afoot. The Walkers and their Latin counterparts were becoming an increasingly hot ticket – but Gazzarri's was not in with the in crowd. Fowley puts it bluntly: "No one ever went to Gazzarri's who had a brain. It was dog shit!"

Johnny Rivers's new home, the Whisky-A-Go-Go, was the place to be. The terms go-go girl and go-go dancer were born there when, during a Rivers show, the female mini-skirted DJ (who spun 45s from a cage above the dance floor) was taken by the spirit of the boogie and began gyrating frenziedly. The crowd, accepting this improvisation as part of the act, went Koo-Koo crazy. The club flooded Technicolor stereo, and right there on Sunset, the 60s flamed into being. Meanwhile, over at old man Gazzarri's, the beat went on as before.

Luckily for the entertainment industry, a town like Hollywood harboured hordes of zombified punters with money to spend and time to kill. So, despite his lowly score on the hip-o-meter, by the end of 1963, Mr G's takings had swollen to such an extent that he was able to invest in another much more accessible venue, at 9039 Sunset. This was the club that would in time become 'it'.

Where Gazzarri went, the Walkers would follow, bringing with them more punters than ever. Kids were queuing around the block and the guest list was peppered with celebrity names. Yet to some, a Gazzarri's was a Gazzarri's was a Gazzarri's.

Fowley again: "Gazzarri's was for the ignorant kids who weren't hip enough to get into the Whisky ... they were just loser people." For young men making such decent dough, John, Scott, Tiny, and their patron Mr G were beyond worrying over what defined hip, and they certainly didn't feel like losers. For much of the coming year, the Walkers continued to alternate noses to the grindstone with the ever-present Tony, Vic, and Manu. The more they played, the more people danced; the more people danced, the more people drank; the more they drank ... and meantime, Gazzarri's coffers would swell. And it wasn't merely about the money. Something of a family atmosphere pervaded the club. Mr G's own mother would often take over the club's kitchen, with a typical Italian matriarchal instinct to feed up the raw-boned Engel and Maus.

Scott, who was at this time apparently estranged from his father, later reminisced at how Mr G had "come-a to a-love-a me like a son". (This was a rare example of Scott's humour making it into print.) True to form, Papa G encouraged his elderly mama to serve the hard-working musicians huge portions of spaghetti and pizza, washing it down with a bottle or three of good Chianti. "Mama Gazzarri always had the pot of sauce going on the stove in the back," slavers Tiny.

Back out front, the band played on and on. Their average audience consisted of the hip, the bad, and the ugly, and, just occasionally, rock royalty. Like any good bar band of the day, the Walkers had a set consisting purely of indisputable classics and current chart hits – usually a lucky-bag mix of both. During a spirited performance of The Rolling Stones' recent chart smash 'Time Is On My Side', Tiny hoofed the bass pedal a little too hard, popping the drum skin. An occasional mishap that happened now and then; no big deal. Except that among the audience as witnesses to this mortal goof were three members of The Rolling Stones themselves. Joshing himself out of embarrassment, Scott turned grinning to the hapless Tiny, and with perfect comic timing hissed: "Get off the fucking stage!" Two thirds of the Walkers would soon meet the Stones, in less embarrassing circumstances. And in a not so far off future life, they would become the best of enemies.

Having gone as far as they could within the cramped circuit of the local club scene, the trio finally made their television debut that January 1964 on the local Channel 9 pilot show, *9th Street A Go-Go*.

LA TV Guide: "Down the street, Bill Gazzarri is excited over being selected, or rather his Gazzarri's club has been selected, by KHJ for their upcoming show *9th Street A Go-Go*. The Walker Brothers plus Tony Vic & Manuel are to be regulars. Programme director Wally Sherwin states, 'The club and its patrons are the kind best-suited for presentation to the general public. Dancers will be auditioned right from the dance floor every Sunday.'

With the Trio tag been lost on the cutting-room floor, The Walker Brothers, as they were now officially known, were effectively the television show's house band. "We were on from the very beginning," confirms Tiny. "We were playing five nights a week in Gazzarri's, plus doing the television show."

Following two successful pilots, where other guests included Jerry Lee Lewis and Sonny & Cher, the show changed its name to the slightly less geographically pedantic *Hollywood A Go-Go*. Television producer Jack Good's legendary *Shindig* followed, and the Walkers were now among the biggest fish in LA's centrally-heated pond.

Jonathan Young, an old associate of the band, had left California a year previously on military service. Now home on leave, he was "impressed at how hot The Walker Brothers had become, being on a weekly TV show as the resident band. I recall how they were introduced as the house group. ... I saw them several times and marvelled at how long their hair was getting!"

Tony Vic & Manuel were not completely mute next to their all-powerful and blond stage buddies. While the Walkers dominated the local television scene, their Latin counterparts had recorded several sides under the name of The Sinners with the producer Nik Venet. A former Capitol Records employee, Venet had produced The Beach Boys after A&R-ing them for Capitol. He had left the label in mid 1964, establishing Ben-Ven Productions with business partner Fred Benson, former manager of Peggy Lee. This new production company also recorded Vic, Manu, and Bob under their own names for Sinatra's Reprise label, and the LP *A Go-Go Hollywood Night Life* was born, followed by a single under the new name of The Sinners, released on Mercury in the January of 1965.

Venet had already met Engel during Scott's previous life as a wannabe boy star, when he was doing television with Eddie Fisher. And now, thanks to the fecund climate of cross-breeding in the Hollywood nightclub scene, Engel and Venet were propelled into each other's orbit once again.

John Maus remembered it from a perspective that even then was tainted by years in the game. "A fellow from Mercury records came in and said, 'We'd like to record you guys' and whatever – I don't know who took that seriously – but we said 'Yeah! What the hell, why not?' I mean we were playing, and so we did it. I suppose it was serious when we actually got to do it. But, I mean, so many people in Hollywood came up to you and said, 'Hey man, would you like the moon? I'm going to give it to you, tomorrow afternoon, on a silver platter!' You get enough of that so after a few years of it you don't pay much attention."

The previous year had been as intense as any hardworking, musically possessed, and ambitious teenager could expect, but the next couple of months would be a crucible. Between the end of 1964 and the dawn of '65, John and Scott would meet the right people in the right places at the right time. As a local small-time musician, Tiny Rogers was a giant success. As a future member of The Walker Brothers pop phenomenon, he was miscast.

Enter Gary.

Scott: "Gary came in one night, to dance. ... He had been working with P.J. Proby and he saw us and said, 'Hey man, I've got a guy who will finance a trip for us to England!' I was dying to go, and John was willing to go for a cheap thrill, if nothing else, right? So we didn't expect anything to happen but thought we'd go over there to goof off – and Gazzarri said we could always come back to the strip, because we were doing so much business."

Kim Fowley: "Up to that point, Scott and John, previous to The Walker Brothers, had never done anything but put out forgettable product. At least Gary had gone to England, gone through the process, learned the formula.

"He could have picked any pretty face, any guy who could sing a chorus, any girl, any talking dog, but he knew how England and the continent felt about rock'n'roll and he knew how to do it."

Gary Leeds, aka Gary Walker, was born Gary Lee Gibson on March 9 1942. He was a native Californian who, for an important part of his development, grew up in a matriarchal household. His parents divorced when Gary was but a toddler, and so he was raised by his mom, grandmother, and aunt. His mother remarried when he was ten, when Gary Gibson became Gary Leeds. An only child, Gary soon developed a passion for music, in particular the jazz drumming of Buddy Rich and Gene Krupa.

"My father used to play the trumpet and we used to go and see Harry James, and a lot of the time the drummer was Buddy Rich," he said. "I'd be standing right next to his kit watching him play, and that did it for me. I knew I could play the drums, I just knew. I used to go and see my grandmother in Los Angeles, and at two in the morning, when I was about 14, I would climb out of her window and walk up the boulevard and stand in front of the drum shop and look in the window and say, 'One day I'll have a set of drums just like those.' The first set I ever had was a wooden set. No famous name, and the first time I set 'em up wrong. Would have been fine if I were left handed. The next set I got was Gretsch."

Coming of age, he tried his hand at everything but music. "I tried working from the bottom up in my father's firm," he would remember. "I worked as a janitor scrubbing floors and washing bottle tops after that. I worked in a factory, but I quit and tried hairdressing. I wanted to be a Sassoon."

Inevitably, his heart overcame his head, and his teen years were marked by membership of various bands, by a passionate desire to become an airline pilot, and by a wacky and inventive sense of humour that would go some way toward sustaining his long and successful friendship with Scott. "I was always friendly with Gary because he has a great sense of humour," affirmed Scott. "He's like Jerry Lewis or Gary Shandling – that great American comic. His humour is timeless and stretches all kinds of boundaries."

As drummer of local Beatles wannabes The Standells, Gary shared agents with John & Judy. The then-omnipresent McKonkey agency was a family-run organisation with practically the entire population of LA's musos on their books. They apparently first met in Hawaii, 1963, while both playing the Oasis club.

Gary Leeds: "The whole connection between all of us was the McKonkey agency, which handled groups who played in these twist clubs. When somebody was sick you just switched around, because we were all playing the same songs. I used to go and watch Scott and John playing across the street in the club opposite. They'd do mostly Top 10 stuff, John playing the Fender lead and Scott doing backing vocals."

Gary, occasionally known as 'Pudding Head' because of his bowl cut, was a natural-born networker and seemed to get off on trading numbers and addresses with his fellow man just for the hell of it. Among the new additions to his little black book was fellow McKonkey stablemate P.J. Proby, who had recently been 'discovered' at an LA party by TV mogul Jack Good. Good had set up a UK tour for Proby on the back of an appearance by the seductively histrionic singer in his successful television show *Around The Beatles*. In an Elvis-starved UK, Proby was the next best thing, and he was instantly and hugely popular.

Back in LA, Gary handed in his resignation as drummer of The Standells when they suddenly became too raucous for his essentially conservative nature. On the way to inform his agent of his decision, Gary bumped into Proby at McKonkey's. P.J. liked Gary and invited him over on his next UK adventure. As a result, while the LA-bound Walker Trio were moving in ever-decreasing circles back at Gazzarri's, Gary was soaking up the UK summer pop scene of 1964 like a mop-topped, amphetamine-fuelled sponge.

Kim Fowley had gigged with Proby on the first leg of his UK tour, as his "minder, manager, pimp, whatever", and was preparing to return to Hollywood when an effervescent Leeds hit London town. "He came over in the late summer of '64. He attached himself to Proby ... as a drummer. He was a good hustler. Did we get on? We were like two soldiers abroad in a wartime situation."

Gary quickly worked out the Proby formula, says Fowley, which he says is also the formula used by a whole range of artists "where a failure would come from America and reinvent himself over there in ten seconds. So, Gary became the master of observing Proby – who was only a demo singer in America and became gigantic in England with a few moves."

Proby: "Gary hung out with me most of '64. I had met Gary at the McKonkey's agency, and I asked him if he'd like to come back to England with me; he said he was a drummer. Of course, I didn't know then that he couldn't play.

"I took Gary on all my tours and everything. I just had him fake it. Cos my actual band was called The Diamonds. They were from Bognor Regis. And I just had Gary tap on a drum. And the band played over him. He couldn't play drums or anything at all. I would use him as a timpani player. I'd give him two sticks and he'd bang away ... as long as he wasn't heard.

"He was living at my house, and I came down one night and found that he had gone through my phone book and everything. So I got up one morning and he'd left. And what I'd found out is that he'd gone through my books and took all the agents' names and numbers. He then went back to the States, borrowed a load of money off of his daddy, and came back with John and Scott.

"Kim Fowley was in the house the night that Gary did that. I was living there, Gary Leeds was living there, Kim Fowley was living there, and my hairdresser was living there. And on the couch was the drummer of The Pretty Things. And there was another guy, too, the roadie for the Stones. I had a real big place, in Ennismore Mews, right off Knightsbridge. Gary was a good hustler but he couldn't play the drums worth a shit. Couldn't play at all."

By the time Gary eventually hustled John and Scott into going to London with him, the two Walkers had already signed to Nik Venet's

Ben-Ven productions. This meant that, through Venet's Smash label, they were now signed to Mercury. Gary was not part of the deal and neither was Tiny. "I just wasn't asked," says Tiny. "I guess they knew which way it was going, and I guess it was on a need-to-know basis only. They just didn't say anything."

Back in the California of late 1964, Venet booked time at the RCA Music Centre Of The World studios. Engel and Maus turned up, seemingly more than willing to accept direction from their producer–manager. Maus: "Nik Venet was a producer for Mercury records, and he said, 'You guys are gonna do this.' He was a pretty astute fellow; he had been responsible for several groups who had become successful. In those days we didn't really pay much attention to anything, so we said sure, why not."

The boys recorded three songs at this session: a cover of 'Pretty Girls Everywhere' (already a minor hit by Eugene & The Fellows), a reinterpretation of The Dalton Brothers' 'I Only Came To Dance With You', and an Engel original – a throwaway dance stomp number called 'Doin' The Jerk'. This uncharacteristically up-tempo Engel original was presumably meant to follow specifically in the novelty dance craze tradition of previous US hits 'The Jerk' and 'Can You Jerk Like Me?'.

Neither the Walkers nor Venet seemed particularly impressed with the results of the recording session, but nor were they exactly disappointed. This new version of 'I Only Came To Dance With You' would remain unreleased, but Venet saw some merit in the other two tracks. Indeed 'Do The Jerk' would earn a large portion of its 15 minutes of fame by clinching the Walkers an appearance in the teen, bubblegum, surf-fodder flick *Beachball*, released at selected drive-ins one year later. (Anyone looking for an insight into the young John and Scott needn't bother with this film – it's a movie made to last one summer, and in that it's wholly successful. There is little to recommend it today.)

For now, Venet was preoccupied with another group, called The Hondells, and they were his priority. Perhaps sensing that the Walkers' true potential hadn't been touched on during these sessions, he suggested another recording date in the near future. He'd be in touch. John and Scott were happy to go with the flow. Back at Sunset and on the set of *Shindig*, The Walker Brothers were as in demand as ever.

Gary's involvement in the recording, even at this stage, was phantom, but he did continue to hustle The Proby Plan incessantly, becoming Tiny's nemesis in the process. Gary had a dream that he, John, and Scott would be reborn as a blonder Beatles in the UK's hothouse pop climate, way across the Atlantic. "The three of us can go to England and make it bigger than The Beatles," he told them. "I'm serious: we've got the hair and the looks and the vocal thing, and I can't see it going wrong."

"Gary was the brains of the Walkers," laughs Fowley. "It was like as if Ringo would have been the brains of The Beatles!"

A hapless Tiny, constantly in demand with other bands, could only watch helplessly, not knowing where all this would lead. "They wanted to go to England ... but they couldn't afford to get over there. Gary Leeds's father came up with the deal where he would pay their way over and everything would be on spec. Well, the kicker was that he could only do that if they used Gary to play drums. So, I got the elbow! I kind of felt like [ousted early Beatles sticksman] Pete Best, for a while. That's just what happened. So they went over there, and the rest is history."

Producer Nik Venet and Ben-Ven Productions were cool with this bold and ballsy move, and a statement was issued to local biz paper *KRLA Beat* that November. It announced grandly that the Walkers had acquired a "two week promotional tour" of the UK for the coming New Year. Bill Gazzarri, despite his street smarts, was seemingly the last to know, kept in the dark until the latest possible hour. John in particular was wary of burning his bridges and at least wanted the chance to come back to a reliable gig if the UK trip went wrong.

The last minuscule explosion in the series of tiny chain reactions that would set off the Walkers bomb was still to come. With flights booked to England for that forthcoming February, Venet called the boys in for the last recording session they would ever create on American soil.

When they arrived once again at the RCA studios in late January to record 'The Seventh Dawn' and 'Love Her', they were giddy with excitement at the prospect of their forthcoming trip. They were also about to encounter the two factors that would parent and patent their place in pop history.

Present was Bernard 'Specs' Nitzsche, known as Jack by everyone except his mother. A second-generation German born in Chicago, he was best known – and was no stranger to Engel – as Phil Spector's arranger. This particular combination of Jack Nitzsche, the 38-piece Spector orchestra that he brought with him, and the song 'Love Her' – originally a B-side on The Everly Brothers' single 'The Girl Sang The Blues' – would change everything. Oh, and the casual suggestion that Engel sing lead.

"Scott got stuck with lead because his voice handled it better," remarked Gary. "There was no jealousy on John's part. That's just the way it worked."

Scott: "It's a marvellous song ... and they were trying to create a different sound. [Nitzsche] asked, 'Who sings lowest?' and that was me, and that's how the sound started."

Ever affable, John did not seem threatened. "The arrangement and the way it was laid out was all done in the studio. That part where Scott just sings with the bass part, that was all Venet's idea, he put the whole thing together. And we sang the parts, basically. He said, 'I want you to do this, and you to do that.' And that's what we did, and the formula worked."

This sound, born almost of accident, was a somehow more European-sounding take on a classic Spector production technique. Fronted by a distinctly un-American sounding baritone, it employed a formula that would, ultimately, make and break The Walker Brothers. It was Nitzsche's input that made the production of 'Love Her' loom above the other US Walker cuts, but that was of little importance to the producer himself.

Nitzsche was dismissive of the recording. Scott sounded too 'white' for his tastes, and he remembered Engel most for being overly preoccupied with hair products (a pomade called Dep – "for men!").

Nitzsche considered the demo version of the song, sung by one Freddie Scott, to be "far superior" to the Walkers' release.

For the Walkers themselves, the session must have had an air of hit-and-run about it. They were leaving for the UK almost immediately, and the inhabitants of the neighbouring studio may have seemed a portent of their new life. Once again, Keith, Mick, Charlie, Brian, and Bill were in the vicinity.

John: "We were finishing the recording and we were going to put some violins on it. So the string section was coming in, and it was in the middle of the night. The funny part about this was that The Rolling Stones had just recorded 'The Last Time' and they were finishing the mixing in the same studio where we were going to put all these violins and things on. They used to come over to Gazzarri's when they were in town, so we knew them a little bit."

Poor Bill Gazzarri himself had finally rumbled that something fishy was going on. Placated by a soothing Maus, he was assured that the Brothers were merely going away on a temporary promo trip for 'Love Her'. He was assured that Gazzarri's biggest draw would be returning home to sunny climes soon. No one saw fit to spare Tiny a similar explanation. "The next thing I knew, the gig on *Hollywood A Go-Go* ended," recalls the big-boned tub thumper. "We were an integral part of making it a success as a local show, and the next thing I knew, they had left! They did everything on the sly so much and stepped on so many toes."

One of their last appearances on *Shindig*, dated January 20, shows John and Scott as exuberant as ever (Tiny and Gary were never featured). The majority of their appearances on this show had presented them bursting with good cheer and sunny southern Californian health. As they bopped through a jazzed-up version of The Beatles' 'I'm A Loser' they seem to consider themselves as anything but, with John in particular beaming encouragement and good vibes toward Scott during the Scott's vocal solo. In addition, compared to their earlier *Shindig* appearances months before, their hairstyles are on the brink of a riot. The thick, blond mops are slathered in Dep and backcombed furiously in an attempt to recapture the old James Dean quiff style that both had worn during the early days of the show. The result of this attempt at follicle censorship is a weirdly futuristic do, pre-empting a bleached Ziggy-styled mullet. It's also perversely at odds with those on the show who do genuinely have short hair and those (mostly British guests) who wear it shockingly long. Scrutinising their golden, collar-length, and ungelded locks, one is reminded of a butterfly about to jailbreak its cocoon.

By piggybacking the Proby tour the previous summer, Gary had left his future in England. John was game for a laugh. A part of Scott was already in Europe, his imagination having perhaps inhabited that foreign place from the first time he had sat spellbound at the cinema through the waking dream of *The Rocking Horse Winner*. He was also pragmatic regarding the music business and any designs Uncle Sam may have had on his future.

Scott: "I'd been aware for some time that my sort of music – ballads and so forth – could sell far better in Britain because, unlike the American public, the British weren't trend-crazy, latching onto surf, then pop folk, then Batman music to the exclusion of everything else. Another reason to leave California was to escape being shipped to Vietnam. When I got my induction papers, I moved away as fast as I could."

And yet, as optimistic and excited as John, Scott and Gary were, nothing was a given. Many of their peers, Tiny included, expected them to be back with their tails between their legs within months.

Kim Fowley: "When they left with [Gary] Leeds it was just another failure going back to England to sleep on the floor. It was just Gary with two morons and some borrowed money."

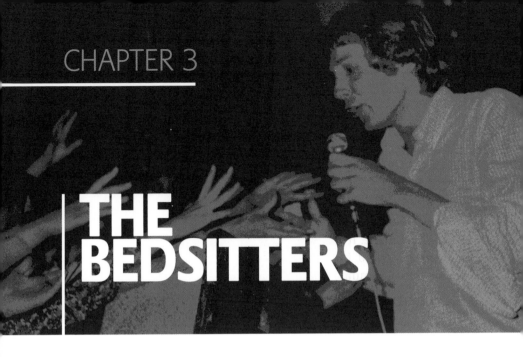

CHAPTER 3

THE BEDSITTERS

Nik Venet called me about The Walker Brothers and said he was going to send them to England, cos he felt they were better suited to break in England. Then silence.

Tony Calder, business partner of Rolling Stones manager Andrew Loog Oldham (2005)

Wednesday, February 17 1965, Heathrow airport, London, 6am. Gary, John, and Scott stepped off their TWA flight into England and wintertime. They certainly looked striking but as far as the other passengers were concerned were just three more anonymous young Americans, perhaps college students taking a year off, or actors of some sort. What was indisputable was that all three were extremely cold. This southern Californian trio had come direct from the sunny LAX airport, utterly unprepared for the harshness of the British winter. "It all looked very strange to me," John would recall some 30 years after the event. "Not at all like California. [There was] white stuff on the ground. Snow!"

Gary quipped that the closest he had come to such weather before was through photographs in the *National Geographic*. His sole trip to England the year before had been at the height of a rare British summer. They had prepared themselves as best they could psychologically, but none of them were equipped sartorially. John wore nothing more than a short-sleeved shirt and a pair of bone-hugging stage trousers (his only pair), which he would rip while leaving the plane. It was hardly a good omen.

Jet-lagged and freezing, and after hours of pavement-pounding because no accommodation had been arranged in advance, they must have thought their Holy Hollywood a lifetime away when they finally moved into digs. The Walkers' debut residence in London was an enormous, draughty, Victorian bedsit at number 1 Onslow Gardens, Kensington (second floor, with balcony).

Kensington was, along with Earl's Court, one of the cheaper parts of central London, with a half decent pad going at £5 a month. Struggling musicians and artists would often share, with transient buddies making a place for themselves on the couch and in the bath. Still, even with the extra body heat generated by three long-limbed Americans sharing one oversized room, the cold still hurt. Extreme weather called for extreme measures, as Gary would testify. "We would go to sleep with so much stuff piled on top of us that we would wake up in the same position as when we fell asleep."

But cold winter nights and bedsit-land itself have always given a good view of the stars, and in classic Tinseltown fashion, a jet-lagged Gary was hustling almost immediately, pumping strange small change into the wall-mounted payphone in the hall.

Kim Fowley: "You have to understand Gary on the phone to Maurice King: 'We're already on Mercury. We already have a worldwide record deal. All we need is your Polish mafia back-up! I've got two great-looking guys who can sing. I'm the drummer.' Gary stole the Proby blueprint and tried to work with it on his own chickenshit level."

P.J. Proby: "When they came over, they didn't have much going for 'em, but Gary's parents paid for them to have a place to live in. Maurice King was an old friend of mine, and he had told Gary's father, 'I'll get 'em the work if you pay the bills'. But Maurice didn't commit until 'Love Her' hit; he wanted to wait and see what he was getting himself into."

Maurice King was a partner with Barry Clayman in Capable Management, at 185 Bickenhall Mansions, Baker Street. Clayman (who was awarded an OBE in 2004) was perceived as the more genteel of the two. "Barry Clayman was a yes man of some sort," reckons Fowley. "One of those faceless guys who probably did the paperwork. Maurice King was larger than life and was a greasy person, like a Robert Maxwell kind of presence, and everybody else was forgettable." Whatever their personal profiles, as a team Capable was on the up. At the time of Gary's fevered phone calls, Maurice and Barry's most successful act was Van Morrison's Them.

Extra income came through a share in the Starlite Club, a nicotine-parched, ale-sodden, after-hours drinking den off Oxford Street. The clientele at this low-budget cinematic fleapit were also members of an even more exclusive club – London's criminal underworld. As one of the gaffers of the Starlite, Maurice King became friendly with proper, real-life, grown-up gangsters, the Krays included.

Proby knew the score. "The Krays were my best friends too. They gave me free rehearsal rooms, big beautiful rehearsal rooms. Every time I was in a whole lot of trouble and everything, they got me out of it." Such contacts bestowed a man with a heavy reputation, and King revelled in it.

Kim Fowley: "The Starlite club was like any bar out of a Dirk Bogarde gangster movie, people standing around acting like wannabe hoodlums ... all that East End crap. Butlins in grime. But, you know, I was 24 years old, and there were dirty girls and chorus girls there, and gangsters and musicians, and it was all very friendly and good food and fun time and no money and ... wow! Oo-ee!

"I didn't push Maurice King too much because he was a bad guy. One day we were having dinner at the Starlite and somebody began arguing, trying to get in and disrupt the dinner. So King's minders went outside with a pitchfork and sorted the guy out. There was a lot of yelling going on in the middle of our dinner. Maurice King promised the world ... and outside, someone's screaming."

Ralph Gurnett was a Capable employee, tour manager, and future personal assistant to Scott Walker. "That's a load of rubbish," he says. "Rubbish. Maurice couldn't hit a fly. He was a coward. He didn't associate with people like that. He was a crook, I know, but he would never do anything like that. Why would someone like Scott Walker have someone like that as his manager?

"My whole take on Capable Management was that it wasn't pretty but it wasn't nasty. Maurice wasn't the ogre people made him out to be. Sometimes I had respect for him, sometimes I had less respect for him."

Proby: "Nobody liked Maurice because he was a very tight, uh, loudmouthed Jew. I mean even his wife couldn't stand him. Mary [his wife] made him sleep in the next bedroom. She made him crawl on his hands and knees to come in the kitchen to get a cup of tea or anything: she was really cruel. They had once been the agents for every club in the North. They lost all that."

Chrissie McCall, soon to be teenage president of the Walkers' fanclub, says: "Maurice was intimidating because he was so much older and powerful. He was 42 at the time and I was only 16, remember. He was a rich businessman with a lot of money and a big house. He had a strong Southern [English] accent. My mental image of him is small, swarthy, with black greasy-type hair. Well dressed. People were afraid of him. If he said 'jump', people jumped."

All of this edginess and King's aura of the outlaw appealed to Scott's dramatically theatrical imagination, a side of his character that was in part responsible for the Walkers' ultimate decision to sign with Capable Management.

But that decision was, for now, some way off. Despite or perhaps because of Gary's incessant hustle – on one occasion the drunken drummer phoned Maurice at 3am – King was not immediately convinced, least of all by Gary, whom he would come to tolerate at best. King would eventually come to idolise Scott at John and Gary's expense, considering them as no more than dead weight.

In the first chilled and teal-coloured months of 1965, such dilemmas were a fairytale away. Managerless and adrift throughout that sunless February, the three endured, suffering in what seemed to them to be something of a Siberian climate. Often they slept fully dressed beneath a cavernous Victorian ceiling, with beds pushed toward the fire and coats and blankets piled over them. All three Walkers had to stay acutely aware of their limited finances. The $10,000 that Gary's dad had lent them would have to last until they had made some kind of break, which would be ... when, exactly? No one then could really know what lay ahead, and while still so very young, Scott in particular had long carried an old head on those shoulders. "Yes, there was that $10k," he said, "but it certainly wasn't a sure thing, as there was no way to guarantee success."

John, typically, had another, more casual attitude. "I don't think we actually came [to Britain] with any intention of working, really. We wanted to check it out. The thing was, in America, everything English was golden, and we thought, 'Well ... ' The opportunity to come here was presented to us and so, being enterprising young men, we jumped on the plane."

Still, whatever it was that they were lacking in domestic utilities was made up for in bullshit and balls. Having already done the jerk, they now did the hustle. All three agreed on a kind of strategy: they would actively promote the idea that they were endorsed by a prestigious 'mystery backer' – which gave them carte blanche to turn down the crummier gigs that were already coming their way.

The long-term plan was that when they did gig, it would be special, causing maximum impact. It was Scott who commandeered this ruse, often to the protest of John, Gary, and their stomachs. "We came near to starvation," grinned Scott. "The other guys thought I'd gone mad."

At least Scott could indulge and find refuge in his love of European movies: decades on, only half joking, he would cite both the draft board and the poor state of American cinema as his dual reasons for leaving the States. Scott admitted that by the time he arrived in London he had seen so many Ealing comedies that just walking the streets made him feel like he was in a film, shoulder to shoulder with "Margaret Rutherford and Terry-Thomas characters".

Alas, man cannot live by celluloid alone, and the already slim-hipped trio were, in their own words, subsisting on "bread and cheese". Seeking to splurge on something slightly more ostentatious, Gary attempted to buy the nearest thing to a McDonalds that was then available in Britain. On entering the local Wimpy burger bar, he set early-60s UK etiquette reeling when the ravenous rhythmist had the temerity to ask for two burgers in a bap.

Gary: "I said, 'I'll have two of those,' and he said, 'Well, you can only have one.' I guessed that was the way it was done over here. But I said, 'Why can't I have two?' He said 'Well, if you eat that one, I'll bring you another.'

"I let it go; being a foreigner, I wasn't sure that was how it was done. But I said, 'Uh … can I have some … ?' and he said, 'No, you can't have any of that on there.' So I had to order the salad on the side and set it up with this sandwich. I said, 'I don't know if I'm going to make it over here.'"

John: "Food in England is a real drag. I can't seem to find good food. There's nothing like a baked potato with sour cream and chives … nothing like it. We take it for granted over here [in America]. Over there, you'll never get one. You'll get a soured cream. Terrible. The meat is funny-tasting. They have a refrigeration problem over there. Meat you buy in the morning and don't eat by evening – forget it. The next day it's gone."

Back at Onslow Gardens, while the anxiety and frustration mounted in the freezing air, refrigeration was certainly not an issue. Occasionally their bland diet would force them to throw budgetary concern to the wind, and the three young Americans would indulge themselves within the exotic food halls of Harrods. Immediate remorse and mild guilt no doubt followed such binges, but despite the bleakness, behind-the-scenes machinery began to move. The Walker Brothers were, after all, signed to Mercury/Smash Records in the States, and Mercury was distributed by Philips in the UK. This was a major force. Compared to the hundreds of other young wannabes freezing their asses off in bedsit-land, The Walker Brothers had as good as made it already. It was surely just a matter of time.

Characteristically taking the initiative, Gary suggested that it was about time they introduced themselves to 'their' record company. After all, they weren't just three bums walking in off the street. There was some kind of business connection – right? Contractually, this was fact, although at first the link did indeed seem tenuous, as Gary noted. "We went over to Philips and they didn't even know we were here at first. And then we walked in, and they said, 'Yeah! You have long hair!' And all that, because Americans at the time had their hair combed back."

As a female of the species, Gloria Bristow, then head of the Philips press department, was one of the first in the industry to recognise their particular potential. "I was coming into work one morning, and they were sat outside in chairs attempting to sun themselves. They were very laidback. As soon as I saw Scott, I thought, 'Gosh! If he doesn't melt a few hearts ... .'"

This brief introductory trip to the Philips offices resulted only in a somewhat vague and muted welcome. True to Gloria's response, it seems the Walkers barely made an impression beyond the female staff. But soon after this meeting, their debut UK single was scheduled for a March release. Something was happening.

'Pretty Girls Everywhere', with its arrangement by diminutive veteran jazzman Shorty Rogers, had been recorded a year previously, at RCA's Victor's Music Centre Of The World studios at 6363 Sunset Boulevard in sunny Los Angeles. Hearing the record again in their frosty bedsit, the three homesick and skinny-ribbed brothers must have felt like wayward pioneers attempting to warm themselves in the light of a dead and distant star. Its impression on the record-buying public would be just as remote.

Sounding slightly summery and vaguely Latin, if the song was heard at all on radio during that freezing March, it would have sounded incongruously at odds with the current climate, both musically and meteorologically. A minor hit in the USA in 1958 when originally released by Eugene Church & The Fellows, the lyrics drew their inspiration from cruising *American Graffiti*-style along the babe-lined boulevards of LA.

Co-composer Eugene Church remembered its origins: "It was one of the first hot days of summer and, everywhere we looked, young ladies were stepping out in shorts, bikinis, little or nothing on, and bro' would tell me, 'Hey bro' man, check this lady.' One lady walked by the car and I sang, 'Everywhere I go, I see a pretty girl.'"

Sonically, the song showcases neither John's nor Scott's voices. Contrary to popular belief, John does not sing lead. Rather, both singers share the melody using an ineffectual hybrid of harmony and duet. Whatever the method, it neutralises both singers. Compared to what was to come, the song had all the potency of secondhand bubblegum.

'Do The Jerk', the flipside, was Scott's tongue-in-cheek attempt to kick-start another dance craze alongside 'The Mashed Potato' or 'The Pony'. In this regard, it has more comic ground in common with Lou Reed's similar adolescent attempt with 'The Ostrich'. Still, compared to 'Pretty Girls Everywhere' it is more engaging and muscular, if only by default. Yet ultimately it fails on all fronts. The melody is hardly hummable and lyrically it's a no-brainer. The groove is as bottom-heavy and unwieldy as a one-man submarine and no particular friend to the dancefloor. Both sides remain oddities: they are among the least Walker-like songs in their catalogue.

Bristow's press department did what it could. Despite an accepted invitation from television mogul Jack Good for the trio to appear on the March 27 edition of his phenomenally popular and hip *Ready Steady Go!*, the release of the single caused little interest. Like gas silently escaping from a freshly-buried corpse, The Walker Brothers' debut single passed largely unnoticed. "'Pretty Girls' was not happening," admitted Scott.

John Maus, already weakened by the lack of sunshine and vitamin D and the paltry diet, was missing his girl Kathy and his lost status. Being one of the biggest fish in the LA pond had come naturally to the guitarist's healthy ego; deprived of all this in freezing, crummy England, John began to crack first. Living in such close proximity, the others could barely fail to notice. Scott said: "Before [the next single] 'Love Her' was released, we were literally in a state of panic. I wanted to stay because I was digging Europe. John wanted to go back to the

States – Gary used to say John had one foot on the plane and another on a banana peel. But Gary wanted us all to stay until it worked out. He was the only one who really believed in it – that The Walker Brothers were going to be something."

Tension was building, and with their debut single dead in the water, John was making increasingly loud going-home noises. One can imagine the spectre of Bill Gazzarri hovering in the dank bedsit air, finger wagging, his singsong voice saying "I told you so" while John held his mop-topped head in his frostbitten hands. How the sunny hills of Hollywood beckoned! All three had graduated to a state of discontent beyond the merely cold, tense, and fed-up, although Scott was buoyed a little at least just by being in Europe. But even his combined love of arty cinema and fear of the draft board was not enough. All three were homesick to some extent, with the 21-year-old Engel occasionally making comforting phone calls to his mom.

On the plus side, the empty days forced the three of them to bond, and they would often go out on day trips together, one time venturing as far as Nottingham's Sherwood Forest, where they hammily play-acted a bow-and-arrow fight. Communal trips to the cinema were less frequent: Gary and John did not share Scott's taste for the avant-garde, although they happily munched popcorn in the dark together during *The Satan Bug* and *The Man From Rio*.

Despite promising noises from Philips and Capable, London still felt a long way from happening. It was not until Allan McDougal, head of Philips press, received a desperate, threatening call from Gary, that any remaining alienation would get the Chelsea boot it deserved.

Gary called from the busy wall-phone in the hall and layed it on the line. "We're thinking of going back to Hollywood, to open a club there for six weeks. There are all these troubles here, mostly over money. It's not worth it, this bother. And I can tell you that, if we catch a plane in a couple of days, we just won't come back. The boys have made that clear."

Having recently acquired copies of the LA master tape, Philips had 'Love Her' in the bag anyway. It wasn't as if they would have to book studio time or arrange for fixers to bring in musicians: the product was ready-made and ready to go. And so they casually let it be known to Maurice and the boys that they would put out this second single, albeit with a minimum commitment. 'Love Her' was practically a no-risk investment, and as such it was released with little fanfare or expectation. Having little to lose, Philips invested frugally.

Back at Onslow Gardens it was now officially spring, but the boys continued their brooding in close proximity to the electric heater, accompanied by the sound of Scott's then-favourite record, Françoise Hardy's 'All Over The World'. Hardy's haunting and prettily wistful voice, lilting over a sweetly sad piano refrain, drifted in the drafty Onslow air, soundtracking an atmosphere that registered imperceptibly above a vacuum.

While Maurice King was keeping his options open, bereft of any tangible success, the boys were resolutely without management, Capable or otherwise. Still, while not fully committing himself, King did apparently placate Gary's father with the occasional soothing transatlantic phone call. Philips' promotional efforts were evident but sluggish, and the trio's exposure was limited to guerrilla attacks on the offices of the lesser pop papers and exposure on offshore pirate radio stations such as Radio Caroline.

Dave Cash was a pirate radio DJ on the *Kenny And Cash Show*. "Our show was one of the first to show any interest in the boys," he says. "We did their first-ever UK radio interview and played 'Love Her' to death. Scott's voice was just to die for. They also did a bunch of jingles and trailers for me and Kenny [Everett]. But the Walkers never actually came out to the boat.

"We were 'in' with about half-a-dozen major record companies, and on our week off we'd go and see Tommy at Fontana, Tony Hall at Decca, and Paddy Fleming at Philips. And we'd say, 'What ya got for us?' And they weren't supposed to be seeing us, you know? Because we were pirates, as it were. The offshore stations were frowned upon. So Paddy said, 'We've got these guys, and this is their record, blah blah.' And me and Kenny thought 'Love Her' was fucking great! So we said, 'Paddy, we're gonna make it our *Kenny And Cash* record of the week.' Then we did the interview at Stanhope Place. And Paddy said, 'Would you like them to do you some jingles?' And we said, 'Wow! Yeah! Would we! Not many, Benny!'."

Gary: "[Radio in the UK] was a shock, because the exposure and the coverage you got was equal to the whole of the United States. I mean, the lady who sold flowers on the corner knew you; it reaches everyone. The coverage compared to the USA's local stations, [where] you were isolated in LA, and another town away wouldn't even know you. You'd have a Top Ten in LA, and then a little further out in San Berdino it's not even in the charts. The coverage you get [in Britain] and everything else is fantastic, for its size."

They followed up such hit-and-miss on-and-offshore escapades with interviews for whoever would listen. Peter Jones, then editor of the fledgling *Record Mirror*, was one of the few in those early days to lend an ear. "It was a bitterly cold morning in February 1965," he said. "We were there at the urgent insistence of Barry Clayman and Maurice King to meet a new group from America's West Coast. They turned up, a few minutes after opening time, jet-lagged and hollow-eyed, for their first press interview in the UK. They looked as if they'd much rather be in bed. But they sat, quietly, too tired even to accept the offer of an injection of alcohol. Nobody – apart from me! – was prepared to spend time interviewing a gang of unknowns."

Above and beyond such concerns, the seven-inch vinyl that bore their name began to take on a life of its own. Slowly, almost imperceptibly, it began to happen. 'Love Her' moved like a bejewelled inch-worm up the charts, increasingly reaping radio play. By late May, it was Top 30 in the *NME* chart. Now new paths were clearing, a fresh destiny was kicking in, and things were happening. As if adhering to some obscure cosmic script, it was exactly now that Maurice King instructed his secretary to draw up the necessary papers, prior to making the call to the Onslow wall-phone. Within hours, King and Clayman were reeling the Yanks into Capable Management's Baker Street offices where, ridden with relief and with John taking the lead, they signed – finally – upon the dotted line. The Walker Brothers were now officially Capable artistes.

Something, somewhere had obviously clicked into place, because almost immediately the Walker profile began to rise. Radio spots bloomed into television appearances – including one memorable spot as special 'mystery' guests on *Juke Box Jury*. They pulled the 'see no evil, hear no evil, speak no evil' three-monkey routine as they were introduced from backstage before a bemused television audience. The trio finally sauntered on, and it was obvious that the BBC camera crews were not prepared for such tall guests. Apart from the slightly shorter Gary, lanky John and Scott initially appeared only from the neck down. Still, 'Love Her' got the panel's unanimous thumbs-up.

As well as pollinating the hearts of the public, the record also introduced John, Scott, and Gary professionally. Key players already established within the industry were gravitating toward the trio at speed, followed by a gaggle of lesser-known faces from the pop periphery. A supporting cast of characters and bit-part players entered, each a necessary cog and wheel in the drama set to unfold.

Among them was Chris Walter, the photographer responsible for some of their most enduring images. He was an entrepreneurial young dude barely out of his teens. "As soon as I heard a new single or artist I thought would make it, or as soon as someone entered the *NME* Top 30, I would set up a photo session. With the Walkers, I'd heard 'Pretty Girls Everywhere' and did my first session just as 'Love Her' came out. Those are the photos from Marble Arch. I heard later that one of them had broken a toe or something during that session, jumping about. But anyway, after that, I just kept doing them whenever appropriate, via their management."

Ready Steady Go! for a while became a second home to The Walker Brothers, although little survives of their performances on this show other than the occasional video, audio recording, and traumatic memory. During an early television performance of 'Love Her', the backing track disappeared as the speaker monitors went down. This left Scott alone in front of a live television audience, caught on the high wire during the breakdown section of the song, when the arrangement shrinks down just to percussion and Engel's low, liquid croon. With nothing audible to sing to, Scott carried on regardless, relying on his own internal sense of timing and pitch. The audience and fellow bandmates watched, enthralled. "I was looking over at Scott, praying that he wouldn't stop," chuckled John. "And he carried on, regardless, except for one thing: it took him both hands to stop the microphone from shaking."

"My eyes were like poached eggs on toast," moaned Scott.

Simon Napier-Bell, the legendary pop manager, says: "I bumped into the Walkers at *Ready Steady Go!*, *Top Of The Pops*, and concerts. It was Michael Lindsay-Hogg, when he was directing *RSG*, who really made their image. His idea was to make them look like trees waving in the wind, filming them from the floor up. I remember the first time he did it, they hadn't liked the cameramen scrubbing around by their feet one bit, and complained bitterly after the first rehearsal. In those days there was no playback after rehearsal, nothing was taped, so they couldn't see what they looked like. Michael persisted with this idea and put up with the grumbling through all the rehearsals and after the show itself [still not taped for immediate playback]. But the next day everyone was talking about how fabulous they looked on the show, and they were convinced. Their problem then was how to give them some semblance of the same image when they were standing on stage in a theatre."

At last it seemed as if the Walkers were on their way, and March 22 saw them embark on their first full-scale tour, where they filled in for The Kinks. It followed an onstage bust-up between the Davies brothers and company that saw Ray Davies go down before the Cardiff audience with a cymbal in his cranium. This opportunity for the Walkers – borne out of violence – would prove eerily prophetic of their own appearances. The female public were waiting to rip them apart.

John: "We walked out on stage ... we were playing as a trio then. We were there for about three or four bars into the first song, and that was the end of that. It was like the whole theatre was on the stage and it was the end. It was over. Bang! I was laying in the dressing room being very hurt. A riot erupted. I had a couple of ribs crushed."

Scott: "We were on The Kinks tour. We locked our dressing room door because there were so many kids. Suddenly, some kind of rock comes hurtling through the window followed by a dozen kids. Gary locked himself in the bathroom, and I'm trying to get the door unlocked. Difficult, because I've got ten youngsters on my back trying to rip the shirt off my back. I'm lucky to be alive."

The reaction made perfect sense to those who witnessed it. As if it could possibly go any other way. But it was hard to explain the science. Dave Cash, as a guest, would often watch the phenomenon from the safety of stage left.

"They were very attractive to girls," says Cash. "You're talking three guys in their early twenties – American guys, no less. Scott's voice could certainly tickle a few fannies. They just had this charisma. There are certain guys who just turn women on, you know?" The object of such affection would soon find it wearying. "Within six months of arriving here, it was like a great mouth and hands coming for you in the night," Scott would shudder from the safety of three decades further on.

Taking over on the tour from the post-Cardiff Kinks calamity, the Walkers were still appearing in their 'original' roles: Scott on bass; John on guitar; and Gary actually tub-thumping. They made their debut at the Leeds Odeon where, if you could make it beyond the screaming, you would have heard such nondescript material as 'Money', 'I'll Be Satisfied', and 'Pretty Girls Everywhere'.

The absence of 'Love Her' from the live set was both conspicuous and prophetic, and a portent of dilemmas to come, but such negativities barely registered for now. Radio Luxembourg and the pirates were converts already, and airplay was spreading to other stations across Europe like red weed from Mars. The US draft board, Vic Tony & Manuel, Gazzarri's, and the rut of LA life were all a lifetime away. Soon, bedsit-land would follow.

The British weather was still pretty harsh, but each packed venue in each quaint English town brought with it the thrill of the new. It felt like it was finally happening. And beyond the petty hardships, the hassles, the grief of travel, the sloppy beds of the cheap hotels, the crappy food, the lack of sleep, the hard, bright climate that caused breath to freeze and vapourise in the early morning air as the gear was loaded into the van ... beyond all this was the hint and promise of something impossibly bright and good.

The Walker Brothers were about to become very, very successful and hugely, massively famous.

Dave Dee: "The first time I heard about the Walkers, we were travelling to a gig. We bumped into another band, and they said, 'Have you heard about The Walker Brothers?' No, we said, what are they like? 'Ever so good but really ... big time. They've got these heavies with them all the time ... you can't get in the dressing room and you can't talk to 'em.' And we had never been used to this, because this was the very beginning of the managers doing the protective showbiz thing, which got the media to talk about them, you know? It made them untouchable."

Gary: "I had told my father, 'I've been to England, and I think we've got a good chance there, especially with Scott and John, because of the looks and the long hair and so forth.' He said, 'What are you going to do when you get over there?' I said, 'Oh, we're gonna go over there and be bigger than The Beatles.'"

CHAPTER 4

TO LOVE SOMEBODY

I was a tape-op for Philips, and the first we heard of The Walker Brothers was when we released 'Love Her'. The first time I saw them was when we recorded 'Make It Easy On Yourself'. My first impression? His voice.

Roger Wake, Philips studio employee (1974)

'Love Her' as a song and a recording can be considered ground zero for The Walker Brothers. Within its high stained-glass-windowed walls and Gothic courtyards, you will find everything there is to either love or to hate about this group. There is the majestic quasi-classical orchestration, with drums that sound like crumbs falling from God's table into flooded mineshafts. The sublimely audacious use of reverb; the almost pitiful sincerity of the gallant lyrics. And running through and above it all is that huge golden skyscraping voice, effortless and gigantic, intimate yet titanic.

The B-side isn't bad either. 'Seventh Dawn' is the sound of America's far West, of rolling canyons and clear blue mountains.

Sounding quite unlike anything they would record again, it's one of the rare examples of John and Scott's voices melding in perfect symbiosis. "I defy you to identify which voice sings which part," enthused John. "Scott's voice is very strong on the lower register but becomes thinner as it goes into higher scales. ... Between us we have a ridiculous range."

Sounding beautifully doomed and new-born immortal, The Walker Brothers' unique sonic sigh was about to cut rose-coloured delta tracks across the blooming adolescent hearts of Britain.

'Love Her' was no overnight sensation. Already six months old when finally released, it had taken over five excruciating weeks to creep to a modest 18 in the *Melody Maker* chart, peaking that June. Almost instantly, it then began its slow descent, although this time the lack of speed in its movement was to be savoured. While no smash hit, it was as solid and impressive an introduction as a Topaz business card.

Even so, the Walkers faced a lot of competition. The UK music press of 1965 was dominated by such transient pop personalities as Herman's Hermits, Billy J. Kramer, and Crispin St Peters, intermediaries like Gary's old buddy P.J. Proby, The Seekers, and Gerry & The Pacemakers, and by the greats: Elvis, Sinatra, The Beatles, and The Stones. Journalists still in search of an angle drew initial comparisons between the Walkers and the other – Righteous – Brothers.

Decades later, John still struggled unsuccessfully to explain away this lazy comparison, making little sense in the process. "The format was the same. It's almost a carbon copy, except that we did entirely different things. ... They were more of a blues style. ... People were always comparing us and there isn't anything to compare. It's just we both happen to be 'Brothers'." As ever, Gary's idiot genius got straight to the point. "There are two of them and three of us. They have short hair and we have long hair."

The success of 'Love Her' allowed The Walker Brothers their own way into the hugely-popular music papers. Like some exotic flower introduced successfully into a reticent alien landscape, the trio's tentative presence within the holy pages of *NME* and *Melody Maker* was at first random and patchy. A column here, a quarter page there, the odd fan letter, a photo of John labelled 'Scott' and vice versa. But then suddenly, seemingly overnight, their copy took on a life of its own, moving speedily toward florid ubiquitousness.

It was what Gary had plotted all along. The table was set, the goalposts wide open, and the quotable Leeds could now riff as he pleased.

On The Byrds: "They originally copied us. They'd come to the LA club where we were working. At that time we were the only group in Hollywood with long hair. They let theirs grow and grow. They would watch how we dressed and played. They did our numbers and caught on to everything about us."

On The Byrds doing Dylan's 'Mr Tambourine Man': "We heard the record, so we plugged it on stage. Everybody thought it was our record for a while. Then about a month ago, it started to climb the charts. We thought, 'What are we doing?' We realised we were helping somebody else's record along, so we dropped it from the act. Vocally, that group is kinda weak, to our way of thinking."

On the future: "We might do an R&B number just to show we can do the junk! You're likely to hear anything from us. We do a very good imitation of The Rolling Stones and we can do the Beatles harmonies as well. We hope to make movies one day, too."

The three took to their newly found if still modest fame like wildfowl to water. They quickly became faces at the in places around town: in particular the Cromwellian, the Bag O' Nails, the Adlib Club, and the Scotch of St James nightclub. Compared to his later incarnation, Scott was still relatively sociable. Laurie Jay was owner of the Scotch of St James (and later Billy Ocean's manager). He remembers: "We would go round to Scott's flat after the place had closed. He had a place on Regent's Park, by the zoo. All the girls who worked in the clubs lived in the same building. This was before Scott went solo and miserable and started playing classical music all the time."

Scott was caught up in the fun and games as much as Gary and John. It was around this time that he met at the Scotch an unknown, later to be called David Bowie. But Scott's true nature quickly began to surface. "I can't stand clubs," he would soon moan. "You see people in their hip gear and it's really funny. They're all such nothing people, and the people who really have got something are probably walking about in the street."

The word was good and the buzz was building, but as far as the greater population of the music industry and the British public was concerned, The Walker Brothers were still something of an unknown quantity. Except, that is, among the little girls. Instinctively, the little girls already understood.

All over the country, the Walkers would find their prey through radio, television, and word of mouth. And the effect on the feminine population was eerily unanimous, like some shared religious epiphany.

"I was in the bath at my mam's house when I first heard 'Love Her'," recalls lifelong fan Margaret Reynolds. "I had a little transistor radio in there with me, and I was listening to Radio Luxembourg. When I heard that voice, I just went cold. It was like I'd gone into shock. And when I saw him on *Ready Steady Go!* it was love at first sight. His face, those long skinny legs, even his hands. And that voice. He was beautiful. I instantly forgot all about Paul McCartney."

Another fan, Margaret Waterhouse, was converted when she saw an early television appearance. "I was only 11 at the time," says Waterhouse. "They were clean, in a smart but casual way, and all three members of the group were good-looking – which was quite unusual then. You usually had a good-looking lead singer and the others were just average on looks. So the Walkers broke the mould in that department. I also think the fact that they were American and not English added to the excitement factor – just a touch more interesting because they came from a faster and flasher world.

"The main attraction for me, though, was their voices: Scott's rich velvet voice with John harmonising in the background just made me melt. The way they stood and delivered a song was simply hypnotic, those dramatic hand gestures of Scott and John's ... this is what made them so exciting to watch as well as listen to."

Future singer-songwriter John Howard was attracted through the printed page. "I read about the Walkers in my parents' *Daily Express*. They looked amazing. Broody and dudey, James Dean shades, black sweaters, tight black jeans, skinny-hipped and gorgeous. I heard 'Love

Her' on Radio Luxembourg. It was a superb gloom-fest, full of foreboding strings, big echoey backing, and a voice from the deepest well of sombreness. And above all this was the sweetest third – above harmony, a husky detached accompaniment to the pleading lead voice. Pop perfection."

The Walkers were a phenomenon just waiting to happen. Most of those stricken were happy to be pleasured passively, while others felt the overwhelming need to contribute. A teenage Chrissie McCall, watching television in Manchester, would become the president of The Walker Brothers' fan club (Northern Division). Forty years on, she remembers the moment vividly. "There was a girl called Sheila that I used to be friends with at school. We watched *Ready Steady Go!* every Friday night. Whoo!, these three nice American guys came on. It was 'Love Her'. And she fell hook, line, and sinker for John. Absolutely had a mega crush on John."

At this point, the communal experience shared with so many other Margarets and Sheilas takes a B-road. "Then later, she said to me y'know what I've done? I've gone and written off to ask if we can run their fan club. I said, 'You what? Are you nuts! We've never run a fan club in our life! We've never even been in a fanclub! What if they say yes?' She said oh we'll cope, we'll cope. And we never thought we'd hear from them. Then we got a note from Capable Management, saying we're already starting one, but would you like to deal with the northwest branch? So we looked at each other and said 'Yeah!'."

Remarkably, it was only after the success of the single that Philips woke up to the cause. David Shrimpton was head of Philips stock control, but until now the Walkers had registered merely as three more pretty anonymous faces. "With regard to what the Walkers were doing earlier on, I really don't know," he admits. "I may be over-emphasising this, but they were signed to Smash/Mercury in the US, not Philips UK. The deal and their ownership of recordings belonged firmly with those in the USA. However, after 'Love Her', people in the office began to take notice.

"My first visual impression of them," says Shrimpton, "was that they were quite tall with skinny arms. They were also very aloof and seemed humourless, with the exception of Gary. They didn't really mix with the staff at Philips and kept pretty much to themselves."

John: "We came over and we went to see the people at Philips Records ... we all said hello, and they said hello – and everybody was polite. We said, 'We're going to be in town for a few weeks. We're just going to cruise around and look at England.' They said OK. I guess about that time, they sent the 'Love Her' tapes over to Philips. The next time we called them up ... actually, we didn't call them up, they called us up and said, 'We want to talk!' So we said OK and went to their office. Then, all of a sudden, we noticed there was a lot more brass in the room, y'know? The first time we went it was like a secretary and somebody else. The next time it was like the vice president of the company."

By the time Gary, Scott, and John had left the meeting at Philips, their world had changed irrevocably. The bedsit was the first to go. Scott and Gary (plus the latter's train set) moved into a furnished flat in Chelsea. Visiting journalists were immediately introduced to the Dadaesque surroundings of the pair's new home. The flat apparently came with an anonymous marble bust, a giant aspidistra, a bedroom adorned with 15 mirrors, and an out-of-work actress who improvised as their secretary.

Holding court, Gary was an interviewer's dream. Buzzing with nervous, happy energy, he hopped from subject to subject regardless of the question. When Gary got going he was like a Yorkshire terrier on speed. "John ... kept coming back to [Onslow Gardens] at ridiculous hours in the morning, and the landlady was going out of her mind and everything. He would insist on playing this one guitar run at about 2am, so we decided to compromise and left.

"We got this new road manager, Claude Powell, just over from the States. He doesn't know how wild the fans are over here, see? We went to *Top Of The Pops* in Manchester, and outside were about 75 kids. Claude's famous last words were, 'Don't worry, I'll hold them back.' He lost his cufflinks, his watch, his jacket ... they did the mash potato all over his face."

The enigmatic 'Claude Powell' was also named as their mysterious backer during early interviews. (The backer was, of course, Gary's stepfather.) Powell would exit their story as quickly as he entered it, leaving the ethereal traces of a fantasy character, most likely made up by the boys for their own amusement during one of those long February afternoons in bedsit-land.

With chart success and new digs came substantial professional allies. Signed to Capable, the boys now had heavy management, who in turn arranged an agent, the prestigious Arthur Howes. Press was initially managed by the established publicist Brian Somerville. In finally signing to Philips, who bought out their contract with Ben-Ven/Smash, they acquired a powerful label that began to contribute its considerable resources to their cause.

To the combined might of these advantages, they added their all-American good looks, Scott's voice, and the combined chemistry and charisma of all three. All of this was caged within the pop epoch of 1965. Success was begging them and the Philips recording studio was wide open to receive.

As Abbey Road was to EMI, so the in-house studios at Stanhope Place near Marble Arch were to Philips. They were situated on the cusp of London's heart and above the Central line – a faint rumble could be felt as the tube trains passed below. During their 30-year existence, the Philips studios would rival America's Stax or northwest London's Abbey Road as a hit factory. The list of those who recorded there is eclectic and comprehensive, including practically everyone who was anyone, chart-wise, between the 50s and the early 80s.

The main studio, Studio One, was 60 feet long, 20 feet wide, and 25 feet high. It has been described as "cramped" by one engineer who routinely recorded full orchestral and choral sessions there and as "vast" by The Who's Roger Daltrey, who recorded there as part of a four-piece. Session-guitarist maestro Alan Parker was among the new recruits called in for the Walkers' first session there. "The studio was a little bit confined," he says, "long and narrow. The control room had a narrow walkway at the back, where we used to stand and listen. So it was a bit restrictive, with all the orchestra and brass, percussion, and singing groups – it was really crammed in."

The entrance to the studio reception was down a stairwell from the street, in through a side door, turning left to go up. The recording space itself was on a raised level, but the guts of the studio were typical of the time.

Roger Wake, then a teenage tape-operator, remembers the studio's specifications with a boffin's clarity. "Physically, there was the studio, then the control room, and then a separate machine room, where the tape machines were. The control room had big windows so that Johnny [Franz, producer] and Peter [Oliff, engineer] could look out and see into the studio. From where I was, in the machine room, we had a little window about three-feet square so I could see into the control room.

"We also had a set-up so that I could hear what was going on in the control room. If Peter wanted to speak to the studio or me, he had a talkback button for both. So I'd be in the control room with all the tape machines, the multitracks, and the stereos and big patch panel, which we would have to operate.

"Philips then had a different patching system to other studios such as Abbey Road, with a patch panel about seven by four feet. Of course, it was all valves [tubes] back then. The first time The Walker Brothers recorded in England, it would have been on an old German valve console. On four-track tape."

Keith Roberts was a budding arranger and a regular at the studio, and although he wouldn't work with John and Scott for a few years yet, he was familiar with the placing of musicians at such a session. "The strings were right down the far end, usually. Drums in the middle, so both sides could hear them. The other rhythm stuff was around the drummer: the guitars and the bass guitar. I'd be in the middle, conducting, so all the musicians could see me. You'd have headphones, one ear on, one off."

The human embodiment of the Philips studio was producer Johnny Franz. He was addicted to (sugarless) cups of tea, dapper in a deep-grey 50s-style pinstripe suit, dark-brown hair slicked back, his groomed moustache pencil thin. He always seemed to have one hand in his pocket, while in the elegant piano-player fingers of the other, a cigarette perpetually burned, swathing him in smoke. Dave Dee, who was tasting his first success with Dozy, Beaky, Mick, and Tich, recalls Franz with a cinematic clarity. "He used to smoke like a trooper. I'd been to his house for dinner and everything. He was a lovely bloke, Johnny, but we used to sit and talk to him and he used to sit and smoke a fag while he was talking, and we used to time how long it took before the ash fell off. Sometimes he'd smoke a cigarette almost two-thirds with the ash still on it.

"He would be talking, and he'd get engrossed with whatever it was he was talking about – whether it was music, or whatever – and the ash on the end of his fag used to get longer and longer and longer. It was a standing joke with us, how long he could get down the cigarette before the ash fell off."

Franz was born in the London village of Hampstead on February 23 1922. He was a bona fide Londoner and a naturally gifted pianist, gigging through the blitz, playing at various nightclubs in the West End during the war.

At some point in his twenties he was involved in a light-airplane crash, when the DH Dragon Rapide biplane in which he was travelling up-ended at Jersey airport. He was a passionate amateur photographer and, dazed and shocked, he had the wherewithal to stagger from the smoke and photograph the wreck. The incident would leave him with a lifelong fear of flying – he would never fly again – and a slight stoop.

Franz served an apprenticeship of sorts, orchestrating for the BBC and working as an accompanist for singers such as Anne Shelton. In 1954, he was appointed as Philips' first resident producer and A&R man, only one year after the company had formed. This was a powerful position. He was generally liked but also greatly respected, as Roger Wake confirms.

"John Franz wasn't really known for having any 'messing about' moments," says Wake. "It's not the sort of thing he did. He wouldn't really lighten up at all. Certainly from a tape-op's point of view, he wouldn't. He always had a copy of *Amateur Photographer* magazine around, as well. He'd be sitting with his legs crossed, reading his *Amateur Photographer* and scratching his balls. Until he accepted you, he was a difficult man to work for. A daunting person occasionally. But everyone loved him."

Many of the musicians employed by Franz remember him as an encouraging, inspiring, benign figure. He was in a position of power but he did not abuse such privileges. It seems he was, at heart, a nice guy who was rarely bored and never boring. "The great thing about Johnny Franz was that he was such a fountain of information, so aware of what was going on in terms of technical innovations and so on," states Dave Shrimpton of Philips, who still has Franz's address book in his possession. He admits to missing him every day. "When he wasn't busy buying Harry Secombe's old Rolls-Royces, he would routine songs in his office, which was directly above the studio, and the artists would learn so much about recording from him."

"He was lucky, in a way," remarks Dave Dee. "He was a musician who loved music and, obviously, he got himself into a situation where he hit producing at the right time. It all came together for him."

Franz was an acutely active A&R man. He had signed Shirley Bassey, after merely seeing her perform on television, and more recently Dusty Springfield. He had heard The Walker Brothers before he had seen them, and was apparently under the impression that they were middle-aged crooners. Upon meeting them, he was somewhat taken aback by their youth, with all three barely in their twenties.

These differences of culture and age would ultimately be positive. When the boy Scott Engel looked at Johnny Franz, it seems something clicked. Instantly, a mutual respect and affection was sparked between them. Franz gave the impression of a refined, somewhat old-fashioned gentlemen, but he was essentially ageless, with an appetite for life that did not confine itself to his peers.

Dave Dee was slightly older than Scott, but he remembers Franz's graciousness well. "I was about 22 at the time, and I used to go and sit with Johnny when we were recording. If you were in a recording session and not involved in some bit of it – the other boys were doing backing vocals or whatever – you'd be sat there twiddling your thumbs. So I used to wander around the Philips building, and sometimes, if he was in his office, I just used to wander in and say, 'You got a minute?' He'd say yeah and we would sit and talk about anything. He was short and chunky, and I couldn't place his age. He was older but he wasn't ... old."

Guitarist Alan Parker: "From what I sussed, Johnny and Scott always seemed to be very friendly and very collaborative. I'm sure Scott had a lot of respect and admiration for Johnny. He was a very experienced man, a producer of a hell of a lot of big artists. There is no hiding from experience. Johnny was a lovely man, actually – and he was a real producer."

"Johnny Franz was old-school," Scott told the journalist Joe Jackson in 1995. "A great piano player for singers. He played for Tony Bennett ... everyone. A great man combined with rock'n'roll players and a young engineer [Peter Oliff] – it was wonderful to be with him."

Soon Engel and Franz would be working together obsessively and socialising, mixing business with pleasure, despite their apparent incongruity. They dined together frequently, either at their favourite local Chinese restaurant, the Lotus House on Edgware Road, or at Franz's impressive residence near Hampstead Heath, which the producer shared with his wife, Moira.

Engel and Franz were both obsessed and possessed by music, and clearly they enjoyed each other's company and talent, discussing arrangements, writing songs, and playing standards together, just for the thrill of it all.

As head of A&R, Franz had a baby grand in his office. Quite often, sessions would be delayed as Scott and Franz ran through the classic American songbook. Gary would sit in as a one-man audience making requests. "I'd be there, giving 'em the most obscure numbers I could think of – you know, old standards and such, and I couldn't catch 'em out. They knew 'em all!"

The resident engineer at Stanhope Place at this time was Franz's number two, Peter Oliff. He was a diminutive man who would perch at the mixing board somewhere between Franz and Wake. When Scott recalled Franz's right-hand man some decades later, his comments implied a parallel yet invisible Walker Brothers: a trio consisting of Scott, Franz, and Oliff.

"[Oliff] was a great engineer," said Scott. "He'd been doing Dusty Springfield and all those people. But although he had a wonderful idea of what a new sound could be, he couldn't quite get it. So I knew what was happening at the bottom end, and that's what made it complete. What Spector did was use two basses: an upright and an electric. Then he used two or three keyboards playing the same thing. One would be an upright piano, [another] a harpsichord. Then he used two, three, maybe four guitars.

"Whereas [Oliff] was just using the basic guitar, bass, drums set-up, with two drummers sometimes. Johnny Franz could read music, whereas Spector couldn't."

That summer, Stanhope Place became the location for recording The Walker Brothers' debut album. John Maus was now assured of a successful stay in Britain and had returned to America to marry his long-time girlfriend Kathy. When he returned to the UK in the first week of July 1965, sure enough he found a tour and a recording session booked for him.

As he was driven to Stanhope Place that morning, Scott was nursing a sore jaw. It was the result of answering his door the night before to a drunken stranger who had turned up at the flat claiming it was his. As Scott started to argue, the stranger had punched him in the face. This was no bad omen, however. Such uncouthness mattered not. The Walkers' debut recording session on UK soil was superlatively successful, aching jaw and all. After all, the very first song of their very first UK recording session was 'Make It Easy On Yourself'.

Gary explained the reasoning behind their choice of song: "[Burt] Bacharach was writing very well at the moment and was quite well accepted, so we liked the song very much, and it was down the same lines as what we'd done before with 'Love Her'. And we thought it would be good all round, y'know? So we cut six sides, and out of those six we figured the Bacharach was about the best."

John found the song. "Jerry Butler had done it," he explained. "And I was an incredible Jerry Butler fan. So I kinda presented the idea to Scott and said, 'What do you think? Should we have a go at trying this?' You know, it's a big task. Jerry Butler's version was so good."

The arranger for those first sessions was to be one in a long line. Ivor Raymonde was a well-respected professional who was best known for some exquisite work with Dusty Springfield. He loved 'Make It Easy On Yourself' and established an instant rapport with Scott and co. "Ah! What a joy to record a song like that," he told BBC Radio London 25 years later. "I mean, the song itself is beautiful. Putting an arrangement to it is absolutely magic. Between Scott and myself, we devised an orchestra that would be The Walker Brothers' band, if you know what I mean. So we had three pianos, four guitars, umpteen Latin American instruments, percussion ... a sound that we hoped would be the 'Walker Brothers' – and, of course, it worked."

Although full credit was given to writers, arrangers, and producers, none of the musicians who made up this Walker Brothers Band was mentioned on the record sleeves. They were, as a rule, paid on the spot, and so nobody kept receipts or long-term records of personnel. Individual names have largely disappeared into the ether, and they do not even find reincarnation in the sumptuous booklets accompanying CD reissues.

It seems, however, that particular producers used the same groups of musicians repeatedly. Franz, Oliff, and Wake would use the same orchestra to record Harry Secombe on Tuesday, the Walkers on Wednesday, and Dusty Springfield on the Friday. A favoured sticksman was the dapper drummer's-drummer Ronnie Verrell.

Something of a legend in session circles even then, Verrell would play on many of the Walkers' group and solo sessions. He would often stretch out on the floor between takes to ease his bad back. Like many of the musicians used at these sessions, Verrell came from a jazz background. He uses the techniques from such an education to great effect in the context of these 'pop' songs. Verrell's rolling tom fills, especially on 'In My Room', 'Archangel', and 'People Get Ready', added an unexpected edginess to the tracks.

His vivid fills sometimes seem as if they are just about to tumble out of time – but they never do. Players like Verrell are typical of the jazz influence inherent in the Walkers' recordings, another unique ingredient in an already quixotic mix. (Verrell would go on to ghost as master-drummer Animal in *The Muppet Show* television series. And incidentally, co-starring in the 1979 *Muppet Movie* beside Animal – as Snake Walker, the 'frog killer' – was an American actor also known as Scott Walker.)

Many of the musicians of the 60s felt that they had strayed from their original musical calling. But pop music was on the rise and it paid well. Alan Parker: "I studied classical guitar originally, and I got all the degrees and all the cups and medals by the time I was 15. All very nice, but you couldn't earn a living at it. So I swapped over to electric guitar. Played with all the big bands in the dancehalls, Tubby Hayes at Ronnie Scott's club, played with Buddy Rich. And you had to learn to sight-read. It was good grounding. I could play anything that was put in front of me."

If someone had suggested to any British A&R man in 1965 that he form and sign up a group consisting of a full classical orchestra, a jazz rhythm-section, extra percussion, and the odd choir, male and female, they would have been shown the door immediately. They would have been laughed out of the office, well before the further suggestion that three young and impossibly handsome Californian dudes should front such a colossal combo. Three 'brothers', whose own musical interests and experience ranged from surf, rock'n'roll, cocktail lounge, Broadway musical, avant-garde, and classical.

As if this was unlikely enough, the actual drummer of the three wouldn't drum. Oh, and the lead singer had one of the greatest ballad voices ever and sounded 20 years older than he was. And they're called The Walker Brothers but aren't actually related. Or called Walker.

However, through glorious accident and design, Philips had inherited these three Californians from Mercury Rcords. In deciding to invest in and promote them as one of their own acts, this bizarrely attractive mutant hybrid is exactly what Philips had before them. Back in the studio, this wonderful new creature named The Walker Brothers was being taken for a test run.

The supporting cast numbered almost a hundred. Among the faceless hordes of hired musicians, it was the electric guitarists, players of a still relatively 'new' instrument, who were beginning to stand out.

Leading lights on the session circuit of the day were Jeff Beck, Vic Flick, and Jimmy Page. Flick would find fame as the man who played the James Bond '007' riff, and Wake asserts that Jimmy Page played on at least one Walkers session. Very rarely would the musicians on the record play with the same artists live.

It is also worth noting that in most cases these were just jobbing musicians. They lived session by session, with little thought for posterity. Alan Parker and Big Jim Sullivan would go on to play guitar for the Walkers throughout the next decade, but at that first meeting, even with the modest hit of 'Love Her' behind the Walkers, the name obviously meant little to them. "I had no idea who they were," admits Parker today.

Sullivan also considered the gig just another job, but even so he picked up on something special. "I worked with 'em right from day one of them coming to England," he states matter-of-factly. "We didn't really know what we were doing. We didn't know we were laying down history. Who were The Walker Brothers? Nobody, until they had hits.

"I was introduced to Scott as we were going up the stairs of the Philips studios. I remember when I first heard him sing I thought, 'This guy's got a great voice.' There are some people whose voices don't suit their face, but his did. He was a cool guy in every way that I could see."

Alan Parker describes the dynamic at these sessions. "Scott was very, very friendly and a little bit nervy, a little bit fractious, I suppose. That was just his personality. But we got on, he and I and John, we got on extremely well, and over the years it developed into quite a professional relationship.

"On those early sessions, my set-up was a little Fender amplifier called a Deluxe Reverb. Guitar-wise it would have been either a Fender Telecaster, a Stratocaster, or a Gibson Les Paul. I would usually play the lead guitar, but if I was working with Big Jim, we would swap around now and then, and he would maybe do it.

"Big Jim would play a lot of the acoustic parts, too, and we'd both do the 'ker-chink' on the offbeat. That would be done on either the

Telecaster or the Strat. I would always take at least three or four guitars with me to the session."

Big Jim remembers the session slightly differently. "My first session with them was for 'Make It Easy'. You can tell it was me because in lots of the tunes there, especially with Ivor Raymonde, I'd be doing the 'ker-chink' sound on guitar. That was my speciality. That's why Ivor used me, because I did all of the cross-rhythms on electric guitar. When Ivor had a session, I was usually on it.

"My amplifier then would have been an Ampeg, and the guitar I used on these sessions was called a National. I'd use a fuzz box when they wanted distortion. Listen to 'Make It Easy'. It sounds like there's two electric guitarists playing two parts, but that was all me, recorded live. I had a footswitch that triggered the tremolo either on or off. Just a pedal. Nothing to it."

The image of an unflustered Big Jim, pretty much playing his parts as he read them alongside a full orchestra – while being recorded live – is an apt microcosm of the whole recording process used for these works. Sound 'preparation', in the dual meaning of the word, was a necessity. This discipline would be ingrained in Scott for the rest of his recording career. Speaking decades later, he was acutely aware of the effects of this particular apprenticeship.

"I come from the old school of recording – and I combine it with the new," he would say in the 80s. "The reason I work this way is because, in the early days when I was working at Philips as a co-producer on those records, I had to have everything prepared. So our albums were done very quickly and live, with a live orchestra. So in my mind I always work that way. I always get everything completely in my head before I go into the studio, because there can't be any mistakes and it helps people work faster."

While the squadron of musicians brought the music to life in their own infinitely complicated human way, the techniques used to record them were, especially compared to coming developments, fairly basic. "Those first sessions were recorded on four-track," says Roger Wake, incredulously. "I think we went to eight-track in 1968. In both cases, when we ran out of tracks – which would obviously happen very quickly on four-track as the orchestra took up most of the tracks – we would mix the existing tracks onto a new four-track, leaving one track empty for an overdub, usually the vocal. This could continue up to four stages of transfer sometimes."

"They hardly had any effects then on desks [boards]," adds Big Jim. "They had reverb, and that, but that goes without saying, it's not really an 'effect'. When I think of effects, I'm thinking of flangers, fuzz boxes, and all that sort of stuff – which we used to put on ourselves, with our amps or pedals or both."

Therefore, to a large extent – and even when taking into account the subtleties of mastering and the variables of playback – the eventual sound of the song as it would sound on vinyl was, by default, already there in the room as it was recorded. It came, in part, from the scores and charts brought to life by the anonymous ranks of brass, woodwind, and strings. Like animals in the zoo, each set of varying musicians adhered to a particular stereotype. "It was a little bit 'them and us' as far as the string players and the rhythm section was concerned," says Parker. "The string players generally kept themselves to themselves, the brass were more ... jovial."

Obviously, such sessions were not cheap, as Maus was inclined to brag at the time. "When we make a record, we have a 25-piece orchestra, with brass, a string section, and an occasional harpsichord," enthused the Mantovani fan. "It costs us from £500 to £1,000, but we get what we want, so it's worth it. We don't go for these beat-group sessions that cost under £300. They're all right for those groups, but they are hit and miss affairs and definitely not for us."

Ivor Raymonde scored the deliciously ornate arrangements with little thought for expense. "Never, never, never, ever worried about money, ever. Nobody ever said to me, 'Look, we can't afford to have ten violins and four violas and two cellos.' You know, if I'd say, 'Well I think we ought to use 16 violins,' they'd say, 'Go ahead and do it.' Providing the money from a recording point of view didn't seem to be a problem."

Much less easygoing at the time was the Musicians Union. The MU kept a strict eye on the activities of all its members and in particular those of the producers. Sessions were timetabled to allow musicians ample travelling time between engagements, and until 1972, when rules relaxed a little, overdubbing was all but forbidden.

Gus Dudgeon (producer of Elton John, David Bowie) recalled: "If you wanted to do overdubbing of any sort, you had to seek permission from the MU, but it wasn't always granted. Sometimes we would only get permission to do a vocal overdub if we produced a doctor's certificate to prove that the singer was too ill at the original session."

This unrealistic ruling resulted in a charade. For the sake of the orchestra et al, the singer would have to 'be seen' singing in front of all present. Rarely would this performance be recorded; the true vocal was recorded after dark and behind locked doors. For self-confessed insomniacs such as Johnny Franz, Dusty Springfield, and Scott Walker, this was not a problem. Speaking of Dusty, Johnny Franz said: "We're both nightbirds. Dusty prefers to record at night, and we take it from there. We just go on 'til we're happy with the result."

For the young Roger Wake, such methods resulted in a bigger pay packet for a harder job. "I would always attend the vocal overdubs because that meant overtime!" jokes Wake, before adding seriously: "But then, your job doing vocals was much harder – dropping in lines and such. We would have to 'punch in' – we were the tape-ops! The engineer wouldn't do it! It's not like it is now, or has been for the last 25 years, where as an engineer I'd have a console and a tape machine in front of me and I'd do all the drop-ins. In those days we were all in separate rooms. Pretty hair-raising when doing a drop-in. And even the evening sessions were three hours.

"It was only in about 1967 that this started to shift, with people like Scott and Dusty, who were so similar in that they were so particular about their vocals: they had to be 'perfect'. If they felt they hadn't sung something properly – even if it sounded perfect to everybody else – we'd have to do it again. Dusty was the worst in the end. It was horrible! She wouldn't let anything go unless she thought it was sensational, and Scott verged on that, but it took him quite a while. Initially his vocals were done quite quickly in three-hour sessions."

CHAPTER 4 **to love somebody**

Such nocturnal shenanigans would come later, when Scott in particular, buoyed by commercial success and Franz's encouragement, would be allowed to pursue his perfectionist aesthetic. For now, the vocals were just another instrument and were recorded as quickly as possible with little fuss or nerve-racking consequences. "It was a pretty frightening experience," said Maus with typical West Coast understatement. "The way we recorded all of the early things we did ... you had to be in the position of knowing what you were going to do. ... Scott and I as a duo, [we] didn't work on separate microphones. Any of the balances and things between ourselves came from ourselves."

Dave Dee speaks of similarly primitive experiences. But for the trained musicians at the sessions, such hit and run tactics were less of an issue. "As a guitarist, I didn't find recording live scary," states Alan Parker. "You had such a good working relationship with the other musicians and with the MDs and producers. To be honest, that's part of the reason why you were booked: you weren't fazed, and you contributed. You didn't just switch the amp on and go 'ker-chink', you used your brain and inventiveness, your imagination."

Scott and John were hardly novices, either, and with the support and planning of all involved, 'Make It Easy On Yourself' took just 40 minutes to record. Ever economical, Philips ensured that Franz used every spare minute of allotted studio time. When the sessions had gone well and finished under schedule, there was always something else that could be squeezed in.

Pirate DJ Dave Cash was an early benefactor of the Philips thrift. "As for the jingles for our *Kenny And Cash Show*, I believe they recorded them during their first session," says Cash. "My contact at Philips, Paddy Fleming, told me it was during the session for 'Make It Easy On Yourself' that they recorded 'em. We got a ten-inch tape out on the boat, with 'lotsa love from The Walker Brothers' written on it. The jingles were not orchestrated, just their wonderful voices with an organ behind 'em. Quite heavy echo as I remember."

Sessions for the album were staggered to accommodate a short UK tour and various promotional duties. This meant that a full day's recording would often follow a chaotic gig the night before, which, depending on the songs scheduled to be recorded, could be both a help and a hindrance for the vocals. Scott was keen to bring his Gold Star studio experience to Britain and would soon be a dominant force both on the studio floor and in the control room.

Dusty Springfield (or 'Dusts' as Franz called her in the studio) had recorded the sublime *A Girl Called Dusty* the year before with the same team that the Walkers were now using, and so to some extent she had already gone through what Scott was now experiencing. "I was asking musicians to play sounds they'd never heard before," said Dusty. "The guys I had to work with were all playing standard basses. I was actually the first person to ask them to play a Fender bass. I was a stickler for getting it just right; I kept saying, 'No, that's not it,' and so on."

She remembered echoing Scott's same approach. "I was wanting to cop Phil Spector's sounds, and I knew that I could. I wanted to be The Crystals and Darlene Love, and [I] knew that there was going to be a space for that in this country, because it hadn't hit here – and I definitely knew that the wall of sound thing could be adapted for England and [that] I was the one to do it."

Franz would not have allowed Scott's input if he had doubted the young singer's ability and vision. Engel was allowed to work beside Franz in the producer's chair, but he knew better than to take it any further. "I picked 75 per cent of the material, because I was a kind of 'producer in disguise' in those days, for some reason. There was a situation there," Scott told journalist Joe Jackson some 30 years later. "It was a personal situation, whereby I wasn't getting any credit for – but I actually did – most of the planning and stuff there. All the stuff that was brought in through Franz was fielded through me, finally, to the end, unless somebody brought in an unusual song.

"We worked very closely together, John, Franz, and I. It was very 50/50. He had a lot of knowledge about how to get an orchestra down in a classical sense. Of course, I had the youth behind me and the excitement of wanting to get it down with everything on, you know? Naturally, it all had to be done at once. We weren't lucky like Phil Spector – we didn't have the same kind of finance. For instance, at the beginning, Phil would be able to go over to the rhythm section on one day. If he didn't like it on that one day, he could take the rhythm section the next day, or the next, and build and build, all on overdubs. We had to do it all at once, everyone playing in the studio, which I think is a hell of a lot more exciting. If you listen to our records in comparison, that's the one thing – because the musicians 'got off' and the sound is just barrelling down on you, you know? It could have been better recorded, but that was the problem, you see. Recording all at once, you can't [improve it]."

Dusty Springfield also kept her 'secret' role hidden from the public. "The magic of my situation with Johnny Franz," she said, "was that he allowed me the freedom to follow my enthusiasm. I never took the producer credit for two reasons. For one, [Franz] deserved it and I was grateful. And then there was the calculating part of me that thought it looked too slick for me to produce and sing."

Roger Wake was there from beginning to end, and he remembers it as less cut and dry. "Scott wasn't at all visible to me as a co-producer during the early sessions. Perhaps he had spoken with the arrangers beforehand," Wake muses.

"Maybe he was more active later on, certainly, but during those early sessions, he was just the singer. Johnny Franz was totally in charge. And what Johnny said went. With all his artists. It was Dusty Springfield and Scott that changed that, with Johnny, but they were the only two that ever did get away with disputing whatever Johnny Franz's decisions were."

This was a rare evolutionary step within the world of popular music. Not only did people like Scott and Dusty have what it took to become stars, but they were also diligent, articulate, and professional conceptualists. Each of them could have made it on either side of the recording console, as a singer or as a producer. The Walkers, and Scott in particular, were about to become pop stars in a way that had never been known before.

Wake witnessed this new phenomenon first-hand and at close range. "They were the new kids on the block," he says, "but the singing was very impressive, the songs were great, and so were the arrangements. They couldn't fail, really."

CHAPTER 5

LOVING HER

This record has got to be big because I want a Bentley!

John Maus (1965)

It would seem blasphemous in retrospect to consider that such a divine birth as 'Make It Easy On Yourself' could abort, but at the time of its release the record's future was far from assured. The single was released in early August 1965, among such variables as Nico's 'I'm Not Saying', Sandie Shaw's 'Long Live Love', and the second long-player by an up-and-coming comedian called Woody Allen. It was a rich and varied era, and the market was wide open for all comers. But not all would make it.

Although the fruits of the Walkers' very first UK recording session received generally good reviews, it was clear from the overall tone that the press had not yet been completely seduced. Dave Clark, reviewing the song in *Melody Maker*, was only slightly less neutral than Switzerland, commenting lamely that it was "nice. Not commercial. A number you can't knock because it's too nice".

Meanwhile, in preparation for this first proper release, a handful of gigs were arranged. As proffered tours of Germany and Scandinavia were rejected, the UK was obviously the priority. To cope with the growing violence of Walkermania, and to fulfil Scott's concept of being a 'sound and an act', a proper, grubby, warts-and-all group of musicians was needed.

The trio decided to foresake their own instrumental duties as well as those of occasional temporary organist Jimmy O'Neill (formerly of The Uglys). In doing so, they attached themselves to a ready-made group: a 'name' backing band called The Quotations who played in a working-class, blue-eyed soul style.

"You're not gonna do 'Make It Easy On Yourself' with drums, bass, and guitar," reasoned John, with classic understatement. "We had this huge orchestra [on thew record]. So what are you going to do when you're playing live? We need a huge orchestra. So we at least needed to have a seven-piece band."

Rehearsing at the grimy Starlite Club, the group grew to nine pieces when they decided that Gary's chops on the drums were not up to the task. The Quotations' regular drummer, Jimmy Pritchard, would cover for him, allowing the on-stage Leeds to be more 'Gary-like' than ever. Although not essential musically, Leeds was a definite presence during Walker gigs, joshing with and baiting the crowd, providing moral support for the nervy Engel, forsaking the drum stool for the occasional song, and generally raving it up. Depending on the backstage mood, Gary was sometimes allowed to open the gig with his own interpretation of 'You Are My Sunshine'. This sunny sentiment was not shared by some of the Walkers crew who, like Maurice, couldn't quite get the point of Gary.

"Gary couldn't play drums," scoffs Ralph Gurnett, who was now a regular member of the Walker entourage. "There was another drummer behind the curtain, and Gary Leeds used to have paper sticks." For those who wondered why Gary was kept in on the deal, John's answer was plain.

"Gary was in The Walker Brothers. When we came here and started having television success, we didn't know how we were gonna do it live. It never crossed our mind. How are we gonna present this live? It never entered anybody's head. And then suddenly it did." He concluded with Zen-like simplicity: "Gary is Gary! So Gary stayed."

While 'Make It Easy On Yourself' moved steadily up the main artery of the *NME* chart, the trio, now ably fortified by The Quotations, embarked on a short skirmish through the otherwise genteel English towns of Great Yarmouth and Morecambe. The packed gigs saw growing hysteria among the largely oestrogen-crazed masses that comprised The Walker Brothers' audience. The result was much grievous harm upon the fragile trio's persons.

"I got pulled off the stage at Rawtenstall Astoria ... I fainted. When I came round, I'd only my underwear left," grinned John dazedly. "Scott had his shirt in ribbons, and they scalped Gary. They wanted noses, pieces of cheeks, stuff like that."

Television was a safer medium and one that was exploited to its fullest. The molestable threesome had a lot going for them in this department. Compared with the average somewhat buck-toothed and lank-haired British beat combos of the day, John, Scott, and Gary were extremely photogenic, space-age sexy, all-American TV eye-candy.

To help promote their third single, they appeared on *Ready Steady Go!*, *Thank Your Lucky Stars*, and the shortlived *Discs-A-Go-Go*, a run of early evening programmes appointed to bring the cheek-boned threesome into the living rooms of the great British public.

It wasn't all plain sailing, however. The Walkers were not just glad-to-be-here happy-go-lucky chancers overawed by the sudden attention. Engel in particular was a showbiz veteran, and the BBC's *Saturday Club* saw a Walkers walk-out when the singer perfectionist decided that technical shortcuts were compromising the band's professional reputation. They did eventually reach an agreement, and the appearance went ahead, but such behaviour, however justified, would begin to garnish Engel with a reputation for being difficult.

Video recordings of these particular appearances are yet to surface, and it is ironic that the one clip for 'Make It Easy On Yourself' that has survived is from a show unaired to this day. Simon Dee's *Discotheque*, a UK pop show in a then-innovative magazine format, was intended for exclusive distribution abroad.

It is an interesting clip. We are introduced to a rail-thin and visibly nervous Gary, who is interviewed haltingly before scurrying back to the safety of his grinning pseudo siblings. There follows an enchantingly dreamy mime through the soon-to-be Number One single.

Apart from looking almost like *Thunderbirds*-puppet versions of themselves, they also appear incredibly young, closer to teenagers than the experienced and seasoned musicians they were. If one was to take away the soundtrack, one could assume they were a folk trio. With Scott strumming on a humble acoustic six-string, John on Fender Strat, and Gary lamely playing at playing the drums, the contrast between their 'performance' and the massive-sounding production is charmingly incongruous. This perhaps illustrates the schism that was at the heart of The Walker Brothers as a group. Clearly, John and Scott were more than capable musicians, yet aside from singing, they never played any of the instruments on their own records. This had been the norm even a few years previously, but with the dominance of The Beatles and the Stones and the subsequent emergence of The Byrds and The Who, this practise was quickly beginning to seem antiquated, un-hip, un-cool, and decidedly old.

The key to their sound was ingrained within the production – and this, of course, included their indisputably fine voices. The production was in itself as much an art as the writing and performing of the song. But it meant that when they toured, even if they could have been heard above the screaming, it would have been impossible for them to recreate such a sound.

Faced with this dilemma, one would have thought that the traditional method of touring would perhaps not have been considered as the first option. A typical tour for a group at the Walkers' level during the mid to late 60s would include as many dates in as many inappropriate venues (civic halls, cinemas) in as short a time as possible. PA systems were crude and transport hampered by the lack of extensive motorways in Britain at that time. As far as being true to what the Walkers essentially were – their sound – it may have been possible that someone would have considered that touring in such conditions was a futile exercise. These kinds of shows were perfectly adequate for the more basic beat combos of the day, such as Dave Dee's group, The Kinks, and even, until *Sgt Pepper*, The Beatles. (No coincidence that they retired from live shows after the recording of *Sgt Pepper*, which was one of the first truly popular albums that utilised the studio as an instrument and was, thus, almost impossible to recreate live.)

But with The Walker Brothers having such a trademark sonic signature, it is perversely appealing to think that their live performances could have been 'limited' to orchestral residencies at symphonic halls in key parts of the country. Nevertheless, evidently, this was not how things were done then, and we would have to wait for Scott's television series for a glimpse into such a reality. This meant that, in essence, The Walker Brothers existed only in the fourth world: that is, within the grooves of their most final and realised records.

This would go some way to explaining the stress that Scott in particular would suffer through the not so merry-go-round of relentless touring.

The Brothers had surrendered their instruments, so the live shows were reduced to a kind of hinterland where neither the artist nor the audience were approaching musical satisfaction. Indeed, this was not the point. All involved were well aware of this paradox.

Gary: "There were so many television shows. Pop shows, where we came over as a very romantic, moody type of group, right? But when we did the stage shows, which no one ever heard ... I mean, you'd come out there, and it would be a wall of sound. I mean, you could have done anything and no one would have heard it. The shows were a sort of ... reverse ... of the records."

The Walkers turned down one major opportunity. Gary: "Ed Sullivan asked us over ... and we said, 'We want three shows, just like The Beatles, or we won't do it.' And he said, 'No, we'll give you two and that's it.' Nobody would back down, so we didn't do it."

Scott: "When you appeared on stage, it was very rare [for the audience]. When The Beatles or we appeared live, we were onstage for about ten seconds, because the stage would be charged with girls. It was because they didn't have any other way to get to you ... there was no video recorders or anything like that. So really getting to you was a matter of life and death."

John said at the time: "We admit our stage sound is nothing like on record. How could it be, without bringing the whole jazz on stage? And in how many places could we do that? We try to sing numbers suitable for [a] small backing, but we have to include our record successes to please the customers. So we do a strung-down version. The fans seem satisfied. Are we content? Well, I guess we have to be happy with the best we can do."

Dave Cash: "I saw 'em live four or five times. I stood at the side of the stage. No, of course, you couldn't hear anything. But when you're a pop star, that's not the point. It's like John Lennon said, about playing Shea Stadium: 'Why did we bother even turning the goddamn amp on!'."

Obviously, for any self-respecting musician, no matter how initially intoxicated by the experience of fame and success, such a tour was a finite ride on a gaudy carousel. For Scott, such exhilaration would soon turn to nausea of an increasingly existential nature.

It must have been quickly, even suddenly, wearying to appear as a mere totem night after night for the gratification of adolescent energies and for the vague benefit of further sales – a nebulous motive, as the records would have sold anyway. Especially for someone as introspective and sensitive as Engel.

Add to this the latent suspicion that the Walkers' lead vocalist had never even principally considered himself as a singer. In addition, he probably felt little more than duty-bound by his professionalism to pander to the expected role of 'entertainer'.

Despite Scott's growing predicament, Gurnett, who saw the show from backstage each night, comments: "He had fun. We all had fun. He had no preferences for playing in one country or another. It was all a muchness. Once he was on stage, he could have been anywhere."

In addition, Scott was beginning to draw attention away from the others, through no particular will of his own. Interviewers were beginning to pick up on the fact that this Number One pop star was not the sort of simpler soul they were used to.

The group were celebrating their chart success backstage with magnums of champagne, prior to a sell-out Colchester show. But the lead singer of one of the most popular groups in Britain at that time was beginning to talk strangely. "Sometimes I don't feel as if I belong here with John and Gary," sighed Scott. "I don't think this whole thing is my scene. I walk around the streets for hours, thinking, wondering, trying to get to know myself. Sometimes I walk so long that I lose all sense of time and forget to show up for appointments."

Following the show, John had an appointment he couldn't miss. He was treated for concussion at Colchester Infirmary. Sue Martin, a freelance journalist who was tagging along that night, remembered the ferocity of the fans' passion, a passion bordering on the pathological. "John was thrown into the pack and walked over, his head trampled and his body kicked."

Engel would escape Colchester relatively unharmed, but it was perhaps only a matter of time. For someone who would later admit to starting out partly because he wanted "to make great music ... with great drummers. That's a bass player's dream", his current floodlit role as an all-singing, all-dancing pop phenomenon was mutually exciting and disorientating.

Gary was as much swept up in the hysteria of it all as anyone, but he was still sensitive enough to his buddy's plight. "What he wanted to do was music. That's what he wanted. He didn't know all this went with it. He liked playing, is all. When we played in Hollywood, he could still go around, get a sandwich or whatever. Here he couldn't go anywhere. Even at a party ... he still was the shy one in the corner."

Becoming a songwriter could only aggravate the situation, and that was exactly what happened next. As the Walkers approached their apex, Scott's true calling began to emerge. "I was writing some very strange little songs for the B-sides. Because you get the publishing [royalties]," he admitted candidly. "They didn't care what I wrote. That's how I got started, you see. They said, 'Well, you can write anything and no one's gonna hear it, because it'll be on the B-side'."

Somewhat disingenuously, he stated: "I had no intention of writing songs before that. I started to write to make money."

Between recording sessions and live dates, Engel would seek writing collaborators elsewhere. His initial efforts saw him sharing early songwriting credits with Johnny Franz, Ivor Raymonde, and backing singer-songwriter Lesley Duncan. Anyone, in fact, other than the most obvious. Throughout their entire history, John, Scott, and Gary would never share any composition credits together. John's reasoning for this was plain: "Scott and I had different ideas about writing songs. [Writing] is a personal deal and it goes where it goes .... . We have different minds and can't write together."

One person who could find enough common ground with the awkward Engel was Lesley Duncan, a Françoise Hardy lookalike. "Scott and I shared Johnny Franz as an A&R man, but we actually met in Don Arden's nightclub in London. Scott wasn't dancing, no. We got talking, I said 'I write songs.' He said, 'I write songs.' So, we said, 'Let's write songs together.'

"We wrote 'You're All Around Me' at his flat, I think. I think we had a guitar and we just tossed ideas back and forth, you know? I sang backing on some of their records, but we didn't write together again. He wasn't a particularly likeable person ... he didn't have many social niceties about him."

At the time, Scott was much more enthusiastic than his writing partner. "I wrote some things with Lesley Duncan. Wait till you hear them! You'll blow your mind. But I'm lazy about songs. I have to have somebody with me. I might get five or six songs on tape and cancel them all out."

Until the 70s, record companies often released different versions of a hit song simultaneously, and in a futile and doomed bid to compete, Decca immediately released a version of 'Make It Easy On Yourself' by one Bern Elliot, which went directly from the pressing plant to the void. As the Walkers' definitive reading of the Burt Bacharach and Hal David song made its way up the charts, Scott took time out to comment on the work of other artists in *Melody Maker*'s Blind Date feature. This perennial ruse was lifted wholesale from *Down Beat*, the classic American jazz magazine: guests are played records without knowing beforehand who the artists are, and they have to guess.

Summing up a playlist that included such obscure and variable artists as Force 5, Steve Benbow, Del Shannon, and The Spencers' Washboard Kings, among others, a buoyantly disappointed Scott exclaimed: "Do you think something could be wrong with your record player? Play me a great record! Everyone's going down the tube!"

He was, however, impressed enough by the Astrud Gilberto record 'Theme From The Sandpiper' to permanently 'borrow' it from the journalist and take it wth him.

The ordeal had left Scott in a rare mood of public gregariousness, and throughout the piece he candidly revealed that he and Franz had considered recording Dylan's 'She Belongs To Me' for their debut album (along with Andy Williams's 'Almost There'). Engel also took the opportunity to give the official Engel definition of Dylan: "Subconscious alliteration – that's what he is."

Concluding a refreshingly cheery feature, he went on to speak of his fondness for country & western lyrics, tipped a hat to the production prowess of Dick Glasser and Phil Spector, and casually revealed the future of pop music. "There are a lot of funky things that I like. But it's the big sound that will come."

John Maus, meanwhile, still had his mind on less corporeal matters. "I've been to look at a Bentley already and is it groovy!" he gibbered. "It's old and beautiful. I had a little ride in it, and you can't hear a rattle!"

The big sound that Scott spoke of had indeed arrived and it seemed that nothing could stand in its way. Not even The Rolling Stones. By September 25, 'Make It Easy On Yourself' had trundled Panzer-like over 'Satisfaction' and was a Number One in both the *Melody Maker* singles chart and in the hearts of pretty girls everywhere. As self-appointed head of the fan club, Chrissie McCall was beginning to feel pleasantly overwhelmed.

"We would send out fan-club magazines. Three a year," recalls the erstwhile teen president. "We used to organise 'Walker holidays' ... it was in Bournemouth. This was the days before computers: we used to write out all the envelopes together by hand. We had 16,000 members in the Northwest branch alone. It was ginormous for two little girls. I was only 16. What we did was join every fan club we could think of to see what they did. We'd never really been interested in a fan club in our lives.

"Scott and John weren't particularly interested in the fan club," says McCall, "but Gary took an interest. He used to sit and sign things, but to be honest we used to forge their autographs. We had to learn how to do it. We'd have competitions: 'Win Gary's sweater' and things like that. The fan club was so big. They just went bazonk! And they attracted girl after girl after girl. Screaming girls. They brought out this incredible lust in young girls. I can't remember how many times I was asked, 'What colour are Scott's underpants?'."

Momentum was building, and the phantom Claude Powell had "returned to Disneyland" just as the Walkers had pupated from contenders to pop gods. It was all happening so quickly.

For John, Gary, and, in particular, their lead singer, the phrase "couldn't get arrested" no longer applied. Scott the hoodlum confessed: "I felt like living it up a little after all the hard times, so I went to this pub and got surrounded by a bunch of freeloaders and a couple of beatnik types. I was drinking beer and whisky chasers and pow! I got drunker and drunker until I was thrown out on the street. Funny thing, none of those freeloaders came to see if I was all right. Instead, the two beatnik painters picked me up – but I was really stoned and started throwing rocks at cars. The police picked me up and locked me up, saying I should be ashamed of myself. I just said, 'Sorry officer,' and the whole bit. Anyway, there were no charges brought against me."

That same week, results of the annual *Melody Maker* readers' poll were released. Gary, John, and Scott came first in the Brightest Hope Of 1965 (International) category and ranked eighth place in Best International Group.

The feeling behind these anonymous voters was expressed in a letter to the *MM* editor, courtesy of one Madeline Noble of Liversedge, Yorkshire. "I'm bored of The Beatles, sick of the Stones, bemused by The Byrds," frothed the fan. "So I'm glad the Walkers have decided to stay in Britain," she wrote. "They look good, sing good, and by golly they do us good!"

In almost direct contrast to such youthful gaiety, Scott, sounding more like a weary frontline tank commander than a pop star, was quoted that same week as saying: "Now we have set a standard for ourselves we must work hard to sustain it."

It was becoming increasingly obvious to fans and colleagues alike that Scott was no mere run-of-the-mill poster boy. While this may have disturbed the more perceptive among those close to him, no one voiced concern. Everything was going to plan – and then some.

October saw John returning to the States yet again, apparently to "protect people like my sister who have no brains. She has this sympathy for derelict young men". In his absence, Scott, Gary, and Maurice met up with Burt Bacharach to discuss the possibility of Burt writing something either in collaboration with or specifically for them, but nothing would come of it.

That month also saw the conclusion of a dispute between Capable Management and Philip and Dorothy Solomon, new business partners of Clayman and King. King was now assured of the Walkers' global success, and while he was happy to share his other acts with the Solomons, the Walkers would belong only to him. And Barry.

On a day-to-day basis, Capable had initially dealt with the more outgoing John and Gary, but it was now Scott who became the group's main man. As well as the most talented, he was also the most savvy. During this period, Scott had the foresight to found a publishing company with his live-work agent Arthur Howes, and he signed an independent producer's contract with Philips. His first gig as a producer was on home ground, as Scott explained.

"I soon started making records for myself – with a buddy called John Stewart, who's in Britain now. We had a scene going with Phil Spector and Sonny Bono back in the States. First guy I'm recording is Gary. Now, Gary is a funny character. He gets this thing going on stage and gets a lot of fan mail. I'd like to see him get a solo hit himself, though maybe he isn't the greatest singer in the world."

Engel explained that Leeds was the only Walker Brother who had not signed to Mercury–Philips, and thus the plan was to record at Pye studios and sell the results to the highest bidder. Part of the production deal at Philips would have required that Scott and Stewart produce a certain amount of acts within a certain amount of time. Where better to start than with the man who in a recent poll had named Scott as his best friend?

To the outside world, it must have seemed as if it were all just happening for the multi-faceted singer, and yet Scott had been working semi-professionally since he was 12. At 21, he was a weary veteran, and already he sounded like someone twice his age.

"I'm the guy they all hate," he confessed. "I produce all the records. I do most of the negotiation with the agency and sign most of the contracts. A great deal of responsibility rests on my shoulders, and when complaints come in, I'm the one who gets it first."

Despite such moaning, outside of their now full professional lives they were still very much like young men on shore-leave. After almost a year in London, all three were beginning to branch out socially.

Pop mogul and star Jonathan King was a close chum of Scott through the 60s, and the two were often witnessed carousing with a gang at the Lotus House, where their drunken dining could be clearly heard from behind private screens. As a personality, King was disliked by many of the industry's less refined movers at the time, Maurice King included. ("Jonathan, have you ever thought about joining the human race?" Maurice is repudedly to have asked him once.) But Scott was enamoured, no doubt relieved at finding a similarly sensitive soul among the hullabaloo. Scott described his new best friend as "the Cocteau of the pop world".

"I think Scott and I met on *Top Of The Pops*, or it could have been *Ready Steady Go!*," recalls King. "In those days, all us 'pop stars' were in a kind of community, like school. We all went to the same parties and clubs and got to meet each other. We got on immediately. He was highly intelligent, and I was at Trinity College, Cambridge, so we started spending a lot of time together and were best friends in the middle 60s.

"I found John and Gary a bit dull. They were more interested in the standard drink–birds kind of social whirl than Scott or I. I got on fine with them but considered them one-dimensional and ordinary."

With the Walkers' overnight success came an overnight power, a powerful rule of attraction. As with all gangs, the social pecking-order ran to its own particular dynamic.

"Jonathan was very good for Scott," says Chrissie McCall. "He grounded Scott when it all got too much. I don't think he was particularly disliked by Maurice, but Maurice didn't like anyone that Scott was pally with because ... he was sort of obsessed with Scott. He didn't like anyone else to become ingratiated with Scott."

Not only had the Walkers caught up with old pioneer buddies like P.J. Proby, but they were on the verge of eclipsing them. Proby, who seemed incapable of taking showbiz seriously, was nevertheless drawn to the game, and he came to the Walker party occasionally, despite their nervy drummer.

"Gary made sure that [Scott and John] wouldn't come anywhere near me," says Proby, "because Gary was afraid of me. He was afraid that I was gonna beat the shit out of him. Which was just stupid. It was very silly. I would have done exactly the same thing that he did – going through [someone else's] address book. So Gary got the wrong end of the stick. I was never mad at him for that. I was only mad at Gary because he had lied and said he could play the drums when he couldn't.

"I was friendly with 'em. I used to go to John's house every Saturday for dinner. What we all used to do was meet up at the Ad Lib club. But Scott and them didn't ... I don't know if they couldn't get a membership, or what, but they were always to be found at the Playboy club. I didn't like it up there. The circle I ran with, The Beatles and everything, didn't go there."

It was noted, particularly by members of The Quotations, that the Walkers themselves rarely socialised together. It was assumed that this was not out of any bad feeling among the trio but because of the amount of time they spent in each others' pockets while working. There was some truth to this, as a tactlessly frank Scott admitted. "I know a lot of people look on [John and Gary] as longhaired morons. They're not. I don't get along socially with them, simply because I don't want to. We just have nothing in common. John is obsessed with talking about his wife, dogs, and cars. Gary is the Casanova of pop, always going on about his birds. I want to talk about music – jazz mainly – and art."

As for the minute dynamics of the band, it seemed that Scott was closer to Gary than John, with Gary giving the impression that he was equally happy pretty much anywhere. John, perhaps partly because he was married, did not seem especially close to either bandmate.

"[Scott and I] just got on really well," said Gary. "We discovered that we had the same sense of humour. It was a terrible thing, when we got together. But John hasn't got that sense of humour."

A desperate need to make it can bring together the most diametrically opposed personalities. The pursuit of fame and success can enable a kind of illusionary context, a harmony of sorts that is born of crisis. This allows individuals who may not even share the same base values and who in any other circumstance might even avoid one another, to spend every waking minute in each others' company, united in their desire for making it.

In this respect, the Walkers were a three-headed beast. It is hard to imagine the naturally shy and self-effacing Engel, if left to himself, pushing his obvious vocal talent onto the agencies and management offices of London on his own.

John, while blessed with all-American typical good looks, an occasionally beautiful voice, and better than average guitar chops, seemed to be lacking in presence.

Kim Fowley would cross paths with the Walkers now and then as they ascended the ladder of fame. His opinion of John Maus never transcended the first impression. "He's just a piece of meat," says Fowley. "Blond granite meat ... just like any model ... and whether he's mysterious, stupid, or boring, it doesn't make any difference, because he's not supposed to be animated like Woody Allen is. He's there to be idolised by knicker-wetting girls, and for that he's very good."

Gary, while having a merely ordinary level of musical talent, was savvy enough to recognise the gifts Engel possessed, how John complemented this, and even where he himself fit into the equation. Using the financial faith of his stepfather and some formidable willpower and spunk of his own, he was then able to approximate the 'Proby Plan' with stunning efficiency. Gary hustled with an engaging verve and energy that his two fair-headed chums lacked.

Whether consciously or unconsciously, all three would have been aware of these facts. So, now that they had 'made it', and made it in such a definite and irrevocable way, it could only be a matter of time before the foundations of such a phenomenon – the three personalities themselves – would begin to tear apart.

In a 1965 'pop profile', Maus is said to have "won a cup for dragster racing [and] has played a lot of American football. He's also an expert surfer and talks about 'hanging five' and 'wipeout'".

By contrast, in a 1993 interview, Scott would reminisce: "I didn't like the average American kid football players and baseball players particularly. I've never been big on American values. I had various things in common with [Gary and John], but not on an artistic level."

Gary's role was that of the lukewarm water between Scott's fire and John's slightly less hot fervor. Everyone involved was aware of their respective places.

John said: "Gary had a pretty tough role because he had to put up with Scott and I. All of a sudden, we went from a trio – which wasn't going to work because of the kind of records we wanted to make – [to where] we had to get a big-band to back us. [Gary] always kept us grounded. Scott and I would tend to get some pretty nutso ideas, and Gary being Gary would say, 'You know, you should think about what you're doing.' He makes you feel comfortable immediately. He was very good ... especially on the road. Gary was the sane one."

Although John and Scott shared a public fondness for Frank Sinatra and the acquired taste of Jack Jones, such common ground was mostly superficial. In fact, while Scott was probably drawn to the artistry of both, John's admiration would have been based on their professionalism and success.

Still, at this point all three were young and open enough to enjoy fame for what it initially is: an exhilarating and joyous ride on a wave of a more metaphysical kind than the type John was used to from surfing back in LA. And, perhaps for an only child such as Scott, such a visceral shared experience allowed him to feel that The Walker Brothers were just that: brothers. No matter their personal differences. Ralph Gurnett: "They were very amicable toward each other. But Scott's heart wasn't in being an entertainer. Gary was the comic. He has a heart of gold. John was in another world."

For the time being, at least, all three were in it together. All for one and one for all.

Between engagements, John and Gary would routinely kick back a little, but as the British winter moved in, Scott could not relax. By the time their Number One was toppled from the top, by Ken Dodd's 'Tears', Engel and Franz were already plotting their next musical move.

'My Ship Is Coming In' would eventually be The Walker Brothers' fourth single, and it was true to Scott's philosophy of perfection. A slab of sound constructed like a Gaudi cathedral in miniature, it came at you sideways on, bottom-heavy with piano and light on understatement. It was no rushed-release follow-up: it charted on its week of release in Britain at Number 36, that December 1965, a full four months on from the appearance of 'Make It Easy On Yourself'.

John explained the reasons for the time lag. "You know, digging up new material is a bit of a problem, but after you've had a couple of hits it gets a little easier. When you phone up a publisher and say, 'I'm John Walker and I'm looking for a song,' it's like, 'How many do you want!' But you have to earn that kind of respect in the business."

As ever, Scott was less frivolous. "We hadn't a number good enough to follow ['Make It Easy On Yourself']. I always insist that everything we record is new, fresh, and right up to the minute. I chatted to Johnny Franz and up turned 'My Ship'.

"We both knew this was it. It meant something to me. I know it's going to mean something to record buyers. I talked it over with the arranger [Ivor Raymonde], then the day before we were to record we started to rehearse. I don't believe in rehearsing for days before a session. We had a fight with Philips. They thought it was too adult."

John Lennon was given the rask of reviewing the single in *Melody Maker*. He was uncharacteristically understated. "I think they're good. But I'm not keen on this type of song. I don't listen to them, really.

Their voices are good, but they overdo the big-voice approach ... still ... it's a hit all right!"

The B-side was the charming lilt of 'You're All Around Me', a pretty mid-paced ballad strung along by its vivid lyrical narrative and rolling piano. Although perfectly engaging, it was hardly of the "mind blowing" variety that Scott had described.

The lead track was a much more formidable composition. Written by Joey Brooks, the song was originally a minor hit for soul singer Jimmy Radcliffe in the States and would be one of the few Walker singles to make an impression in their home country, making it to Number 63 on the US *Billboard* chart.

The instrumental hook of the song can be heard immediately in the stirring intro through a three-note riff on the piano, played in its lowest octave and no doubt reinforced by electric and double basses for good measure.

The piano player was yet another jazzman – veteran pianist and arranger Reg Guest, who would soon become another convert and collaborator to the Engel cause, arranging some of the best material Scott would write while still a 'Brother'.

Decades later, Guest would reminisce about his relationship with Scott. His insight goes some way toward explaining the obvious and frequent rapport that Scott enjoyed with many of his senior colleagues, Franz and Guest in particular.

"This was special," Reg fondly recalled two decades down the line. "I've thought about this recently, and I always knew it was special – and with respect it wasn't John or Gary. I knew that Scott was a creative artist, but I also knew that he wasn't a chart performer. He was also to most people a bit weird, I suppose; reclusive. There was something very private about him, but we were very friendly.

"I don't think I'm particularly unusual," said Guest, "but I have the ability to understand artistic people. I just sensed his whole persona. He's been mistreated all along the line, and they would rely on people like me to get through to him, which was dead simple. Once you sympathise with someone, it's no problem. So with me, he had the opportunity to go as far out as he wanted – and he did. He went his own imperious way, and it got him into trouble, but he's been proved right in the long run."

With 'My Ship Is Coming In' steaming its way to the Top Three and the recording sessions for their debut album completed in its wake, the boys were allowed a rare breather. Maurice King issued a statement to the press declaring that, from now on, they would be "more choosey" about the types of tours they would embark upon. King's biggest earners took the opportunity to treat themselves. Gary and Scott celebrated their recent chart success by taking in Lionel Bart's *Oliver!* in the West End, and the three then set about acquiring wheels to match their status. Scott part-traded his Ford Comet for a £180 jeep, Gary bought a Marcos, and John finally had his Bentley. "When I see other Bentley owners it's all thumbs-up," he beamed.

Perversely, Scott celebrations meant that he wasg picked up by the law again. "I was singing and shouting my head off in Oxford Street [and] some police officer told me to shut up, and I didn't," he admitted. "Again I was lucky. The police recognised who I was and my management picked me up before the press could find anything out."

By the time recording sessions for the now eagerly awaited debut album drew to a close, Reg Guest had been quickly promoted from pianist to arranger. It was a mutually agreeable arrangement, as Reg was aware. "This was a great opportunity for me to make music. And I kind of sensed it back then. I just knew that this was good stuff. We could just sense the talent we had in each other; him to use me for his backings and me to be one of the few who could see just how good he really was. When he heard some of the sounds in the studio for the first time, he was thrilled to bits. I thought good, I've got it right."

With the bulk of the recording complete, autumn saw the Walker army on the march again, although this time, true to Maurice's word, they had "quit the ballroom scene". John once again reasoned why, and the specifics were beginning to sound like a mantra. "Things got so hectic, we had to get out of playing ballrooms for a while. We would have our clothes ripped off. Scott ended up beneath a pile of chairs. He almost didn't make it." In Dunstable "girls got my shirt off in three minutes, and then they got Scott. So there we stood – shirtless. I looked around and saw Scott climbing up a balcony."

Theatres would be the venues of choice on this tour, and a new recruit joined the band. Billy Bremner, a young streetwise Glaswegian guitarist, was the new boy. His induction to the Walker world was, as with most showbiz coups, a matter of being in the right place at the right time.

"I was playing with these Irish birds [The McKinney Sisters] and we were asked to be on one of The Walker Brothers' first big tours in Britain, as part of the package tour," explains the plain-speaking guitarist. "The first time I saw them, I was watching the crowd and listening to Scott and John sing; it was great. It was so different. No one was doing anything like it. I thought it was terrific. There was no one at the time doing this huge-ballad stuff on stage, with that big vibrato vocal.

"Then they would do the up-tempo stuff, and, to be honest, they weren't really good at that. After that gig, I got to know The Quotations, and when they fired Bobby, the guitarist who was playing at that time, they asked me if I'd like the job ... and at the time I thought this was great, because I'd never played in front of so many people. So I said yes, and that was it."

Everyone got along well enough, but there was little fraternising between the stars and hired hands once the job was done. "It was them three guys and then it was us, the band. And we really didn't mix with them a lot. When touring, the band would travel by bus and Scott, John, and Gary in cars. We would socialise on tours, but there was none of that when we had time off."

The switch to theatres was perhaps more aesthetically pleasing but it did little to chasten the teenage girls of October 1965. If anything, the mania went up a notch, resulting in further hospitalisations for the trio, their colleagues, and the fans themselves. Road manager Drew Harvey, who suffered spinal injuries on this tour, explained how the opening of each show was carefully choreographed. "The Quotations would play the James Bond intro, and the lights would be spotting through the audience ... then, from off-stage, John would sing a line, then Scott would. Then a crescendo where they would sing together ... . The curtain would go up and [Gary would] be playing the drums [and] the crowd would go ballistic. Scott knew how to milk an audience because of his professionalism and his upbringing – he would play the audience."

Considering the by-now predictable reaction of each audience, this nightly ritual was an exercise akin to putting out fire with gasoline. Typically, Scott would tease the audience, getting just close enough for the faintest touch of a female fingertip before jumping back into the bosom of the stage. Yet Scott wasn't showbiz slick enough to always pull back in time, and audience photos from this period show a bemused Scott rolling around the heads of the audience, clinging grimly to his microphone, the shirt literally being ripped from his back.

Beat Instrumental magazine wrote about a typical one-nighter. "Their act is lost in one big zany conglomeration of ripped clothes, demented fans, and wilder-than-wild bouncers. To be fair, The Walker Brothers do try to give value for money. They will not stop singing unless it's necessary. John and Scott have entirely different images. John, the taller of the two, makes a rather impressive figure on stage. In true American western style he 'stands tall' and rock-like until he crumbles into the sea of fans. Scott is an 'all go-croucher'; he moves about, twists and turns, until he is brought down to earth by the many grasping hands."

Within a few short years the idea of a smiling, half-naked Scott belly-surfing the crowd would be unimaginable. However, on this tour the boys were still indulging in a kind of honeymoon period. The reviewer noted that little music could be heard, although snatches of "spot-on harmony" slid out between the ravenous screaming, accompanied by the inevitable dull thump of sub-audible bass frequencies.

Despite Billy Bremner's vivid image of a quivering Scott belting out 'Love Her', few ballads were featured on this tour. The set consisted of indestructible up-tempo stompers such as Jackie Wilson's 'That's All I Need', James Brown's 'Out Of Sight', and Rufus Thomas's 'All Night

Worker". But as we have seen, The Walker Brothers live was hardly about the music. As far as the fans were concerned, John, Scott, and Gary could have come on singing nursery rhymes.

Jean Markwell, a fan, remembered: "I saw The Walker Brothers playing live at Grantham Drill Hall on October 16 1965. It was a dancehall, and there was no seating. During the warm-up, we were dancing at the front, near the stage, so that when the Walkers came on, we were right at the front. Between us and the stage were the bouncers, who were pushing us back, and behind us was the force of the crowd pushing forward. It was extremely hot, and the girl next to me stood heavily on my foot, with her stiletto heel. I thought I was going to faint with the pain and the crush, but there was no space to slide to the floor.

"They finally came on, and we soon forgot about everything else. We felt euphoric for days afterwards, for actually having been there. However, I can truly say we never heard a word they sang, due to the screaming, of which I'm sure we must have contributed to."

Margaret Waterhouse: "It was mass hysteria. You certainly couldn't hear anything – or see anything, come to that. My ten-year-old sister and I were terrified as people stood up on their seats to try and see more. God knows how Scott, John, and Gary must have felt up on that stage, looking out over that frenzied sea. It was difficult to tell which songs they were singing."

For the Walkers themselves, simply getting in and out of the venues was another performance. Increasingly detailed plans were drawn up, often verging on the theatrical. Initially, it all seemed straightforward enough. Scott, John, and Gary rarely travelled with The Quotations; instead, they would shuttle to and from the stage door in either a Jaguar or a Rolls-Royce. Their driver, a veteran of Them and Byrds tours, was road manager Bobby Hamilton. As mob scenes escalated around each arrival and departure, so did the trio's insurance premiums. In the short dash from car to stage door, clothes and hair would be torn, flesh bruised, limbs sprained, and the car vandalised. As a result, over the course of their touring campaigns they improvised, drew up, and implemented different strategies.

Sometimes, John, Gary, and Scott would arrive heavily disguised through a 'secret' entrance, perhaps ushered in through a kitchen. A local police escort began to accompany their car in every town. Sometimes they would travel in the police car, leaving decoys – policemen posing as Walker Brothers – with their road manager in the doomed Jaguar.

As the sacrificial coppers pulled up at the venue, the fans would descend, piranha-like, upon the hapless impostors. Meanwhile, suitably covered by this diversion, the true objects of desire would hurl themselves from panda car to pavement. Inevitably, this action would trigger some chemical sixth sense amongst the pack, instantly alerting the ravenous teenagers to the foul deception afoot. Instinctively, they would change targets, casting aside the dazed and mauled officers like so much bad rubbish. Shoal-like, they would descend as one upon the fragile threesome; further police officers falling heroically before the mascara'd and beehived wake.

Such extreme happenings called for extreme measures. Someone, somewhere came up with the idea of crash helmets. Indeed, it must have been excruciatingly painful to have random locks of one's precious mop ripped out, night after night. Adding motorcycle helmets to their Carnaby Street wardrobe was an ingenious and gimmicky measure that soon became the norm.

At this time, John lived with his wife in a flat near Regent's Park. If the gig that night was at the Tooting Granada, Bobby Hamilton would first collect Scott and Gary from St John's Wood, going on to pick up John. Scott and Gary would then be treated to the sight of John kissing his wife goodnight at the doorstep as he left for another day at the office, crash helmet tucked dutifully under his arm.

Alas, the ingenuity of such plans, plots, and props were sometimes not enough, as Gary himself would recall with all the lucidity of a wartime veteran. "We would wait until about four o'clock in the morning, and then we would leave – with those crash helmets on. Of course, everybody thought it was a big publicity thing, but it wasn't. That was for real. They were ripping your hair out and everything. John's head was cut wide open about three times.

"I remember one incident with a girl about half the size of us," said Gary." I guess she must have been about 12 years old. She grabbed hold of John's hair. I was screaming, 'Let go! Let go!' because the whole crowd was surging and it was getting to the point where everything was going to collapse, including the hotel! So I finally hit her in the face – she screamed, but she still held on. There was nothing else for it but to hit her. I just felt the end was coming and we were going to be underneath ... . We were going to get killed."

Amid this frothing sea of adolescent hysteria came the launch of their debut album, *Take It Easy*. Despite the strange and unflattering choice of photograph for its cover (taken by legendary photographer Terence Donovan), the album could not fail. Propelled by the current success of 'My Ship Is Coming In', a brief cabaret run, a multitude of good press, and appearances on *Ready Steady Go!* (December 3), *Top Of The Pops* (November 25) and *Scene At 6-30* (November 26), among others, by Christmas the record had sold in its hundreds of thousands, peaking at Number Four in the *NME* album chart. Track by track, it runs as follows.

'Make It Easy On Yourself' is the classic Number One, still played regularly on radio but never played live by the Walkers.

'There Goes My Baby' (Nelson–Patterson–Treadwell) is almost identical to The Drifters' version, aside from the vocals – and there are a lot of vocals, from Scott, John, Lesley Duncan, and co. Seductively primitive sounding, the recording captures a feeling of joy, abandon, and commitment that is absent from many Walkers recordings. It also sounds like a band effort, with a sublime Ivor Raymonde string and brass arrangement seamlessly weaving together the complex vocal harmonies and wonderfully exuberant drumming.

'First Love Never Dies' (Morris–Seals) is a widescreen epic, and the arrangement brings to mind the work of film composer Jerry Goldsmith (whom Scott admired).

Sandy Moore, a fan, said: "The thing that got me when I first saw Scott singing [this song] on TV was how sincere he seemed." This is evident more than ever in Scott's delivery. Endearing vocal glitch and all, it sounds less a performance, more a confession.

Although John takes the lead on a pleasing, if restrained, version of the Martha & The Vandellas classic 'Dancing In The Street' (Stevenson–Gaye), he does not now recall recording this, or its distant musical cousin, 'Land Of A Thousand Dances'. The typical 'Holland Tunnel' sound effect is noticeably lowered, allowing focus on the somewhat neutered backing vocals and muted brass fugues. John's vocal is deceptively throwaway. On closer listening, his phrasing and pitch are immaculate.

Although 'Dancing In The Street' sounds mediocre beside the definitive Motown version, it is a dollar bill bearing the signature of Picasso when compared to the infinitely more bland and popular versions that would follow. Sadly, this was the only Marvin Gaye song that any Walker would ever get close to.

'Lonely Winds', a throwaway by Doc Pomus and Mort Shuman, follows. Other work by this New York writing team would hold far greater relevance for Scott in the near future, but his voice was of the wrong shape to suit most up-tempo numbers. Within the shallow parameters of the song, the performances are as convincing as ever, thanks to Scott's nevertheless impeccable delivery and the huge recording resources available at the Philips studios.

'The Girl I Lost In The Rain' was written by the then unknown David Gates, who had yet to join Bread and write 'If'. It was a personal favourite of John's, and a song that may have influenced his own writing in this period. An eerie flute figure introduces a mood equally reminiscent of both the Parisian Left Bank and Victorian alleyways. Blinded by their rain-sodden fringes, the narrators trail listlessly along deserted boulevards and dead-ended avenues, fully in keeping with the romantic image imposed upon them.

'Land Of A Thousand Dances' (Kenner–Domino) is next up. Such a romp was never suited to the essentially sombre beauty of Scott's voice, leaving this version sounding a little too correct and courtly. It was a live favourite, and they would regularly open shows with an extended version. They also performed the song repeatedly during their early television appearances. Scott and John would often accompany the song with their own self-invented dance moves – Scott coming across as an awkward and stilted school prefect, while John was as graceful and fluid as a panther on goofballs.

'You're All Around Me' is one of the first Scott Engel originals to be recorded in Britain. Written in collaboration with Lesley Duncan, it is a perfectly executed watercolour of early-morning London suburbia.

'Love Minus Zero' is the first of four Bob Dylan songs to be covered by the Brothers. The melody here, as with most Dylan covers, is much more realised than on the original.

'I Don't Want To Hear It Anymore' (Newman) is a perfect song and a perfect performance by all concerned. Dusty Springfield recorded her own version around the same time, and although she and Scott would have used the same studio, crew, and musicians, it's interesting to note the differences. The original Walkers master of this goes on for almost a minute longer, showcasing some fine vocal ad-libbing by the 21-year-old singer. Scott and co would go on to cover many of Randy Newman's songs, but this was the first. Scott: "I've always been into Randy Newman, even when I was working around Hollywood. I think he's the closest style to what I write and he ... has a wonderful feel for the human heart."

'Here Comes The Night' (Pomus–Shuman) is not the song by the Walkers' fellow Capable stablemates, Them, but another take on a Drifters' classic.

'Tell The Truth' (Pauling) marks one of the few appearances by The Quotations on record, and they are assisted enthusiastically by vocal group The Breakaways. John: "I probably was a little more inclined to do music that was up-tempo than Scott was, because my voice would lean to that a little easier. It was more my style of singing." Scott: "Some of the tracks were rushed and sound unbelievably bad. But some things are really beautiful." Big Jim Sullivan: "At the time, going from session to session, the Walkers were well respected. I really think those recordings have stood up."

With their uncommon good looks, across-the-board material, and strangely mature-sounding records, Maurice King's golden boys were beginning to extend their appeal beyond the teens. Not only did the little girls understand: so, too, did their mothers.

Margaret Waterhouse: "I remember coming home from school one day to be greeted by a comment from my mother. She said, 'You know, I think Scott Walker is a young man who has been let down in love.' I asked her why she thought that, and she said she had been listening to his records in my room while I had been at school that day, and she said she had felt really sorry and sad for him. She had been moved in much the same way that I had."

By the end of the year, the Walkers' success in Britain was almost total. For John, however, it was a case of finally getting what one needs and not what one wants. And perhaps there was something prophetic in the sudden fate of his much-lusted-after Bentley.

Gary: "You know that Bentley John bought, the only thing in his life, the one thing that he's been raving about? It fell apart. The sunroof snapped open forever. The windscreen wipers won't work when the rain pressure is too hard, and the heater is jammed. Yesterday he told me the door has fallen off."

CHAPTER 6

1966

I think being part of a very popular group is really a great deal of fun. A lot of people decry being famous and this and that. Actually, I think they're lying.

John Maus (2004)

By the New Year, 'My Ship Is Coming In' was peaking at Number Three and The Walker Brothers had become an entity greater than the sum of its parts. They were an unstoppable force driven by a momentum no longer dependent on the will of Gary, John, or Scott, their managers, their agent, or their producer. It was as if, at this time, Britain not only wanted them – it needed them, demanded them, had a right to them.

In Alan Yentob's excellent 1974 documentary on David Bowie, *Cracked Actor*, Bowie compares the sudden ascent of fame to waking up in the back seat of a car as it goes from zero to a hundred in less than three seconds. Scott was both exhilarated and terrified by such acceleration, slumping beneath seatbelts in the back seat, his hands jittering and juggling between the Scotch and the pill bottle. John was simply thrilled, a glass of finest Bourbon in one hand, a pair of brand new tailor-made cowboy boots on his feet and a movie-star grin spattered across his Hollywood features. Leeds, meanwhile, was completely unfazed. If destiny was driving, Gary was in the passenger seat, a sloppy grin on his face and his head out of the window.

High in the slipstream of sudden celebrity and status, the non-drumming drummer was never truer to his essence. Terminally extroverted, Gary could not rest. A supernatural networker and a perpetually-in-motion PR man, Gary could not be stopped, even by a case of bronchial pneumonia.

As the holiday period dissolved along with the black snow around London's streets, Britain began to shake off the post-Christmas hangover, easing itself back into the monochrome grind of the five-day week. Meanwhile, Gary – no doubt the type of annoying character who gets restless on holidays – although feverish and sick, was doggedly present at the helm, ready to advance the cause that much further. Speaking from his sick room at the St John's Wood hotel, between pillow plumping and brow-mopping by a nurse called Arpy, Leeds delivered the latest screed from the Walker mountaintop. Bedridden but driven, his ten-stone-one-pound frame swathed in perspiration, Gary's gaze wandered lazily between the journalist's notebook and a Christmas present from Scott's mum: a novelty set of slippers, made to appear as a pair of naked, oversized, human feet.

"I'm not going solo," he croaked, emphatically. And then, with the impeccable comic timing that so endeared him to Scott, Leeds launched into an account of the recording of his forthcoming solo single.

"It took The Quotations about four hours to figure out the number, and me about ten minutes to do the vocal. Scott and John Stewart have done a great job producing it … . The record'll probably make it and Tony Bennett and Frank Sinatra will kill themselves … . I heard a lot of people singing on the radio and I said, 'I could do better than that.' Scott said, 'Oh yeah? Why don't you make a record?'

"I wanted to do something really funky, like the Stones. This one's really slangy. I like to do all the screaming things, dirty and sexy. What the girls like, I guess. I don't play on it, you know. I just stand there and rave. CBS had the best offer. That's the main thing, grab the money while you can. Up 'til now the fastest thing we've done was 'Land Of A Thousand Dances', and even that wasn't fast enough for me."

While The Walker Brothers were fast approaching the status of household names, those households seemed more interested in John and Scott than the guy who had actually instigated the whole phenomenon. Aesthetically fascistic TV directors, who ruthlessly instructed their camera crews to focus on the glamorous vocalists, did not help Gary's profile. The relatively ego-free and easygoing Leeds was rankled to the point where he wondered out loud if he wouldn't get more airtime as a dancer. For once, he wasn't just joking – miniskirted audience members did indeed attract almost as much camera attention as the pop singers they grooved along to.

He had already put this theory to the test the previous year when, during their performance of 'Everything's Gonna Be Alright' on the *Ready Steady Go!* Christmas Special, a white polo-necked Gary had abandoned his kit. Descending into the snakepit of the audience, he could be seen frugging wildly with a lady who, as the term groupie was not yet in common circulation, may have been reasonably referred to as a 'band bird'. This was a type wholly endorsed by Gary 'Alfie' Leeds: "[Band birds] are kinda groovy ... I think clothes make or break a girl. I really dig short skirts – the shorter the better. I love all girls. My ideal girl, as everyone must know by now, has long hair, a well-shaped pair of legs, and a flat stomach, in that order." His ideal partner at this time, if it were not for a few fundamental differences, could have been one of his closest colleagues: she would be "blonde, kinda quiet, real affectionate".

Gary's lack of musical presence in the Walkers was not just down to his perceived ability or confidence as a musician. Certain factors at this time meant that it was very common for many groups not to actually play any instruments on their own records. Even groups as indisputably credible as Them and The Kinks sometimes bowed to pressure from their producer and used session men. Ringo had not even played drums on 'Love Me Do', the debut Beatles single.

Session schedules were strictly regimented in all aspects, yet sometimes, because of the number of personnel involved, particularly so in the case of the Walkers, these sessions were still exceedingly expensive. Producers like Johnny Franz had to come up with a particular quantity of high quality material – material that had to compete with some of the greatest records ever made – within a tight schedule. Timing was a crucial factor, and the resulting pressure was considerable. Franz was, at the end of the day, an officer and a gentlemen. A consummate professional.

To this end, across the board, it made the utmost sense to use other professionals. Not only could session men usually sight-read, but also they could play with both impeccable feel and timing, while still completing the job quickly. Even an able bassist like Scott saw the sense in this, admitting that with such fine session players at their disposal, it was pointless for the Walkers themselves to bust their chops. But then if Scott had to prove himself at all, he was doing so as a singer.

The Walker Brothers' very real success – a smash album and three Top 20 singles, including a Number One – meant that even if they did not appeal to your taste, they were taken seriously. Gary, while at the heart of this pop phenomenon, was absent from the recordings and a superfluous musical entity during their live shows. He was not, at this time, considered seriously as a musician by anyone who knew him.

Hollies drummer Bobby Graham: "I worked with him on the Proby tour, and as far as drumming went, he wasn't a player as such, not really. He may well have asked to play on the records, but Franz decided who was gonna do what. He was the boss. The producer always was in those days; the artist had very little say in what was going on. I knew Gary reasonably well socially, and we never really talked about it." Billy Bremner: "Gary was useless. And he knew that. [Live] he could do whatever he wanted, because there was another drummer sitting behind him ... so Gary could stand up, fuck around, and do what he wanted."

Kim Fowley: "The Beatles weren't The Beatles until Ringo joined, no matter how many drummers they had before. So it's irrelevant how many drummers the Walkers had before Gary, because when Gary joined, then it became the big deal."

Dave Cash: "I thought he was fun! He was the only one of the three you could get down the pub. He was the only one who laughed and he was the one who gee'd up the conversation. He had a big personality and he used it. And I thought he was a very good drummer. It's just he was no Phil Collins."

Andrew Loog Oldham: "Gary Leeds was the Andrew Ridgeley to John and Scott's George Michael."

Among the staff at Philips, Gary's non-involvement was considered a taboo subject. No one would speak about it openly. It was probably assumed that he could not play at all, whereas in fact, while no Elvin Jones, Gary was at the least a competent drummer. No recorded evidence of Gary's ability would appear until the release of his first post-Walker album with The Rain.

On the Walkers' live shows, it is hard to gauge the quality of his contribution, as he always played with soft sticks and in tandem with another drummer – usually James Butcher of The Quotations. Even on the live recordings that do exist, only one kit seems present, which is perhaps due to how instruments and which instruments were mic'd up.

Perversely, it was only at their soundchecks that John, Scott, and Gary would play together. Borrowing instruments from the supporting musicians, they would relax their pre-show nerves by cranking up the amps and having a blow, all three running through old blues standards together. And yet even this rare attempt at letting their hair down was tarnished.

A year of being pop stars had seriously taken its toll on their musicianship, and this filled John in particular with self-loathing. "We hadn't played together since we left our nightclub gigs back in the States, but we were just getting back to standard [on the Kinks tour] when we decided to blow it and leave it to the group. Now we have a blow with all the guys on the shows before the curtain is up and, believe me, I'm terrible now. I've never been this bad on guitar, even before I started playing. It's really disgusting. I try to do little runs, which I used to be able to do with my eyes closed, and I just muff them up! Still, perhaps if I sat down and took my time I could get back in shape."

Even Gary was bemoaning his "wasted drumming ability". And yet, what to do? This 'secret' Walker Brothers Trio would be banished from the stage well before the punters were let in. Taking their place on the cramped stage, The Quotations would shoulder the responsibility of the (practically inaudible) sound, allowing John, Scott, and Gary to get on with their role-playing. The tedium of such a ritual meant the shows became increasingly eccentric. Scott gleefully took over Gary's kit on occasion, bashing away with Butcher behind a raving loony Leeds, whose solo spots included the proto-punk of 'Turn On Your Light' and 'Ooh Poo Pah Doo'.

Some shows even had Leeds miming to Scott's off-stage Sinatra impression. The spotlit drummer, often outfitted in a custom-made suit of shocking pink, would throw his whole hammy heart into the mime, emoting passionately to 'Strangers In The Night', screwing his eyes shut in mock concentration. The teenage audience, hysterical as ever, seemed oblivious to such surreal japes. It hardly seemed to matter which Walker Brother took the spotlight. The girls continued to throw themselves at the stage.

Beyond such pantomime, the ghosts of master drummers Gene Krupa and Buddy Rich lingered. Gary was still in touch with his original musical passions. He would ritualistically and meticulously set up his own kit every night, insisting, in spite of its inaudibility, that "it must be positioned perfectly".

Despite playing such a minimal role musically, Gary was clearly appreciated by the public. (Scott claimed, perhaps diplomatically, that they all received equal amounts of fan mail.) Gary was held in high regard by his two 'siblings'. Scott would call Gary "one of the most human and one of the funniest people" and would credit him with "the greatest amount of humility of anyone I've ever met". Chrissie McCall, often in the presence of all three at once, recalls in particular: "Scott was so protective of Gary. He knew they wouldn't have made it if it wasn't for Gary. Gary was hilarious. He had quite a juvenile sense of humour, but, conversely, it wasn't irritating."

It was acknowledged by those in the know that Gary and his family had in effect set up the Walkers and was thus responsible for the whole crazy shindig. While many of those at Capable Management held him in affection – "He 'ad an 'eart of gold!" recalls Ralph Gurnett – the idea that this 'joker' was to be held ultimately responsible for the Walkers and thus in some indirect way all ensuing successes – well, this must have rankled Maurice considerably.

Maurice was irked both by the duality of Gary's innocence and by his lack of musicality. To think that in some weird way Maurice owed everything to this clown must have caused some degree of nocturnal teeth-gnashing. "Maurice had no time for Gary," confirms McCall. "He thought Gary was a waster." And yet, obviously, Gary was more than just the court jester.

Gary said at the time: "Having a solo record means so much to me personally. It's something I need. It makes me more than the little guy stuck at the back playing the drums. I want to be the Walker who's known and accepted. People know me as kinda friendly, noisy, always fooling around and that. But that's not the real me. I'm pretty quiet when it comes down to it ... I guess I'm pretty serious. I'm always thinking I think too much."

The song to set the Gary debate straight was a grimy, low-slung, infectious throwaway. In the light of Gary's obviously wounded ego, it was appropriately titled 'You Don't Love Me'. His vinyl debut was co-produced by Scott and John Stewart, who also wrote the B-side, 'Get It Right'. It is slightly too polite to be garage but rough enough around the edges to completely evade any comparisons to the monolithic recordings of his group. He is no worse a singer than many and, in fact, his voice has a stupefied, grotty quality that suits the song perfectly. In keeping with the Gary 'zaniness', he does not even play drums on his own single.

Perhaps because of budgetary constraints – the single was paid for by Scott and John's Alec-Noel productions, to be sold to the highest bidder – it was, as noted by Gary, one of the rare Walker recordings to feature their actual live band. Not that all of the band members shared Gary's enthusiasm for it. "It was awful," states Bremner. "Scott wanted me to play that particular riff and I really didn't like the guitar sound. But that's what he wanted, this toppy Telecaster sound."

Yet it is this sound that dates the record so agreeably. While not best suited to the process of digital remastering, the seven-inch must have sounded great grinding from a jukebox somewhere in the depths of 60s Soho. Bremner and Maurice aside, this spunky debut had more than enough fans. Mick Jagger reviewed it favourably in one of the weeklies and the record hit Number 26 in the *Melody Maker* chart. By April it had sold 60,000 copies in the UK alone.

Fulfilling the needs of their production deal with Philips, Alec-Noel productions also found time to produce various tracks for Dutch beat group, The Motions, plus 'Tears On My Pillow'/'Crying My Eyes Out' for CBS band Carol & The Memories, and 'Light' by Fontana group Finders Keepers. John would also try his hand, producing 'On The Beach'/'Sadie The Cleaning Lady' for Finders Keepers, although none of these sonic excursions would match even Gary's success.

'You Don't Love Me' was less the beginnings of a serious solo career and more a minor diversion, a footnote in the Walker opus; a holiday, even, for the spotlight-weary Engel. While no one except the hard-hearted few begrudged Gary his fun, the main concern was, of course, the trio. Further television appearances for the Walkers continued through January, with the boys appearing on TWW's *Now* and ATV's *Lucky Stars.*

Back at Baker Street, Capable confirmed another manic UK tour that took up most of that rainy April. But just as The Walker Brothers had at last got it together and were basking within the all-golden, all-affirming light of commercial success, each member seemed suddenly and publicly concerned with stating their individuality.

John announced plans to record and release a guitar instrumental; Engel and Stewart launched their own label, Super Records; and Gary, buoyed by the warm response to his solo foray, sombrely announced to his transfixed public that he saw it as his duty to forge ahead in his solo career. He added: "We will all be solo artists, except that we will all sing together on stage and make records together." Such a nebulously dizzy statement is to be expected from a young pop star drunk on the first frothing draft of fame. But the phrase "make records together" falls short in describing that which would follow.

'The Sun Ain't Gonna Shine Anymore' had been written by the archetypal classic songwriting partnership of Bob Crewe and Bob Gaudio less than two years before. They originally gave the song – built around a mere two chords – to their Four Seasons friend, Frankie Valli, who was the first person to record it.

Valli's interpretation was a minor hit in the USA, did zilch elsewhere, and while a pleasingly albeit middle-of-the-road listening experience, his take would sound like a low-calorie demo recording compared to the version to come.

Bob Crewe: "When we were writing 'The Sun Ain't Gonna Shine' we were writing it specifically for Frankie to sing. That particular morning was so grey, and I looked at it and I said, 'The sun it ain't never gonna shine no more.'"

Bob Gaudio: "Frankie walked by our little writing room ... we were in the Atlantic building at the time. He heard it and said, 'That goes nowhere, it's mine.'"

Once released, the record did go nowhere, chart-wise. But Crewe had enough foresight to make sure he took a copy with him on his next trip to London. As he handed the Valli single to Franz, he told the producer to "jump on it".

A copy subsequently found its way to Maurice King's house, where, over dinner, Scott heard it for the first time. His pop producer's instinct kicked in right there at the dining table, and he decided instantly that he would cut it.

"Because of the way they'd recorded [the Valli version], it hadn't been a hit. But I could hear that it could have been a hit. ... So, we took it in with a lot of other stuff. And it was just a terrible session all round."

As ever, The Musicians Union ruled with an iron baton. Although the Walkers were now Number One recording artists, their recording sessions still adhered to a strict timetable, perhaps more suited to the black-and-white austerity of the postwar 50s than the dawning Technicolor age-of-Aquarius 60s.

Scott explained: "In those days, we had to go into the studio with four tunes. This was standard. Some kind of Philips economy or some such dumb thing."

Roger Wake: "The session [for 'The Sun Ain't Gonna Shine Anymore'] would have been like any other Walker Brothers session and would start at 10am. And because of the MU, it was a three-hour session. We'd break for a lunch hour and then do afternoon sessions, two 'til five."

Scott: "Just as we get a nice atmosphere and feel on the disc, everyone gets up as one man and off they go for a tea break. The feeling is completely lost. For this particular session, they had booked a couple of very deaf guitar players. It was really bad. And you know at the beginning it just has to be acoustic guitar and some horns ... and these two guys couldn't cut it. So we went into some of the other songs, which were easier for them to play."

John: "The first time I heard it, I heard a hit song – I did not hear a hit record. The first time Scott and I recorded it, it wasn't going to be a hit either. It's an incredible song. The problem is, it's one of those songs that you really had to do some work on to make a record of this song. It's dramatic [and] lends itself to being a very powerful piece of music or a very quiet piece of music. It was funny. The first time we recorded it we didn't get it. We listened and said, 'We just did what Frankie Valli did.'"

Scott: "At the end of that day, Johnny Franz said, 'OK, let's put the vocals on.' And I said, 'No way. We have got to cut that song again – that song's a hit. That's one of the only ones I know for sure. I'll put anything on it. I'll put my mother on it – it's a hit!'

"And I had such a big argument with the top people at Philips, who weren't gonna let us record the track again, man! I couldn't believe it! It was a fucking nightmare. And so I had to bite my knuckles."

Dave Shrimpton: "The session rules weren't an exclusive policy of Philips, they were standard Musician Union rules at the time. Most people were professional enough to be able to get what they wanted in that time. Sinatra would sometimes cut as many as four or five tracks within a session."

Drummer Bobby Graham: "It's unusual that we would have done

another session for the same track. I don't remember that. If the guitarists really couldn't cut it – and that's unlikely as they were all professionals – then the producer would have postponed the session and just called up reserve guitarists immediately, and we would have waited until they got there. An arranger like Charlie Katz, whom I recall had arranged the session, he wouldn't have booked 'deaf guitarists'."

Scott: "Anyway, we finally recorded it again at a session the next day and managed to get some good guitar players, and we got the whole thing together."

John: "Philips weren't happy with us at that point, because that was a very expensive session and we had to do it again."

Gary: "You had four or five pianos creeping in there, playing the same note. And the 'Holland Tunnel' effect, with the echo on. Five or six drums playing at the same time. The echo was sometimes turned up, but not the actual instruments."

Bobby Graham: "There was only myself on drums. And if it wasn't me, it was someone like Ronnie Verrell. But never two drummers at once. Lots of percussion, sure, but never two drummers together, that I saw. The drum parts themselves were written like any of the other parts, and the directors who used me on sessions knew that I wasn't the best reader in the world, so for the drum fills, they would just write 'fill in' and leave it to me to do what I wanted to. They were happy with me doing it just the way I felt. What I often did was play fills against the beat rather than with it, and I got that directly from Phil Spector's drummer, Hal Blaine. If you listen to the Phil Spector Christmas album [*A Christmas Gift For You*], you'll hear those sorts of fills played all over that album, and I just copied 'em."

Roger Wake: "It was also a new sound for us in the studio. We were used to a more ... 'natural' sound. The orchestras were usually recorded as they sounded, whereas this Spector thing was just over-the-top; very big echoes and lots of rumbling basses going on. Whereas we were used to having someone like Harry Secombe in – even on the same day – and we'd have the same orchestra, but the sound of it would just be purely orchestral. So, we broke away from the classical sound. This was the first time Johnny Franz and the arrangers over here tried to emulate Spector – at the same time trying to make it a little bit different."

John: "It took us a little time to figure out, but when we found the right space to do it in, the song just … I mean, they played it as an instrumental – we hadn't even sung a note – and we listened to this thing and said, 'Damn! That's Number One!' It was a killer.

"Then, when we did the vocal, we had to figure out what we were going to do with it. Scott and I had to split parts. We switch parts halfway through the song because it doesn't work as a straight lead with harmony. Between he and I, it was real group effort to get something done … I looked at him and he looked at me, and it was just like, 'Well, if it never gets worse than this, it'll be fine!'

"I can honestly say that it was the first time that I had ever walked out of the studio knowing for sure that not only was it going to be Number One but that it was going to stay there. And it did."

'The Sun Ain't Gonna Shine Anymore' was released on February 25 1966 and was instantly and unanimously accepted as a classic. It spent 14 weeks in the UK chart, four of those at the topper-most of the popper-most. In fact, it was a hit in every country it was released in, hitting Number 13 on the US *Billboard* chart. The record sounds as if it's been around forever and is haloed by an implacable timeless quality. If it is tied to the 60s in some people's minds, it is perhaps because of a more sinister connotation.

One spring evening, in 1966, at 8.30pm, infamous gangster Ronnie Kray marched into the Blind Beggar pub in London's Whitechapel and put three bullets through the face of gangland rival George Cornell. 'The Sun Ain't Gonna Shine Anymore' was, courtesy of the bar's jukebox, the soundtrack to a murder. As Cornell slumped to the floor, Kray fired one more shot into the ceiling to cover his (and Cornell's) exit. The bullet apparently ricocheted around the pub several times before lodging in the jukebox itself, causing the seven-inch vinyl inside to become stuck in one groove: "The sun ain't gonna shine anymore … anymore … anymore …"

'Mad' Frankie Fraser: "At the time when Ronnie come in and shot 'im dead, that famous song was playing. And after he shot him dead,

Ronnie said, 'That's certainly right, the sun ain't gonna shine anymore for George.'"

Transcending even this noirish association, 'The Sun Ain't Gonna Shine Anymore' is as perfect-sounding a hit record as ever was. Thirty years later, even Scott would acknowledge as much, admitting modestly to the Irish journalist Joe Jackson: "I hate to say it, but it is a great pop record."

Indeed, everything is right about the Walkers' interpretation, from the now iconic intro to the beautiful snatch of Engel falsetto at the tail end of its fade-out. (Alas, this appears only on the original seven-inch and video.) A promo film was made to accompany the song, which shows the boys resplendent in their shining youth, strolling through the erotic sculptures of Stockholm's Millesgarden.

The B-side was much more than the usual filler. 'After The Lights Go Out', written by Scott's best buddy John Stewart, evokes perfectly, once more, the kind of myth-like scenario from which, in the eyes of the public, Scott would never fully escape: the pretty boy-dude with the old man's voice and the world at his feet. All the same, he'd rather stay in tonight, thanks. A winter sun sets across the threadbare bedsit floor, finding the narrator alone, as the tap drips, the clock ticks, and yet the silence is deafening.

"Nobody can say ['After The Lights Go Out'] is a happy song," mused The Jesus & Mary Chain's William Reid some 20 years later. "But it makes me feel good. It might sound depressing, but it doesn't make me feel the least bit depressed; it makes me feel happy that the record actually exists. You might not be able to explain what the lyric means, but that's not what I want. I know what the lyrics mean, but I couldn't tell you."

Applied to The Walker Brothers' best work as a whole, Reid's words could be a perfect summation of their appeal. Despite its portentously doomy lyric and title, 'The Sun Ain't Gonna Shine Anymore' and its perfectly matched B-side are, ultimately, transcendently beautiful listening experiences. The A-side in particular makes the prospect of eternal night sound uplifting.

It's also a testament to The Walker Brothers' unique chemistry that this song was never a substantial hit for any other artist, despite numerous versions recorded before and after this release. Still, even those who made up said chemistry had a hard time in breaking down its formula. "It's a difficult song to sing, although it doesn't sound it. It just is," groped John. "There were certain things that we did with the music. ... If you're not bringing something special to the material, don't do it. And I think that what we did with the songs we recorded, I think we found ways to do them that were very unique, and I think they had their own kind of life. And if you wanted to go and cover those, you'd have to do something special to the song – and those songs are not exactly easy songs."

Gary was, as ever, more succinct. "We have this sophisticated style. By sophisticated I mean something in between The Rolling Stones and Cliff Richard."

Released in early spring 1966, the single was a phenomenon, causing an instant and inedible impression upon the British pop consciousness, in a week that included the release of The Who's 'Substitute' and The Kinks' 'Dedicated Follower Of Fashion', and in which John Lennon's thoughts on the relative importance of both his band and Jesus Christ dominated the tabloids and broadsheets. Despite the increased demands on the Walkers' time that such success entailed, the three pop stars made room to develop their extracurricular interests, and even Scott was not above retail therapy.

Gary: "We used to go through Foyle's bookshop all the time like it was a sweetshop. Any time Scott thought about writing a book, he'd then give up immediately after leaving the place. There used to be a little place in Soho Square that [sold] classical records, and he'd go through everything ... the Andre Previn thing with the L.S.O. when that was around ... we'd get one version of Rachmaninoff and then another and see how they'd treat it. ... We'd sit up 'til all hours listening to these things. A lot of the time, it'd bore me to death; he'd give me some opera and say, 'You'll love this.' And I still haven't opened it, funnily enough: it's still in the box and cellophane."

When not attempting to pull Gary up the cultural ladder with him, Scott still found time to take in *Our Man Flint* at the movies, catch up on the latest releases by fellow crooners such as Frank Sinatra ("It embarrasses me to be compared to Sinatra, I'm nowhere near as good") and Jack Jones (the Guv'nor), while also sharing a trade secret: the leggy singer got his jeans to fit by wearing them in the bath.

Scott was now a regular at Ronnie Scott's jazz club, and yet he still found enough hours in the night to foster healthy feuds with the likes of Eric Burdon and Mick Jagger: The Animals' Burdon had dissed the titanic 'Sun' on *Jukebox Jury*, stating his preference for black soul music. "I don't understand this coloured soul bit," Scott retorted. "To me, the greatest soul singer in the world is Frank Sinatra."

Scott's problem with Jagger and his then-beau, the model Chrissie Shrimpton, was perhaps more complex in its motives and much more visceral and comical in effect.

Scott: "Chrissie Shrimpton seems to have something against me and I know Mick Jagger doesn't like me. Apart from trying to elbow me off the dance floor where I was with a girl ... I was sitting in a club below a balcony on which Jagger had a table. A cigarette butt was thrown down. At first, I thought it was funny. Then another came down. In the end, I lost my temper and threw a handful back up. Things were quiet after that. We fellows seem to hit it off with The Beatles but the Stones don't like us."

Gary: "[Jagger] uses my cigarettes to throw at Scott. I can't smoke 'em afterwards cos they're full of Scott's hair."

Chrissie McCall remembers that the Engel–Jagger feud, while blown out of proportion by the drama-hungry press, did have its basis in truth. "I think it was because Jagger saw Scott as a challenge, didn't he? Let's face it, you couldn't even compare voices, could you? And when it comes down to the looks department ... ."

Perhaps Scott's inability to bond with fellow celebs like the Stones was simply down to an unwillingness to play the game or a simple shyness, or both. "I respect my privacy," he would say, "and I suppose I'm rude in other people's eyes. I stick to myself [and] don't hang around clubs." Even those who worked with and respected Scott knew for sure that they were dealing with something different, particularly in comparison to his contempories. Big Jim Sullivan: "Scott was an enigma. He wasn't the kind of person that could be your friend. He wouldn't really mix. He must have had good friends, but he seemed a bit standoff-ish ... whereas John was always really friendly. John would say, 'Let's go and have dinner tonight,' and we'd go out to Flanagan's or somewhere and kick up the sawdust. But Scott was never like that. He wouldn't let his hair down. He was shy."

Such meditation on the Engel character would have little consequence. There was simply no time to consider such traits. The Walkers were being sucked into the eye of the storm, and there was work to be done. Maurice made a phone call, and the fabric of all three Walkers' time rearranged itself accordingly. First, there was a warm-up residency at Tito's in Stockton (where Scott found the week of cabaret much more to his taste than the constant grind of driving/hotel/onstage insanity that constituted touring). Then a 27-date grind duly began, kicking off at London's Finsbury Park Astoria on March 2. Unbelievably, the Walkers, who were now as big as they would ever get (which was the biggest in the country), found themselves below Roy Orbison on the bill, following Lulu. Lulu's inclusion on the programme would mean that, even backstage, Scott could not be free from the female attention that seemed to plague him so.

Lulu: "The first person to bruise my heart was Scott Walker. I toured with him for six weeks, and it was like an ecstatic torture. I went to bed dreaming about Scott each night, listening to young girls call his name from outside the hotel. At the concerts they swooned and became hysterical, reaching their arms up toward him. I watched from the side of the stage thinking, 'Please pick me!'."

Scott's guests in the audience at the Finsbury Park show were his mother Betty and Aunt Cile, two islands of normality among a heaving sea of teenage insanity, and undoubtedly the only females in the vicinity who did not covet Scott romantically. Both senior Engels were reputedly bemused by the hysterical reaction toward their Noel, and perhaps they were only half joking when, on meeting up with Scott afterward, they put on the whole 'starstruck' bit, claiming that they were now not worthy of his time.

Beyond such surreal events, Scott and company were confined to the regimental order of the touring life, while the world beyond went on, seeming increasingly to revolve around what was now Britain's biggest pop group. EMI attempted to release an album's worth of early Engel and Stewart tracks, preceded by their excellent take on P.J. Proby's 'I Only Came To Dance With You' as a single. Philips barred the releases, blowing both out of the commercial water. As one decoy went down, another popped up, when the head of Liberty Recordings threatened to release his archive recordings of an adolescent Engel. Maurice instructed Clayman to get their solicitors working on that, too. During a few rare hours off, while Scott prepared to meet with Franz to discuss the next album, Gary and John gamely turned up at a Kensington charity walk on the spring morning of April 22. After the starting pistol fired, the (literal) Walkers barely had a chance to leave the gate before Gary and John were bundled away for more interviews and rehearsals.

Even their manager was called on to perform beyond duty. One week later, Maurice King would be hosting the *NME* poll winners' concert. Among the star acts he introduced was, of course, a group called The Walker Brothers. Engel, Maus, Leeds, and King were now omnipresent. John wore a t-shirt cut off at the midriff, causing some members of the audience to suffer 'multiple fainting', bouts of swooning interspersed with just enough consciousness to allow another black-out. The most famous pop group in Britain was also the busiest, and they had no time for such restful bouts of oblivion.

Between the dressing rooms and hotel rooms, Scott crammed in some interviews. Speaking to the ever-present Keith Altham, he attempted to end the Jagger feud with what sounded like a stilted compliment, offered up a succinct definition of existentialism, expressed admiration for Orson Welles and Italian screen goddess Claudia Cardinale, and rather preciously bemoaned the fact that he was expected to perform his hits live.

John, meanwhile, confessed that he didn't think their records were commercial enough – a perverse statement, as 'The Sun Ain't Gonna Shine Anymore' would remain at Number One for the duration of the tour. As if this weren't enough, an unknown Liverpudlian group called

The Berries announced their intention to record an Engel song as their debut single. All three Walkers barely had time to turn down a cameo in the forthcoming Bardot movie, *Two Weeks In September.*

As the madness rolled on, this tour was fraught with chaos – even compared to the usual hysteria. Roy Orbison fractured a leg on a day off, motorcycling at Hawkston Park; Marlene Dietrich was inadvertently trampled by Walker fans in Birmingham; Gary was kidnapped as a part of a charity stunt by students; and John lost consciousness amid a gaggle of gals in Chester, thus forfeiting the following night's date in Wigan.

The closest Scott came to any physical harm was when he became paralysed with fear during a flight over Liverpool, when the plane started bleeding oil. By comparison, when Lulu went down with laryngitis in Cardiff it seemed like an Ingmar Bergman film festival. By the end of the tour, at Maurice's suggestion, an amiable agreement had been reached, and Orbison would be playing below the obvious stars of the show. Scott wasn't that impressed by the Big O, finding him too genial and eager to please, but John admired Orbison's operatic voice and respected his professional success, often watching the black-clad Texan from stage left.

The tour ended a thousand sodden seats later, on a Sunday, at the Coventry Theatre. Chaos reigned, with Scott entering the stage on a pushbike amid a tsunami of screams. He then hijacked the drumkit and, with John on piano, they accompanied a hollering Gary, eventually closing the show with seven curtain calls. Back in London, the Lotus House, everybody's favourite Chinese restaurant, was booked out for the end-of-tour party.

Lulu's longing remained unrequited. "I thought I was hiding my feelings, but Scott realised I had a crush on him," she would reminisce decades later, no doubt slipping back into the persona of her blushing teen self once more. "I looked all calf-eyed at him and would get flustered talking to him. All he did was pat me on the head and treat me like a little sister."

Scott had escaped the tour physically unmolested, but by the time the 27 dates were over he nevertheless felt mentally ravaged and generally exhausted. Even Maurice could see the kid needed a break.

That summer Scott declared his intentions to cut his hair and attend the season's bullfights in Spain. The Walkers camp duly went on holiday to Marbella.

Gary: "[Spain] was bad for the first few days. No one would talk to us. They looked at our hair and kinda steered away from us like we were hobos. Then a millionaire guy came up and talks to us and everyone wanted to be friends all day. They thought we were The Beatles or something."

Ironically, by the time the boys were back in blighty, John, Gary, and Scott were bigger than The Beatles – in the UK, at least, where their fan club subscriptions outnumbered those of The Beatles and the Stones. Following the apocalyptic success of their last tour and single, it was time for the Californian Ringo to go out into the world and spread the Leeds creed once more. Preceding the release that May of his second solo single, 'Twinkie Lee', Gary took to the hot seat on the BBC's *A Whole Scene Going On* and popped up on TWTV's *Now* scoffing a bag of fish and chips. In promoting the "revived rock'n'roll" of his new single, Gary spoke with some insight. "I probably get more of a kick out of singing than the other two guys, because I'm not really a singer."

Following the dual excursions of Marbella and 'Twinkie Lee' (another minor hit), the Walkers' carousel ground on. A tour of Germany in late May saw them play Hamburg's legendary Star Club and the local US army base, and on Bremen TV they mimed to 'The Sun Ain't Gonna Shine Anymore', 'Land Of A Thousand Dances', and Dylan's 'Love Minus Zero'.

They were banned from a Copenhagen hotel for making too much row in an elevator, and there was anguish when John lost one of his favourite Stratocaster guitars in Munich, but the boys returned to the UK in early June, heading straight for Stanhope Place, where they put the finishing touches to the new album. Their confidence had grown and the experience was a little more relaxed compared to the *Take It Easy* sessions a year before. Tape operator Roger Wake remembers John, in particular, being more confident than ever during the sessions, asserting himself vocally and in terms of the material chosen.

The schedule was unremitting. Following another all-nighter with Franz, John and Scott would head for the Starlite Club to rehearse for a bouquet of Blackpool dates in August and September. They spent spare hours fulfilling celebrity duties, such as arriving by helicopter at Brands Hatch motor-racing circuit to present a trophy to the winner. Scott did not attend, but this was not just down to his hatred of flying. He was becoming recognised as a major vocal talent and, even if only because of his natural professionalism, he was busy honing his craft. John was less concerned in working on his God-given talent and had no problem spending his time at the race-track with Gary while Scott laboured elsewhere.

"I am working on my own, studying breath control and phrasing," he confided. "I'd like to be able to put that styling into a song that Sinatra does in 'A Very Good Year'. That would mean a lot to me."

To help him achieve such heights, Franz sent the lead singer – still only 22 – along to the late Freddie Winrose, a vocal coach then based in Denmark Street.

As with so many of the older male professionals Scott would come into contact with, he and the singing tutor hit it off immediately, striking up a respectful and affectionate rapport. They would work together on and off until the late 70s. Winrose's main ambition was to eliminate Engel's liquid vibrato.

With Scott's apparent natural ability as a singer, Sinatra was often the most obvious and stated comparison. Sinatra had worked on his own breathing and phrasing from an early age, swimming lap after lap at the local public baths in order to increase his lung capacity. He would also submerge himself below the water, holding his breath in increasingly long bouts. This would help him sing a phrase without interruption, having more breath to use at a time. Singing a line as it's spoken or written is hard to do within one breath, but if it can be done, unbroken, the marrying of lyric and melody sounds much more and natural and effective as a result.

Scott was a fan in particular of Sinatra's 50s albums and would have been aware of the technique. But he did not apparently follow Frank into the swimming pool, instead building up his lung capacity by attempting to hold his breath for a block at a time as he walked the streets of London. Scott respected Frank Sinatra the singer, but by the summer of 1966 he was growing disillusioned with Frank's output. Reviewing 'Strangers In The Night' as a guest of *Melody Maker*, the young pretender to the throne was unforgiving in his assessment. "Sinatra degrades himself by doing this rubbish. I love Sinatra, but when I hear him going all Dean Martin, it sickens me. The phrasing at which Sinatra usually excels sounds like a train labouring uphill. The man is not equipped to swing any more. He doesn't need the prestige of a chart number."

Maurice simply believed that his young charge was the next Frankie and was not shy about saying so, often loudly and in company. Few argued. Fellow Capable client Tony Hatch was in agreement with his manager and, as a musician himself, was arguably better qualified in his assessment.

"[Scott's] voice had a naturally warm and deep resonance, yet he could hit the high notes without straining or closing the throat," says Hatch. "His diction was perfect and his intonation was always spot-on. More importantly, he always thought carefully about the lyrics and sang them straight from the heart, not from the song sheet."

Such talk obviously raised questions about John and Gary's roles. If Scott was on the way to becoming the new 'chairman of the board' then where did these two fit in? To some, and Maurice in particular, they did not even come close to their obvious equivalent: Dean Martin and Sammy Davis Jr. Even Sammy played better drums than Gary, and while John was acquiring Dino's penchant for a drink, any similarities beyond this were purely coincidental.

As ever, with the Walker star in full ascent, there was no time to brood upon such irregularities. That July 8, shortly after announcing a (subsequently aborted) seaside-resort tour with Ike and Tina Turner, the Walkers were given an entire episode of *Ready Steady Go!* to themselves, hosting it as well as choosing the guests. The group performed together and did solo spots, with Scott performing a sublime slow-motion version of The Beatles' 'We Can Work It Out', while John soloed on Petula Clarke's 'I Couldn't Live Without Your

Love'. The show was timed to promote the new single, '(Baby) You Don't Have To Tell Me', apparently chosen by Gary. Coming after 'The Sun Ain't Gonna Shine Anymore' it sounded odd, like something of a sideways step, a concession to compromise.

'(Baby) You Don't Have To Tell Me' is amiable and overly bombastic, as if Mercedes-Benz had designed a go-kart, and was their first wrong foot since 'Pretty Girls Everywhere'. The B-side, 'My Love Is Growing', is the perfect counterpart, mirroring the relative mundanity of the lead compared to the previous three milestone singles.

John: "I screamed the loudest for this one – production-wise, it surpasses anything we have ever done. There are 40 guys on this session, and you can hear 40 sounds on the track. This is really The Walker Brothers on this one. I love it." Gary: "No one liked that, for some reason; they didn't want to hear it. They wanted to hear the one voice, the melody, and the 'Holland Tunnel', and that was it."

Scott: "It's kind of a concession – many people wanted us to have a dance number, something up-tempo. They didn't think we could do another ballad. At the moment, it seems like me and Johnny Franz against the world."

Although the Walkers were the crowned gods of UK pop that summer, when the disappointing single peaked ominously at Number 13, Scott was suddenly under pressure. He reacted, violently, against himself. The results were dramatic, and some of the responses were less sympathetic than others.

Andrew Loog Oldham: "Jonathan [King] called me and Tony once and said, 'You must get up to Regent's Park. Scott is having a breakdown; he's snapped, he's talking to the hedges.' I thought, 'Yeah, all on half a bottle of Mateus.' [Rock photographer] Gered Mankowitz and I went around to Scott's, banging on the door, shouted through his mailbox, and told him to stop acting like an old poof and do the decent thing and put his head in the oven."

Following the dubious publicity from reports that their singer had apparently attempted suicide on August 19, The Walker Brothers' second album, *Portrait*, was released. The cover shot was slightly better than that of the first album and was also taken by a celebrity photographer – this time the legendary Cecil Beaton. A separate print of the photo was included within the sleeve. The album matched *Take It Easy*, reaching Number Three.

While the album was a step forward, it was never going to be much of a surprise. "They didn't tell us exactly what material to pick," Scott admitted, presumably referring to the combined might of Philips, Franz, and his own pop sensibility. "But they'd tell us the kind of material they wanted. It had to be ballads. It had to be the two voices."

Portrait begins with 'In My Room' – and this is Scott solo by any other name. If, in the tradition of shows based on Queen, Abba, Buddy Holly, and the rest, they ever turn the public myth of Scott Walker into a West End or Broadway musical, this song would surely kick off the first act. The introductory fanfare seems to suggest thick red drapes opening up onto a stage-set version of Scott the super-bachelor. A man alone, distinctly by choice, brooding over terrifying profundities in a cold-water flat, the floor splayed with dead flowers and Mateus Rosé bottles. A room where horrifying realities have come home to roost, a room that is of a time and place where John and Gary are not even conspicuous in their absence.

A song of Italian origin, 'In My Room' is one of those perfect Walker moments: deeper than it is wide, clocking in at a deceptively short-sounding 2:31, the string and choral arrangements impeccable, exquisite. It is reminiscent of some of the sub-Spaghetti Western pop-song soundtracks with which Ennio Morricone was experimenting in *A Pistol For Ringo* and so on, and yet the effect as a whole is vastly superior. The slightly over-dramatic dynamic of the arrangement and lyric – the song verges on camp – is given complete individuation and credibility by Scott's impeccably deadpan vocal.

'Saturday's Child' marks the debut appearance of a 100 per cent sole Engel composition on any Walker Brothers LP, and it is also one of the few Engel songs to sound as if it was written on the singer's first instrument, the electric bass guitar. This is apparent in the heavy four-string riff that is an obvious nod to Spector's arrangement of Ike and Tina Turner's 'River Deep – Mountain High'. Yet, even as Engel's newfound confidence makes its presence felt, the results, while impressive, are ultimately unconvincing. The tune is a bittersweet throwaway, and Reg Guest's formidable arrangement pumps the song up to a stature it neither warrants nor sustains. Few Engel songs would again sound so rhythmically driven, and that's no bad thing. The levity of his voice and, to a much lesser degree, the 'heaviness' of the lyric – one can draw a direct line between the subject matter of this song and Scott's earlier outspoken opinion on the mid-60s London club scene – both kill any chances this had of becoming a dancefloor favourite. In short, Scott just doesn't sound convincing at this BPM. If nothing else, it works as a bridge between the gorgeous opening of 'In My Room' and the moribund prettiness that follows on 'Just For A Thrill'.

John: "I thought ['Just For A Thrill'] was one of the greatest songs I'd ever heard in my life. And the whole gist of the song was: you broke my heart just for a thrill. I mean, come on! Stick the knife in deeper! I just love the song. It makes sense to me."

John's amber croon wears this Ray Charles standard well enough, but in the context of this album, it's hardly anything one would want to hear here. Where the previous arrangement nodded brazenly toward Phil Spector, 'Just For A Thrill', with its lush, effortless strings and chocolate-coloured trombone solo, signposts Sinatra's arranger, Nelson Riddle. However, where Sinatra had the history, presence, personality, gravity, and destiny to make any number of MOR standards become more than they were, John merely sounds perfunctory, petty, and pretty.

It is revealing of the growing gulf between the Brothers that it's not until the fourth song, 'Hurting Each Other', that John and Scott appear on the album together. For neither the first nor the last time, John really does sound like a backing singer rather than a counterpoint, as Scott strolls through the melody with Teutonic efficiency. Impressive as it is, there is something casual about his performance. It's another engaging filler (and a hit for The Carpenters six years later). By now, the dark, blood-red promise of 'In My Room' seems another career away.

The lyrics of the creaky jazz standard 'Old Folks' are an exercise in stultified sentimentality. It is an odd juxtaposition to imagine Scott singing such words and then perhaps leaving the studio, however reticently, for a nightcap at the Cromwellian or the Ad Lib club. (Guy Peellaert's and Nik Cohn's book *Rock Dreams* features 'The Ad-Lib', a painting that, intriguingly, shows a regal Scott mingling with John, Paul, George, the Glimmer twins, et al.)

The choice of 'Old Folks', even then, would have seemed better suited to a more established and sexless crooner such as Des O'Connor or Perry Como. One wonders on hearing such offensively inoffensive material where Scott's head was. Awake, aware, and essentially hip as Scott was, how must he have felt to be putting out material like this alongside 'Paint It, Black', *Miles Ahead*, and *Revolver*? It is, as ever, impeccably arranged and sincerely sung, and the final vocal verse ends in a style that would for a time become the singer's trademark: the sustained and vibrato-less melting away of the last word. (See also 'Copenhagen', 'Rosemary', 'The Summer Knows', and 'A Face In The Crowd'.)

The spectre of Morricone returns on the Brothers' take on the Gershwin classic 'Summertime', and the promise of the opening 'In My Room' is fulfilled. Despite having apparently "wrecked" their voices the night before the session by getting carried away on stage, and regardless of Scott's subsequent criticism of the rhythm section ("The bass player and the drummer fell apart"), 'Summertime' is a pinnacle, a blue mountain, one of the best things they recorded.

The voices are flawless, falling skyward like cranes out of a cedarwood forest, sitting together in perfect harmony like the vodka and kaluha in a white Russian cocktail. Neither voice overshadows the other. This song alone is argument enough against the foregone conclusion of Scott's solo career and one of the few recordings that warrant the literal meaning inherent in 'The Walker Brothers'. Scott's voice seems to give birth to John's, and vice versa, as each respectively relinquishes and takes up the lead. The big-band arrangement, illuminated achingly by wide-open spaces, occasionally hints at Gil Evans's superlative work with Miles Davis in the 50s.

The timing of the drums is imperfect – in particular, they seem to stumble beneath the frayed conclusion of Barrie Martin's raw sax solo. However, this just adds to the odd and disquieting atmosphere of the piece. There is a sense of the sinister throughout. And this, ultimately, is the Brothers' strength: they are singing about the joy and promise of summer, and yet the whole scene seems set in an oddly minor key, an atmosphere of marine twilight. They have either completely subverted the meaning of the song or found some deeper more disconcerting truth beneath; within the height of summer, there is the echo of the coming fall. It's a highlight not only of the album but also of their career.

Next, the Walkers gracefully assimilate Curtis Mayfield's 'People Get Ready', and the result is a fine version of the Impressions hit. Ronnie Verrell's drumming and Scott's phrasing in the latter verses are particularly alluring. On some vinyl versions, the string coda swings delightfully from left channel to right and back again.

'I Can See It Now' is an utterly beguiling Franz–Engel collaboration. Scott rarely sounds passive or casual when singing words he has written himself. This alone is usually enough to lend even an Engel-by-numbers piece such as this the edge over bog-standards like 'Old Folks' and 'Take It Like A Man'. Scott sounds fatally blond and nonchalant against a painterly Ivor Raymonde arrangement, Big Jim does his guitar thing, sibling John croons along dutifully, and somewhere over the West End rooftops a broken-hearted dolly bird is striking 'Engel' from her address book.

'Where's The Girl' is the first of two Leiber & Stoller songs covered on the record, and along with 'In My Room' was Scott's favourite cut on the album. It paints a vivid picture of a recently female-less apartment, bringing to mind images of a classic Jack Lemmon movie from the late 50s or early 60s. It's another transcendent (solo) performance from Scott with a particularly sympathetic accompaniment by Ivor Raymonde, the strings soaring to match Scott's balletic vocals. The young singer seems to be taking delight in matching the expansive melody octave for octave. Many have based careers on such moments, and yet this was probably the last time Scott ever sang this song.

The tracklisting is completed by 'Living Above Your Head' – similar to 'Saturday's Child' in groove, tempom and effect, but never quite living up to the promise of its gorgeous intro. The album plays out with a solo John vocal on a mediocre mid-tempo cut of Leiber & Stoller's 'Take It Like A Man' and then ends with John and Scott's choirboys-at-a-mafioso-funeral rendition of 'No Sad Songs For Me'. It was the soundtrack to a million teenage daydreams.

In private and in public, Scott was sometimes generous in his praise for John's contributions, but he also spoke truthfully, if not tactfully, in his official statement summing up the album as "a creative cataclysm by three people, Reg Guest, Johnny Franz, and myself".

Neither Gary nor John argued the point – in public, anyway – but such bold statements of such bald facts could not have endeared Scott to either. "Who can you insult if you can't insult your friends," Scott had quipped cheerfully in the *NME* summer special a few weeks before.

By the time the Walkers started a Swedish tour that September, riding the wave of their latest chart success, all three were operating on increasingly different wavelengths. Although Scott temporarily lost his voice in Stockholm, for John and Gary the tour was business as usual. Regardless of any backstage problems or personal grief and hassles that they may have encountered, they always displayed professional conduct on stage and then let off steam afterward, clubbing, mingling, carousing, sightseeing, much like any other 22-year-old pop star abroad. Scott's heart lay elsewhere, however. The divide between him and his bothers was widening.

"I was in Sweden for a short tour," said Scott. "I was convinced that I would meet Ingmar Bergman. I was naive enough to think that it would be sufficient to walk about a bit in Sweden to come across somebody who would introduce me to Bergman. But when I talked with people in Sweden they just tried to change the subject the whole time. They couldn't imagine something more boring than discussing Ingmar Bergman. I was quite shocked."

Gary: "He used to take me to see all the Bergman films. He was really into all the existential stuff. He used to take me to see *War And Peace*. It lasted about 35 days."

CHAPTER 7

FINAL IMAGES

Both [Gary] and John are much more materialistic than me. I don't honestly care much about money. John counts his very carefully. ... I want to make records, look after publishing music, all that sort of thing. It's all being carefully planned. The Walkers: fine. However, it's not the end of my ambition.

Scott Walker (1966)

The pop world in which the Walkers moved was at this time measured by innovation and a seemingly insatiable appetite for novelty. Technology was catching up with imagination, and imagination, fuelled by the revolution in psychedelics, was catching up with itself. Recording technology was becoming increasingly complex, and by 1968, eight-track studios would be the norm. Over at Abbey Road, The Beatles' engineers were coming up with all kinds of mechanical hybrids within the studio, crudely lashing tape machines to each other in an attempt to keep up with their bosses' need for tools to match vision. Elsewhere, the space race was in full ascent, and domestic jetpacks and lunar discotheques were apparently but a tomorrow away.

In the midst of all this, day and night at the studio, Engel and Franz sought to refine their sonic formula, making subtle adjustments and progressions within each recording. While Philips were wary of any drastic sonic reinvention – if it ain't broke, why fix it? – the public and press were beginning to tire of what seemed to be the same old sound. The refinements that Franz, Oliff, and Engel were making with each release were lost to the ears of both paymaster and punter.

While the alchemy of production was subtly changing, the base material remained the same. On September 16, one more platter of sonic melodrama rolled off of the Engel–Franz production line. Yet another Bacharach–David tune, 'Another Tear Falls', was chosen at the suggestion of guitarist Billy Bremner, who'd seen Gene McDaniels sing it in the 1962 movie *It's Trad, Dad*. A mid-paced ballad woven from black thunder and a squadron of teardrops, the song pressed all the right buttons but left little of an afterglow. It was, in effect, the Walkers on cruise control. Although it would fall short of the Top Ten, peaking at 12, no one could know then that it would be their most successful single for another decade.

This record's B-side, 'Saddest Night In The World', is unique among the canon in that it features Scott singing a 100 per cent John Maus original. For anyone even slightly aware of the delicate dynamic of their friendship, this lends the piece a touching poignancy. Much less orchestrated than any of their albums' tracks, it is almost folksy and intimate by comparison. An interesting, key-hopping chord progression drives it toward the perfect finale: a brief soliloquy by Scott and harpsichord that puts the whole song to sleep beneath a blanket of snowy strings. If this were film, it would be Godard in Carnaby Street. It's interesting to speculate if John wrote this with Scott in mind and raised his game accordingly, as it's among his best writing of this period.

Prior to the group's first headline tour that autumn, the Arthur Howes Agency booked the Walkers into a short residency with Bill Haley & His Comets at Paris's Alhambra music hall. By the Walkers' admission, they and fellow support act The Spencer Davis Group were blown off the stage by the original cow-licked rocker. The promoters paid for travel and accommodation, but on this occasion the Walkers would have to meet the food and bar bill. Over the course of a few days, in spite of John's gastronomic fussiness – he had a problem with 'funny tasting' French eggs in particular – they ran up a bill of £3,000, a not inconsiderable sum in 1966. On returning to England, they were met by an under-the-table offer of management from Brian Epstein. True to his own particular moral compass, Scott declined, saying that he did not want to "be involved with the Beatle money".

Ballooning bar tabs aside, lack of privacy was a particularly stubborn monkey that Scott could not shake from his back. As if the exhausting schedule of promo, writing, recording, and gigging wasn't enough, all three found themselves having to change their phone numbers at least weekly. They would also have to move flats several times a year, often under cover of darkness. Such a lifestyle does not anchor one psychologically.

Chrissie McCall: "Scott moved into a flat on the Fulham Road, and he had these very heavy velvet curtains, stapled together because he was so paranoid about fans finding out where he lived. When he'd just moved in, he rang Gary up absolutely mortified. He said, 'I've only just moved in here and they've found me already! There's hundreds of them out there!' And it was nothing to do with that. It was football fans at the local football ground in Chelsea. And he was convinced they were fans who had found him. When Gary told him the truth, knowing Scott, he wouldn't have felt silly, just relieved."

Still, Scott was barely home long enough to be truly bothered by such noise pollution. As autumn came, Capable let the clockwork toys out of the box again. October heralded an exhaustive and exhausting 33-date tour with support from The Troggs and Dave Dee Dozy Beaky Mick & Tich. Apart from the novelty of concluding the tour with a Royal Gala performance before the Duke of Edinburgh at the London Palladium, it was the same old scene.

Scott: "The tour is 33 dates long – out of greed. Not my greed: I'd rather do one date and have it perfect. My mind will be completely blown after this one. I'll be working all night, writing, and then travelling all day. For the teenagers, this is a very exciting tour, and I think we shall draw a different audience from the last one with Orbison. This one is for the fans."

Dave Dee: "We all used to travel in a bus, but the Walkers didn't. They never came on the bus. Still, I got very friendly with John – and Gary. They were always quite amenable. I never really quite worked it out with Scott. Whether he was shy ... I mean, they used to have two guys, minders, with them all the time. Scott, I think, didn't like being around a lot of people. I think he felt a bit like a goldfish in a bowl.

"The minute The Walker Brothers went on stage, you couldn't hear anything. How they ever heard whatever they were singing I will never know, because the girls just used to scream the theatres down. I wouldn't say it was violent; it was just mass hysteria. We used to encourage it. Oh yeah! You know, it was the days of the real screamers. It could be quite frightening, if they got hold of you en masse. But, by the same token, that's what you were there for. They were the audience and wanted a piece of you, and we used to encourage it a lot of the time. I don't know if the Walkers did. I don't think they had to.

"The screaming went on all through the whole show, but it got a bit louder when The Walker Brothers went on. I mean, he was a very good-looking young man, and the three of 'em on stage looked good. They were a very good-looking bunch of lads, and they would up the tempo from however many decibels we would get. You'd sometimes be doing two shows a day, a matinee and an evening show, and you'd have the kids from the first show outside the stage door, screaming for Scott, screaming for John ... they used to hang outside, hundreds of 'em, in the street ... just ... screaming."

The Walkers found some musical relief from the fans' exhausting adoration by jamming Freddy King and blues shuffles with their support acts at soundchecks. Scott, though, would usually make for the relative quiet of his hotel room, where he would continue to work on songs for a new EP and a screenplay for a "surrealistic pop film with a contemporary of Ingmar Bergman's" – a collaborator whose name he couldn't pronounce and therefore could not remember. He also voiced plans to emulate The Righteous Brothers' successful reinterpretation of 'White Cliffs Of Dover' by having the Walkers record a Spectoresque version of Vera Lynn's 'We'll Meet Again'. While both plans no doubt served Engel well during his touring downtime, neither came to fruition.

Beyond the refined think-tank atmosphere of the Engel hotel room, it was almost business as usual. While the audiences were as bewitched as ever, the press on this tour was less enraptured than previously. Of the opening night's show at the East Ham Granada, the *NME* wondered aloud: "How long can Scott keep carrying the other two? Their act is virtually a one-man show. John and Gary may as well have stayed home."

Such statements would cause powerful repercussions within the enclosed Walker camp, although they were rarely verbalised by the Walkers themselves. As hurtful as these critical perceptions may have been, they were not seen as false. Chrissie McCall was often backstage when some naive roadie would innocently read the previous night's notices out aloud. "But it was all true," she says, speaking for all who were there. "That is the sad fact of the matter. We all knew this. It wouldn't be talked about. Scott took it all with a pinch of salt anyway. He really was disinterested in the press; he wasn't putting it on. John would deal with it by getting drunk."

Without even trying, Scott was coming to dominate, on and off stage. Big Jim Sullivan speaks for the majority: "Scott was the presence. His voice was everything. As it is on the records. You can't get away from that fact."

John's response was surprisingly easy-going, philosophical, or, increasingly, intoxicated. But he would maintain a sunny and surprisingly sensible attitude. "The media focuses on who the lead singer is, and it wasn't a situation where Scott was the lead singer of a group and nobody else was singing. Basically, our sound happened because of [our] harmonies. That was how it worked."

DJ Dave Cash, like McCall, was also a regular backstage presence at their shows and was sympathetic toward those in Scott's shadow. "John was one guy who never got enough credit, I thought. His voice was absolutely essential to making the sound of The Walker Brothers.

Scott got all the accolades and John should have got more than he did. As for Gary ... Gary was a great PR man, the jumping around, grooving guy. He was TCB – taking care of business. But Scott was the focus of attention ... that's just the way it happened. I don't think there was any mercenary move by Scott to take over the whole thing."

Whatever the perception of the public and press, it all came down to the dynamic of the group. And this was becoming increasingly skewed. John Maus: "What did concern me was when we started having a lot of ideas that started becoming very separate: separate ideas about what to do with the music and how to do the music. And it got to the point where working on material, picking the material for new albums and things, was not fun any more. ... There seemed to be problems over settling on pieces of material. At that time, I'd rather be on the road than in the recording studio: that's the truth."

For Scott, the novelty had worn off, and any affair he ever had with life on the road was over. "Touring was pure hell. You were driving from London to Glasgow in a van in one night. On the other hand, you're young, so you can take it. We were ill most of the time. A lot of bands were very sick with colds and stuff, and we were southern Californians, so we were ill more. It was a living hell."

Contrary to the widening divide, it was announced that John would produce Gary's next solo single, although even Gary, an innocent musical eunuch in anyone's eyes, hadn't escaped the scattergun onslaught of John's Scotch-and-cola-fuelled comments backstage at the Manchester show. "Gary is very easy-going and a good friend, but he's been put into this raunchy rock'n'roll category," proclaimed John between mouthfuls of Jack Daniels. "And these records he made on his own – they were really not very tasteful. Distasteful, in fact. He's capable of better things." Gary was seen to make a sharp exit as John turned up the discontent to 11. "My pet bitch is being compared to Engel. He's a lead weight [pulling me down]! He's moody, irresponsible, and a pain in the neck – but he's got talent."

Almost instantaneously, the public were up in arms.

Anonymous fan letter to *NME*: "I wasn't a fan of J Maus before ... but now! Just who does he think he is? Can't he understand Scott *is*

The Walker Brothers? Hasn't it ever occurred to him that as Gary and Scott get on well together, it could be him who is the 'pain in the neck'? John is so jealous, it's unbelievable. I only hope his fans are proud of him."

While the fans too began to separate into biased camps, Chrissie McCall sums up the dilemma. "The problem was that both John and Gary wanted to be pop stars but didn't quite have what it takes, while Scott did. And he didn't want to be a pop star. He really didn't want it. It wasn't an act. It scared him."

Amid the bickering, exhaustion, and bitchiness there came some respite. True to the slow-delay nature of royalties, it was around now that money from the first big successes began to roll in, and following the release of *Portrait*, publishing options were taken up and fulfilled. By necessity, any income that made its way past Capable would be divided among the three Walkers unequally.

Gary: "All I remember is they said, 'We'll put you on a retainer and pay your flats and that,' and gave us about £40 a week. And everyone else was making about £8 a week! So I thought, 'We're all right.'"

Gary was neither a published composer nor officially signed to Philips, but he was unarguably due an equal slice of the box office, and in addition probably had a separate deal with Capable that kept him afloat when the band weren't gigging. So he was doing very well indeed for a man in his early twenties. By the end of the year, he had moved into a centrally located £25-a-week flat with The Hollies' Graham Nash, and as an early Christmas present to himself, he splurged on some sophisticated sound-surveillance equipment, à la Gene Hackman in *The Conversation*. Visiting journalists would often find Gary eavesdropping on tourists chatting in Trafalgar Square, a couple of miles away. On the other side of town, Scott, who had moved into a basement flat on his own, was apparently less concerned with material things, to a scarily naive degree. "I've just never been able to do things by numbers. Maybe that's why my management looks after my financial affairs today; I don't keep my money in a bank. They hold it instead."

Perhaps it wasn't so much that Scott was careless with money, just uninterested. "Scott was quite frugal," claims McCall, "while Gary and

John were spendthrifts. They were pop stars. They loved it, they thrived on it ... they loved the sports cars, the shopping trips, and the lifestyle. Scott's big treat to himself was to buy a good book or a piece of art. Or a Mini, while Gary and John had sports cars – a Marcos each. While Scott had that same duffle coat for years."

John, meanwhile, claimed that the main thing on his mind was the music, the choice of songs, and, just as importantly to him, how they were presented on stage: "You get so busy taking care of all that stuff that you don't think about the other things. Least, I didn't. You probably are lucky if you get the rent paid. We may have been making a fortune, but we weren't getting it."

There were carefully-muted rumours that King's balancing of the books left something to be desired, and certainly some parties were openly attempting to milk the Walkers cash-cow and keep the proceeds for themselves. Engel's pre-pubescent self came back to haunt him from 50s America for the second time that year when his old label, Liberty Records, released an EP of soprano Engel. The record overcame the court injunction, slapped on by King via Philips to little effect. The antique recordings were released to mass uninterest on November 4 – overshadowed by the news that a frail Scott collapsed at a *Billy Cotton Band Show* rehearsal after an "allergic reaction to Aspirin". It got much worse when a car hit Engel's lifelong best buddy, John Stewart, the following weekend. Stewart suffered substantial head injuries and returned to America for private health care, apparently paid for by Scott. But the boyish pipedream of Alec-Noel productions was over. So, tragically, was Stewart's enormously promising writing career. By the mid 70s, he had recovered enough to work at Tower Records on Sunset Boulevard, a few blocks from where the dream had begun.

Despite Engel's shock and grief, the show had to go on. The Walkers eventually fulfilled the obligation of their Palladium show before the Duke of Edinburgh on Tuesday November 29. Opening with a sensible white-bread rendition of James Brown's 'I Got You (I Feel Good)', the group then busked through a rather moribund-sounding medley of 'Make It Easy On Yourself' and 'The Sun Ain't Gonna Shine Anymore', followed by a sterling version of the current EP track 'I

Need You'. The highlight was 'Summertime', introduced by minimalist guitar and screams of "Gary!", "Scott!", and "John!". Thanks to BBC engineers, for once the voices of the Walkers themselves are audible during a live show in addition to the screaming teenies. The backing band is inconsistent – during the instrumental break, they almost but not quite take flight, and on the verses, they fluff chord changes while the drumming wavers in and out of the beat. But John and Scott sang up a treat. Maus, in particular, sounded unusually powerful and fluent, and excelled. Post-show, all three dutifully lined up to shake hands with royalty, although, to Maurice's chagrin, Scott declined Princess Margaret's invitation to party the following week.

With the tour completed and the madness temporarily abated, the frazzled three attempted to return to a relatively normal speed of life. However, for Scott, the bends came on regardless, and his attendance at the screening of Cliff Richard's *Finders Keepers* movie proved the final straw. On December 3, Scott booked into Quarr Abbey monastery on the Isle of Wight.

Scott: "The retreat has no religious significance. I am going simply to find time to think and to sort out my life. I went to learn Gregorian chant, and they had a special system of the square notes ... this was one of the only places they taught it. It was a nice little break, and you got to learn things as well."

Chrissie McCall: "Scott was much more deep and profound [and] academic than John and Gary. They were nice people but simpler souls. Although, in a way, Scott was simpler again, because his lifestyle was very simple. He would have made a good monk, Scott. He could deal with solitude: it didn't scare him."

Scott left the monastery two weeks later, at the request of the monks, whose mediations on the eternal were now being interrupted daily by screaming mobs of teenage Engel freaks. When the time came for Scott to move on, he had already forged another friendship with an elder: the head music monk, father Altham Dean. Dean had connected with the young singer, and a bond was struck. On leaving, he presented Scott with a key to the monastery gate, an open invitation to return whenever he needed to. The young apprentice eventually attached the key to a chain, and would wear it around his neck like a talisman throughout the coming years. It was perhaps a symbol, a source of comfort and strength for when the pop life got too tough.

If forever changes, then the pop world is a planet in constant flux. Trends were mutating and, far from the relative serenity of Quarr Abbey, late November 1966 saw the release of the most unsuccessful Walkers single since 'Pretty Girls Everywhere'. Having turned down an offer to sing the theme to the James Bond movie *You Only Live Twice* some months before, Engel and Franz composed a worthy counterpoint as the next Walkers single: 'Deadlier Than The Male'.

It was hardly laden with hooks. It's the marine-blue verses that draw the listener in – the chorus is little more than a brief descent over which the excellent title is draped – but the song nevertheless is an understated Walker classic. Loneliness rarely sounded sexier while Scott sang of "Walking streets / You'll never know / When the night comes." John hovers above, anointing the chorus with a luminous harmony. The piece is also subtly knowing and even slightly self-mocking, moving with shark-like stealth toward some unutterably lovely petit mort. The B-side, 'Archangel', is even better; it is simply one of the best things Scott ever wrote and recorded. He obviously wears his new-found love of classical music on his heart sleeves, and the result is mortifyingly seductive, an eerily lunar-like hymn to melancholia.

Reg Guest: "That was fabulous. It's well over-the-top. I think Scott was into Sibelius; he was always quoting symphonies to me: 'I want it like Sibelius's Seventh Symphony.' We used the organ in the Leicester Square Odeon. I remember writing strings, brass section, and giving it a thumping huge beat."

Perhaps this latest offering was just too refined – too beautiful for the charts of the day – and the single withered commercially. It stalled in the higher 30s, its fate certainly not helped by a complete lack of promotion. That December, the UK's three most famous US citizens had to go into exile as their work permits expired. In order to satisfy the immigration authorities, they would have to spend six months without working in the UK. Rather than have the boys experience anything like a holiday, Capable made sure the time would be well spent elsewhere. They booked extensive tours of the continent, Australia, and the Far East. As for the UK, they could not be seen to do anything that approached work, and this included promoting their new single. All three kicked back in their respective pads and watched 'Deadlier Than The Male' shrivel in the winter sun. Gary got in a few interviews the day before the permits expired, once again soothsaying the Walker future in his own idiosyncratic terms.

"We'll be looking for a new sound," he said. "We're not satisfied. We don't even know what we're looking for. All we know is we're going to use this time to find it. When we start working again, we'll be different Walkers, even if we're substantially the same, if you get my meaning. We're not aiming to lose anything. There'll be Engel's operatic bit and Maus soprano, but we'll be adding something of value. We hope."

Meanwhile, the rumour mills, boutiques, and gossipy bars of London were ebbing softly with the subject of the Walkers' future. While the trio themselves were publicly quoted as positive about their unified destiny, this was the result of a deliberate strategy, aimed at keeping the fans as shiny happy record-purchasers. Ironically, the title of a new EP released that December said it all: *Solo Scott, Solo John.*

For the most part, this latest release trod water musically. John kicks off his solo side with a smouldering, erotically narcotic vocal on 'Sunny'. It remains one of his finest performances, the sound of slow fire on a hot Baptist night. The low-lit orchestral arrangement flows like liquid resin through a John Barry-type score, and the whole thing just simmers. It's the perfect companion piece to what comes next: a perfectly poised gambol through 'Come Rain Or Come Shine' that sees John once again steering his voice to the bull's-eye. Based on these renditions alone, John would have nothing to worry about if the band did split; the supper-club circuit of the world was his oyster.

Scott contributes his take on the title theme from the movie *The Gentle Rain* and, while perfectly adequate and routinely charming (and perhaps because, today, 'Orpheus' still reverberates in our inner chambers), the whole thing falls flat and dry. It's because we know he can do so much better. And he does, on his own companion composition, 'Mrs Murphy'. It's a 22-carat Engel classic: an intricate, almost show-tune arrangement, by turns lush and intimate, marrying an explicitly narrative lyric and melody. And surely Scott is singing about himself? "Upstairs in 22 / The tall boy stretched / Just like a cat / Put his hands behind his head / And lay there whistling out of tune / Thinking of a dream he'd had." Blossom Dearie, the jazz singer who wrote 'Long Daddy Green' about Scott, said: "'The Gentle Rain' is the perfect combination, a beautiful song and a perfect singer. I also admire greatly that wild, crazy, marvellous song 'Mrs Murphy'."

The EP charted modestly and was packaged in a sleeve depicting one of the worst portraits ever of Scott. By comparison, the photo of John looked like a king far too regal for any earthly kingdom. The release pricked the ears of some in the business: in the event of a split, maybe John would take the prize?

Still forced into temporary exile by the British government, the Walkers began 1967 with an Australasian tour. By most accounts – Scott's excepted – the jaunt was a riot, with the headliners getting along famously with fellow bands on the bill: The Yardbirds and, Engel favourite, Roy Orbison. The opening gig at Sydney Stadium continued in the Walkermania tradition with 17 girls ending the day in hospital.

Billy Bremner: "Australia was good ... Orbison was nothing like you'd think. He was a party animal. Crazy guy. Anyway, we all got on extremely well. It was very chummy. Lots of practical jokes."

Scott: "The pressures were nearly always outside of the group – until the Australian tour, when things began to brew up within the group as well. It came to a head when I turned up late for a show and nobody would speak to me."

For the engine-room boys like Bremner, the tour was perhaps just another particularly memorable gig. Yet for Scott, the carney had gone on long enough. It's possible that, back in London, prior to the Walkers' return, Franz had let his bosses know that their flagship act was en route to an iceberg. Eager to make hay while the sun was gonna shine, Philips released yet another Walkers single in the group's absence. Only a year before, Franz and Engel had been deliberating over each release like alchemists, weighing up the timing and commercial trends against the quality of the production and the song, and then and only then allowing a release.

But as 1967 opened, Scott was already focusing on other horizons, and Philips could be a lot less discerning. This did not pass unnoticed. "If there's any ill breeze blowing, you seem to get an awful lot of studio time," noted John. "[The record company] always have one or two things in the can. So they started pumping out various bits and pieces." Had the new single been released earlier, it would probably have been as famous as one of the classic songs for which the Walkers are now known. As it was, the single was as magnificent as anything they had ever done, and was aptly titled, considering the coming circumstances, but it flopped, peaking at 26. In a business where timing is often crucial, the majestic 'Stay With Me, Baby' was born too late. The B-side, a strangely schmaltzy Engel original, 'Turn Out The Moon', was the not unattractive sound of Scott playing publicly to his own myth, but is still no more than Engel-by-numbers.

In the meantime, back at Baker Street, Capable had managed to reinstate The Walker Brothers' work permits ahead of schedule. Maurice was privy to the deepest dynamics of his group and knew the lay of the land better than anybody, and yet it was obvious even to the lowliest secretary that as far as the Walkers' future was concerned, a weird ill wind was a-blowin'. Anyone with even a remotely vested interest in the Walker industry felt the need to make the best of this fantastic dream now, before the beautiful boys awoke and broke the spell.

Sessions were hastily booked at Stanhope Place in anticipation of their return. By the time they were heading back to Britain via Europe – on February 27 they were captured in concert at Paris's Locomotive club through a broadcast on *Ready Steady Go!* – the equilibrium among the group had forever changed. Ultimately, the very same things that gave them success were limiting them: the soap opera aspect of their personal relationships; the adoring yet oblivious crowds; the golden cage of their big, big sound. Perhaps in an effort to overcome the familiarity of their workplace, the final sessions for the last album were marked by an almost hysterical overindulgence.

Scott: "I went crazy, of course, and demanded more and more. At first, my demands to use two pianos, two bass players, and say three guitars, as opposed to, say, the one guy who would use one bass player, one piano, et cetera, were outrageous. They didn't know what I was going to do with them – but I knew, you see. Then, as the albums progressed, I just got more and more guys into the studio. After the second album, it wasn't fun any more.

"And the sound – I mean, people said, 'What a fantastic sound!' But if you listen to the three albums back to back, the sound gets to really drudge on a bit. You start to feel, 'Oh God, this is all too much.' It's like too many chocolate cakes in one go."

Guitarist Alan Parker: "Having played on all their albums, I could see that toward the end it got a little bit fractious. Scott had taken a greater interest in it – in every single aspect of it, even when we were laying down rhythm tracks."

Scott had little left to prove at this stage, such were the rules of the game. "As they became more famous and sold more, they had more leeway. I mean it was obvious, anyway, that Scott knew what he was doing," remembers the then adolescent tape operator Roger Wake. He also notes that the relationship between Engel and Franz was more sound than ever. The young Californian had brought something vital to the A&R man's table. While most of Franz's musical relationships (Dusty excepted) were one-way streets, in this case it was different. Engel engaged, inspired, impressed, and delighted the older man. While the Walkers may be ending, the Franz–Engel partnership was in full bloom.

"Johnny Franz had a great relationship with Scott, and Scott trusted him," acknowledges the songwriter and arranger Tony Hatch, who was often in attendance at the studio sessions. "Scott was very experimental and innovative, and Johnny let him go down these exciting and untried roads, while giving him loads of support and signing the budgets. Johnny let Scott do his own thing but helped him all the way."

Franz would become a trusted ally through good and bad times. John and Gary would never touch him in anywhere near the same fashion. Despite the growing strength of the Franz and Engel union, for many concerned, the recording of the third album was becoming more like just another day job. The very studio itself was beginning to grate, as other Philips artists were only to ready to testify.

Dusty Springfield: "[The Philips studio] was hard because there was only four tracks, and so you were stuck with the internal balance on any track. You'd end up with some maniac putting a bass on the same track as the strings, and by then, you know ... . It was an extremely dead studio. It sounded like someone had turned down the treble on everything – and it was essential to get an edge on things. I couldn't get an edge. There was no ambience; it was like singing in a padded cell."

Tony Hatch: "Unfortunately, the [studio] curtains made it so dead it was pretty awful for most of the musicians except the rhythm section."

Scott took time out from co-producing himself to produce Nicky James's commercially doomed single 'I Need To Be Needed', while all over town, rumours were rife that this Walker Brother would soon be ascending toward his true potential and shedding John and Gary like sandbags from a balloon. With the majority of the final album now in the can, their next tour was announced as their last. Scott was still talking of a collective future, but it was clear that things would not go on in the same way.

The final tour included a bill as schizophrenic as the headliners' state of mind. Any rabid Walker fan who had long saved for that precious ticket would hold in their trembling hands admission to a show that also featured Cat Stevens, Engelbert Humperdink, and The Jimi Hendrix Experience.

John: "[Jimi] and I used to get to the theatre a little bit earlier and we'd sneak out onto the stage and have a little play for a little while before the whole thing started. ... Jimi didn't even have to have a good guitar, you know? He was a player, and some people are just really magical that way. And he was."

When, on the tour's opening night at the Finsbury Park Astoria, Hendrix set fire to his guitar for the first time, the burning Fender sent out smoke signals signifying the end of one pop era and the beginning of another. Unsurprisingly, Hendrix would dominate the tour's press coverage. By the time the Walkers came on, they were yesterday's sunshine. The old fashioned and suddenly passé nature of their stage show was made more apparent within minutes of Scott's arrival. After the usual expansive build up by The Quotations, Scott entered stage-left – only to be engulfed by a manic female fan of Amazonian proportions. As Scott lay beneath her expansive form, the band stuttered to an astonished halt and the curtain came hurriedly down. By the time the show started again, everything went on as before, yet it was also clear that things would never be the same again. For the audience, this was their final chance. The Walkers would tour no more. The carnival played out, for one last time, as insane as it had ever been.

Peter O'Flaherty, bassist with Simon Dupree & The Big Sound (best known for the unique-sounding hit 'Kites'), found he and his group slotted into the bill at the ABC Theatre, Blackpool. He remembers the Walkers swansong with a rookie's clarity. "Most of the audience were girls, who were at the show just to scream. The area was in complete chaos when we arrived ... surrounded by screaming girls who were after the Walkers, but anybody who remotely looked like they were a member of the band was fair game and could be torn apart. It would have been easy to lose an ear, a leg, or a more private part of the body if they could get a hold of it.

"Looking down from the window of our dressing room on the second floor, we could see the chaos below. The police were having a hard time controlling the fans, so they'd called in the mounted police. A few of the girls were prepared for this, because they had bags of glass marbles. They'd throw a handful of these under the horses' hooves. These could make the horse buck and throw the rider off. A stressed police inspector came into our dressing room and told us to keep away from the windows or he would have us arrested for 'inciting a riot'.

"Before the show, I wandered around the theatre [and] around the stage area I saw a hysterical girl being pursued by the security guards. Her face, hands, and legs were covered in blood. Later, somebody told me that to get into the theatre she'd crawled through a small broken window and cut herself to pieces on the broken glass. She was eventually restrained and taken to hospital. When The Walker Brothers did their act, we stood in the wings to watch. There was so much screaming, we never heard a thing that they did. It was a bit pointless."

The final Walkers album, *Images*, was released that April, immediately charting at Number Six and gathering their best reviews yet. The band's long-playing swansong begins with 'Everything Under The Sun'. It has a stirring start, courtesy of Ronnie Verrell, but it's soon clear that the song is in one of the few keys that does not suit Scott's voice. The backing track, although impressive, sounds suddenly leadened by familiarity. Both vocalists sound tired, distracted, and ultimately unconvincing. Reg Guest's spirited arrangement does its damnedest to spark the embers into fire, but the whole thing is doomed beneath one of the most insincere vocal takes Scott ever put to tape. He argued against Maus and Franz's wishes for this to be released as a single and won. But this would be scant consolation.

'Once Upon A Summertime' was apparently Scott's favourite at the time, but this vapid, string-drenched, sentimental offering is closer to the type of album-filler that was usually John's fault.

Scott's composition 'Experience', a spontaneously joyful polka, is a vast improvement and evokes images of carousing at Bavarian beerhalls and Black Forest chateaus via *Fantasia*-era Walt Disney. The author sings the challenging cinematic lyrics impeccably – the colour of his voice and phrasing are as pure as melting mountain snow. Unlike most lead singers, he is also able to blend in with the chorus, barely discernible above the other male voices during the "Here's to Emily..." refrain.

John's sleepy drawl through an unnecessary cover of 'Blueberry Hill' sounds even more somnambulant and pointless coming straight after the uplifting exuberance of 'Experience'. The saccharine strings and cooing vocal group that drench the burnt-oak grain of his voice don't help. It would have been more effective stripped back to John, the piano, the saxophone, and the overflowing ashtray.

Another Engel original, 'Orpheus', raises the bar again. Scott had recently discovered and fallen in love with classical music, and 'Orpheus', with its Bach-like refrain, bears the love-bites of this infatuation. Paradoxically, Scott owed his introduction to this particular form of 'high art' to the screaming teeny fans that irked him so.

Scott: "I was living around Primrose Hill. There was this tiny little record store on a roundabout at that time. I was being pursued by some wild girls at that stage and I ran into this store. And this guy behind the counter closed the store up and kept me safe until some help arrived. I got chatting with him. His name was Terry Collins, and I got friendly with him and his wife. He knew everything about classical music and he introduced me to it. I introduced him to jazz, so it was a trade-off, and I just became an addict from then on."

Although Scott had seen *Orphée*, Jean Cocteau's cinematic adaptation of the Greek myth, the lyrics, music, and mood of this song bear no resemblance to the movie – or its plot, for that matter. Yet the song is truly cinematic in its grand scope. "Sure, that could have gone back to seeing the movie originally," confirmed Scott. "Yet again, I really can't remember, because I was so out of it. But ... cinema was a huge influence on those songs, in the broadest sense."

If 'Blueberry Hill' seemed an utterly pointless Walkerfication of a ubiquitous standard, their take on 'Stand By Me', Ben E. King's best-known song, is an unmitigated success, bringing out the composition's full potential by dint of the Walkers' big budget and slightly skewed aesthetic. Throughout their three albums, the Walkers would cover many songs made famous by The Drifters. Superficially, the arrangements are very similar, and Scott was a fan, up to 'Under The Boardwalk'.

Sadly, one song covered by The Drifters that Scott never tackled was the sublime and eerie 'On The Horizon'. Listening to Ben E. King's excellent version, it's hard not to imagine Scott singing it to a Wally Stott arrangement.

'I Wanna Know' is a generic, unoriginal 'original' by John; sounding so over-familiar that one could imagine it had been around since the late 50s. Nevertheless, it's a convincing blue-eyed soul footstomper, presumably written with live shows in mind. Conversely, 'I Will Wait For You (Theme from *Les Parapluies De Cherbourg*)' is another seemingly effortless Scott performance, framed within an exquisitely tasteful arrangement. Scott obviously had an appetite for the film songs of Michel Legrand, although it's debatable if the films they came from were to his taste.

'It Makes No Difference Now' could almost be Jack Jones, if not for the masterful vocal. During the verses, Scott is singing at the lower edge of his range, evoking a cracked and stained erotic quality. John joins faithfully on the chorus, their voices fitting each other so perfectly you imagine orchards of roses simultaneously blooming in sympathy the world over. The lead singer's occasionally idiosyncratic pronunciation surfaces on the yawned "never" during the second verse (listen to how he sings "enjoy" on the *Scott* album's 'Best Of Both Worlds'). This kink is always endearing. Perhaps it's a subliminal response to having an almost-too-perfect voice?

Like last year's B-side 'The Saddest Night In The World', John's 'I Can't Let It Happen To You' is a perfectly formed evocation of Jean-Luc Godard in Carnaby Street. The inconsistency of Maus's writing gives the impression that occasional beauties like this plopped fully formed into his skinny lap. A confident and present vocal is interestingly set against new combinations and textures: a Farfisa organ; busked percussion; a homely piano. And, rare occurrence, no strings. And the brass is limited to a 'Penny Lane'-style French horn solo.

Scott's 'Genevieve' lilts like a chandelier aboard the Titanic and, lyrically, it has him playing (unconsciously or not) to the public Engel myth to wonderful effect: "I guess I'll always be the same / A drifting man / Without a name." The gossamer-like beauty of the result is as if supreme Spaghetti Western auteur Sergio Leone had directed *Hamlet*. It was John's favourite song from the album.

Considering what was to come, the choice of the valedictory 'Just Say Goodbye' as a closer seemed appropriate and must have provided the soundtrack to many a teenage tear-soaked sleepless night. The last song of, arguably, the last true Walker Brothers album is no great departure in terms of arrangement, composition, or production. And that makes some sort of sense. It is interesting to imagine that in some far-off frozen dimension, John and Scott are singing this song to each other even now.

The album's release coincided with some heavy television exposure. Once again, the Walkers headlined *Sunday Night At The London Palladium*, on April 2. Oddly, this second appearance was much more schmaltzy than their debut. As usual, they open with a medley of their two Number Ones, with 'The Sun Ain't Gonna Shine Anymore' (what there is of it) sounding drained of all grandeur. It gets worse, when Scott, sounding as insincere as possible, croons the intro to 'My Kind Of Town': "It sounds like corn but I was born / In Hollywood / And Hollywood sure means a lot to me." He is joined by 'brother' John on the amended chorus: "London is! Our kind of town."

Scott recovers his dignity on the theme from *Doctor Zhivago*, 'Somewhere My Love'. John sounds slightly more comfortable throughout, with the bulk of in-between patter falling to his smoky drawl, but the Ravel-esque bolero of 'What Now My Love' brings things mercifully to the end.

The tour continued, but the atmosphere between the John and Scott camps became increasingly strained. Scott would often go AWOL between soundcheck and gig, on one occasion only turning up during the third song. These passive–aggressive antics infuriated the usually mellow Maus, whose own moods were not balanced by an increasing affinity with the dressing room's complimentary bottles of Scotch.

Gary was an impotent witness throughout. Chrissie McCall: "I felt sorry for Gary. He was like piggy in the middle. He loved John and he loved Scott, and ... they barely spoke. Gary and John wanted to carry on but Scott couldn't really give a shit by this time. He wanted out."

The last show was back in London, where the glorious madness had begun. The atmosphere was as hysterical as ever, albeit tinged with a definite melancholy. Even though this was, apparently, the last show of the last tour, few fans in the audience that night believed it so. Backstage at Tooting's Granada, following the riotous show, Capable announced to the press that The Walker Brothers were over. Out on the deserted stage, a luckless MC attempted to announce the same news to the crowd. The relief in the dressing room was tangible. By now, Scott and John were not talking, and the strain of hiding the obvious truth had become unbearable.

Scott: "After seeing our last Palladium performance, I think I really got things into perspective and made up my mind to quit the group. It's a nasty feeling watching a show like that. I was so embarrassed and full of shame for myself and the rest of the group. It was the last straw. I was disgusted. I want to be free. I know everyone knows that Scott Walker's a difficult person to work with and only works when he wants – when he's ready. Well that's right! I'm not singing 'til I'm ready. I had to work with the Walkers because I was with two other guys who needed the bread and one of them had a family to support, and so on. Money just isn't important to me."

John: "I knew we couldn't go on. Now the only thing I regret is that the fans are getting a raw deal. If they liked all three of us, now they have to buy three records every time. We tried to pull together, but I now know I could never be compatible with Scott. Mostly the difference is musical. I wanted to go one way and Scott wanted to go another. The spark was beginning to fade as a group. Now it will come back to us individually. We all had so many things on our mind that we couldn't get out in the group. So, I feel free, really."

Gary: "I have sadness because of everyone involved. [Next] I'm recording with Graham Nash of The Hollies [but] there's nothing definite like a release date or anything yet. I don't see why there should be a hurry. [Nash and I] leave for a holiday in Morocco on Sunday."

The final single, a pointless cover of The Ronettes' Mann–Spector–Weil song 'Walking In The Rain', was a damp squib among the Walkers' sonic legacy. Doubtless, Scott had stopped caring and was more concerned with the first Engel solo release than the final Walker Brothers one. The single was received with indifference and stalled in the UK, like 'Stay With Me, Baby', at Number 26. As with all true goodbyes, it satisfied no one. "Scott wasn't keen on our last single," said John. "But it did have a commercial angle."

The Walker fan club, once the biggest in the country, downsized overnight. Chrissie McCall: "When they split, we said to the fan club members, 'OK, the band have split, but you can continue your membership in whichever membership you want.' So Scott's fans could be in Scott's fan club until their membership expired, and Gary's could be in Gary's, and John's could be John's. Scott got the most. But John and Gary did OK."

Possibly as one final publicity stunt to aid the ailing single, May 13 1967 was given as the official last day of the band's existence. An army of hormonal teenagers, suddenly feeling very old, marched the miles between Baker Street and Barry Clayman's house in Maida Vale. It was perhaps more a march of mourning than of protest. These girls would never love again in quite the same way that they loved the Walkers. Gary, arguably capitalising on his true talent – a flare for synchronicity – met his wife on the march, at least, and they would marry 15 years later. As the gnashing of teenage teeth and the wailing of adolescent hearts receded, the objects of their sorrow were ultimately relieved.

Scott: "It was fun for the first six months, and within a year it becomes a drag. They would just run us into the ground – just getting you from one gig to another, flying all over the place – you didn't know if it was day or night, and your money wasn't coming in regularly … it was a nightmare."

John: "We were very young. Personality-wise we didn't have a problem, because he understood me and I understood him. As far as that went, there was never a personality conflict. It might have been, to some degree, artistic conflict."

Ralph Gurnett: "There were three of them and, out of the three, there was only one good person and singer. I'm biased, but it was Scott Walker."

Kim Fowley: "They split while still looking and sounding reasonable: so now it's been 35 years, so it's like dying when you're young – James Dean will always look like that. [The same goes for] Jim Morrison – they will never age."

John, speaking on Saga Radio in July 2005: "No one ever read me harmonies. … We knew what we could do."

CHAPTER 8

SOLO SCOTT, SOLO JOHN

I'd like to make a public apology for the poor quality of some of the records I've made. Kids have ordered them before they had a chance to hear them, and four of them were really bad.

John Maus (1970)

Following the split, John was first to wet his flowing locks within the choppy straits of a solo career, and by the spring of 1967, he had already recorded a batch of songs scheduled for an almost indecently hasty release.

The trio, when they finally imploded, were not the commercial Goliath they had been, but they were still a formidable force with a stellar track record. Many in the industry would have reasonably expected the boys individually to outdo their previous success as a group. With an average age of 24, all were still young and, if anything, they looked better now – more refined, less goofily adolescent – than they had on arrival. Philips confirmed such confidences that June by individually signing both John and Scott to five-year contracts.

Hopes were high, and it seems that John was as good-naturedly caught up in the flow as anyone. Including the fans he would be apologising to within a mere three years. "I had a tendency to pretty much kind of go along with what my manager and record company were saying," he admitted. "It became odd, because all of a sudden I found myself doing things that I probably wouldn't have done had I thought about it a bit more. I kind of rushed headlong. I think Scott took a smarter avenue."

Splitting the management team between them, John chose the more retiring Barry Clayman. Given Maurice King's reputation, one would assume that John had chosen the saintlier of the two, if only by default. It wasn't necessarily so. Scott would later brand Clayman a "hustler" who had forced John into a rush-release recording schedule.

Yet, in that brief and brightly-lit hinterland between the end of a group career and the beginnings of a solo one, the vibes were good. Big-money film offers were coming in daily to the Clayman office ("I wanna be in movies," drawled John) and television and radio spots were practically open-doors. If John wanted to take it to the people, then any venue could be booked, anyplace, anytime.

A full month before his debut record release, John was strutting the boards again, making his solo debut at Paris's Palais des Sports in June, with a small live band consisting of John McCain on guitar, Martin Clark on bass, Stuart Fordham on drums, and Quotations stalwart Johnny B. Great on keyboards. The show was so well received that the promoter invited John back to play the prestigious Paris Olympia that coming August.

This French triumph was followed by an offer to write four songs for film director Franco Zeffirelli's *Romeo And Juliet*. John, surely touched that such an offer had not automatically gone to Scott, savoured the compliment as he ploughed zestily into a brief tour of Britain's classier seaside venues, conquering Torquay and Great Yarmouth. Temporarily free from Engel's shadow, John saw a sunny outlook and endless opportunities.

But if John's managers went to bed dreaming of supper clubs and James Bond theme songs, the client was, deep down, just a guitarist. On the purest base level, for John, it all came down to the music. Free of the ornate and impossibly beautiful formula that the 'big sound' of the Walkers had become, a formula that had ultimately suffocated the trio, John was excited again. John: "Even if I am the biggest flop in the world, I'll not regret having lost The Walker Brothers ... though we're all sticking to the surname Walker in the future. ... I'm an old blues guitar player, and if tomorrow afternoon somebody says, 'Let's go and play some blues,' I'm ready. I'm experimenting in the studio. It's difficult to say what kind of sound I'm after. I'd say it's somewhere between the basic feel of someone like Hendrix and the big voice sound of the old Walkers. For me, it's a matter of finding a new rhythm."

Potential songs for the album were pitched to Maus via Clayman and Franz, while session-fixers were hastily called and musicians booked. All confirmed to congregate at Stanhope Place in late March and early May for a big-budget widescreen production.

It must have seemed business as usual to most in attendance at these sessions. Cosmetically, it would have appeared like another day at the Walker Brothers hit factory. Yet two of the most obvious elements were missing: Engel and Franz. As such, John's forthcoming album could be compared to a mere movie-set version of the real thing. It would look and sound the part, but on further inspection it would betray a complete lack of substance. The surface was as beautiful as ever, but beyond this was an airy blond void.

Perhaps in part, John could blame his lack of ultimate success on his own easygoing nature. Without doubt he was a victim of the then music-business equivalent of Hollywood's star system. Whereas Scott would, in this regard, eventually be seen by his 'bosses' as box-office poison, John lacked the sense of direction or obstinacy to go one way or the other. He was a pop star, but he was not a Beatle or a Stone; he had no real proven credentials as a musician or a writer, and his superb vocal talent had been artificially dimmed by such close proximity to Scott, like a star in the daytime cancelled out by the sun. In fact, he was unproven as anything but a pop personality, a 'face'. As far as Philips, the accountants, and Johnny Franz and Barry Clayman were concerned, he would do as he was told.

By mid May 1967, the bulk of the album that would become *If You*

Go Away, plus the single 'Annabella' (and its B-side) and an outtake, 'She Cried', were in the can. They were recorded at the Philips studios using many of the veterans of the Walker Brother sessions, although Franz was notable by his absence, committing himself instead to Scott and Dusty, with all three recording schedules overlapping.

If You Go Away was arranged by Reg Guest (bar one track from Keith Mansfield, who also arranged the non-album tracks recorded at the same sessions), so it is no surprise that in terms of recording technique, the album did not stray far from the sonic palette previously prepared by Franz, Oliff, and Engel. Perhaps to compensate for the more delicately ethereal tones and range of John's voice, the arrangements are at times spared the full-on Wagnerian bombast of previous productions. In place of the expected turn-it-up-to-11, full-on, Holland Tunnel overkill, the woodwind, for example, is featured much more prominently. Such delicate tones provide a pleasing counterpoint to the vocal, matching John's more earthy timbre. These delicacies would add a faintly English olde worlde feel to the album, a faux Edwardian flavour that no doubt matched John's wardrobe at the time.

Fans of John's mostly latent songwriting talent, examples of which had until now appeared sporadically, may have expected an album's worth of similarly understated and seductive gems. Indeed, at this time John was writing more songs than ever before, but only one of his would appear on the album. The lack of original Maus material was probably down to the misguided A&R advice of management and John's lack of confidence in his own abilities, and so nothing of the calibre of 'Saddest Night In The World' or 'I Can't Let It Happen To You' made it to the album.

It's generally acknowledged that, compared with Scott, John was a passive presence in the studio. This was seen by some as simple West Coast cool. "He was very laidback," recalls guitarist Alan Parker. "Compared to Scott, who was much more edgy, John was very … cool. Nothing seemed to fluster him." The arranger Keith Mansfield had a similar impression. "I met [John] in Johnny Franz's office … he was very pleasant, very laidback, y'know? All 'hey man'. I suppose you would say he was a pretty cool guy in today's vernacular." As hip and affable as he was, no one could say that John was a studio visionary in terms of capturing his sound, but he was undoubtedly a good musician, with all the usual sensitivities associated with such a vocation.

John: "Growing up, I liked the big string orchestras – Mantovani. Film theme music has always intrigued me, it's always so grand. It seemed to me you could do popular music in the same kind of form ... I did manage to pretty much be able to record the material I wanted to record, [but] when we were in the studios, I never really understood. It always seemed like the engineer could get you what you wanted, but I never knew how he did it."

Keith Mansfield: "I remember little input from John as far as the arrangements went. In those days, artists wouldn't have anything to say on the studio floor. At most, they might say, 'Oh I don't like this, I don't like that, can you change the other.' There was a very rigid hierarchy in place back then and, basically, the further up the ladder you went, the more power and sway you had. Someone in John's position would have maybe found it easier to do as the producer told him.

"As for the studio environment, well, everyone used to smoke, for a start, and of course there was no such thing as air conditioning. Without a doubt, too, there was a drinking culture back then – particularly among the brass players. Listening to the album almost 40 years on, I do think John sounded like a different guy on each track, almost. I couldn't say if it was because he'd had a drink on one particular day ... because I wouldn't have actually been there when they did the vocals. As you know, officially, they were supposed to record the vocal with everything else, but invariably the singer would return to the studio at about 11 at night as darkness enveloped London.

"As far as The Walker Brothers went – I wasn't much a fan of pop music then, I loved the big-band era. My involvement was purely as an arranger. Saying that, I was there for the benefit of the artist, and I always put them first, John included."

With the bulk of an album in the can, the sessions were put temporarily on hold while Philips and Clayman deigned to road test their new investment. John Walker's debut single that summer was 'Annabella' backed with the prophetically titled 'You Don't

Understand Me'. The A-side was written by Gary's flatmate and ex-Hollie, Graham Nash, and while it retains the little-boy-lost-in-the-rain sentiment of some of the Walkers' most memorably mawkish and self-mythologising moments, it has enough quirkiness and charm to stand alone as a true solo single.

It kicks in with a decidedly Vivaldi-meets-'Eleanor Rigby' vibe, thanks to a close-mic'd and resolutely reverb-less string quartet, and the first impression is that this is what a Walker Brothers demo would have sounded like – if they had made demos, of course. By the time John's slightly off-key vocal comes in – he sounds like he's barely made it to the microphone in time – the blueprint of his 60s solo career has already been mapped out.

Compared to the mighty Walkers, 'Annabella' sounds a little rushed and slightly low-budget. At the same time, it has an enormously goofy, slightly stoned charm, played out to an undercooked arrangement and the kind of vocal that suggests the singer is perfectly balanced somewhere between the microphone and the drinks cabinet. It's a classic jukebox record.

If The Walker Brothers at their best were widescreen and Technicolor John Ford movies, then Maus's efforts are the made-for-television equivalent. Not necessarily worse as such, but rarely as big, and with a skewed Saturday-afternoon allure all of their own.

John's own composition, 'You Don't Understand Me', is grittier – a grinding, acoustic-driven thing bulked up by a modest but high-cholesterol horn section. It shows perhaps an influence of Neil Diamond, whose material was being pitched to John at this time. It also sounds touchingly authentic, in part due to the rare conviction in the singing. As a vocalist, John, unlike Scott, lacked the questionable advantage of being able to sing almost anything and have the listener find it engaging and believable. It sounds immediately apparent when John believes in the material. His own compositions often resonate with a truth that is lacking when he sings the material of others. 'You Don't Understand Me' turns out to be much more believable and rewarding than the majority of his forthcoming album.

John's views on his debut seven-inch platter were as modest as its sales. "I liked it and was as satisfied with it as a song and a production. The most important thing to me was not to sound anything like the old Walker Brothers records."

'Annabella', all two minutes and 15 seconds of it, came out at the height of the summer of 1967, hung around the UK charts for six weeks, peaked at Number 24, and then went wherever it is that ex-hit singles go. Astoundingly, it would be John's only British solo chart entry. "Its sales were an advance-order hangover from the old Walker scene," he explained grimly.

And yet just prior to its release, who could have known this would come to pass? Still hugely famous, demonically handsome, and utterly up for it, John spent the next few months on a promo blitz of television, radio, and print media. Simultaneously, the undaunted Philips-powered colossus lumbered on, arranging further recording dates for early autumn. Johnny Franz, as Philips's A&R man, heard the initial sessions and thought that something was missing. He suggested that additional material should be recorded before an album release could be considered. In the meantime, John was kept busy with more promotional duties and sporadic tours, while Franz continued to concentrate on Scott, whose own debut album was nearing completion.

As John left the unseasonable gloom of the Philips offices after yet another meeting of pluggers, management, and A&R, he may have sensed on some animal level that the reverberation from the fallout of the colossal Walker Brothers was fading. Ultimately, he was, in his own words, headed for a "crack up", exiting stage right as Scott flatfooted onto the world stage once more.

While John was storming provincial stages with the zeal of a Southern preacher man, Scott Walker had long ago wearied of the treadmill of studio and promo and touring. Increasingly true to his contemplative nature, the most beloved Walker Brother had been in no rush to capitalise on the success of the group. In fact, he would later recall that he suspected his own solo effort would flop, and he figured that if it did so, then he may as well flop "in style". The consequence of this fatalistic attitude was that he neither rushed into the marketplace nor felt particularly pressured to please Philips. And so, up until the last moment, Scott had, in his own words, "laid back". This is probably a deceptive phrase for what was in essence a period of intense preparation.

There is a popular saying that a band has a lifetime to write its first album and six months to make its second. True, certain tracks of certain Walkers albums had been 'Scott solo' in all but name. But for all the arguments as to how much of a 'group' The Walker Brothers actually were, compared to the Stones or whomever, the trio were perceived by the public as a group and marketed as such. Few whose spirits were lifted by hearing 'The Sun Ain't Gonna Shine Anymore' blast out of a transistor radio on a hot summer's day cared about the mechanics behind it. Those who bought every record, every magazine, and who fell asleep every night beneath the frozen gaze of Walker pictures on their wall, they cared even less. And together, the blond brothers were allowed to lean on each other a little. No matter how as co-producers of the work Scott had been increasingly committed and John, to a lesser extent, the listener's focus was still allowed to wander like a lazy spotlight within each Walker Brothers LP. This worked to the advantage of Engel and Maus, allowing both to experiment in style and form without ever suffering the full responsibility of coming up with A-sides or entire albums.

This time, Scott would have no such buffers between him and the listener. Despite having a recording career that went back almost a decade, Scott's next album would be effectively his debut. Scott was game. "I'm writing songs now, and I want to get more experience of life into them. The only way for me to do this would be to go to Paris, Czechoslovakia, or Moscow, but time isn't on my side now. I can only write about the people and things I know." He added, touchingly: "I belong to the I.C.A. [London arts centre] and that helps a bit."

Scott conceived his material during the spring and recorded it during the silly sunny season of 1967, but the surrounding 'summer of love' informed his work only by default, as he later admitted. "I saw that you didn't have to write 'flower power' songs, which I didn't want to do, cos I hated that period. I didn't like hippies."

This is underlined by the complete absence of Scott as even a footnote in many of the books written since about this fertile period. Scott obviously had a passionate, profound, and sincere interest in what at the time was considered 'left field' culture: foreign films, the 'beats', existentialism, modern jazz. And yet there is no mention of him in Barry Miles's various books on these movements during this era, or in Harriet Vyner's 2001 biography of the infamous Chelsea art dealer, *Groovy Bob: The Life And Times of Robert Fraser.*

Miles: "You won't find Scott in my book, or [books by] Mickey Farren or Jonathan Green, because he was not part of the underground scene. I saw him sometimes in places like the Scotch of St James, but from my perception he was part of the pop world, a very different thing."

Scott did not mix with the McCartney-funded Indica gallery crowd; he did not get high with Brian Jones while listening to pan-pipe music; and he most definitely did not join in on the satellite-broadcast chorus of 'All You Need Is Love' (although Gary did). In some respects, Scott seemed closer to another incredibly popular maverick of this time, the comedian Tony Hancock. Scott's self-education and interests were, as ever, solitary pursuits. One of the few memoirs of this period to mention Scott are those of Andrew Loog Oldham, *Stoned* (2001) and *2Stoned* (2003).

Tony King, Loog Oldham's business partner, said: "Andrew loved 'The Sun Ain't Gonna Shine Anymore', and he loved Scott Walker and his whole drama-queen image: the tragic poet with the booming voice. He'd say, 'Oh God, just listen to that.' Of course, he'd make Mick and Keith listen to all of his favourite songs as well. Whenever Andrew liked something, the whole world had to hear about it."

Tony Calder was Loog Oldham's partner in Immediate Records. "We first saw [the Walkers] on *Ready Steady Go!*," says Calder, "and they were magnetic. It soon became obvious that Scott started to come out of his shell behind John and started to shine. Andrew and I started to focus on Scott: we were looking at a future mega solo nightclub star, Jacques Brel-cum-Bobby Darin à la Frank Sinatra."

Andrew Loog Oldham himself said: "Jonathan King told me I'd like [Scott] and encouraged me to get together with him and Scott 'for a chat' – told me how much we'd have in common."

Calder: "He was going to record solo for us. Scott was the star; we were fans; that made it great: he could have been the mega star. Maurice King threatened us with violence, then issued an ex parte injunction to prevent us interfering with his management contract. We didn't respond; we were after the recordings. We knew we could manage Scott through his records. Maurice King came to see me one night with a gun. He said, 'You're not gonna take my boy! I'll fucking shoot you!' I said, 'You're not gonna fucking shoot me, or else you would have done already.'"

P.J. Proby: "[Maurice King] liked to think he was a gangster but he wasn't. He was just a loudmouthed Jew who, at one time in his life, had ruled the North."

Ralph Gurnett: "Maurice would never threaten anyone with a gun. All these stories about Maurice being a gangster are a load of old rubbish. I know what Maurice King was, and he wasn't a very nice person, but 'big teddy bear', that's about the best definition you can give him."

Calder: "We had come into a business run by two sad old men [King and Barry Clayman], and Andrew and I really revolutionised the UK record industry. I mean, Maurice King? Barry Clayman? Probably a failed variety act, another dodgy no vision agent. Johnny Franz was an old-time A&R man, always well dressed but old-fashioned, meant well but a little pompous, hated Andrew and I. Barry Clayman, tacky Gilbert O'Sullivan – sad. Maurice King didn't know how big The Walker Brothers were.

"Scott was there ready to record," Calder continues. "I negotiated the deal. I mean, what a fucking star, but I couldn't deal with him. Even Andrew couldn't cope with him. Scott Walker was the only artist Andrew shut up for. Scott was talking about Brel; we were talking about Mort Shuman. He was talking about I-don't-know-what, something about philosophy. I thought, 'What's all this about? My idea of philosophy is a Number One hit record.'"

Loog Oldham: "Scott Walker was attractive, but I made sure I never really spoke to him, because I knew, up close and personal, he'd bore me. He was neurotic boy blue, one sigh away from being a wanker. The idea of him was better than the reality.

"I was concerned that Scott was really Richard Davalos and that John Walker would turn out to be James Dean. Scott had great pipes, emoted great, but I didn't need another Brian Jones drain in my life. I couldn't have done anything for him; we'd have got on each other's nerves. We could not have handled him. I was mid electric-shock treatment and out to a long lunch of no use to Tony or Immediate or my own name. We were bored and Scott was boring."

Such power games must have frayed Engel's already fraught nerves. To be weighed down by such heavy professional, personal, and public expectation was exasperating, particularly at a time when he was beginning to find himself, both as a person and as a writer.

Scott: "Everything I was seeing at that time in movies, or reading at the time, probably influenced me. Then, when I got out on my own, I realised I could do all these things ... it was a surprise to me, as well, coming into it as a singer and then as a writer."

It is unrealistic to suppose that such a dyed-in-the–wool old-school wheeler-dealer as Maurice King would have been sympathetic to the emergence of such a rare butterfly. He was a businessman who, depending on who you ask, bordered on gangsterdom. Ralph Gurnett recalls: "Some days I had more respect for Maurice, sometimes less. The way it was in those days was that if you had a big act like The Walker Brothers, it was a licence to print money." King was a man whose eyes were back-lit by neon visions of Vegas every time Scott walked onto stage, into his office, or just plain walked. Such visions were exasperated only by having to share them with the likes of frighteningly hip upstarts like those Oldham and Calder types.

Scott was barely into his mid-twenties. To be the focus of such pressures must have made the day-to-day business of everyday living an ongoing drama. Unable to authentically lose himself in the traditional perks of his profession – drugs, girls, the popularity of the public and the press, the perma-massage of ego – he turned instead to booze (Scotch), music (classical and jazz), cinema (foreign), prescribed medication (sleeping pills and Valium), and self-actualisation (writing).

The work – the songs, the recordings, the records – would justify any amount of hassle. And while he found himself as the increasingly frayed rope in the King–Loog Oldham tug-of-war, an unbearably bearable role, such associations did provide Scott with a unique way into the heart of the *Scott* album through the Belgian godfather of chanson himself, Jacques Brel.

Scott: "I discovered Brel cos I was having a drink with Andrew Loog Oldham. Three or four weeks before, I had been dating a German girl from the Playboy Club – who played Brel and kept a bottle of Pernod under her bed. She used to play Brel records, and cos she spoke French, she'd translate them. I thought, 'This is incredible!' And bought the lot immediately. And I was talking to Andrew about this, and he said, 'Funny you should say that, because there's a guy in New York – Mort Shuman – who has translated Brel and has got a demo of them and is trying to get a deal for them.'

"When I heard Brel, it showed me that it could be done. I'd never heard anyone else who could write like that – not even Dylan. I thought, 'That's for me,' and recorded them right away before anyone else had done them."

Brel, a Belgian singer-songwriter and a lyrical force of nature, had established himself in France as something of a legend in his own lifetime. By the time Scott discovered his work, Brel had been living in semi-retirement for almost a year. Brel's songs for the main part are uncompromising and direct, portraying a world-view bordering on the dramatic, perverse, and nihilistic. And yet he expressed such sentiments so eloquently, with such sincere wit and authenticity, that the songs usually transcended their bleak subject matter.

Through full-on confrontation of subjects most writers avoided, Brel would achieve a redemptive catharsis that was both beguiling and often amusing. They were, on some levels, the antitheses of 'All You Need Is Love' or 'San Francisco (Be Sure To Wear Some Flowers In Your Hair)'. Brel was the anti-hippie.

It's possible that Scott found expression for himself in Brel's canon that otherwise would have gone unexpressed in either his own material or the material suggested by the trusted Johnny Franz. One could easily imagine the following from Jacques Brel as an Engel quote from this period: "I am not a poet and I am not a musician. I make songs, that's all, never more than eight a year. I haven't that many things to say. ... I'm obsessed by those things that are ugly or sordid that people don't want to talk about, as if they were afraid of touching a wound that might soil them."

Scott: "Brel was a reflection of the times I was going through – all sorts of dark images, which I associated with Brel. His own interpretations of his own songs, in many ways, were very different from mine. I certainly didn't want to copy him. My intention was to take the material and try and do something else with it."

From this point on, Scott seems to have become infatuated with Brel and his work, for a couple of years at least. He even occasionally dressed in the classic chanson style – black suit and tie, white shirt. It's true to say that the intense passion he felt initially for Brel's work was the key to his long-awaited debut. As Scott explained to the writer Joe Jackson in the mid 90s: "What you have there is the enthusiasm of Shuman and [Eric] Blau finding this stuff, and then you have – if my records are any good – the enthusiasm of me finding the work and wanting to get into the studio as quickly as possible and cut 'em live. I got those translations and set up those sessions as fast as I could, and that energy is probably what comes across."

Prior to any new and substantial release, Scott was breathing air that to an extent was still bittered by the fallout from the spring split. His nerves would have barely been steadied when, following the announcement of live dates for that August, a psychotic fan smashed every window in his new Mini. Whether Scott felt sincerely responsible for the moods of his fans or not, his honesty in interviews was endearing. "I'm genuinely sorry that the group split up on bad terms. John and I don't speak, which is stupid and childish. I'm not entirely happy now. I'm one of those people who are never happy about anything."

The album was preceded by a summer tour, debuting with a residency at Stockton's Fiesta Club on August 6 and taking in further runs at Great Yarmouth and Blackpool. Unlike John's new group, none of the Quotations survived Scott's switch to solo status. From now on, Scott would be backed by a more refined group of musicians, in keeping with his new 'adult' image and aspirations. Legendary jazz man Ronnie Scott, an associate of Scott Walker's, was only too happy to assist. "I spoke to Scott in my nightclub one night, when I knew he was going solo, and suggested getting something together. I knew he was not just a pop singer and had very good taste. I got in arrangers like Wally Stott, Jimmy Deucher, Stan Tracey, and we had three days rehearsal. Nothing way-out – nice arrangements and a little jazz."

The shows were a success, reviewers commenting on a newfound confidence in Scott's performance and an audience altogether more reserved and appreciative of Ronnie Scott's ensemble. Engel was clearly happy with the new set-up. "Ignore me; just listen to the band!" he implored. And in part, his usual stage nerves may have been soothed by some subtle self-suggestion. "It's really a warm-up period for me. I'm not going to set the world on fire. I'd hate to walk dead cold into the Royal Festival Hall or Albert Hall without working out first."

Back at Bickenhall Mansions, Maurice King was earnestly pursuing his ultimate dream of managing a worldwide megastar, while his golden boy trod the boards. Calder and Loog Oldham may have been uppity brats in the eyes of Franz and King, but they clearly knew a star when they saw one. Now Maurice had seen the competition off with his sub-Cagney shenanigans, backed up with a perfectly legal argument, it was all going like clockwork. As Maurice closed in on negotiations with the BBC for a Scott Walker television special, cash-shaped sweat patches bloomed across his tautly tailored Savile Row shirt. First Britain and then Vegas. And then across America, which, as far as Maurice was concerned, was the world.

The rest of the planet seemed in accordance. Scott lookalikes were peppering the pages of the music press: Keith Relf, Peter Frampton, Dave Garrick, David Jones (soon to be Bowie). To a lesser extent, John Walker would, perversely, have to be counted among them. In contrast to any other solo Walker record, Philips went all out in promoting Scott's debut. Full-page ads were placed on the cover of *NME* and *Melody Maker* and reviews and interviews were rife, rampant, and generally very positive. If anything, this record was even more highly anticipated than The Walker Brothers' debut had been, a mere two years ago.

Released in the late summer of 1967, the album, simply titled *Scott*, was a smash, peaking at Number Three and gracing the UK album charts for 13 weeks. The cover has become iconic, and it is interesting to compare it to that of John's (as yet unreleased) debut. While John's cover would have a diffused, painterly quality, Scott's appears to have been taken by a war photographer. Both are highly stylised and heavily romantic images, and yet it is obvious that the cover of the (then) forthcoming *If You Go Away* features John as a mere model, posing. The picture of Scott seems violently authentic, candid, and true. The songs within were in accordance.

Scott begins with Brel's 'Mathilde', a storming, frantic romp compared to the relatively polite original. It roars elegantly with all the power of a divine manifesto. But even this impressive opening is dwarfed by what comes next: Engel's own 'Montague Terrace (In Blue)'. This song is as perfect as its title and has become the one solo recording that epitomises his audience's frozen romantic perception of the 60s Scott Walker. It is one of the most dynamic songs from the Engel canon – the verses glide like carps in a bluegreen lagoon before crashing into mile-high waves that blot out the sun – and yet the song is also one of his most intimate. The lyrics take us on a voyeur's tour through the rooms of London's young lovers, via a map of "thighs full of tales to tell", eyes like "pregnant pools" and "cold blue fire". The Wally Stott arrangement serves the song perfectly while Scott's voice climbs and descends octaves as if gravity were not invented. (The song was apparently based on Scott's visits to two friends – a couple – who resided in a mews cottage in London's Montague Terrace, which was demolished in the 70s.)

Cynthia Weil And Barry Mann's 'Angelica' follows, a song that Elvis turned down; previous covers by P.J. Proby and Gene Pitney were less good than Scott's version. It is again a perfect snapshot of rainy lovelorn city streets, beautifying heartbreak and heroic romantic loss.

In spite of his committed version of Tim Hardin's classic 'The Lady Came From Baltimore', Scott would say of its author: "Hardin wrote some good songs, but generally speaking he wasn't that big an influence on me."

'When Joanna Loved Me' is pure Tony Bennett, Scott showing off his easy range with the divine closing line "And the month / Is May." It's no coincidence that Brel's 'My Death' follows this, highlighting the best aspects of both songs. Featuring one of the chanson's most powerful lyrics, it is set to an arrangement that tangoes toward hell in a most delightful manner and was a favourite of the young David Bowie.

'The Big Hurt' was a US hit for Toni Fisher in 1959 and was also recorded by Del Shannon and, years later, Nick Cave. Scott's version is a robust romp set to a groovy march and a string arrangement that revels in its own voluptuous beauty.

'Such A Small Love' was another self-penned number, a distant cousin of 'Montague Terrace' drenched in tears and cheap wine ("dago red"). The lyrics apparently reflect on the funeral of a friend.

André Previn's 'You're Gonna Hear From Me' is a nod to the older ranks among Scott's fans, as is the intricately arranged 'Through A Long And Sleepless Night,' originally from the 1949 movie *Come To The Stable*.

'Always Coming Back To You' is another Engel composition, a sliver of a song, one of his 'snapshot' pieces when compared to the epic scale of 'Montague Terrace' and 'Such A Small Love'.

The album closes with the Brel classic 'Amsterdam'. It's a triumphant end to an accomplished album, with an arrangement that toward its finale threatens to burst its breeches. Bowie was still listening and would cover this song during his *Pin-Ups* sessions a few years hence.

Scott had managed to present differing styles that when combined worked as a whole. This was a rare achievement that owes something to the unifying compound of Scott's excellent voice. Further to this, not only was he blessed with a great voice but also he could sing. It was a rare and winning combination.

The excitement triggered by hearing the Brel records in a playboy bunny's flat had paid off. Brel's official reaction was unrecorded, but Scott happily recalled: "I heard through Brel's wife that he really liked the versions I'd done. I had a chance to meet him when I was in Paris one evening. He was doing La Mancha – a show there. I was too nervous to meet him ... I thought, 'I can't possibly ... this is one of my big idols'. And I didn't do it."

Autumn promotion included a further handful of ecstatically-received cabaret dates and an appearance on *It Must Be Dusty* on September 19. Dusts introduces this as Scott's first solo television appearance, and almost before she has finished, Scott is just suddenly there. Almost running on, he barely makes the microphone in time, ripping into a charged rendition of 'Mathilde' that seems less like a lover's lament than a call to arms.

Hands shaking, legs each as thin as one of Gandhi's halved, Scott gives a performance ferociously compressed, racing toward petit mort. He sings the climax so intensely that at its finale, he appears to reach for the ground as if he's stopped a bullet. The version of 'When Joanna Loved Me' is calmer by default, although the trembling singer still seems uncomfortable in suit and skin.

Scott's appearance on the Eamonn Andrews talk show a few days later was even more vivid, explicitly revealing a man both powerfully focused and yet seemingly at cross-purposes with the main axis points of his life: his muse, management, and his nature. Certainly he was no typical guest pop-star on the promo circuit.

When writing at home and working in the recording studio, he worked harmoniously with his self and with his talent toward some tangible sonic goal: in other words, the finished album. Yet on television, beneath the harsh glare of the studio lights and the oversized BBC TV cameras, the gulf between his character and his success manifested itself as a discreet and profound irregularity.

Appearing alongside James Coburn, a fellow American and spiritual journeyman, Scott ran through a Guinness-smooth and Jack Jones-esque version of 'When Joanna Loved Me' before settling on the couch. Here he revealed himself as an uncomfortable, paradoxical, uncompromising, and intriguing guest.

Host: "After the break up, you became a recluse?"

Scott: "Yeah ... well ... I'm always trying to do this. I live like this. It's a strange thing ... for other people to grasp onto, but this is the way I like to live. Or else I go away to concentrate. I'm trying to find what it is I want to do, which is the important thing. And to write down what I think is the truth in songs, you know? ... I did shut myself in."

Host: "What's the result of this?"

Scott: "About three songs! That's all. But that's good enough. Because I believe that ... I believe in trying to tell the truth to the people that I'm trying to communicate to – and it's a thing I have to do constantly."

Host: "Is this to sort out you as an artist or you as yourself?"

Scott: "It's to do with the traumas of being in town. The traumas of having agents and managers and everybody on your back, and I just don't like to live like that. I require a bit more privacy than most people. I believe so. And this I earn. I don't believe a personality belongs to his public 24 hours a day. ... I think his work does and he does, in as much as you're watching me now. But in as much as where I live and I live it by myself, I'm a free man, you know?"

Host: "Most people would envy your life. What went wrong?"

Scott: "I don't consider it a problem, first of all. It's not a problem with me, it's a way of life with me, and a way of life that I like. I like minding my own business and watching everybody ... right there, instead of sort of getting involved, really. That's all there is too it. Everyone wants to escape, and that's the problem. If it's not drugs then it's meditation ... we're all trying to get out of here ... and ... you can't deny it, even if you do it through God. We're all trying to get out."

Scott was entirely committed to an album he wholeheartedly believed in, and so, no doubt to the relief of Maurice King and Philips, was relatively game for promotion.

One of his most wonderfully incongruous appearances occurred when Scott invaded the 'I've Got A Lovely Bunch Of Coconuts' atmosphere of *The Billy Cotton Band Show* to recite a haunting and slow-burning version of Brel's 'My Death'. Admittedly, he made a token gesture at sugaring the medicine by preceding it with an up-tempo reading of the jazz standard 'More', but then, ignoring the adolescent yelps of the female audience, he gravely intoned in familiar languid tones: "Thank you very much. I have an album that is released tomorrow. And on it is a very, very marvellous song by a person that I idolise very much, named Jacques Brel. And this song deals with death and his aspects of it. He laughs at it, drinks at it, and sleeps with it. I hope you like it. It's called 'My Death'."

As this strange, sad-sounding, eerily beautiful music drifted out of television sets across Britain, perfuming the provincial air with a charged exoticness, many of the more casual Walker fans must have paused mid tea and biscuit to ponder what it all might mean. Hardly typical light entertainment for a Saturday evening, and all the more wonderful for it. Back on *The Billy Cotton Band Show*, at the song's end, the crowd went hysterical. Whatever he sang, this was Scott Walker, after all.

Scott gave his final television appearance that month, the night before leaving for Russia. He appeared on *Dee Time*, a show almost certainly taped a few days before. The inclusion of a cool, soberly-suited Scott – fawn-brown velvet and a lime-green button-down Oxford shirt like the one Miles Davis wears on the cover of *Milestones* – provided more odd juxtapositions. Amid the animal screams and lusty squawks of young girls, the object of their desire talks coolly with the hipper-than-thou Simon Dee about visiting Moscow and meeting and collaborating with revolutionary people's poet Yevgeny Yevtushenko. The plan was to put the hero-poet's verses to music. But Scott would ultimately blow the meeting, blaming a "hangover". (He would, however, reference Yevtushenko on his fourth solo album, attempting to "link lyrics by Sartre, Camus, and Yevtushenko to Bartok modal lines".)

Scott was a regular on Dee's show (and, incidentally, it was there that John would meet his second wife). Scott and Dee seemed to share a mutual respect. In one of the countless pop annuals bearing his name, Dee would write: "Scott Walker is the original lost soul of pop. Locked behind a barrier of non-communication, you get the impression he is living totally alone in his own little screwed-up hell. Actually, I feel, like Sandie Shaw, all he wants is to be left alone to have some peace and quiet. ... His music gets better and better, and that's all that matters."

While Scott was in Russia on his officially Soviet-sanctioned, culturally-rich state visit, the results of the *Melody Maker* annual poll were announced. They featured Scott as its eighth brightest hope and its fourth best singer. It was barely five months since the group had disbanded, and Maus and Leeds were not featured in any category.

It had been a somewhat disorientating year for John. He had started 1967 as the prettiest star and yet had worked as hard as any rookie all through the spring and summer. By the time his second single, 'If I Promise', was released in November, the line "I haven't slept in a month of Sundays" would sound less like a songwriter's cliché and more like a simple statement of fact.

The audio recordings that survive from John's live television and radio appearances during this period often portray a singer who sounds exhausted, remote, directionless, and, occasionally, somewhat tipsy. Appearing on Ed Stewart's Sunday show on BBC radio, for example, John mumbles through his A-side, missing and slurring cues, sounding utterly unconvinced and unconvincing. Whie John lacked both the artistic focus and success of Scott, his career, while seeming superficially to revolve around music, was now becoming just a job.

John, a blues guitarist at heart, was very tired and increasingly emotional. "I felt like jumping off the roof about 14 times. I couldn't get myself together, and when you can't do that, you're really in a bad state. I was drinking too much, and I didn't care about anything. I didn't go around smashing people up, but I got a bad reputation for being totally unreliable. TV-show people weren't sure if I'd make it on time. And I think I told a lot of people to go away, which is not cool."

John's radio sessions often featured B-sides and album tracks in addition to the current single, and the Ed Stewart guest spot featured a competent amble through the Sinatra standard 'Nancy With The Laughing Face'. As usual, John is most convincing on his own composition, the fine jazz-blues of 'I See Love In You', a superior song relegated to a B-side.

Further promotional appearances reveal a somewhat forced and nervy professionalism. The singing is improved, but as an interview subject, John sounds more enthused when talking about his passion for stock-car racing than the record he's promoting. He frequently sounded lost in interviews, with the terminally easygoing John owning up to his own almost nihilistically casual attitude in such matters. One could almost hear the shrug of his soul when he confessed: "I can adapt. On television, they want the ballad stuff –

CHAPTER 8 **solo scott, solo john**

that's fine. If I go to Germany, they want the longhaired beat stuff, and that's fine by me too. I'll become a longhaired rocker."

While John no doubt followed the wishes of those to whom he paid 20 per cent, it is hard to imagine the kind of mutant fan who would find all these genres appealing: supper-club crooner; blue-eyed soul singer; perky pop performer. Perhaps Clayman and company saw the music as secondary to John's pin-up appeal? Perhaps movies were the ultimate goal? In which case, the material was almost irrelevant and just something to hang over John's photogenic physical frame. Regardless, Philips continued to book studio time, and the remnants of his delayed debut were completed in November.

The second single, meanwhile, was 'If I Promise', again fading to two minutes, 15 seconds exactly. It is jaunty and juvenile, perky and petty, with a flute part so irreverent that it sounds as if Gary Leeds is playing it. Lyrically, it could be called 'Annabella II'.

John had little opinion one way or the other. "It's ... uh, an American song, I think. Jerry Reed wrote it. I like it cos it has a different sort of rhythm and things. I heard it on a demonstration disc. I hear lots of them. I either love them or hate them. I loved this one. I believe Tom Jones might have done it, but ... I certainly handled it differently from Tom."

The B-side, John's own 'I See Love In You', is vastly superior in every way: in its composition, arrangement, performance, and production. It is a solid, convincingly bluesy ballad smattered with a transcendent orchestral arrangement and a lead guitar part intriguingly redolent of John's own playing. The song is both spacious and brooding, with a vocal allowing his full range. Admittedly, it's not obvious single material, but the clear contrast in quality between this and the A-side – not to mention much of the forthcoming album – must have raised unanswerable questions within the singer-songwriter's mind.

The *Daily Mirror* called it "the flipside of a flop" and it was – everywhere apart from the Netherlands, where it charted apologetically at Number 21. Philips were not in the game of giving up so soon, however. They had invested sizeably in John, and the draining schedule of television, radio, and magazine promo and touring would continue, flop or no flop.

While John sweated it out beneath the unforgiving lights of television studios and supper clubs, Scott returned from Russia via Denmark, where he would witness a Saturday night drug-raid on a party in Copenhagen. He headed, inspired, to the Philips studios to begin recording his second album.

Little had changed in his absence, although press coverage of Gary and John had become patchy to the point of non-existence. Scott, meanwhile, reaped more than his fair share, even dominating the letters pages, which reverberated with the moaning and groaning of Walker Brothers fans who felt that their hero wasn't giving enough of himself to their succubus-like needs. Again and again, his shadowy nature and spartan public appearances were criticised. And yet, in true schizophrenic adolescent love–hate style, these same fans turned out en masse to protest at the BBC's 'banning' of Scott's new single, Brel's 'Jackie', that December. Mini-skirted hordes hoisted banners on the steps of Broadcasting House in protest.

"We've not banned it," went the official BBC statement. "We're just not playing it." The 'ban' was accredited purely to the risqué lyrical content. As a result, pre-taped appearances on television shows were cancelled. Characteristically, Scott turned to hipper shores to promote these first fruits from the recording sessions of his forthcoming sophomore solo work, *Scott 2*, and played a handful of ecstatically-received live shows in Europe.

Despite the initial furore, 'Jackie' – backed with the powerful freakout of Scott's own 'The Plague' – was at least allowed late-night plays on the BBC. (Simon Dee, on his mid-morning show, was one of the few to rebel, and was eventually fired by the Corporation for his trouble.) In addition, the singer was able to promote the show on the independent ATV and on late-night BBC television, after the watershed. Coupled with a rabid fan-base and the obvious quality of the song, this led to an eventual, if modest hit. The single peaked at Number 22. The irony in Scott charting with a single he wasn't even allowed to promote properly would not have been lost on the Clayman–Maus camp. Scott himself was surprised. Catching his breath during yet another television appearance, he admitted: "I'm shocked. It's unbelievable [and] I really do sincerely have to thank all the people who did buy it, all the people who were sensitive enough to listen to a beautiful lyric, instead of picking out a lot of dirty things and thinking a lot of dirty things. It's a beautiful lyric. It's Jacques Brel's lyric and he's an art form ... and all the producers and people who played it are wonderful. I haven't been able to plug it, and that's been the rough thing about it." Cue screams.

One of the few British television shows on which he did appear was Frankie Howerd's, on December 22. It rivalled even *The Billy Cotton Band Show* in its apparent inappropriateness. Scott performed a fruitily camp version of 'Jackie' perched on a banister in a set resembling something between The Old Bull And Bush and a Wild West saloon. Changing out of the familiar cord jacket, he stepped into a ridiculously frilly white shirt and a pair of stage trousers so high-waisted that his knees seemed in danger of troubling his elbows. Scott also played the romantic lead, Jack, in an overlong comedy panto skit based loosely on *Cyrano De Bergerac*, surely paying for all those whining letters written to the *NME* criticising his aloofness. The skit seemed to go on forever, and at one point comedian Howerd, referring directly to Scott, ad-libbed to a nonplussed audience: "Ooohh! He needs some aggravation. He's been a bit uppity of late. Some aggro may make him tour!"

While Scott's conscience was able to endure such compromises, his body ultimately rebelled. Weakened by a punishing schedule of writing, carousing, and promotional duties, he was found unconscious on the floor of his flat by Ralph Gurnett. Appendicitis was diagnosed. Even so, Scott, regaining consciousness in hospital, immediately discharged himself before surgery. "The guy had me all booked for the operating theatre last night, and I said, 'Oh no, you're not cutting me up!'" Scott joyfully recounted. "And I split. I'm just gonna wait until the next blow comes and hope I'm near a doctor."

Christmas was coming, and for most this would mean a break. But not for The Walker Brothers. The new year would be dominated by a short Japanese tour. To Gary and John, at least, the prospect of these gigs, booked by Arthur Howes way back when the Walkers were still Brothers, must have beckoned like a relative holiday. After an annus horribilis, John in particular was relishing being a mega star again. "[Scott and I are] on the same bill, which is amazing. It's something we started before we split up, and it was a legal commitment, so we decided that it was best not to, you know, cause any nasty relationships. It's gonna be a big mess around for us, you know?"

Gary and Scott, Maurice King and his wife Mary Arnold, plus an entourage, all took off from London on New Year's Eve 1967. John would be joining them from Los Angeles. He couldn't wait. "You know, if you could pick one country and say, 'This is your number one success,' I think Japan was that. It was kinda fun," John said later.

Kiyoko Kojima, a fan, said: "When I heard 'The Sun Ain't Gonna Shine Anymore' on the radio in 1966, Scott's voice and the beautiful melody made a great impact on me. At the same time, I think, I saw them on a very popular magazine called *Music Life*. Of course, I rushed to the shop to buy the records.

"When they came to Japan for the first time, I went to the airport with a bunch of flowers, which I threw to Scott when they came off the airplane. But later, when they came out after passport control, I saw John with my bunch of flowers: what a pity!

"The Walker Brothers were the second group, as far as fan numbers, who received such an enthusiastic welcome from their fans. When I saw them singing 'In My Room' and 'Land Of A Thousand Dances' on TV's *The Music Of The World*, I got allured by them, especially by Scott ... and I was forgetting Paul McCartney.

"What I liked most was Scott's voice! His golden baritone, his velvety, cavernous, and virile voice. Then the marvellous harmony caused by John and Scott's voices. Their refined looks I liked, their elegance. Thanks to that one TV programme, their popularity was the same as The Beatles. In a short time, Scott got the first place as the best male singer, defeating Paul McCartney. In *Music Life*, we could always see the photos of Scott, John, and Gary and could read articles about them every month."

Although the boys had made promotional tours to Japan before, these were their first gigs. The concerts at Osaka Festival Hall on January 2 and 4 1968 (recorded for future release) were followed by further gigs at the Tokyo Hilton Hotel and two gigs at Korakuen Stadium. The shows were rowdy both on and off stage, with the Walkers and their Japanese house band sounding irreverent, saki-soaked, and frequently out of tune, sometimes seemingly in different keys. The atmosphere suffuses such technicalities, and Scott especially sounds as if he's surrendered gamely to the occasion. All three come across as simply going with the flow, having fun with a set that included classics by The Beatles, Motown, and ... themselves.

Another Japanese fan, Tamako Chang, said: "I saw them on TV many times. My unforgettable scene was when they appeared on TV and Scott wore the Japanese school uniform, a typical boy's one. Black uniform suited him well. John and Gary didn't wear it. After their visit, 'Land Of A Thousand Dances' was very popular in Japan. I went to a concert in Tokyo. It was full of screaming girls at the Budokan. Scott was very bad at playing guitar."

The Osaka shows, filmed and supervised by BBC producer Barry Cawtheray, were shown the following evening, and the touring party assembled in the suite of 'Babee Beads' (as Gary was known on this adventure). Despite numerous calls to Scott's suite, he declined to join them in watching the gig, perhaps still suffering post-traumatic stress disorder from their final London Palladium show.

The remainder of the trip was both industrious and restful. John was escorted around the bars and spas of Kyoto, while Scott and Gary slept, and all three converged to record a television advert for Fujiya chocolate. The tastefully tacky ad featured all three of them holding up chocolate bars while intoning the brand name basso profoundo. Although they appear to be clothed in traditional Japanese dress, the clothes were actually from The Beatles' Apple boutique in London. The soundtrack was another treat altogether, a snatch of brooding melancholy music as dark as the confectionary it lauded, sounding like an outtake from the forthcoming *Scott 2*, with Scott crooning the brand name as sincerely as any Brel lyric. The advert launched a campaign that rewarded fans who sent in ten Fujiya wrappers with a life-size Walker poster.

Following a tough year and a healthy cash injection thanks to the Japanese trip, John flew to Hawaii for a holiday while, thousands of miles away at Stanhope Place, Philips at last prepared for the overdue release of his debut album.

Scott and Gary, industrious and entrepreneurial by turns, stayed on to record with Japanese beat group The Carnabeats. Gary had instigated this meeting of east and west. "We had a few days left that were free," he said, "and we saw The Carnabeats play, and I asked if I could play with them, because I thought they were very good. Some friends of ours said we should meet them, and they were at a recording session one night, and we stopped into see them and said, 'Let's do a record together, it'll be fun.'"

Scott produced both tracks, writing lyrics to the A-side, 'Cutie Morning Moon' (backed with 'Hello Gary'), that were inspired by an early-morning moon after a late-night recording session. The single would help raise Gary's profile in Japan to emperor-like proportions for a while. As the single was hurriedly pressed, Gary and Scott both flew to LA to visit family before eventually returning to the UK.

The new year of 1968 was to be one of make or break for John. Soaking up the Hawaiian sun, he held onto both a large Scotch and the benefit of the doubt.

Professionally, Scott was on firm ground, and while Gary was unproven, his future seemed as sunny as his demeanour. The Japanese trip had been a blast for all three, and Gary and Scott in particular had planted seeds for future solo careers in fertile soil. Yet Gary still failed to translate as a musician in any language.

Ai Takano, drummr with The Carnabeats, said: "At first, I was amazed that [Gary] couldn't play the drums very well. I used to tune the drums with a very high tension, but Gary and Scott tuned them lower and lower. Scott produced it [and] we learned a lot from him about recording techniques. Gary used to make us smile because he was kind of dopey – I can't believe that he was able to become a famous musician."

CHAPTER 9

THE FALL AND RISE OF JOHN AND SCOTT

I went to Rome in 1967 wearing a blazer and tie, and when I came back in 1968, everyone had long hair and was dropping acid. It was known as The Acid Summer.

Bruce Robinson, writer and film director

John Walker's *If You Go Away* album was released by Philips somewhere between Boxing Day and New Year's Eve 1967. Although in the main it had been completed well before *Scott*, Philips had held John's debut back in favour of allowing Engel's debut as much room as possible. By the time Maus's firstborn was allowed out, almost nine months after its recording, it was as if all post-Walker Brothers expectations had been fulfilled by the success of their lead singer. As a result, Philips afforded little promotion to this particular beautiful orphan.

The cover was a treated photograph depicting John as emotionally shipwrecked and exquisitely lovelorn. Waves broke behind him upon some wintry beach as he stood staring into the lonely mineral wind. His Orphic features expressed the kind of 'strong enough to hurt' insignia that we would later associate with the 'new man' phenomenon of the mid 80s.

There were typically gushing and nebulous sleeve notes by a top DJ of the time – the evergreen Tony Blackburn. The album's cohesive theme arguably dealt with the day-to-day concerns of a modern breed of man. John represented a new kind of pedigree among 60s pop icons: over-sensitive, nature-loving, classless, and just as attractive – if not more so – to those that he was attracted to. Sadly, in John's case, it was a pedigree that would become extinct on arrival.

'The Right To Cry' (Goffin–King) opens with a typical Reg Guest pizzicato string figure, although as an intro it is brief to the point of sounding truncated. It is as if the fervour behind getting John out into the public and commercial marketplace has somehow manifested into the opening bars of the first song on his debut album. Ironic, in the light of its delayed release.

Vocally, there is already an improvement on the quality of the A-sides (none of which features here) in both sonics and performance. It's apparent that more time has been taken over recording in terms of set-ups and takes. John sounds confident in diction and key, and the lyrics immediately bring us into a theme that crops up repeatedly on his singles: "When you went away / You took all my pride."

This image, of a man left lonely, the jilted John who is not afraid to cry, who lives by his 'pride', wounds easily, and is usually, emotionally, the passive partner, is one that occurs not just on this album but repeatedly in Maus's songs, in his own material as well as that chosen for him. Perhaps this lyrical trait first surfaced in John's own songs and its theme then carried on throughout material either written or chosen specifically for him. Perhaps it was the other way round. Either way, the effect is often unsympathetic and not entirely convincing.

The bridge to the chorus is reminiscent of one of the later Walker Brothers singles, 'Stay With Me, Baby', but this time what follows fails to deliver, flattening out with nothing but John's vacuously impassioned oh baby!s and unconvincing no! no!s. The players are nothing if not professional. However unengaged guitarist Big Jim Sullivan was with the material at the time, his percussive guitar parts run like clockwork throughout, with all the comforting regularity of the rising and falling signal of a bedside heart monitor.

Although the middle-eight slips into something altogether more atmospheric, the tension is pricked by a rare example of the vocalist over-singing. The tuning lapses and, in addition, John sounds almost oafish. It is as if in feeling he has something to prove he instantly fails to do so. The result is clumsy and uncharacteristically heavy-handed. Previously, even at his most lacklustre, John had always retained a balletic and feline grace.

While John wasn't acting in any movies, he was frequently recording songs that sounded like movie theme songs. 'Guess I'll Hang My Tears Out To Dry' (Cahn–Styne) in particular sounds like a potential soundtrack to one of Jane Fonda's 60s romantic comedies. Such a safe, much-covered number, best known by Frank Sinatra and Ray Charles, could have easily snuck into *Barefoot In The Park* or *Sunday In New York*.

It employs a refreshingly restrained arrangement, mostly using only the top end of the orchestra, and the drums are brushed rather than pounded from beneath a sea of reverb. John is clearly making an effort and, but for the last few notes, he pulls off a sublime performance that remains a favourite of his to this day. John: "It's a great song. I love the arrangement. I really like orchestras and big violins and all that stuff, and this one is just loaded with it."

From the team who gave John his only solo hit, 'Reaching For The Sun' (Duncan–Nash–James) appropriately sounds like a cousin of 'Annabella', right down to the close-mic'd string octet. Such a relatively sparse approach suits the singer, whose vocal strengths bloom best when not forced, when he's not trying too hard. And while he does not sound as over-relaxed as he did on 'Annabella', it is as if he is relieved here not to have to pit his delicate timbre against the usual orchestral army. For a few tantalising bars, it's as if the old men managing him have issued charge for Sir John to lay down his Carnaby Street drapes and ruffs and groove awhile.

It can't last, and following a refreshing blast of summery cor anglais, the arrangement soon swells to overdone proportions. It ends, as ever, well before the two-and-a-half minute mark, leaving us with a niggling insight into what could have been but never was: an album's worth of stripped-down, concise, rhythm-driven vignettes.

The velvet collars, flowing cuffs, and frothing ruffs are back in force for 'Good Day' (Duncan–Nash–James). It begins with the ending of The Beatles' 'She's Leaving Home' thanks to an exquisite harp figure, ushering us regally into the court of one of John's feyest vocals. One can almost see him peek-a-booing radiantly from behind oversized papier-mâché sunflowers amid a television set long since spoofed by Austin Powers and 60s-period Spinal Tap. "Colour me a rainbow / Dream me a dream," croons a doubtless velvet-shod Maus, tiptoeing ethereally through some candy-coloured cellophane orchard of the mind. Disney-animated bluebirds flutter by enchantingly. A drum kit made of lysergic lemon sherbet and liquorice skin kicks in, awaking a choir of ambrosial fairies high on plasticine and the pill. "Hello green grass / Let me see you grow / Hi there water / Let me hear you flow." The whole delivery is so unselfish, so sincere, that only the hardest-hearted remain unbeguiled. We can only mourn the bank-holiday television special that never was.

'If You Go Away' (Brel–McKuen) is one of Jacques Brel's most covered compositions and was, in the 60s and early 70s alone, interpreted to varying degrees of success by Nina Simone, Dusty Springfield, Neil Diamond, Tom Jones, and, of course, Scott Walker. Although John's is one of the earliest English-language versions, it is also the least known. It is interesting that it was the title chosen for the album. The dominant mood of the LP is not particularly one of romantic estrangement, although if there is a lyrical thread, then it is that of the rain-sodden boy-child expecting hot coffee and kisses, only to have the front door slammed into his face.

Of those other versions of 'If You Go Away', it is Scott's which is closest to John's (Scott would record his a year later). Using a delicate and predominately orchestral arrangement that lushly enfolds his cappuccino croon, John's version here lacks any regular rhythm section, which together with a sparse use of percussion suggests a womb-like atmosphere. The presence of over-dramatic timpani breaks the mood a little, but overall it's as convincing a treatment as any from this period. John sings "Shadow of your shadow" as opposed to the often-used "Shadow of your dog," a clumsy translation credited to the American singer and composer Rod McKuen.

It has been suggested that Brel wrote this masterpiece from the point of view of one of his own mistresses. This is a more than plausible idea that goes some way toward explaining why so many male interpretations of this song err on the overly theatrical and ultimately unconvincing. "No one mentioned Jacques Brel to me in the pop business before Scott did the Brel songs," said John. "And funnily enough, I didn't even realise that Jacques Brel wrote one of the most beautiful songs, 'If You Go Away'. I didn't know he wrote that. He was just an obscure person."

'So Goes Love' (Goffin–King) is one of the very few Walkers tracks to feature an electric guitar through a wah-wah pedal. Perhaps the tour with Hendrix rubbed off on John after all. The woodwind refrain is an intriguing counterpoint, and both flavours are a refreshing presence. Such textures rarely appeared on any Walker-associated recordings, although it's arguable that they were wasted on such an unengaging, mediocre song and performance.

'It's All In The Game' (Sigman–Dawes) is an overly cluttered version of the 50s standard previously covered by Brooke Brenton, Dinah Shore, and the future Elton John, Reg Dwight. John Maus sounds polite, professional, and supper-club smooth, if a bit lost among the plethora of guitars, percussion, and more guitars.

The lovingly arranged and impeccably performed version of yet another over-familiar song, 'Nancy With The Laughing Face' (Silvers–Van Heusen) – even in the sleevenotes described as "this beautiful old standard" – illustrates the Achilles heel in John's immediately post-Walkers solo career. While everyone involved did a good job of interpreting such wholesome and tasteful material, the result was often just that: a good job, thorough and bland. Within a business so dependent upon the variables of timing, fashion, nepotism, and good old-fashioned luck, producing 'mediocre' work in itself does not guarantee an artist's lack of success or otherwise. Quite often, an occasional inferior release by an established and beloved artiste such as Sinatra would attain greater commercial success than the same superior releases by an unknown. In such a case, timing and public interest would coincide and dictate freakish results. For instance, out of countless recorded versions of David Gates's classic 'If', it was Telly Savalas, who as a singer could not even talk in tune, who had the biggest hit.

By having Maus cover such material as 'Nancy With The Laughing Face', it's conceivable that Philips and Clayman saw him fulfilling the demand for a hipper, younger, better-looking Bobby Darin or Tony Bennett. Unfortunately, in hindsight, it seems there never was any such demand. By concentrating on such material, *If You Go Away* would be stillborn.

'It's A Hang Up Baby' (Reeves) is a further example of the kind of R&B-lite that John did much too often. It's hard to imagine anyone wanting to play this when Jerry Lee Lewis's version was available. As part of an album, coming after 'Nancy With The Laughing Face', it serves only to make both sound incongruous by comparison. In the context of a debut release by a relative unknown, this would have been forgivable, but coming from such a 'name' as John was, at the time, baffling. There is some redemption in the lazy nod to *Revolver*-era Beatles with some lively Ringo-style fills and the Harrison-esque guitar, but even that is blighted somewhat mid-solo by the throwaway vocal ad lib scattered lamely across it. Perhaps this was to serve as an example of John's 'raunchy' live act or as a concession to less discerning though no less fruitful foreign markets.

Of the self-penned 'I Don't Know About You', John said: "My songwriting when I was a lot younger probably wasn't ... I didn't write deep emotional things, I just wrote the kind of things that came into my head, and it was like a learning thing ... you kind of experiment when you first start writing."

Those who admired previous lovelies such as 'I Can't Let It Happen To You', 'The Saddest Night In The World', and 'You Don't Understand Me' would have noted the writing credit on the silver Philips label and expected another slyly gorgeous classic. Alas, despite a promising intro reminiscent of Neil Diamond's 'The Boat That I Row' or 'Cherry

Cherry', the song quickly slides into the subsoil previously excavated on the album by 'It's A Hang Up Baby'.

Listening to such accomplished readings as the next track, 'Pennies From Heaven' (Burke–Johnston), it's perhaps a shame John didn't go all the way and follow Sinatra into the realm of the occasional concept album. The Maus equivalent of *Songs For Swinging Lovers*, *In The Wee Small Hours*, or *Only The Lonely* would have rendered such material much more palatable. As it is, sandwiching ornate and sentimental lushness between two weak rockers only highlights the shortcomings of all involved and the album as a whole.

Despite mildly encouraging if scattered press and the spirited shows that John put in to promote his debut, the album received very little airplay and was bargain-bin fodder within weeks of its release. John's presence in the press at the time was exceedingly slight. His reaction to what must have been a mammoth disappointment is unrecorded. Still, while the record buying public had abandoned him, at least he still had his looks.

Dave Shrimpton of Philips: "I seem to remember it didn't sell too badly, although obviously not as successfully as one of Scott's. You must remember,]John's] appeal was very much to the impressionable young female population at the time, and his good looks would have been worth extra sales of 10,000 of his album. His voice was pretty good, actually, and he sounded not unlike Tony Bennett."

Chrissie McCall, still involved in the individual Walker fanclubs, witnessed in person the effects of Maus's good looks. "I remember him coming up to the Granada TV studios, and he brought me a suitcase full of fanmail. And of course, John is six-feet-four and I'm five feet ... so we must have looked quite odd as a pair. And we were walking down Manchester's King Street on the way to the television studio and, you know, this is one hell of a good-looking guy. I actually thought John was far better looking than Scott. John's got classic features, brilliant bone structure. Though I never fancied any of them. I could appreciate John and Scott were very good-looking. Gary became very good-looking, because he had such a great personality. So I remember walking down King Street and people were just turning around and looking – staring. I don't know if it was because they knew it was John Walker or because it was this drop-dead gorgeous, tall, tanned fit guy."

Looks aside, who was John Walker without The Walker Brothers anyway? A blues guitarist trapped in the body of a heart-throb, steered by a manager who was pushing him into the mould of, if not another Sinatra, at least a Bobby Darin or a Matt Monro?

Superficially, compared to Scott, John seemed less hung-up about things in general. This natural, easygoing affability allowed him to surf the wake of the split with a less troubled conscience than some. As far as doing the right thing concerning his artistic and personal aesthetic, it is likely that John did little more than listen to the rush-release manifesto put forward by Barry Clayman, pausing briefly to take breath, before simply going for it. What 'it' was exactly, and what it meant to get 'it', was not the point. Whereas Scott's attitude to his work was becoming increasingly European and almost Protestant in its ethic, John seemed happy to be more typically West Coast about it all. He would look back fondly even on this low period.

"It was exceedingly busy, no free time," he recalled. "If you weren't touring, you were in the studio. If you weren't in the studio, you were doing press or travelling someplace. Something was always going on. It was chaotic and fun." By replacing "fun" with "hell", one could as easily attribute the above to Scott – and this illustrates the fundamental differences between the two. Although as a singer Maus was now free of having to stand next to one of the greatest pop voices of the 20th century for a living, he was, to some extent, at least as a musician, a victim of comparison.

Ralph Gurnett, who now worked solely with Scott, was unsympathetic: "[John] never did anything about it. He just followed the trend, you know? Whereas Scott was writing all the time and coming up with ideas all the time, John had a drinking problem."

By early 1968, less than a year after their break-up, the commercial stock of the 'other two' Walkers had crashed dramatically. Prior to a forthcoming February release, Gary was a mere bearded rumour, and John would find himself involuntarily forced to exit stage right when Scott deigned to slouch from the shadowy studios into the spotlight once more. As far as the latent army of ex-Walker fans were concerned, apart from the weird few, it was Scott and Scott alone who was the vortex for both their attention and their pocket money. This was a troubling state of affairs for John. While he toed the party line as best he could and played the game accordingly, it seemed that the less Scott did of both, the more successful he was.

Scott weighed barely over ten stone (140 pounds), was anti-showbiz, socially reticent, and obsessed with his work, yet his fame and success cast giant shadows over the British pop landscape. These shadows were wildly out of proportion with his true nature, spreading out above him like the exaggerated shapes in a 20s silent horror movie. Such shadows bestowed a heavy cloak over the Clayman–Maus camp, resulting in a darkness within which Maus would have to learn to struggle, endure, and thrive.

Although John was about to release only his third single in less than a year, it seemed that, for him, the war was already over. Meanwhile his ol' buddy, the kid who used to play occasional bass in Judy & The Gents, the guy who only ended up singing on 'Love Her' by accident was now reaping massive commercial and critical success with increasingly obscure-sounding records. There he was, putting out hardly fashionable and increasingly strange-sounding material by "some French guy" (Brel was of course Belgian), and yet finally hitting home-runs beyond the female fanbase. It wasn't even that John wished ill upon Scott. Scott was obviously a major talent and worked damn hard. But did John's failures have to be so total by comparison? Such harsh realities and the subsequent mounting pressure from label and management must have made John feel like he'd been fighting for his 'solo' life an awful long time.

John was apparently drinking more than ever, and his marriage was, like his Scotch, on the rocks. (He and Kathy divorced that August; John later admitted he had married far too young.) By March 1968, as the latest hopeful round of promo began again, John was, in short, a man with a beard. "Everyone's got a beard these days," chirped DJ Dave Lee Travis on the German syndicated *Beat Club* television show. "Me, the producer and ... John Walker!" Cut to John on stool.

Impeccably polo-necked, cowboy-booted, his hair bleached and blow-dried, two months growth blurring his sharp features, he did perhaps look less like a contender and more like Clint Eastwood's hairdresser. Strumming a gorgeous acoustic 12-string guitar, he mimed his way louchely through his new offering – a sensual and languid version of Dylan's 'I'll Be Your Baby Tonight' (released in direct competition with a version by the English psychedelic band Blossom Toes).

John's vocal on this track is toasted, the sound of smoke rising through air. The line "Bring that bottle over here" is particularly convincing. Although the backing is almost comically pedestrian, the strain of overwork perhaps beginning to show on arranger Keith Mansfield, Maus carries the song effortlessly, sublimely evoking the sentiment of the song. The kids stayed away in their millions. The B-side, another Dylan oddity, 'Open The Door, Homer', is slightly less beguiling, although worth a listen if only for John's bald Dylan impression in the opening bars. Rarely does John sound closer to the hillbilly stock he occasionally played as a child actor.

By the time Scott had returned from a Paris recording session that April (where he recorded the theme to Robert Hossein's Leone-lite western *Une Corde, Un Colt*), a panicking Philips had already rush-released a Maus follow-up. 'Kentucky Woman' (Diamond) slipped out that spring. If it were not for the stellar ascendancy of Neil Diamond himself, perhaps John's reading would have stood a chance. As it was, Diamond was by now successfully metamorphosing from worthy songwriter into Elvis-esque superstar, cuckolding John's version into oblivion.

While it cracks along at whiplash pace, its tempo ultimately neutralises the song. John is uncomfortably close to the top of his range during the chorus and sounds like a man close to hysteria. The B-side is, as ever, depressingly superior. The self-penned 'I Cried All The Way Home' sounds like a companion piece to the Morricone-imbued ballad Scott had recently recorded in Paris. It is dramatic, lean, moody, and accomplished, like a tuxedoed cowboy in a Spaghetti Western.

By the late spring, even Gary had enjoyed more solo single success than Scott and John combined, and in this regard, the drummer-jester must have been relishing his return. In February, he announced the emergence of his new group, Gary Walker & The Rain. Consisting of former Masterminds guitarist Joey Molland, ex-Universal bassist John Lawson, and Paul Crane of The Cryin' Shames, their Scott-produced debut, a sublime version of The Classics' minor hit 'Spooky' (backed with 'I Can't Stand To Lose You'), could potentially top the single success of any solo Walker so far. Gary was rightfully optimistic. "It's taken me a year to get things together, because I wanted people to forget about me as part of The Walker Brothers. We believe we've made a better version than The Classics' single, which may as well be a demo disc, and we've eliminated the sax in favour of a guitar. They'll never stop us!"

Released that spring and sounding groovily stoned and ridden with theremin, the single was stopped when a high-court injunction was brought against singer Paul Crane by his old management, preventing him playing or appearing with the group. As a result, all pre-booked television and radio spots were scuppered. By the time the injunction was lifted and promotion was allowed, with appearances on BBC's *Top Of The Pops* and *All Systems Freeman*, the moment had passed and the splendid single evaporated, leaving not even the equivalent of a wet patch upon the pop consciousness. It would, alas, be The Rain's most successful release outside of Japan.

Although Philips had been initially interested in the group – a promo copy of 'Spooky' exists on the Philips label, but it was eventually released by Polydor – Franz and company were almost exclusively focused on the fulfilment of Scott's potential. After months of disciplined work at the Stanhope Place studios, his second solo album was ready. The vibe at Philips was exceedingly positive and the public and media were in accord. In early April, trundling over the corpses of the recent Maus and Leeds records, *Scott 2* was released to majestic reviews and enough sales to take it to Number One.

It was packaged in a cover that showed the singer looking like Jack Jones's doppelganger, and a free print of the same image was included in initial copies. ("It's really none of my business how they package a thing ... I mean, I don't see any of the covers until they're done," an evidently uninterested Scott admitted.)

He was by now more candid than ever in his interviews,

shamelessly admitting that he hated live work and did it purely for the money. He mused that he was neither surprised nor disappointed by his solo success, and when asked by Keith Altham in a television interview if he missed the good old days, Scott's reply was equally honest. "I don't miss those times ... the only thing I do miss is ... well, I miss the guys, you know? I really miss the fact that somebody's there to take it off your shoulders with you, you know ... I have to take it alone now, that's the only difference, and I don't like to do that ... really. But I'm learning to." Such an effort was not wasted on the development of his character. "I've had to come out a hell of a lot. I've had to ... I feel better in myself. Better than I ever have."

While John still wittered amiably in interviews about the model of his new car, Scott, on the eve of a new solo album, spoke of his new-found philosophy. "I believe in existentialism," he told Altham. "I believe the theory works. I believe in certain writers. And their theories work for me, better than meditation or things like that."

Scott: "The first reaction [to *Scott 2*] in England was, 'Well it's nice, but it's not commercial.' They didn't listen to it a lot. They just sort of put it out. When I got round to recording maybe my second album, with some of my songs on it, people started to listen a bit to my songs. But nobody really took me seriously as a writer until about my third or fourth album."

'Jackie' (Brel–Jouannest–Shuman) is a perfect opener to an almost damn-near perfect album. Sounding like the cousin of 'Mathilde', this encompasses all the storming energy and boozy confidence of Engel at his peak. As a lyricist, Scott would never indulge in such fanciful, rich wordplay – the lyrics here seem almost to pile on top of one another – but he seems to revel in being able to sing such a busy song. Live versions often featured Scott ably miming in his finest chanson style.

'Best Of Both Worlds' (London–Black) features one of Scott's most dramatic vocals. He sings from the seabed during the verses before exploding in the sky on the perfectly arranged chorus. A rare kink comes through in his pronunciation of "enjoy" ("enjoyah") but even this is utterly beguiling, sounding like a majestic P.J. Proby on horseback.

Scott had a good ear for up-and-coming songwriters. As with his appreciation of Randy Newman, he was also an early champion of Tim Hardin's writing, although as Engel himself would confess, he was impressed by the work and not the man. His version of the classic 'Black Sheep Boy' is as clear-eyed and upright as its author's own version is bleary and stoned.

'The Amorous Humphrey Plugg' is one of the first bona fide 24-carat Engel classics. The marriage of music and words (on the surface, a straightahead narrative) is forged in heaven. Although the arrangement is rich and intricate, it's also perfectly poised. There is nothing extraneous about it. Few could get away with a line such as "Pavements of poets / Will write that I died / In nine angels' arms" – but the voice and melody are so strong, so true, that such a sentiment sounds almost ordinary in this context. Humphrey Plugg is apparently a character from an obscure series of American children's books.

'Next' (Brel–Shuman) is another lyrical tour de force by Jacques Brel, displaying the blackest comedy in this account of a mobile army whorehouse. Scott relates the loss of innocence in one of his most expressive (some would say camp) vocal performances.

'The Girls From The Streets' is a hymn-like epic and has often been criticised for being 'Brel lite', but although the lyrics are as narrative as anything Brel ever wrote, the music is beyond anything the chanson would have attempted. This is one of Engel's most heroic-sounding compositions and one where he fully utilises the forces available to him. The detail of instrumentation – from the tiniest percussion instrument to the grandest choir – is staggeringly impressive.

'Plastic Palace People' is another Engel classic and perfectly poised upon the precipice of self-indulgence. The arrangement is once again lush and dense but not a moment too long or overdone. The lyrics are among his most enigmatic and disturbing, as a radio listener admitted ten years later during a Capital Radio phone-in. A distraught-sounding female nervously asked Engel if this song was "about what I think it is". The auteur's response was deadpan: "Uh, yeah."

Perhaps on the advice of comrade Franz, Engel felt that the world was not yet ready for a full-on album of originals, and thus his records were still peppered with quality fillers such as 'Wait Until Dark'

(Mancini–Livingstone–Evans). Actually, such middle-of-the-road standards work well in this context, making the originals sound stranger and the Brel songs darker. 'Wait Until Dark' was the theme song from the movie of the same name.

'The Girls And The Dogs' (Brel–Jouannest–Shuman) follows; it is Brel at his lightest, with a pepped-up arrangement to match.

Scott's interpretations of Burt Bacharach and Hal David's material were rarely definitive. Aside from 'Make It Easy On Yourself', he usually tilted the material slightly, adding a darkened, smoky veneer. He sings their 'The Windows Of The World' as if he has all the time in the world, and the marimba-anointed arrangement is a refreshing counterpoint to his deep mahogany tone.

'Boy Child' is prefigured in the misty, billowing arrangement of 'The Bridge' (Engel). It seems to float mid-air, free of the earth it straddles. (Incidentally, the name of the song's protagonist, Madeleine, was also the heroine in Brel's eponymous song of 1962.)

As with 'Wait Until Dark', 'Come Next Spring' (Adelson–Steiner) is an impeccably constructed and likeable slice of MOR.

The chart-topping album graced the UK charts for 18 weeks. Scott Walker was a Number One recording artist – with the emphasis on artist. And though he became increasingly private from this point on, he was far from a passive presence in society and certainly not apolitical. As the pop world seemed to move in harmony with Scott Walker's vision, Maurice King would have raised an eyebrow at his singer's latest request.

At the height of his commercial success, Scott phoned-in his instructions for a newspaper advert that he wanted placed in *The Times*. Was it a 'thank you' to his manager and all at Philips? A public declaration of gratitude at his fans support? No. With an album at Number One and London as his potential playground, Scott Walker would nevertheless stand up and be counted.

From *The Times*, Wednesday April 3 1968: "Fellow Americans in London required to join campaign committee supporting Robert Kennedy election bid; 60,000 eligible votes in Britain are important and must be contacted – Please call Scott Engel 01-836 0535 or 6185."

CHAPTER 10

JOANNA AND THE JAZZ LIFE

I don't like to work. I don't like live shows. I like to record and write, but I don't particularly like to work live shows, so I lay off doing them – and then when I'm broke, I start again.

Scott Walker (1968)

In the afterglow of a Number One album, Scott was in the luxurious position of being able to pick and choose his next move. For his less fortunate Walker brothers, the options were shrinking. While John applied alcohol to his wounds, Gary & The Rain marched dutifully on. A UK package tour at the end of April saw the combo opening for The Kinks and The Herd – led by Scott lookalike and 'face-of-68' Peter Frampton. Although the shows were well received, the group made little lasting impression outside of their own universe. Chrissie McCall was part of that universe. "Touring with The Rain was so much fun. Gary didn't seem to get down over the lack of success with each Rain single. He just looked to the next."

"We don't have to worry," joked Gary, the gag wearing thin. "We've had no hit records, never been on TV, and no one's ever heard of us!"

As successful as Scott was, his manager, typically, saw one step beyond. If *Scott 2* had got to Number One, then surely they could top that with *Scott 3*? To this end, Maurice convinced "the next Sinatra" to release a single altogether more palatable than any of that Brel stuff. Buoyed by the recent commercial success of his and Franz's joint artistic vision, and always a sucker for a great song, Scott acquiesced and opted to play the game, recording what would be his most successful solo single ever, the Tony Hatch–Jackie Trent ballad 'Joanna'. Languid and subtly world-weary, it was Scott pulling off his Sinatra–Bennett–Jones schtick with awe-inspiring grace and sincerity.

Gary: "I was never sure of this 'Joanna' thing, cos I always kept questioning [Scott], right? We'd be in some wine bar or something, and I said, 'You didn't write that, did you?' And he said, 'What makes you say that?' I said, 'I'm really suspicious about that, if you wrote that and you're not telling anybody.' And he gave me a funny, strange look. But I've always suspected he wrote that."

Tony Hatch: "When my demo of the song was first sent to Scott, he suggested some subtle but perfect lyric changes. We were delighted with his contribution both to the first and last stanzas and offered him a royalty share of the lyrics. Amazingly, he declined the offer and just said that he loved the song and was happy to leave us with the full songwriter shares. He recorded the song with a beautiful Peter Knight arrangement. Everyone was delighted with the record."

Scott said he didn't suggest it as a single release. "I was on my way to Yugoslavia and I said I didn't want a single released. Then someone at Philips said, 'But you must have a single released.' And then someone else says 'Yes! That's a good idea!' You know how these things go. [But] there can be no more of a sincere approach to this kind of thing. I don't think it can do any harm, cos the production is good. It's a fairly good record. It can't do that much harm; it can't do that much good.

"I'm not known to be [romantic]. Because most people say my stuff is cynical. But I like to write one of these things occasionally. Of course, this was done by Hatch and Trent, but I adjusted the lyric.

When I go to films and things and I'll see something, and I'll cry ... I have a great abundance of sentimentality."

The release of 'Joanna' was accompanied by a minor court appeal, this time by a Maureen Malone, secretary to Chris Blackwell, the founder of Island Records. Malone claimed that she, in fact, wrote the melody, originally for a song called 'What Went Wrong'. The accusation was thrown out and the single, propelled by its own obvious quality and by good television and radio promotion, including slots on *Top Of The Pops* on April 25 and May 16, peaked at Number Seven in the UK. The song became beloved particularly among the British public, and more than a few children born in its wake that spring were christened accordingly.

Perversely, Scott did little to acknowledge any gratitude he may have felt toward such overwhelming public support. Later that May of 1968, he appeared at the 16th annual *NME* concert at Wembley Pool, topping a bill that included a still psychedelic Status Quo and the besotted Lulu. Clad in typical existentialist uniform, Scott made a dramatic entrance in a cool cord suit and black roll-neck sweater to deliver a raucous rendition of Brel's 'Amsterdam'. The crowd loved it, clapping wildly as, unbelievably, the singer promptly left the stage. The applause petered out to a confused comparative silence and many a furious letter to the *NME*. What kind of headliner did one song! The plan had apparently been to do 'Joanna' as well but, on being told that his band, The Mike Leander Orchestra, did not have the sheet music, Scott simply walked.

"I don't plan anything ... I do it spontaneous," reasoned Scott, stating what was now becoming the increasingly obvious. "That's why I don't make plans for shows ... I don't know what I'm gonna do. I like to surprise myself."

Less suprisingly, he did embark upon the expected rounds of television and radio appearances, appearing for the second time on the hugely popular show of his Philips stablemate Dusty Springfield. Sounding relaxed and inspired, Scott lays down a dryly-funky 'The Lady Came From Baltimore' before amiably doing 'bits' with the hostess. Leaving this attempt at light humour swiftly behind, they get down to business, kicking off into a spirited duet on the hymn-like 'Let It Be Me'. With two such supreme voices inhabiting one song, the result can only be slightly disappointing. Although Dusty plainly tries to hold back, singing for the most part beneath Scott's strident tones, she cannot fully mask her inherent power, and like a stalemate in a game of scissors–paper–stone, both singers cancel each other out.

Between the constant engagements and dates, private cars, and trains, the pressure was turned up to 11, and it was now that Scott began to be more public than ever about his fondness for a drink. In The Walker Brothers' day, it had been the light wine of Mateus Rosé. Now it was Scotch. He drank at home and socially. Jonathan King: "I've always lectured him about his heavy drinking. In a place like the Scotch of St James, he used to get me out drinking, but I didn't join in. He soon found other friends to go around with drinking."

Years later, speaking from a much more sober perspective, the singer was just as candid. "In the 60s, everyone was either drunk or stoned. I was a very heavy drinker for years. ... It was crazy, that whole time, because we were taking sleeping pills to sleep at night ... we were drinking so much. I was writing off that. ... I was emotionally fuelled by all kinds of things, booze included, I'm afraid."

Still, compared to the competition, Scott was a health freak, as Rolling Stones manager Andrew Loog Oldham pointed out. "Scott always looked like half a bottle of Mateus Rosé would put him away."

The mixed media of 1968 – television, radio, the newspapers – was heaven for a Scott Walker fan. Articles and news items appeared in the *NME* and *Melody Maker* seemingly often just for the sake of it. For a celebrity renowned for the value he placed on his privacy, the more interviews Scott Walker gave, the more candid he became. Once-familiar topics had now been exhausted, and the fatigued singer would often be allowed to ramble off into fascinating stream-of-consciousness monologues, usually with a drink close to hand. Scott, who had long accepted interviews as part of the game, now seemed to be using them as public therapy sessions. He had a particular affinity with Nick Logan, a hip young freelance writer at the time who seemed to completely disarm his subject.

Sat at a table in a private drinking club in Soho that summer, Scott – who, along with nameless other multitudes, was still in shock and mourning for the recently assassinated Robert Kennedy – gazed down at the masses two floors below and launched gently into a melancholy soliloquy with only Logan, his notebook, and hundreds of thousands of *NME* readers for an audience. "It's my thing in life, I feel it's my duty, to uncover hypocrisy everywhere and to throw it in people's faces," he stated wearily. "We have got to love them all ... we must hope for them and try. I know that really, in my heart, I cannot change anything, but I must try."

A letter written by Scott himself would follow up the *NME* article. In it, he protested that the chat with Logan had been put across inaccurately and incompletely. Yet Scott's protest was worded in such an obtuse and eccentric manner that he merely reinforced that perception of himself. He was an obviously overworked, tired, and emotional formalist (not a formulist).

Scott to the *NME*: "I was made to look like the great deliverer of the human race, as if I thought myself capable of leading hoards of brutalised, twisted children to see the almighty light of day. ... As I chase my thoughts like a madman, I am no modern day Quixote, attempting to battle windmills."

Such sentiments must surely have been over the head of his manager. But whether they rang distant alarm bells or not, Maurice King carried on as normal, flying to New York that summer to discuss film offers on his client's behalf. Back in Britain, the palely loitering singer took his philosophy to the people, sharing a show with Dave Dee Dozy Beaky Mick & Tich at the Bournemouth Pavilion on June 16. This was followed by sold-out one-nighters at Birmingham and Brighton. Three proposed tours were also announced: one of Japan with Gary & The Rain; a UK one with jazz drummer Buddy Rich; and a November solo tour of the then apartheid South Africa, using local musicians as his band. The latter would only happen, Scott insisted, if he could play before non-segregated audiences. This was a bold decision at a time when many of Scott's peers – even groups he regularly toured and propped-up bars with – took up such offers routinely, taking good money to play for exclusively white audiences. Predictably, the proposal quickly ran into difficulties when the South African promoter made it obvious to Maurice and Scott, through their new agent, Harold Davidson, that 'mixed' audiences could not be guaranteed. Scott immediately withdrew from the tour until such an aberration was rectified – in writing.

The South African promoter refused to comply with the wishes of Scott's conscience, and the tour was cancelled, reportedly forfeiting the singer £35,000 and Maurice and Davidson their respective commissions. John would, similarly, turn down a later offer for the same reasons, albeit with much less publicity. The letter pages were once again rife with Scott-themed missives, this time in support of his anti-apartheid stance.

A planned appearance at the Majorca 68 festival was cancelled in favour of the Japanese tour by Scott Walker and The Rain, so the ever aviophobic Scott now had time to set off for Japan via the Trans-Siberian Express. The naturally paranoid singer was barely two days into his journey when suspicious KGB men apprehended him.

Scott: "I got kicked out because I brought in tapes. Yes! I was spying! I had, uh, all these jazz tapes I'd made, and we entered the border in the middle of the night, and they got on the train like Nazis. They were doing the whole Nazi bit, and they took away my tapes and my tape recorder. And when I got to Moscow, I got the next plane back. ... Thing is, I was heading to Japan on the train, I was going on a 17-day journey on the train cos I'm terrified of flying ... and I was taking these tapes with me. I had earphones and everything ... I had this marvellous tape recorder, and it's never supposed to break down. ... War correspondents use it in Vietnam when they're getting bombed, and I had this thing. So I took it, and I taped all my favourite albums, and was playing them like crazy. It was the only relief, on a train for 17 days, so when they took that away from me, I just couldn't go on. I just had to get on a plane and go back, I was so panicky, y'know? ... I love the Russian people, but the government ... I'm worried about the Russian artist under this regime."

Gary and The Rain's itinerary went ahead as planned, and they arrived at Japan's Haneda Airport on the 9:40pm direct flight from London. Arriving to jubilant if slightly smaller crowds than usual, ironically, Gary looked the least like a member of The Walker Brothers compared to fellow bandmates Joey, John, and Paul. All three had adopted Scott Walker haircuts and poses and, indeed, listed him at the time as their 'favourite singer' in a Japanese Q&A.

The ten-date tour that July, supported by The Carnabeats, was successful and fun – most pictures from the trip show them surrounded by sake and grinning insanely while opening piles of presents. They also worked off stage, booked into local studios to record demos. Their schedule was such that they could barely find time to leave Tokyo. They must have been reticent to leave. Although they could barely get arrested elsewhere, in Japan they were pop gods – to such an extent that Philips Japan circulated a special promotional record to provincial radio stations. It consisted of three minutes of groovy muzak over which Gary apologised for not being able to meet everybody in Japan personally. At this point, it would have been hard for Gary not to believe the hype.

While some Japanese fans wailed publicly at Scott's omission from the tour, incredibly, Scott now had the ultimate alibi – the KGB was to blame. Even Maurice couldn't argue with that, allowing Scott to take the opportunity of this welcome down-time to book himself into a nursing home. After seven days of rest, Maurice sent a car to take his suitably rested charge directly to BBC's Golders Green studios. *The Scott Walker Special* that Maurice had been working on was finally recorded on August 12 and 13, with a broadcast scheduled for later in the year.

Following the cancellation of the recent tours, Scott was as aware as anyone of his increasingly eccentric reputation. "I taped two shows for the BBC. The reason I taped two shows was, I think, not for me but as a safety net for the BBC, because my reputation as being unreliable is renowned ... and I don't think they figured I could do one show completely in one go."

With the television specials wrapped, Scott, guitar case in hand, was on the run again. He immediately caught a ferry to the south of France for what he stated was to be a proper holiday. He returned refreshed two weeks later to the results of the annual *Melody Maker* poll. A phone call from Maurice confirmed the manager's if not his client's greatest hopes: Scott Walker was the man. In 1968, the pop youth of Britain voted Scott Walker as the top male singer above Lennon, McCartney, Tom Jones, and Elvis. *Scott 2* was voted Number One album of the year. While all around him were celebrating, Scott, at the centre of it all, was eerily still.

Such accolades brought greater freedom artistically and bigger recording budgets, but at what price? The point of it all was that the writing and the songs came from a quiet, private space. By now, Scott was pop's most visible man, with little time to indulge in peace and solitude. Thus, the key to a true success was in an equilibrium he would struggle to maintain.

While Scott began to write again, the heat was off as the BBC screened the first of his specials later that month, to great acclaim and more than decent ratings. The Capable office was now inundated with offers of further specials, supermarket openings, charity gigs, and movie offers. Scott deflected all by going on his third holiday in as many months. He announced he had just beaten a bout of typhoid and headed abroad again, this time on "a working holiday" of Tunisia, where he would mentally prepare for the forthcoming package tour, a tour he freely admitted to doing "solely for the money".

If the South African tour had been cancelled because of its inherently fascistic nature, then the October 1968 tour, with Scott headlining above über-pop fluff acts Love Affair and The Paper Dolls, was an example of democracy gone mad. It began at the familiar Finsbury Park Astoria on October 12, and the audience was, as ever, mainly populated by the female of the species. But men were now attending in increasing numbers.

David Boon, a fan, recalls: "It may seem odd now, but it was the norm in those days for cinemas to be requisitioned for pop tours, despite the inadequate size of the stages. It was a great atmosphere, but the excitement grew to such an extent that by the time Scott was due to appear, the compere, Mike Quinn, had to ask for hush, saying that people had come to hear *that voice*. Predictably, even that was greeted by surround-sound screams. "The curtains opened to reveal Ronnie Scott's orchestra, minus violins, although still looking slightly cramped on the small stage. Scott clomped on stage, wearing shoes that appeared too heavy for his slight frame, casually dressed in black trousers and brown jacket and tie, to the strains of 'Jackie'. Amazingly, the crowd calmed down completely with only the occasional scream, which was hastily hushed. 'Main Street Mission' was great; I'd never heard it before. 'Make It Easy', 'If You Go Away', and a new song to me, 'We're Alone'. Marvellous, but all too short." Although acceptable live recordings exist of Brel's 'We're Alone' – not to be confused with the later single, 'We're All Alone' – it seems Scott never attempted it in the studio.

"The final number," says Boon, "was 'Amsterdam', which perked the crowd up somewhat. Bearing in mind that Scott was wearing very tight trousers, it got to the part where he sings about the sailor whose 'teeth had rotted too soon' and 'he gets up and laughs and he zips up his fly' – which Scott mimed, driving the ladies among the crowd wild."

Although the shows dutifully fulfilled all expectations, the usual contingent of pen-happy fans wrote in to the weekly papers to complain about the brevity of the set, a criticism also voiced by the ever-present Keith Altham in his *NME* review. The audience, consisting of the screamers of old and those who came genuinely to listen, were at cross purposes. Many thought that the package tour, with its sugar-sweet-pop opening act of The Paper Dolls, sent out completely the wrong signal to prospective punters. Surely, Scott was a 'serious artiste' now?

Maurice King was not pleased with such a tacky showcase, finding the support acts distasteful by comparison. The Paper Dolls themselves were also upset, complaining that Scott had been aloof, remote and standoffish.

"Scott talked to no one," moaned one anonymous and disgruntled band member. "[He] just used to stamp on stage and then stamp off and into a waiting car and away – either that or he hid in his dressing room." Faced with a padre-like Keith Altham on national television the following week, Scott went through a very public act of contrition. "They seemed to overlook the fact that nobody tried to talk to me either. I didn't see people clamouring at my dressing room door to try and talk to me. I go on as I am; I wasn't aware that I was putting people off in that way. If so, I'm very, very sorry. I didn't mean to. It's just the way I am, I suppose. I was doing a job and that's all I look at it as: a job."

In the same television interview, Scott told Altham that he would never tour again, bemoaned the fact that he had trouble raising cash for film projects, and concluded by admitting to an apparent extreme laziness. In this last instance he was surely being too hard on himself: that November saw him embarking on projects with Jonathan King, jazz guitarist Terry Smith, and old army buddy John Maus. The proposed Engel–King musical, based on the legend of Cyrano de Bergerac, would be abandoned at early stages and never surface. (Back in late 1966, Scott and King had edited an issue of *Granta* magazine, published in January 1967 and focusing on many aspects of the pop industry. Probably the only substantial Engel contribution, however, was the epilogue, written in a breathless Kerouac style.)

Much of that month was spent completing the Terry Smith sessions, which had begun in August. Using an impressive line-up of musicians, including Kenny Wheeler and Tony Fisher, Scott replaced Franz in the Oliff–Wake equation. As a result of the *Fallout* album, Smith would, among other things, go on to top *Melody Maker*'s Most Promising Instrumentalist Of 1969 poll.

"Many musicians like Terry fail to win wide recognition," read the LP's liner notes. "Their talents are enjoyed mainly by the cognoscenti who frequent jazz clubs. But sometimes their work comes to the attention of a wider audience – more usually through the appreciation of critics or those fellow members of the profession who have a real ear for true musicianship. Such a man is Scott Walker."

Smith: "I first met Scott Walker at Ronnie Scott's club in August of last year. Scott was interested in jazz and seemed to like my guitar playing. So, when Ronnie Scott formed a band to accompany Scott Walker in cabaret, I was included in the line-up. Scott asked me if I had ever done an album. I told him I hadn't – so he said he was doing some A&R work for Philips. And that's how this album came about. In Scott's own words, the motif of the album is 'happy jazz'." The album would be released the following year and enjoyed favourable reviews, Scott's production in particular being praised by *Melody Maker*, the original jazz paper.

The next exercise in the packed Engel itinerary was to hold out a helping hand to John Maus, whose career had hit an iceberg.

John: "People don't believe me when they ask me what I've been doing and I say 'nothing'. Actually, the most I've been doing is sitting on the floor of my flat overlooking Regent's Park with a bottle of wine, writing songs. It's very cheap wine. I'm not a writer really, and I just can't write soul hits or something. Scott produced my record after I told him I was writing. It's easy for him and me to get in the studio after working together for so long. I had dinner with Scott one night and he said it would be a good idea to get together."

The resulting single, 'Woman', was possibly the best thing Maus would ever write and record, a rolling, golden sea of gorgeousness that displays him at his most mature, seductive, and regal. Everything about this undulating, lazily burning ballad is just right. The string arrangement prefigures what was to come on *Scott 4*, and as a singer, John never sounded better. Pitch-perfect and effervescent, he sounds like a bar-bound angel with dirt in his wings and vintage cognac on his breath.

John and Gary would seem to bloom under the direction of Scott the producer. It's a shame no full album was ever completed in such circumstances. The B-side, 'A Dream', another Maus composition, is also another corker, soaked in 12-string and evoking the best of David Bowie's Deram period. It is lush, incandescent, and slightly sinister: Maus at his best. Its author was charmingly honest about his best work to date. "I wrote that in '67 and it was a surprise to me. You don't always like what you write, but I liked that."

Obviously disillusioned with Barry Clayman, John had re-signed with Maurice King, and this, coupled with the quality of his new Scott-produced single, must have raised his hopes on a par with those of the spring of 1967. Inexplicably, this supreme single stiffed everywhere. Despite a higher-than-usual promotional campaign by Philips and some decent press, the single drew no airplay at all.

As John turned aghast once more to the drinking cabinet, one could only conclude that the BBC and the rest had decided that there was space for only one Walker on their schedules and that his first name was neither Gary nor John.

The one ex-Walker Brother allowed an almost guaranteed public platform for his particularly private expressions did not waste the opportunity, heading back into Stanhope Place studios that busiest of Novembers with Franz, Stott, and Oliff to record what would become *Scott 3*. The recordings displayed his classical influences more obviously than ever before, but this most serious of young men was not precious about such a source.

"I get pleasure out of [modern classical composers]. It's a pastime. Cinema is a pastime," Scott told Nick Logan. "I am not competing with pop writers or Brel. I don't believe in pop art. What I do is polish up an antique, so to speak, and bring something new to them. Classical composers have made huge leaps but have progressed without becoming unmusical."

While John met with Maurice at the Lotus House to discuss what it was they could possibly do next, Gary dreamed of salvation in Japan, and Scott continued to clock in at the studio, working not only on his own opus but on yet another extracurricular project. In early December 1968, he took some time off from his own labours to produce an album showcasing another one of his favourite contemporary young jazz players, Ray Warleigh.

Liner notes for *The Ray Warleigh Album* described Warleigh as a "saxophonist supreme" who has "lent his talent to such bands as Alexis Korner, Eric Delaney, Ronnie Scott, and later the group formed to back Scott Walker. Scott recognised the talents of young Ray and produced this record. It's a beautiful reflection of the way a saxophone can sound when played expertly with feelings."

The album, recorded on December 13 and released in the following year, had little in common with the more esoteric progressive jazz that Scott was digging at the time, and the result veered more toward pleasantly middle-of-the-road muzak than the jazz fusion just around (on) the corner.

Warleigh: "I can't remember how I met [Scott], but I ended up as his musical director for his live band for a while. The title of my album was Scott's idea, because his had been called *Scott*, *Scott 2*, and so forth. He sent me a few tunes that he thought would be good, and together we picked the ones we thought would be most suitable. They were mostly standards, a couple of McCartney pieces.

"We did the album at the Philips studio, and it was very nice. Must have been a reasonable budget. There was an orchestra. It wasn't often I was off with an orchestra. The record could have been better, but no one discussed it with me ... the arrangers talked to Scott. And I think he more or less said, 'Do whatever you want,' or, 'Make it modern.' And then Johnny Franz heard it and told us to tone it down a bit.

"[Scott] was a good bloke. That much I remember. He was pretty secretive. He wore his dark glasses a lot. He didn't say that much. As far as I remember, whenever he went out, he always had his collar up and his dark glasses on. He was into Miles Davis and Ravel and all that: he knew what was going on. I wasn't particularly aware of the stuff he was writing. As a musician, I was too involved in my own stuff at the time."

While Scott worked himself to the point of fracture, his video-taped image also did the rounds. Back in TV-land, the BBC aired the second of his television specials, filmed three months previously. The reviews and the ratings were a glorious bookend to a triumphal year, a year that ended with a very public display of sobriety and unity from Engel and his manager.

Among the more frivolous Christmas messages placed by his peers as ads in the music papers that December, Scott and Maurice's stood out in its sereiousness. "A prosperous, peaceful '69," read the message, beside which an angelic Engel, seemingly lit by candlelight and anticipating the Eucharist, gazed beatifically heavenward.

Scott also sent a new year greeting to readers of the Japanese magazine *Music Life*. "Hello, readers. Happy New Year. This is Scott. I'm speaking from my flat ... somewhere in London. As you know, I was ill for quite a long time and had to be in bed. But now, thanks to everything, I'm fully recovered and feeling fine. At first I'd like to say to all my fans, I couldn't be in Japan last July, so I earnestly hope to be there. I wish to see you soon, as soon as we can set something up with some promoters in your country.

"It's about 8 o'clock in the evening here roughly ... I don't know for sure because I don't keep watches or clocks in the house. They have a tendency to make me very nervous. I'm dressed in corduroy pants, brown corduroy pants and a brown sweater: my usual casual sort of gear.

"I've been producing some jazz LPs in England for Philips recently, for some talented musicians, some new young jazz artists, hoping they'll be a big success in this country although I really don't think so. The English aren't very fond of progressive jazz. But I'm hoping to get them released in America and Japan where's there's a lot of market for this kind of thing.

"I've been composing quite a bit lately. Most of the stuff I've been tearing up, though. I'm nearer to completion of my third album. I should be finished next month and I'm hoping for a release in February if things go right.

"Not much has happened here in England. The weather is freezing and winter's setting in. And so is the fog. When you walk down the street you run into people and lampposts; it can be very embarrassing. It all depends on how you look at it, you know. I'd like to conclude by saying 'Sayonara' and, once again, a happy new year."

CHAPTER 11

A LONER

People have got to understand that there are more important things in life than a hit record for me. I think my real fans understand that; 'fans' is such a silly word. Most of my public are intelligent and sensitive enough to realise that I do not want adulation. I don't want to be idolised. I want respect for my privacy and recognition for my work. If I don't get it, I'll quit!
Scott Walker (1968)

Scott saw out the year, as far as the public were concerned, by singing 'Black Sheep Boy' on Esther & Abi Ofarim's BBC television special. While on set, Scott met up again with Esther's manager, Ady Semel. Johnny Franz had introduced Scott previously to Semel during an Ofarim session at Stanhope Place. As reserved and as civil as Maurice was bolshy and brash, Semel was smoothly dressed and self-contained. He and Engel were developing a rapport that would bloom unexpectedly within the coming year of 1969.

While Scott was approaching a kind of summertime within his own life, flowering through his work that came gloriously into being, John and Gary slid inexorably into the professional equivalent of a Russian winter. Even Gary's supernaturally sunny nature had taken a severe thrashing these last few months. Only the year before, burning bright in Japan, he had been working with The Carnabeats and about to storm the Top Ten with 'Twinkie Lee'. Gary had seemed on the brink of an Emperor-like fame in that country, with the world to follow. By January 1969, all possibilities had seemingly shrunken down to this one sole territory.

Lack of sales and a low, low profile profile meant that the *Gary Walker & The Rain Album No 1* was not released outside of Japan. Partly because of this, original copies have sold for thousands of pounds since the early 70s, and the record has been widely bootlegged on vinyl and CD.

The record itself is a patchy delight, with the Scott-produced singles sounding especially accomplished and vibrant. As with Brother John, Gary seemed to make more of an effort when working with Engel. The rest of the album, compared to the singles, is as inconsistent as Gary's drumming, but there are highlights. The opening track, 'Magazine Woman', written by Joey Molland, follows lyrically in the tradition of The Who's 'Pictures Of Lily' and the Bob & Earl hit 'Harlem Shuffle', celebrating the power of self-love through pornography. Sounding like The Beatles' 'Taxman' as interpreted by Hendrix guesting with The Electric Prunes, the tune lollops along groovily for almost five minutes – an epic at the time. Gary's drumming is not quite up to the task, the irregularity of his timing its sole constant. The fills are clumsy and unimaginative, but nevertheless, like Gary himself, it is ultimately charming.

'The Sun Shines' is a paranoid Kinks number via Chas & Dave. 'I Can't Stand To Lose You', one of Gary's compositional debuts, is a gormless stomp around a damp cul-de-sac. 'Market Tavern' is another Molland number and a charmingly melodic ballad of a pub, inhabiting the same territory as some of Bowie's Deram-era songs – which were being recorded almost simultaneously at the

Pye studio. The remainder of the album veers between these highs and lows. Despite the variables in production and of Gary's contributions, The Rain's first and final album is ultimately an engaging, inventive chunk of roughly-hewn British psychedelia that was allowed no room at the Pop Inn.

In bright contrast, Scott went from strength to strength, with sessions for his new solo album concluding early in the year. In addition, the BBC, impressed by Scott's two specials a year before (and by their ratings), picked up on the option of a television series. *This Is Scott Walker* ran for six weeks from March 1969, appearing at 9:50pm every Tuesday evening and making Scott one of the most visible recluses of the year. The show was, in its day, very successful, achieving good ratings to the extent that it overshadowed its ITV rival, *The Tom Jones Show*, by a considerable margin. Scott was no fan of Jones The Voice, and in a moment of self-indulgence he may have allowed himself a perverse smirk.

It was BBC policy at the time to re-use video tape for the sake of storage space, and as a result none of these shows now exist in the BBC vaults. All were efficiently recycled. All that exists of many of the *Scott* shows are audio recordings, albeit of occasionally excellent quality. These were recorded directly from the television set on to a reel-to-reel two-track as a favour to a Scott-mad daughter by a doting dad who just happened to be a sound engineer. The recordings he made are surprisingly hi-fidelity.

Chris Pountain, a fan, recalled: "In 1968, I was fortunate enough to secure tickets to one of Scott's BBC TV shows. It was most memorable to me because what was happening could actually be heard, unlike The Walker Brothers' concerts I had attended at Hammersmith Odeon and Finsbury Park Astoria, when the screaming was sometimes deafening. The BBC audience was hushed unless responding to the clapboards. There were overhead TV screens interspersed throughout the auditorium, which afforded us an excellent view of close-ups as the cameras zoomed in.

"On screen, it seemed that Scott descended some rather splendid-looking stairs in the opening sequence to the tune of 'Joanna', but in reality the staircase was far less grand. It appeared to consist of wooden crates covered with white and blue crepe paper. As Scott bounded down the steps like a young gazelle, one of them gave way under him – but the trouper that he was, he was unfazed and did another take, his rather large feet avoiding further mishap.

"When his guest, Kiki Dee, was due on set, he looked genuinely excited to be witnessing her performance. With almost boyish enthusiasm, he even pushed up his sleeves and started hauling the grand piano Johnnie Franz had just played off centre stage, well before the stagehands arrived. During the show, Scott performed a duet with Kiki Dee, the Billy Eckstine and Sarah Vaughan number 'Passing Strangers'."

The shows were tele-recorded at the Golders Green TV Theatre and were routinely broadcast a fortnight later in most UK regions, with the exception of Scotland, where a local quiz show was shown instead (prompting furious letter-writing to the *NME*).

The format of the programmes was pretty typical for a light-entertainment show of this period, and often the shows incorporated visual effects that were, at the time, no doubt state of the art. The material swung between standards and a good helping of Brel and Scott's own compositions, the former performed both by Scott and his guests, some of whom were obviously chosen by Scott personally. (See this book's Appendix II for an episode guide.)

The duality inherent in such a choice of material lends each show an almost schizophrenic edge at times. At one point, we are treated to the liquid melancholy and atonal strings of Engel's own 'It's Raining Today' immediately following an endearingly schmaltzy arrangement of Charles Aznavour's 'Who (Will Take My Place)'. This is in part a symptom of the friction between the star of the show and its sometime producer, BBC veteran Johnnie Stewart.

Stewart: "My reaction was mixed. The thing is that I question the material he used in the series. I would like to hear him sing some good standards as well as his own particular style of songs, like Brel's and his own compositions. I think he is a good singer, but he could be even better if he only sang a wider range of material. Some of the songs on his *Scott 3* album are great, but they're not really box-office material. They've got limited appeal. His songs really are a bit samey, I suppose. If you're going to be a name artiste, you can't stay with 'in the mind' songs all the time. You have got to do ballads and up-tempo stuff, the lot, much in the same way as stars like Tony Bennett and Frank Sinatra. They are great because they have such tremendous scope."

Scott does not come across as a natural television host, and the idiosyncrasies of his personality in such a context sometimes portray him as awkward and flip, even as vaguely arrogant. Nevertheless, this is a common complaint among the terminally shy, and he is clearly making an effort. The overall effect is beguiling. The spots that feature Scott and Johnny Franz alone together are quietly touching, and the mutual affection and respect between them is obvious.

Ultimately, the show may be seen as a record of a man in transition, unsure how to leave behind the showbiz expectations placed upon him while pursuing the purity of his own destiny.

Stewart: "[Scott] is such an interesting and intelligent person, and I'd like to get to know him better and know what makes him tick. I've worked with him since the early days of The Walker Brothers, when I was producing *Top Of The Pops*, and he has changed a lot from those days. He is much more of a person, much more mature. And although he has this supposed image of being a moody, difficult person, he seems to be much more friendly these days, which I like very much.

"It's true that you can be discussing things with him and he'll seem miles away," Stewart continued, "but I found him very co-operative. Mind you, he should be, since he is completely inexperienced as far as a TV series goes. He has an awful lot to learn. But he got better with every show he did. At first, he said he was scared stiff of having his own show, but as the series went along he got more and more relaxed. His speech, too, was very natural, for he doesn't put on airs and graces."

Prior to Scott's appearance on each show, a portentous voice, impeccably BBC-accented, intones emphatically: "Ladies and gentlemen … *this* is Scott Walker!" And each show began and ended on a variation of the 'Joanna' theme. The introduction was usually in a big-band style;

the outro affected more of a 'lounge' feel. Scott would dress formally for the first part of the show, in suit and tie, slipping into something more casual and comfortable for the latter segments.

The shows were well-paced, sustaining an even standard of quality. While no truly big names appeared, there was a plethora of interesting and sometimes unlikely guests, ranging from The Dudley Moore Trio and Gene Pitney to the classical guitarist John Williams and organist Billy Preston. Neither Gary nor John appeared, during a time when both were fighting for their professional lives.

And fighting they were. That suitably wet February saw the release of The Rain's second UK single, 'Come In, You'll Get Pneumonia'. One of the most ambitious things The Rain ever did in their short life, it is a ridiculously overblown opera in miniature and the closest Gary's new band ever came to sounding like his old one. The vocals sound uncannily like a hybrid of Gary and John combined. Yet, alas, airplay was scant, probably hampered by the wonderfully offbeat title.

No such irregularities would hamper Scott, who, striding stilt-legged across television, radio, and paper press, seemed commercially invincible by the time his third solo album was released in March 1969. Even so, such pop success seemed increasingly inconsequential to an artist who admitted that his own current favourite musicians were Beethoven and Brahms.

As with 'Montague Terrace (In Blue)"' on *Scott*, 'It's Raining Today' (Engel), which opens *Scott 3*, ranks among one of the most perfect compositions that Scott ever released. It flawlessly marries both his melodic pop sensibility and his passion for the avant-garde, combining them within a lazily effervescent arrangement. It was inspired by the teenage Engel's Greyhound trip across America. "I saw the seamy side of life on that trip – some funny things," he said.

'Copenhagen' (Engel) is a hymn to his long-term girlfriend Mette and the location of their pre-marriage honeymoon. The last word, "carousel", is sung in a style that Engel made his own, bending the note high and leading it out into a vibrato-less infinity.

The self-penned 'Rosemary' and 'Big Louise' both show Scott flexing his narrative muscles, as the observer watches the world go by, his life defined by his distance from it. These pieces were less full-blown songs and closer to exquisite snapshots, watercolour Polaroids.

'We Came Through' (Engel) is an uncharacteristically up-tempo and attacking number, complete with sound effects. The cannons are reminiscent of Beethoven's 'Wellington Victory' and Tchaikovsky's *1812 Overture.*

With an arrangement inspired by Delius, 'Butterfly' (Engel) was as close to classical as pop music got in 1969, although Scott was well aware of his own limitations. "I could never have been a classical music player. I don't have the patience. I have very bad hand-to-eye co-ordination."

'Two Ragged Soldiers' (Engel) was inspired by a photograph of down-and-outs in *Time* magazine, another classic example of Scott looking outside of himself.

The Brel covers that completed the album – 'Sons Of', 'Funeral Tango' (both Jouanest–Brel–Shuman) and 'If You Go Away' (Brel–Mckuen) – were also the last that Brel himself would ever record, and they were much more recognisable as complete songs, with full arrangements, intros, bridges, and choruses. And yet it was precisely because Scott's own songs – '30 Century Man', 'Winter Night', 'Two Weeks Since You've Gone' – were often no more than slivers or lushly-orchestrated memos that, beside the fully-executed Brel covers, the album worked as a whole.

'If You Go Away' is the pinnacle of the Brel–Engel material. The version on *Scott 3* stands among the best interpretations ever recorded of the standard. This was the sound of a soul torn in two in slow motion. It made the heart ache for heartbreak. It was, according to Ralph Gurnett, "one of the greatest English translations of that song ever heard".

In combining Brel and Engel, the album achieved an exquisite balance that Scott would never attain again. Not only would the work boost Brel's reputation and publishing revenue, but also it proved cathartic for others involved in Engel's vision.

Reg Guest was on board as one of the key arrangers, and for him it would be a peak experience, as he recalled fondly years later. "I did look back at that period and I suddenly realised that for about six months I'd been in total euphoria all that time. When else does this happen to you? Everything was right ... I was working on meaty material, going to the studio, being in control, getting recognition, being treated respectfully. With Scott, you're into the blood and guts."

Some would have expected such words to have come from Scott himself, but as ever he was too busy moving forward to stop and smell the flowers. Philips gleefully encouraged him, and their promo efforts included full shop-window displays and generous amounts of ad space in the inkies – although it was hardly necessary. This was Scott's moment, and his public lapped it up, taking the elaborately packaged *Scott 3* disc into the Top Three.

The sleeve was a gatefold and, although unaccredited at the time, stalwart photographer Chris Walter was involved all the way. "I took the photo of Scott on the cover, the one reflected in the eye," he recalls. "I did the rest of the album, too. I remember we drove around London one Sunday morning in Scott's Mini, looking for gargoyles and tramps to photograph."

A beautiful sepia-tinted picture of Scott was included with the album, the first to show him smiling. Walter didn't see this as a big deal. "Scott never seemed to have a problem with being photographed. He was a little more serious than most, maybe."

By this time, Scott was a bona fide sex symbol, mature enough to appeal across the board. Pop writer Penny Valentine wrote: "[My great aunt] used to think Scott Engel was the most handsome boy she'd ever seen on television. And *she's* over 80!" But the subject of such unwanted affection was less impressed. "Sometimes I imagine people seeing me as I see myself," Scott reflected, "coming out of a newsagent's early in the morning before I've shaved or woken up properly. Maybe I've had a heavy night into early morning and I look terrible. I can imagine somebody's saying, 'My God, is that Scott Walker?' But, you see, it is."

As with the previous hit 'Joanna' and *Scott 2*, the new single, 'The Lights Of Cincinnati', released that May to sustain *Scott 3*, bore little relation to either the LP or Scott's mindset at the time.

Beautifully produced and overly sentimental, the countrified ballad was a lushly arranged sheath of corn – and a weirdly inappropriate choice for someone as young and in their prime as Scott to be singing.

He was as aware of this as anybody and much more honest than most. "I don't want to be put in any kind of compartment. If you listened to my single, you might get the impression that was the way I was going, but if you listen to my album you must see I'm not. Everything goes hand in hand in this business. If you don't put out a single, you are under pressure from the public, who pressure my record company, who pressure my manager, who pressures me. It's the one thing I can't abide about this business."

An example of the gulf between public and private persona is illustrated by 'Overgrown Paths', an Engel original recorded at the same sessions as 'The Lights Of Cincinnati'. It was as complex and as layered as 'Cincinnati' was homely and straightforward. An ambitious and sprawling foxtrot through the gardens of a fragmented mind, it remained incomplete, along with the contemporary 'Desperate Ones', (both sound as if they only have guide vocals), and to date has not been released.

Although dismissive of 'The Lights Of Cincinnati' in the press, Scott dutifully promoted it on *Top Of The Pops*, verging on a self-conscious bout of giggles during "Suddenly I'm back there / In that old rocking chair." The record would no doubt have appealed to the older contingent among his fans and made it to Number 13.

With such relentless success, perhaps King and Franz were sensing some sort of approaching watershed. Many of Scott's contemporaries, much less the head honchos at Philips, could not understand where the singer of *Scott 3* was coming from. Philips understood the smooth, crooning ballad schtick – surely, this was what the public ultimately wanted, too? If the left-of-centre, modern neo-classicism of *Scott 3* had made the Top Three, what would an album of safe and proven 24-carat classics sell? So it was that while Scott holidayed in Greece, Philips released yet another album in late June 1969: *Scott Sings Songs From His TV Series.*

THE IMPOSSIBLE DREAM

This more overtly commercial offering included Scott's versions of Rodgers & Hammerstein's 'I Have Dreamed' (from *The King And I*), Charles Aznavour's 'Who (Will Take My Place)', Bacharach & David's 'The Look Of Love' (recently made famous by Dusty Springfield in the James Bond spoof *Casino Royale*), and Kurt Weill's 'Lost In The Stars', among others. Dave Shrimpton calls this "the only album on which Scott really swung". It too peaked at that unlucky Number 13.

Scott Walker's summer of 1969 came in a pivotal year for a singer whose career was now little short of schizophrenic. The recent release of two very different albums seemed to point his career south and north simultaneously. He was a performer who hated performing and a pop star who loathed public adulation. As a writer, he was approaching a point of crystal clarity in his work, and he was recording and releasing work that was both commercially successful and critically acclaimed.

Yet this was still not enough for either Maurice King or Philips Records. While Johnny Franz would have been more than happy to pursue Scott's original vision for as long as he was allowed, the challenging nature of songs like 'It's Raining Today', 'Plastic Palace People', and 'My Death' were uneasy listening experiences for Franz's bosses, no matter how many they sold. Maurice, meanwhile, still dreamt of managing his very own Sinatra, of breaking Scott in Vegas ... America ... the world. Scott 'got away' with doing things such as cancelling South African tours because on some (usually neglected) higher level, Maurice identified with the singer's strong moral core and respected both this and his obvious talent. As for Scott, part of him was a Sinatra-like crooner, and part of him did feed off showbiz pap, so he was thus able to maintain a balance that pleased all parties, including himself. This balance was explicitly illustrated by the aesthetic ocean separating 'The Lights Of Cincinnati' and its flipside, 'Two Weeks Since You've Gone' (from *Scott 3*).

Scott was capable of perusing both destinies signposted by his most recent albums. But to do so would have been ultimately impossible. No one person could deal simultaneously with maintaining two very different careers within one business. Scott would have to choose between left-field singer-songwriter or supper-club singer. In this regard, Maurice King symbolised the latter. Although Scott would have ultimately made the decision for himself, in the dying summer of 1969, the US draft board made it for him.

Astonishingly, Scott had finally been called up to join the war in Vietnam. Although he did at this point bear an uncanny resemblance to the Hawkeye character in Robert Altman's movie *M.A.S.H.*, he was probably among the least suited recruits that the US Army could have enlisted.

As ever, and without going into details, Maurice assured the nervy Engel that he would "sort it", and after some clandestine phone calls, the two flew to New York. As far as the British press was concerned, they were off on a mission to meet and discuss lucrative film offers with top Hollywood producers. In reality, Maurice had arranged for medical papers to be drawn up declaring Scott as homosexual and, consequently, unfit for service. The documents would be false, obtainable only at a price. Once they were in New York, the draft board duly processed Scott, and on evidence of the false papers and the interview they dismissed him from potential service.

While Scott and Maurice killed time in their respective hotel rooms, prior to the flight home, Maurice was approached by his 'fixer', the lawyer who had orchestrated the deception and now wanted paying. After sending the lawyer hither and thither, Maurice eventually caved in and paid, and in doing so lost more than a few thousand dollars. Scott was furious at how Maurice had handled it. Mary Arnold, Maurice's wife, recalled decades later: "When Scott found out about the money, it broke his heart. He lost his trust in Maurice."

Scott and his manager had passed a point of no return in their relationship. The singer was notoriously, almost puritanically transparent in his need for his personal relationships to be built on a basis of strict mutual trust. Maurice had known this most of all and had not only breached this personal covenant between them but also had endangered Scott legally – and all for the sake of a few extra grand. Perversely, it was not as if business was slow: the manager could hardly plead poverty. His gross mishandling of the situation pointed at something beyond even pure avarice. His number one client was no doubt left feeling vulnerable, disgusted, and shocked. On returning to the UK, Engel's brooding temperament would not have been cheered by the cabaret dates he was contracted to play that July.

On July 27 1969, Scott was yet again playing the part in Blackpool. Supported by David Macbeth, Linda Scott, and The Rockin' Berries, and backed by the Ronnie Scott band, Scott found that this role was quickly wearing thin. Ray Warleigh was the musical director and remembers Scott's predicament with good-natured amusement. "In the UK, we had been doing a lot of working men's clubs up north, variety clubs, stuff like that. We tried to appeal to a kind of sophisticated audience, but mostly you got 13-year-old girls ... who liked the look of him, I suppose."

At the time, Scott spoke plainly. "I'm doing this concert because I have to do it, but, you know, it's not me."

"We were very, very much a backing band," continues Warleigh. "There were a couple of solos: I played one on 'Black Sheep Boy'. It was pretty much what he wanted to do, and we simply played the arrangements. If you're playing to these kinds of audiences, there has to be a certain kind of sound they would want, so you simply couldn't play anything too avant-garde. It wasn't the right kind of venue in which to do anything esoteric."

A typical show kicked off with the band playing two introductory instrumentals before Scott bounced on, launching into 'Mathilde'. The set continued apace, including expected classics such as 'Make It Easy On Yourself', contemporary interludes like Dion's 'Abraham, Martin And John', and one of his best (but unrecorded) Brel interpretations, 'We're Alone'. Tim Hardin's 'Black Sheep Boy' was a perennial, beside a jazzed-up version (as yet unrecorded by Scott) of 'Stormy Monday', with an instrumental break broken up by a blustery Terry Smith solo.

The audience had been respectful and appreciative at the matinée show, but by the evening performance something was beginning to crack and blister. Introducing 'Joanna' and 'The Lights Of Cincinnati' in that familiar, considered baritone, Scott stated before a bemused audience: "I'm now going to sing a medley of my hits in the past year.

I'm joining them together, because they are boring for me and this way they won't take so long."

Under the obvious strain of playing two shows a day, and deeply troubled by his current management hassles, Scott was mixing prescribed medication with Scotch. And then going on stage. As a result, he appeared slightly eccentric to some members of the audience, an impression reinforced by the singer cueing in the aptly-titled 'Black Sheep Boy' twice during the same set.

For a musical purist like Scott, who had been singing professionally on and off since he was a child, mistakenly singing the same song twice in one set and introducing two other songs a tad too candidly was about as punk rock as it got. And yet, in the context of these Blackpool cabaret dates, the effect was as if he had done a Hendrix and set fire to Warleigh's saxophone reed. Warleigh himself states categorically that "I never, ever saw Scott drunk" yet remembers something "odd in the air" on that particular night. Warleigh concludes by joking: "Surely, you'd think that with two versions of 'Black Sheep Boy', the audience would be happy at getting more than their money's worth."

The opposite was true. At the end of the show, peeved and disgusted audience members did go so far as to ask for their money back. Bad feeling was echoed by the usual flurry of disgruntled letters to the press. By now, Scott was an artist at war with himself, and this visceral inner conflict was manifesting itself on stage, in person, and even among the public and press.

"I could sense that the critics were becoming confused, y'know," stated Scott. "They were becoming impatient and confused. I had a feeling of decline, at that time, in sales. My work was getting better, but the sales were getting less. Everybody kept saying to me, 'Why don't you get a decent producer from the States ... and record blah blah blah, and it'll be a hit record,' and that really got to me too. I really got annoyed at that. This was the last thing I wanted to do."

With the cabaret farce behind him, by the time Scott Walker got to London, he had decided what he would do. He would balk the Vegas route and follow his heart as well as he could. To this end, he sacked his manager. Maurice King was devastated. King's response is not recorded, but his wife remembered: "Not even Maurice could talk his way out of that. [Now] Maurice's whole life was shattered. He had lost his prestige. He was never the same man after Scott left him."

"Maurice worshipped Scott," confirms Chrissie McCall. "At one point he was going to have a wing built on his house for Scott to live in. He recognised Scott's talent and he idolised that talent."

Resolutely ignoring King's pleas and protests, legal and otherwise, Scott got on with his future. Now 'self-managed' by default, he treated himself by cancelling a further week of cabaret at Wythenshawe's Golden Garter Theatre and by publicly announcing a name change. This would signify no major conversion, no Cassius Clay–Muhammad Ali rebirth. He was simply dropping his public past. From now on, he would be known as Scott Engel.

Recording sessions were immediately booked in this name. Suiting the sense of a new beginning, Stanhope Place was unavailable (it was undergoing long-overdue renovations). Olympic Studios were booked instead, a sprawling space often used to record symphonic orchestras and movie soundtracks. Free of John and Gary, Maurice, and 'Walker', Scott Engel fixed the Quarr Abbey key to a chain, looped it around his neck, and immersed himself in *Scott 4*.

As usual, Johnny Franz was aboard to aid and abet, although engineering duties were shared this time by Peter Oliff and resident Olympic engineer Keith Grant. Scott stalwart Wally Stott would write the majority of the arrangements, sharing them with another new studio quantity, string co-arranger Keith Roberts.

Roberts: "The first thing I'd do is ask Scott and Johnny what kind of instrumentation they would want. Obviously there would be strings on there, but also other things. I would be presented beforehand with a demo and a manuscript. If there was a demo, it would have been an acetate or even just a tape. Scott may have recorded it in his home ... just him singing and playing guitar. But you'd also have some music, top lines, chord symbols, and the words, the melody line and the harmonies on top. Johnny Franz said, 'Give me a ring when you've had a listen, and we'll discuss what kind of orchestration you'd like on the session.' So I had a listen, phoned him, and said, 'I think we need some French horns.' He said, 'Are you sure we need those?' But I could visualise them on this particular number. And he went along with it. As it happened, they probably only came along for a half session, I remember.

"Anyway," says Roberts, "once all this was fixed with Johnny, then I'd get the recording date, two weeks hence or something like that. I'd be listening to the demos during that time, [and] some of the ideas may have been suggested by Scott Walker."

Scott: 'I've always been able to go to an arranger and have a pretty full idea of what I want. If you don't have the right arranger, it's very difficult ... you can pull him through it – but you can tell he's struggling. Wally Stott was a great arranger, and it never happened. He would not only take what I gave him, but he would come back with something even more."

Angela Morley (formerly known as Wally Stott) recalls: "I'm flattered that Scott would say such things, but then he did have a lot of say in the way those arrangements were done."

Parts of this record were to be as intimate as anything Scott had yet recorded, half an ocean away from such beautiful bombast as 'Love Her' and 'Best Of Both Worlds'. The album is not nearly as soaked in reverb as these past glories, and it is all the better for it. Despite the sonic shift, some of the musicians on *Scott 4* went as far back as the sessions for 'The Sun Ain't Goona Shine Anymore' .

Guitarist Alan Parker had been a witness since day one. "Scott was quite witty – he had a great sense of humour. But he could always counter this by being ... 'uptight' is too strong a word. More like edgy. Tense. By *Scott 4*, he was much more intense, to be honest. Still a nice guy, but much more intense. Almost going slightly introvert." The auteur himself had long since passed the point of cutting corners.

"No one really knows how hard I work on my songs," Scott confessed at the time. "I put every ounce of mental energy I have into them, and concentrate as much upon the melody line as the lyrics. In fact, more upon the melody than anything else, because I feel it is often neglected in popular songs."

Keeping true to this ethic and to both the charged atmosphere at Olympic and the quality of the material, the sympathetic sessionmen worked quickly and efficiently, but never blandly. Scott, free at last of so much excess baggage, was able to focus more intently than ever. His intensity, distilled somewhat by the diplomatic Franz, would have been inspiring for all concerned. Still, even for a big-budget man like Scott Walker, the processes of making such a complete sounding record were strictly governed by time. The songwriter, now at his peak, would not actually hear the complete arrangement of each of his songs until they came to be recorded.

Scott: "[Arranging is] not an easy thing to do, because it's not a visual thing. We can storyboard the movie ... we can draw pictures of what it should look like frame by frame, and people can see that – but not with music. It's a different thing. And we didn't have synthesizers to try it out on first. We only had a live session, and it had to be right that day. No tracking. That day."

Keith Roberts: "As an arranger I'd put all of the instruments down on the score, but obviously musicians can't read off of that because every instrument is on there. So each instrument would have to be copied out separately, and each player would have his own score. The drummer wouldn't see what the trumpet or the strings are doing: he just has his own individual part. So everyone would hear the whole thing for the first time as they played it.

"We'd overdub choirs, usually, and things like that, but most of it was done on the day. It wouldn't be that exciting for the musicians. Don't forget, they were going from job to job, playing on jingles and that. It was a job to them. They may get a buzz out of it and think, 'Oh, this is good,' or something, but then after that session is over they are on to someone else's.

"The words were very important to me as an arranger. You need to get some definition. I'd accentuate a certain lyric with a timpani, for instance, on this track. On a [certain] song, I wouldn't have powerful trumpets going; you'd have blended strings and delicate instruments.

"Scott and Johnny Franz wouldn't actually hear what was going down until that day. They would not say, 'Let's have a look at what you've done before we go to the studio.' No. They would hear my ideas on the day we recorded it. Scott might have been hearing something slightly different as we rehearsed the piece, and he'd mention it to Johnny or me.

"Scott would be listening in the control room, or he might come out to the studio to listen. When we started, he might even have stood next to the conductor. You'd do a few rehearsals first, before recording, cos there might be some mistakes in the score. Then you'd rectify those and do a take. Go sit in the studio, and Johnny Franz would be listening back to the take, and he might say, 'OK, we're going to have to do another one. Do another take, if we could, please.' Very rarely, someone would come up and say that the artist wasn't happy, or whatever. The producer wouldn't want to pay for overtime if he can help it.

"I think I [arranged] about three or four of the songs, and Wally Stott did the rest. And all of mine were recorded in one day."

The opening track – all are credited to Engel – is 'The Seventh Seal', transparently based on the Bergman film of the same name. The object of such an exercise, an almost complete transcription of film into song, is curious, and the result almost totters into the abyss of self-indulgence. At points, the piece seems on the brink of collapsing beneath the heavy narrative, but it is saved by the masterful arrangement.

'On Your Own Again' harks back to the vignettes of *Scott 3*, and 'The World's Strongest Man' takes us in a direction that Scott touched upon tantalisingly but never fully perused. It's a compact, fully realised, melodic pop song that is both romantic and sincere but never corny or sentimental.

'Angels Of Ashes' is among the least successful tracks, a country-tinged dirge that waltzes alone in ever decreasing circles.

Scott described 'Boy Child' as "one of the songs I'm most proud of. It marks the apex of the album and of the first phase of his solo career. The sonic equivalent of a Monet painting, the piece seems to exist outside of regular metre and timings. It is the sound of Engel confronting himself come judgement day, and we are witness as his own ghost leads the singer through endless rooms of billowing white cloud, fog, and illuminated mist.

Although the lyrics are among his most poetic and allegorical, at times they seem to be his most plainly biographical: "Boy child / Mustn't tremble / Cos he came / Without a name." Although the album features many beautiful contenders, the promise of each leads to this one song.

'Hero Of The War' is as topical as 'Boy Child' is timeless: it's a *Picture Post*-style account of a war veteran returning home crippled. Scott: "There are several compositions of mine, from my fourth album, that fall into the long narrative style that Dylan does. And those are the ones that have aged more so than some of the others, though that too is probably because they are political. Though not overtly so."

'The Old Man's Back Again' is a cousin to 'Seventh Seal' and again comes close to collapsing under its lyrical weight. It's saved by the drunk, dry funk of the rhythm section, acoustic bass and all.

From the same place as 'The World's Strongest Man', 'Duchess' is a slow, aching ballad that sounds like a less weary, blue-eyed Neil Diamond.

Following a starry 12-string introduction, 'Get Behind Me' attempts to rock, but the effect is lumpen rather than heavy.

'Rhymes Of Goodbye' is yet another average countrified waltz, and the title keeps in with Scott's habit of ending albums with a lullaby bye-bye.

Within a matter of weeks, *Scott 4* was in the can. True to Philips' scrupulous budgetary concerns, at the end of the session, Keith Roberts was not even allowed to retain his handwritten arrangements. The meticulously pencilled score sheets were handed in to Philips' administration, where they were filed away and, ultimately, lost.

While *Scott 4* was being processed by Philips – packaged and mastered, outside in the marketplace – Philips gave John Walker one last roll of the dice with the sexed-up ska shuffle of 'Yesterday's Sunshine', scored by Roberts and produced by Scott. It was another perfect pop moment that was cast into oblivion by radio producers with no taste and a fickle public. As a consequence, John was dropped.

Although he almost instantly found another less luxurious home at the terminally uncool Carnaby label, the rushed singles and the subsequent patchy album would do nothing to re-establish his reputation or illuminate his fading star.

This Is John Walker, the last Maus solo record of the 20th century, featured tantalising signs of life, in particular the epic and angry opener, 'Sun Comes Up', but John's originals were conspicuously absent, and the remainder of the album drifted into a directionless and mawkish slush. As unbelievable as it seemed on the eve of Scott's first true masterpiece, it would take far longer for him to fall the same way, but fall he would.

Without Maurice King as a powerful go-between, Philips could do little to force Scott into promotion and much less persuade him to revert to the Walker brandname. Before leaving for Amsterdam just prior to *Scott 4*'s release, Scott Engel granted scant time to the press and flatly refused to appear on either television or stage. There was also a sense within the weekly papers and among the dividing fanbase that Scott, in refusing to play the game all the way down the line, had blown it, and deservedly so.

Up until now, everything Scott Walker had released in 1969 had been a substantial hit. *Scott 2*, released only the previous year, had been a Number One. *Scott 3* had made it easily to Number Three. The *Sings Songs From His TV Series* album had reflected the source show's popularity, charting at Number 13. His latest single had achieved the same position. Although it may have been seen as indulgent by some to release another solo album that November, no one could have been prepared for the consequences of such an act. As it was, practically nobody bought *Scott 4* upon its release and it did not chart.

Scott gave no comment at the time, but years later he was able to reason with the calamity, blaming it in part on his culling of the Walker surname. "I tried to kill it – but it confused a lot of people, and that's part of the reason why the record didn't sell that much, because people didn't know who this was. First of all, I just wanted to bury ... Even up to that point people were still saying 'of The Walker Brothers'. I just thought: get rid of it!

"I had two audiences. There were people who regarded me as a serious singer of standards and things, and then I was doing this other kind of record which people thought was just loony. So nobody knew what to think, y'know? You didn't get people thinking he's that kind of singer, or he's that kind of singer. They didn't know how to focus, and it did more damage to me than anything else, because people were confused about it."

Andy Farmer, a fan, said: "It is remarked that the release of *Scott 4* was met with 'widespread apathy'. This is not entirely correct. At that time, I was working in the retail side of the record business, and Scott's insistence that the record be put out under the name of Noel Scott Engel confused many record-buyers ordering stock. Those who were Walker fans [like myself] being the exception. Plus, shops were filing it under E, not W, and with little promotion, that meant that even browsers looking for Walker product wouldn't always come across it. Talking later with other people in the business, I consider this one ill-considered act had more to do with *Scott 4*'s failure than any apathy on the part of the general public."

Perhaps in some sense Scott hoped for this commercial suicide. Maybe he was moving toward a long-desired anonymity. Jonathan King, still a friend at this stage, comments: "He did hate the adulation; he hated being a celebrity. He actually, deliberately, gave up fame. It wasn't a question of doing things that were less commercial or whatever: he deliberately gave up fame because he didn't like anything about fame."

Professionally, Chrissie McCall was only marginally involved at this point. Now no longer working for Scott, she was able to view the latest development with a clear perspective. She was not at all surprised at Scott's exit. "[Fame] never sat comfortably on him. And people say, 'So what? He could have given it up at any time,' but while he was in The Walker Brothers he felt a certain responsibility to Gary and John. And he wasn't stupid. He knew that it wouldn't last forever. So, you know, take it while you've got it, if you like. And do what you want with it. It's opened doors for him that would otherwise never have been opened. So it served its purpose. And I don't mean that he was coldly calculating about it. In a way, he was flattered by it. And I don't mean in a big-headed kind of way. It scared him that all these people wanted a piece of him, wanted to touch him, wanted to scream at him, that he couldn't have deep and meaningful conversations with people, because it was all superficial."

The reviews were mixed and the general feeling was that Scott, in pursuing his own vision to the exclusion of all else, had exhausted the public's patience. In this respect, *Scott 4* was like a rose at the height of its bloom, finally and fatally outweighed by its own voluptuous beauty, crumbling to the touch. 'Boy Child', in particular, was a testament to the duality of fulfilled potential and commercial suicide.

Scott followed the news from his retreat in Amsterdam. He was far from immune to this new failure, even going so far as to write personally to the author of a favourable review in the British pop paper *Record Mirror*. Scott the auteur was winning the war over Scott the MOR singer, but at the price of sales, recording budget, and, ultimately, commercial freedom. The abject commercial failure of his most artistically successful work was both confusing and depressing for the man. It marked the beginning of a new and arduous era.

Scott: "Y'see, you gotta figure the state of mind I was in, in a foreign country in total isolation. And a friend brought me over these reviews and [I'm] seeing things like, 'For Scott Walker freaks only, and even heavy for them.'"

CHAPTER 12

SO LOW 70s

The early 70s, that was the worst period of my life. That's when everything escalated, my drinking and everything else.
Scott Walker (2005)

Scott saw in the decade from his new home in Amsterdam, which he shared with both his long-term girlfriend Mette and their giant St Bernard (alternately known as Rasmus or Nosey, presumably after Mette's father or Scott's favourite childhood toy respectively). Having been a bona fide star throughout most of the world since late 1965, it was time to reacclimatise.

Consciously or not, Scott was true to his perverse nature in choosing to come down to earth in the capital city of illicit substances. Although not a dope smoker himself, he still liked a drink and, as a relative unknown in the Dutch city, was able to indulge in the life of occasional barfly. He spent many days drifting from pub to pub, unhampered by the usual hassles of celebrity and seemingly an age away from the accursed blessing of Walkermania. Back in Britain, true to the pop market mentality, the general population assumed that

Scott had simply quit both Britain and the music business. Scott would scorn such hearsay as nonsense. "It's a huge myth, man. I haven't left England at all. I now have an apartment in Amsterdam and one in London, that's all. I just commute between the two ... I had to get away. The phone was ringing constantly. Someone wanting to sue me, someone wanting me to make a record."

Far from abandoning Britain, it was around this time that Scott was taking official steps toward becoming a naturalised British citizen. *The Times*, Thursday May 7 1970: "Notice is hereby given that Noel Scott Engel of 17 Bolton Street, London W1 is applying to the Home Secretary for naturalisation and that any person who knows any reason why naturalisation should not be granted should send written and signed statement of the facts to the Home Secretary of State, Home Office (Nationality Division), Princeton House, 271 High Holborn, WC1."

Aside from this move toward British citizenship, Scott Engel allowed himself a season of indecision during the early months of 1970. He would later reveal that he had considered retiring from music during this period. While it is hard to imagine what kind of employment outside of music would have suited him at this point, it's possible that he could have taken up the reins of academia once again. Not that such a choice would be so cut and dried, financially. It's doubtful that someone who admitted to having to put himself through the grief of live appearances simply because he "needed the bread" would be able to pull off such a radical and sudden change of lifestyle. Alternatively, he made token gestures toward putting himself on the market again as a session player – almost instantly betraying the flippancy of such a notion by admitting that he no longer even owned a bass guitar. Perhaps by "quitting music" he really meant quitting singing.

With no gigs or studio bookings, he was once again a civilian, and like so many of the under-employed, he gleefully turned to the cinema as a means of using up the hours, visiting the local movie theatre with Mette up to four times a day. If Scott was looking for a new career that still paid well, the obvious step out of music may have been into movies. While he may have been able to bag a reasonable part in an upcoming flick thanks to his celebrity and looks alone, he had already decided on which side of the camera he belonged.

"I have no aspirations to become an actor myself, but I would love to direct. That's more of a reality now than ever before. I've seen some great continental movies recently, like *The Damned*. And some of Visconti's things. I saw *Easy Rider*, but the only thing I liked about it was Phil Spector's appearance as the pusher at the beginning. My idol has always been Orson Welles. I wish I was Orson Welles – he produced *Citizen Kane* at the age of 25." Ironically, the coming years would to a certain extents ee Engel's career parallel Welles's wilderness years.

Back in London, Philips issued the first of what would be a legion of compilations. Although generically titled, *The Best Of Scott Walker* was refreshingly Engel-heavy in content, and the resulting publishing royalties would allow Scott further time and space in which to muse.

Free of management hassles and physically removed from the corporate hierarchy of Philips, Scott could relax in one of the most domestic set-ups he had yet experienced. Within such relative silence, ideas began to slowly bud and bloom, and by summertime, between indulging himself in the cinema and the pub, the prolific Engel had begun to write again.

Ever restless, Scott and Mette took off to Greece for a month that September. Using the fragments, concepts, melodies, and lyrics that had germinated in his Amsterdam apartment, he began to elaborate these themes into songs. He was writing his fifth solo album already, and within the month he would be recording it.

Although Scott was physically far removed from the 'suits' at Stanhope Place, his agenda nevertheless was affected by a pressure to compete in the marketplace. Now that he was moving back into the game, he did so at a pace. It was as though if he moved fast enough, the commercial failure of *Scott 4* could be erased and, in doing so, he could hook up with the mighty momentum of 1968 once more. The pressure was on to have a new solo album out by Christmas 1970. Scott would come to regret such indecent haste. "I wrote [it] in two weeks, because I was trying to somehow bridge the gap ... I was trying to find out what the hell it was they wanted me to do ... which was dumb of me. It was written in two weeks, and it sounds it to me. I should have kept pursuing what I was pursuing."

The result was that he was forced into a compromise. *Scott 4* had consisted entirely of Engel originals, and it was a plateau he had laboured hard to reach. He would now have to give up such hard-earned privileges. If the first four solo albums were to Scott Walker an approximation of what *Citizen Kane* had been to his beloved Orson Welles, then what was to follow would be Engel's own equivalent of Welles's *The Magnificent Ambersons*.

Johnny Franz's support of Engel was well known within the business at this time, but even Franz had to answer to somebody. There was always someone higher up the corporate ladder. Scott was, at least, realistic. "When I started having trouble after my fourth album, when they didn't really want to let me write any more, [Franz] tried a little bit, but there wasn't a lot he could do, because he would be putting his job on the line. And of course my fourth album hadn't sold that many, so he couldn't say it was a success – 'let's do it again,' you know?"

By the time Scott flew back to the Philips studios that autumn, he had accepted the necessary evil of compromise. He'd agreed to split the album down the middle: one side hosting the songs he'd finished in Greece; the other consisting of a bunch of standards. Something for everybody. Surely. And it wasn't all bad: Maurice King and all his legal threats were at last history, and Scott had a new manager in the shape of Israel-born Ady Semel.

Scott and Ady were both frequent presences at the Stanhope complex and had become familiar with each other over the previous year. Johnny Franz made their introduction as manager and artiste official. Compared to the worst of King's indulgences, any new manager could only be an improvement, if only by default.

Yet not everyone thought Scott had made the right choice. Ralph Gurnett recalls cryptically: "Johnny Franz said it was the worst thing he ever did. Ady Semel wasn't Scott's person." As a man, Semel was immaculately tailored and effusively cultured. As a businessman, he was bold and radical; he immediately took the manager–client relationship one step further by sharing writing credits on half of the forthcoming album with Engel himself.

As Scott is quoted as referring to Semel as his "censor" it is unlikely that they composed together in the accepted sense. If such an unusual move was not purely a financial one – Scott paying his manager a delayed commission through a share of his publishing, for example – it seems more likely that, in such a role, Semel's contribution to the songs would come after the fact. Semel would be given completed songs and then simply make suggestions toward curbing some of their 'indulgences' – indulgences that Scott naturally utilised so beautifully. If the songs 'came through' Scott in the classic shamanistic ritual familiar to many artists, they then had to go through his manager thanks to a much less mystical tradition.

Dick Leahy, a former Philips employee and future head of GTO Records, says: "It sounds almost certainly a financial thing. But then if it was a way of paying commission through publishing, you wouldn't need to credit him as a writer for that. You could make a separate arrangement. It could have been a tax thing. But it certainly sounds like a financial thing to me. Did Ady Semel suddenly come out after this album and be a writer? It's the kind of thing that used to happen a lot in the 50s."

Ray Warleigh: "Scott was a fairly indecisive person. I think he was glad that Ady was going to look after him and he wouldn't have to make too many decisions. Ady was like an ultra-smooth Jewish businessman. Extremely polite, extremely kind, proper. And he was a very nice man all round. Very generous, if I remember rightly."

It is probable that Semel's influence related exclusively to the lyrical content. In addition to the five Engel pieces, Semel is credited as contributing to the lyrics of several of Esther Ofarim's songs. Such Machiavellian goings-on did not hamper the birth of these new blues. Even compared to the quick turnaround of previous albums, the new record, '*Til The Band Comes In*, was completed with almost indecent haste, with the master tapes finalised by early November.

The usual team had been employed and divided. Wally Stott arranged the Engel originals on side one, while Peter Knight scored the cover versions on side two. Franz and Engel were producing, although, as ever, only Franz would receive any sleeve credit. Going by Semel's literate and fluent liner notes for the album, it seemed that he and Scott shared a natural love of high culture as well as a mutual respect for each other's solitude. In a questionnaire he completed some years earlier where he was asked for his favourite attributes in a man, Scott answered "Silence." Conversely, Semel would often attend Scott's press interviews as an equal, something Maurice King would have kept well away from. But then King had also left Scott's writing well alone, too.

In anticipation of the new release, the 'reclusive' singer, perhaps in part inspired by Semel and undoubtedly refreshed by his recent honeymoon period in Amsterdam, gave more of himself to promotion than many may have expected. Particularly when compared to the media silence that accompanied *Scott 4* – and perhaps because of it.

He had also gone back to the famous trademark name, his reasoning behind such a symbolic move illustrating a new weary fatalism. "Well, that's a concession ... it's a name ... fuck it, I don't care, y'know? A name doesn't mean anything to me. So I'm not going to stand fast on a name."

It was harder than ever before to get Scott television spots, but the press and radio were still relatively easy. Sounding both refreshed and laconic on Dave Cash's BBC Radio 2 *Be My Guest* show, Scott Walker, as he was once again known, confirmed that he had recently acquired a new flat in London. He added perversely: "This is where I started, and I recently said this is where I'm gonna end."

Although the album was already a projection of a divided soul, its author would add to the schizophrenia by adding another element into the equation. "I'd like to be able to get in a position that Rod McKuen was in with that *Man Alone* album for Sinatra," he told Cash, before shooting down the idea. "But then he's his own best PR man and I'm not. I can't really get into that. But I'd like to do something for Bennett."

Although it is easy to imagine Tony Bennett ably covering 'The War Is Over' and, in particular, 'Time Operator', it is also perversely tempting to imagine a bizarre scenario where Scott Engel would end up writing such gorgeous jazz-MOR standards for Scott Walker to sing.

Scott continued: "I'm really fond of a quote by Miles Davis: 'Look, man, I'm not stepping forward or backward, I'm just heading in another direction.' And that's what I like to think of myself as doing every time. Writing in different directions. I want to be more accepted as a writer than I have been."

Dave Cash: "My main memory of that interview is just that it was very professional. I respected him tremendously. After the *Be My Guest* interview, we went to the BBC canteen, and we were talking politics. We were both very for Kennedy, who was facing Nixon at that time. Richard Milhouse did not make it, as far as we were concerned. We were both at that time left of centre, shall we say. I enjoyed talking to him about that, because he was very cool, a very intelligent man, and very moralistic, too. He always mentioned Jacques Brel every time I saw him in the 70s. I thought, 'Well, here's an American guy, lives in Europe, and he really digs a Frenchman.' I found him to be a very complicated man, and as he matured he became more complicated, because he understood more and he questioned more. He seemed to me to be a very lonely man."

Full-page adverts were placed in the weeklies showing a smirking Scott in a chic designer Japanese windbreaker. The accompanying headline, "A major breakthrough by a major artiste," certainly suggested that Philips had not lost faith, but the "special Scott album giveaway" competitions in the same magazines and the life-size, fold-out posters given away with initial quantities of the LP betrayed a subliminal desperation.

This was heavy promo – more push was given to this one Scott Walker release than to the whole of John's catalogue – but Philips' release of the album was as flawed and botched as the record's content. The title track was released as a single in Holland, with copies hurriedly imported into the UK as a trailer for the album. The press release described the work as "a musical interpretation of life in a block of flats at a frozen moment in time," an idea Scott had first voiced back in 1968. While this seemingly ignores the second half of the album completely, it does raise the question as to why such an album was rush-released to compete in the harshly competitive and utterly unsympathetic Christmas market. Not that it mattered, as distribution of the disc was so erratic that most copies did not surface in record shops until January. In retrospect, Scott was as bewildered as anybody by such a hopeless marketing strategy. "So, they mixed it with a lot of other garbage and put it out, and, of course, it didn't sell."

The record itself is a lovable mistake. If the previous Scott Walker albums were increasingly gorgeous offspring, then *'Til The Band Comes In* is their pretty-eyed, club-footed sibling. It begins with 'Prologue', which, like all of side one, is co-credited to Engel and Semel. Many would have assumed the opening bars to sound like the beginning of a typical day for Scott at the time. Purely instrumental and minor key, all chocolate cellos and BBC library sound-effects records, the piece acts as the overture to the forthcoming movie in sound.

Scott: "You can hear the sound of children: it's a very visual moment. I like film music; I respect Jerry Goldsmith and I admire Alex North. They belong to a bygone age, which was very rich and interesting. Unconsciously, [film music] has always influenced me, even before opera and the great works, because I have always spent lots of my time sitting in the dark listening to films."

'Little Things (That Keep Us Together)' is often compared to Brel. While it was the only Engel composition to appear on the 1981 compilation *Scott Walker Sings Jacques Brel*, the association ends there. It is in fact one of the most original Engel songs, utilising an attacking tango rhythm and stream-of-consciousness lyrics that recall nothing before or since (other than 'Overgrown Paths', from a couple of years before, which at the time of writing remains an unreleased Engel composition).

'Joe' is a political saloon song – with both a capital and lower-case P – a kind of Engel companion to the BBC *Play For Today* series that was so popular on British television at the time. Wally Stott provides a convincingly faux-lounge-bar arrangement over which Scott croons deliciously. The cutting line "A postcard from Sun City / Was found laying by your side / A kind of desert place / Where old folks dry away" obtusely references Scott's very public falling out with a South African promoter a few years previously.

'Thanks for Chicago, Mr James' is one of the most sublimely melodic and compact tunes that Scott ever recorded. A soaring string refrain opens up on a narrative borrowed from 1969's *Midnight Cowboy*, set to the chiming of tubular bells and a laconic vocal. Scott's harmonies on the ebullient chorus conclusively illustrate one of the tragedies of his old group. Scott could easily sing John's part, but John could never pull off a Scott. At less than three minutes, this perky piece of ear-candy would have been a contender for a single two years earlier.

Although 'Long About Now' is ably sung by Esther Ofarim, it never quite transcends Scott's familiar stylistics. (There is apparently a demo of this track with Scott singing the lead.) One can also imagine Dusty performing this to wonderful effect.

'Time Operator' features a deliciously parched Scott vocal that is perhaps attributable to his realisation that sometimes a vocalist can be too confident and the results therefore predictably smooth. It includes the memorable line: "You just picture Paul Newman / Cos girl he looks a lot like me." A biopic of our hero made around now could have featured either Newman, Redford, or McQueen in the lead role.

'Jean The Machine' is another *Play For Today*, alluding once again to Scott's personal political sympathies (the left). The arrangement is half-baked, however, and it's the most incomplete and rushed-sounding piece on the album.

'Cowbells Shakin'' is another touching portrait in sound, a snapshot of struggling immigrant workers ... although by this time, the album's stated concept seems to be wearing thin. As a "musical interpretation of life in a block of flats frozen in time" it succeeds in purely literal terms but lacks emotional impact or any clear conclusion.

The two closing Engel originals seem to have little to say about those characters mentioned so far, and perhaps that's the point. The widescreen ''Til The Band Comes In' and the intimate 'The War Is Over', where it sounds as if Scott is singing from his bed, are, again, lush and impressive ... to little effect. There is a sense that Scott himself has lost heart in his original vision and, as a result, the arrangements and performances sound less committed than those on *Scott 4*.

The much-maligned 'inferior' second half of the record is probably born out of the disappointment of the first half. The idea persists that perhaps if Scott hadn't been 'forced' to record this 'schlock' we would not have been denied a masterpiece. And yet the Engel originals on side one of the original vinyl release show no true progression of Scott as a writer. In fact, he admitted as much when paraphrasing Miles Davis's quote on the *Be My Guest* show. *'Til The Band Comes In*, even side one, was the sound of Scott going sideways.

The 'schlock' side has many rewards for those who are fans of Scott merely as a singer. If side one sounds a little like outtakes salvaged from *Scott 4*, then the 'covers' side sounds like superior leftovers from *Scott Sings Songs From His TV Series*.

'Stormy' (Buie–Cobb) is not a promising beginning, however. This is the sound of Scott embarking on half a decade of bad habits. His voice was always too heavy for up-tempo fodder such as this, and he sounds like he knows it. His heart was never light enough to bear such fripperies. 'The Hills Of Yesterday' (Mancini–Webster) is more apt. Scott had admitted to a great weakness for sentimentality, and his voice wears such weepy string-soaked songs as this beguilingly.

The corn-fed hillbilly stomp of 'Reuben James' (Ertis–Harvey) makes 'Stormy' sound like 'My Death' by comparison. This is the sound of Scott Walker in gingham, chewing a wheat stalk, and swigging from a jug o' moonshine. Only minutes before, he had been singing of "Commie plans" and male prostitutes. The gulf between such extremes is the measure of this album's failure.

'What Are You Doing The Rest Of Your Life' (Bergman–Legrand) is as seductive and lithe as an opium-scented serpent. The original version was sung by Jaye P. Morgan and featured in the Academy Award-nominated 1969 movie, *The Happy Ending*. Scott ends his performance with a transcendently sung "you ..." that threatens to last forever.

'It's Over' (Rogers) is Scott as cowboy, high-plains-drifting across the prairies of his youth. It was always a role he played well, and the quality of this finale is more than the album promised.

The record was, as Scott admitted, a rushed affair, but even so, this was not its true failure. It was a schizophrenic attempt to appeal to as many different markets as possible within one sitting: country &

western, supper-club, ex-Walker Brother devotees. Side one ably catered for fans of Scott the singer-songwriter, but even these numbers were below par when compared with previous trophies. And, worse still, it seemed as though Scott himself knew it. For the first time, he sounds resigned and unsure on a record. For someone who had previously sounded like a supremely confident artist, the effect on the listener is disturbing. But by now times were moving on, and few enough were listening anyway.

Margaret Waterhouse: "After *Scott 4*, well, it all went very quiet indeed. He seemed to have died a death, at too young an age in my opinion, because after *Scott 1*, *2*, and *3*, at least, I thought he was going to be the next Frank Sinatra, or so the music papers of that time would have you believe. Then, one day, I think it must have been about 1971, quite unexpectedly, I was browsing round the record department of a large store in Leeds, and whose face should I find peering out at me but a handsome, well-tanned Scott Walker on the front of an album called *'Till The Band Comes In*."

Margaret was among the few to find it. The release campaign was as good as aborted by a seemingly unfocused record company, the concept of the album was flawed from the start, and the LP picked up scattered, low-key, mixed reviews. Radio play was stark and after dark, if at all. Scott's movie-star looks, glorious commercial past, and inarguable vocal talent were still good for the occasional television spot, including an incongruously majestic version of the title track performed on the Simon Dee replacement, *The Derek Nimmo Show*. But such efforts were akin to putting lipstick on a scarecrow. Token attempts at promotion were academic, and the album was launched below radar, crashing on take off.

While it apparently sold better than *Scott 4* had done initially, *'Til The Band Comes In* failed to chart or make an impression outside of Scott's unfashionable and increasingly alienated hardcore fans.

Undoubtedly, the dual nature of the disc was a concession to the bosses at Philips (soon to become Phonogram). With the Engel originals on one side, separated from what Scott himself would later describe as "cornball schlock" on the other, the work had fallen with a soundless thud between two stools. The commercial impact of the record would decide which route the singer-songwriter would be forced to take.

The lack of any serious single seemed to suggest that the company almost immediately lost faith in their product. As such it was probably a given that their signing would follow the dire plan mapped out by the 'schlock' side of the experiment. As his latest work tumbled into the dark chasms of the global bargain bin, Scott must have known what was to come next, and he steeled himself for it.

While Mette set up a new European base for them in Copenhagen, Scott continued to spend his time in the UK in a large flat near Regent's Park, a locale that would, within the mythology of his own life, become symbolic of bad times. Decades later, from the safety of a new century, Scott would recall grimly: "I'd bought an apartment, which was giving me nightmares, a huge place I was wandering around in, like Xanadu [the mansion in *Citizen Kane*]. ... I thought, 'What am I doing in here?' And, of course, I got rid of it as quickly as I could. A lot of it was drink, years of drinking, bad decisions. I was unable to make decisions."

In the wake of the commercial stillbirth of the latest album, there would have been no further sympathy within Philips for Scott's original material. As his status shrank, along with his sales, so his leverage in the company as a creative force diminished almost overnight. For all his romantic gypsy fantasies, Scott was essentially realistic and anchored by a heavy stoicism. Whatever his personal agenda, motives, and feelings, he was still a singer with a contract. Signed to Philips for at least two more original albums – reissues and compilations were unlikely to fulfil such contractual obligations – he was undoubtedly, like most recording artists, 'unrecouped' and in debt to his label. In music business terms, the stellar commercial success of *Scott 3* was light years away.

He was also still working with the familiar team – Johnny Franz, Peter Ollif, Wally Stott, Peter Knight – and the glory of their previous triumphs together must have made the last two commercial failures seem even more total by comparison. As ever, there was not one credible explanation as to why *Scott 3* had hit Number one and *Scott 4* and *'Til The Band Comes In* hadn't even charted. He was once again using the trademark name, and his recent material was as strong and accessible as it ever had been. No one could say that the glorious string-bleached charm of 'Thanks For Chicago, Mr James' was difficult or obtuse. The reasons for Scott Walker's sudden lack of sales were as intangible and subtle as the reasons for The Walker Brothers' sudden success, but it was only natural that the victim of both would try to explain such negative phenomena.

"The sort of material I had been writing just isn't a saleable product," Scott reasoned. "I wasn't disappointed about *'Til The Band Comes In* because I knew all along it wouldn't sell. If you become too happy, too satisfied, with what you are doing, you become Engelbert Humperdink."

Stalwart fan Margaret Waterhouse had another less sophisticated angle on his dilemma. "Scott was fighting an uphill battle with the music trends of that particular time, it was all T.Rex stuff and more 'teenrock' type music being flavour of the month. A seriously good singing voice like his just didn't seem to fit in any more."

Fashions had changed, tastes had shifted, and many of the screaming teens had become mothers. Approaching one's thirties is a cause for reflection and personal evaluation among most men and women, and Scott may have felt as if his life up to that point had taken him to a kind of creative and professional cul-de-sac.

This was a new experience for him. Learning the rules as he broke them, he would, down the years, come close to regretting this period. "I was still under contract, so I had to make a lot of albums I didn't want to make to finish the contract and get onto another contract. They were giving me money to stay on recording these mediocre albums – these nothing albums. I needed money to live ... so I kept making money because I didn't want to work live. So you become a whore from time to time, and that's it. And it gets worse. You get worse inside yourself."

It is possible that Semel and Engel could have gone to court in a bid to expunge the contract, but Scott's character did not fit with such an aggressive tactic, even if his new manager had agreed. Scott was all at sea. "I didn't know what I wanted to do. I know I needed money ... I knew that the company was not going to drop me at that stage, because they just weren't. I couldn't afford to sue them or anything, so it was just easier for me to stay there and wait and see what happened. Just wait my time out."

The timid ripples caused by the belly flop of *'Til The Band Comes In* soon played out into a shallow nothingness, leading Scott back to Copenhagen, where he would invariably muse on the meaning of these latest (non-)developments. In some senses, the release of the album had done little other than seal the immediate fate of Walker as an original singer-songwriter.

Perhaps in many ways he envied brother John, who had by now exhausted almost all commercial faith and was, by the end of the year, without a management, publishing, or record deal. Free, in a sense. His last two single releases, 'Cottonfields' and 'Over And Over Again', were of high quality but may as well have been released in theory only. It had seemed at the time that the superb 'Cottonfields' might have been in with a chance. Early notices had been promising, as John almost too eagerly pointed out at the time. "In the past, every review I had made reference to Scott or The Walker Brothers. I've been winning battles against things like that for a long time. ... On 'Cottonfields', reviews were talking only about the record I made. Only one mentioned Scott. That's my cross to bear, as it were."

Tragically for John, 'Cottonfields' clashed with a simultaneously-released Beach Boys version of the same song and, as a result, it didn't even leave the starting gate. If Scott's press people were finding it hard to get their man free advertising space, then John's people could barely be blamed for not even trying. For a man whose adult life so far had been gobbled up by insane itinaries of touring, recording, and interviews, the newly found spare time at least allowed the 26-year-old to spend the bulk of his days at his local pub, which throughout most of 1970 was the bar at London's upmarket Hilton hotel.

John, whose looks seemed unaffected by his unhealthy lifestyle, had been separated from his wife for two years, and many of his originals from this period seemed to deal with this very subject.

Having lost both his home and his public life within the space of 18 months, he was now at a loose end, often giving what remianed of his press interest an audience while he drank – a lethal combination for a man in John's position. Such sessions found him obviously disillusioned and embittered. He was even bemoaning the fact that the public often referred to him as Scott in the street.

"It's funny," he sighed, "Scott and I were so alike to look at, that people thought we were brothers. The trouble was that Scott always got the limelight. He ended up with all the credit for making the group as big as it was. But I did more than Scott and Gary Leeds put together. And, take my voice off Walker Brothers records, and what have you got? A big, fat nothing."

Following his final single for the Carnaby label, John found himself at more than a loose end. When confronted with this, he had simply shrugged, took a hit of Scotch, and resolved to go beyond it. A freak hit in Spain with 'Huellas Del Mañana' offered some new options and, for a few weeks of 1971, John was apparently seen in the company of his two female backing singers, wandering off into the hills of southern Spain to embark upon an improvised tour of local tapas bars.

Scott was allowed no such respite. Back in London, Philips considered how best to next exploit their investment. Although an old-school professional and a company man all down the line, Johnny Franz still held great affection for his former golden boy. So, even though word had apparently come down from the top that there was to be "no more of this Scott Walker shit", Franz sympathetically sought out material that Scott could at least empathise with.

The result of this search was the vocal theme to a new movie adaptation of L.P. Hartley's classic novel *The Go-Between*. Name singers were queuing up to record the title song, a drifting, haunted ballad by Legrand & Shaper called 'I Still See You'. Scott was among those hustling and was given the chance of a crack at it. He seemed happy enough at the prospect. "I recorded the song because I dug the film. It's a beautiful song, and I've always admired Legrand."

Hal Shaper, the song's lyricist, gave Scott his blessing among the many other contenders for the song and attended the recording session at Stanhope Place. Shaper had worked harmoniously with Scott on a previous occasion in Paris on a one-off, 'The Rope And The Colt'. Three turbulent years had passed since then.

Arriving at the Philips studio, Shaper was disturbed by the obvious change in Scott's personality. Scott had brought a companion with him to the session – probably Mette – but was also accompanied by two bottles of vodka. According to Shaper, Scott acted with all the classic temerity of a spoilt slightly-past-his-prime Hollywood movie star, suggesting changes to the script in the form of psychedelicised lyrics and a new musical arrangement. The Philips studio would express their discontent by cutting the singer's budget.

The singer was 'pissed', in both the American and British vernacular – annoyed *and* drunk. "Do you know I have a helluva job getting studio time? I had to do the single in one hour. I want to be able to take six hours if that's how long is needed."

Whatever the difficulties of its birth, the resulting single is a golden child. Regardless of how much vodka was or wasn't consumed, no negative effect is apparent on the final product. The singing is vintage Scott: pitch perfect, deep, warm, and gloriously melancholic. The B-side, 'My Way Home', is even better and a unique song in the Engel canon. Poised angelically between the singer's countrified future and his lushly orchestral recent past, there is little to connect the unadulterated sentimentality of this song with his other writing of the period. Lyrically, there is a possible link to 'It's Raining Today': it seems to hark back to the teenage Engel's Kerouac-esque travels across America. The translucently lovely score suggests as much, referencing once again the panoramic desertscapes and rich valleys of a Jerry Goldsmith treatment. The voice is classic, romantic, mid-60s Scott Walker, as fluid and as pure as the melody it gives life to. He would never use this voice again.

Scott performed an opaquely elegant version of the A-side on the 200th edition of ATV's show *The Golden Shot*, to little avail. The song's parent film, *The Go-Between*, was a hit, but the single, released in October 1971, barely a year after the flop of *'Til The Band Came In*, died on the vine, taking the sublime B-side with it. 'My Way Home' would be hidden for decades, rarely resurfacing on compilations and not appearing on CD until the mid 90s.

Semel and Engel turned down an offer from an independent promoter to perform all-original material from *Scott* onward at the Royal Albert Hall. Scott: "It was to be a concert of my songs, but I had been away a while and forgotten most of them." The pair instead decided to go the way of the supper club. After the briefest rehearsal period, they put together a series of 45-minute sets for a residency at the Frontier variety club in Batley, West Yorkshire.

These would be the first gigs Scott would perform while not at the top of his game and the first that were not balanced by a more satisfying recording life. Some punters saw the singer as uncomfortable, even disgusted, during early numbers. There was a feeling from some that Scott was forcing himself to sing – a bad sign for a vocalist who had always sounded nothing if not natural.

The sets consisted mostly of solo material and the occasional Walker Brothers hit. There would be no Engel originals. On and off stage, Scott tried to sound convincing: "They paid me superb money. They did very good business, the band was great, and, generally, things were as good as they can be for something like that."

Scott took the money and ran, spending the bulk of 1972 at home in Copenhagen. While Franz and Philips pondered the next Engel-related move, Mette had become pregnant. Their daughter, Lee, was born in August, and the couple married in Las Vegas soon afterward. For the first time in a long time, songwriting was not on the agenda.

Scott: "I never would write when I knew nothing would be recorded, because it would make me feel too bad. I stopped worrying about it at that stage. I let John Franz choose practically every song, y'know. I didn't think about it. I was just taking the money. Everything, as far as your art goes, gets pointless. It's just throwing it out of the window ... but that's just the way it went. They wanted to give me songs that wouldn't be banned any more, so I'd sing Jim Webb songs. In the end I would take the money so I wouldn't have to work at all ... so you get spoilt."

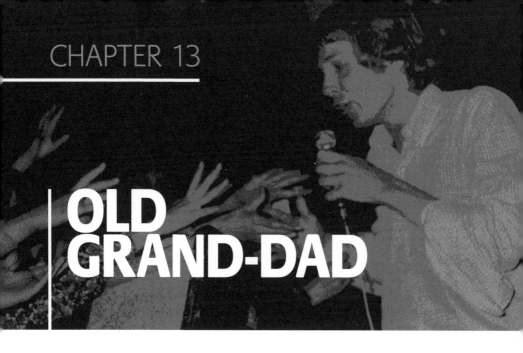

CHAPTER 13

OLD GRAND-DAD

I just sat back and copped money for whatever it was they wanted me to do. If they wanted me to do movie themes, man, I would pick the best movie themes that I thought were possible and I would do them ... Sinatra-type stuff ... I'll imitate anybody. It was down to that: whatever it was that needed to be done.

Scott Walker (1977)

By the early 70s, concept albums, typified by Marvin Gaye's *What's Going On*, The Who's *Tommy*, and David Bowie's *The Rise And Fall Of Ziggy Stardust And The Spiders From Mars*, were increasingly in vogue. (Although that hadn't helped the half-baked attempt of *'Til The Band Comes In*.) Philips and Johnny Franz decided that the next Scott album needed a unifying theme. With this, perhaps Franz also sought to impose focus upon an artist who had resigned himself to being lost. All the same, Franz tried to assure Scott that in time they would return to the real work: the continued fulfilment of Engel's own muse. For now, they would have to kowtow to the industry authorities. Until fashions changed and the public came around again, the brief was to record inoffensive, middle-of-the-road material that could be easily processed, marketed, and sold. This new phase would duly kick off with a concept album, and in this instance, at least, the theme was something close to Scott's heart: the movies.

It was also decided that some new blood might add some inspiration to proceedings. Robert Cornford – a major player who had also co-founded the London Sinfonia and was an associate of jazzmen Evan Parker and John McLaughlin – was appointed as the exclusive arranger for the next album.

It was recorded quickly and professionally – or, as far as Scott was concerned, carelessly – at Stanhope Place. For the first time since *Sings Songs From His TV Series*, Scott Walker was nothing but an interpretive talent. While that talent was being expressed well under par, the decision to do covers only would at least allow the album a consistency that was grievously lacking in his previous effort.

The Moviegoer opens with a far-from-obvious selection, 'This Way Mary' (Barry–Black) from *Mary, Queen Of Scots*, introducing the gentle, careful pace that dominates the album. The arrangement is substantial, considered, and as tasteful as the vocal. While the tune itself is insubstantial, the overall effect is sincere and harmless. (This track was destined as the B-side of the single 'The Me I Never Knew'.)

Scott's take on the vocal version of Nino Rota's 'Speak Softly Love' (the theme from *The Godfather*) is plain gorgeous. It drifts heavenward through incensed air, like smoke from a thousand snuffed candles. The backing is sympathetic and authentic, with some tasteful mandolin work. *The Godfather* was one of the few films referred to on this album that Scott may actually have appreciated.

Neil Diamond's lilting 'Glory Road' from *W.U.S.A.* is one of the rare instances where Scott, Marvin Gaye-style, overdubbed his own vocal. The tempo is drifting incarnate: neither too fast nor too slow, the effect gently stoned and aching.

'That Night' (Shifrin–Gimbel) from *The Fox* and 'The Summer Knows' (Legrand–Bergman) from *Summer Of '42* are sung from the heart of tuxedo country: impeccably arranged, cosmetically beautiful, but lacking heart. 'The Summer Knows' is the superior of the two, its arrangement echoing the style of Wally Stott (and it would not have sounded out of place on *Scott 3*). Scott seems to connect with the lyrics and the performance is edgier.

'The Ballad Of Sacco And Vanzetti' (Morricone–Baez) from *Sacco And Vanzetti* trounces the pious original. Scott's number draws completely on the Morricone aspect of the song and grooves it up magnificently, with a bleached cowboy swagger.

'Face In The Crowd' from *Le Mans* opens with a sonic reference to Gershwin's tone poem 'An American In Paris', with trombones mimicking car horns and speeding traffic, but this is as interesting as the piece gets. Ultimately, the song is as unfocused and meandering as the Steve McQueen film it comes from.

'Joe Hill' from *The Ballad Of Joe Hill* is Scott at Dean Martin's worst. He sounds soused and ashamed to be singing such corn-starched sludge.

Scott sings an insincere version of the mawkish Christian ballad 'All His Children' (Bergman–Legrand–Bergman) from *Never Give An Inch* and it is as low as he gets on this record. At times, it seems as if his vocal has been muted between phrases, to cut the sound of his own self-loathing laughter. He sounds as if he's at once inebriated and chewing tobacco, mocking himself and affecting a country-bumpkin accent throughout.

It's surprising that Franz allowed such a cut to be released. The poor reputation of Scott's work between 1970 and 1977 rests on rare and occasional blunders such as this track, 'Joe Hill', and, from *'Til The Band Comes In*, 'Reuben James'.

By contrast, Andre Previn's 'Come Saturday Morning' from *Pookie*, a song that would ordinarily register as nothing but a pretty distraction, sounds colossally beautiful.

'Easy Come Easy Go' (Green–Hayman) from *They Shoot Horses Don't They* is the jazziest track on the album, with a weary Scott singing soulfully to a sparse trad-jazz accompaniment of bass, drums, and piano. And yet, as pleasant as it is, this tender song highlights his restriction as a vocalist just as much as the rockin' uptempo numbers he had attempted in The Walker Brothers. Scott's voice is just too handsome for jazz.

If the idea of the album was to play on Scott's well-known love of cinema, then the choices were as inappropriate as the cover, which showed the singer half swallowed by a Stetson beneath the superimposed image of a giant ticket stub. The effect was half-hearted and tacky – as a philosophical Scott himself recognised some years on. "They're useless records, you know? And in a sense, I was thinking about this, maybe it's better to have had that awful gap [between *'Til The Band Comes In* and 1978's *Nite Flights*] than to have made a lot of half-assed art records like a lot of people did. You know what I mean? To just not quite get up to the standard in the time, and to have that behind you. I would rather have gone off totally and experimented with standards and had that experience than not."

There was no lead single and scant promotion: Scott's most recent television appearance had been with Sandie Shaw, on ATV's *2Gs And The Pop People* in July. The album, released in October, stiffed. Expectations had been low anyhow, and few involved had held out any real hope. There was a feeling of disappointment, but no one was surprised. Scott himself was resigned to the point of being a virtual bystander at his own career.

By early 1973, Scott was broke again and treading the dreaded cabaret boards, at Fagin's nightclub in Manchester. Ex-fanclub president and Manchester resident Chrissie McCall was there to witness the low. "I had been sent over to Fagin's to see that Scott had everything he needed in his dressing room. He always wanted a TV set in there. He also wanted to work out how to get from his dressing room to the stage as simply and quickly as possible, as he hated that walk. He was always so nice to my mum. She adored Scott. At Fagin's, she barged into his dressing room, and I was mortified, but he was so polite, offering her a drink. I think Scott lacked confidence. I've seen him on stage close up and he's physically shaking, his hands are shaking."

The audiences were split between hardboiled fanatics and the casual punter who would have been unable to tell Scott apart from any other crooner. As much as he hated these gigs, it would have been hard for Scott to offend. He self-medicated his nerves with Valium and Scotch backstage, but such was his stage fright that by the time he walked into the lights he at least felt sober. He sailed through the midnight show with the usual professionalism, tainted only by a barely discernible self-loathing. Once the job was done, he didn't hang around, beating a hasty retreat with Semel in his orange Volkswagen.

Once settled back in London, Scott dutifully continued to punch the clock with Franz and Oliff at Stanhope Place. It was common knowledge now that Scott was just seeing out his contract. Philips chose not to dwell on the dismal commercial performance of *The Moviegoer* and ushered their signing into the studio for what, mercifully for all concerned, would be his final Philips album.

The singer, who had been most public in his search for a philosophy during his early solo career, had obviously arrived at some kind of understanding with his current predicament. Speaking to a French journalist in the early 90s, he outlined his survivalist philosophy from this time. "I've never been someone who wanted to sort of suck my thumb and get a foetal position or something going behind the couch there. I mean, I've never had that. Sure it bothered me, of course, but it didn't crush me. It bothered me that I couldn't write a record. Sure. But I felt, well, it's more … it's just as important to exist as write. It's really important, that. People think, 'Oh God, my work is everything,, but it isn't everything. Existence is worth everything. So I wasn't dead, you know?"

Commercially, the records continued to expire on arrival. The liner notes to the 1973 album *Any Day Now* say: "To describe Scott Walker as an outstanding singer is something of an understatement. To this much misunderstood artiste, good music and good singing are the loves of his life." While this was true, it did not apply here (and whoever was misguided enough to write such notes did not put a name to them).

The portraits of Scott adorning the sleeve had him looking catatonically pissed-off. These final Philips sessions must have been tainted with a sentimental sadness. All involved – Franz, Oliff, Knight, and many of the musicians – all had known and been enraptured by Scott while he was at the top of his game. The last four albums had seen his commercial stock plummet, and this final Philips album, recorded as little more than a contractual obligation, was the lowest point so far. Most would have been aware of all this before heading into the studio, and yet, ultimately, any melancholy would have been neutralised, certainly in Scott's case, by relief and liberal doses of Scotch. This album would free him, and while there was no guarantee that things would get better, they surely couldn't get much worse. For the first time, Scott recorded his vocals indecently quickly: in one day. side one before lunch; side two in the afternoon.

Burt Bacharach & Bob Hilliard's 'Any Day Now' ushers in Scott's final Philips phase. The sweet woodwind arrangement is at odds with Scott's sad, sad vocal. Lyrically, the song ruminates on the inevitable collapse of a love affair, but Scott sounds as if it's happened already. This first song introduces a new-sounding singer – despondent, unwell, not merely heartbroken but just plain broken.

Jimmy Webb's 'All My Love's Laughter' is the first of many superfluous, mournful refrains, with Scott lapsing once more into his 'country' accent.

The snazzy airborne arrangement of 'Do I Love You' (Pelay–Le Govic–Dessca–Piolat–Anka) comes as some relief following the graveyard lullabies of the opening tracks. Scott is not yet checking the studio clock, and while he seems detached in the verses, the muscular chorus buoys him up and has him singing with an old-school, clear-eyed conviction.

'Maria Bethania' (Veloso) was one of the last tracks recorded. It is among the oddest and most eccentric of Scott's career. He sings in a cod West Indian accent above a dry, rubbery groove, the sound of a man past caring. The pitching on the chorus is among his worst recorded. And yet the quality of the song, the unique parched rhythm, and the sumptuous, flighty string arrangement mark this above such expertly-executed fluff as 'That Night' or 'This Way Mary'.

Randy Newman's 'Cowboy' sounds like the morning after the night before. Scott atones for sins against himself, singing to comfort himself: a yearning, low-slung, brooding meditation that hints at what could have been. The arrangement and choice of song suggest that Engel actually had some input during its recording. The vocal sounds sombre and exhausted, resigned beyond defeat.

'When You Get Right Down To It' is the sound of BBC Radio 2 circa 1973: that is, polite, tranquillised, tasteful, and toothless. Scott is going through the motions, but as ever there are always surprising moments: the lovely nylon-stringed guitar break and Scott's playful ad-libbing in the outro.

Scott had first covered singer-songwriter David Gates's work less than a decade earlier – which must have seemed a lifetime ago – when he and John recorded 'The Girl I Lost In The Rain'. Of the many versions of Gates's classic 'If', Scott's take for *Any Day Now* here is among the most accomplished and expensive sounding. Scott is convinced by the melody and committed to the lyrics. The result is a performance of opaque purity.

Bill Withers's 'Ain't No Sunshine' sees the kitty-hipped Scott get raunchy to little effect, his heavy voice exaggerating the darker tones of the song. 'The Me I Never Knew' (Black–Berry) was issued as a single, with Scott making a television appearance to promote it. Prime 1973 MOR, it has aged well. Everything about Scott the crooner is geared toward such material, with the tempo and key deliciously matching his natural singing range.

Another Jimmy Webb number follows, 'If Ships Were Made To Sail'. The backing of just strings and piano is immaculate. Scott sings: "If I could go / To Alpha Centurai / There I would be / A-livin' there." However, as lovely as it is, the song fails to take off.

'We Could Be Flying' (Colombia–Williams) is one of three arrangements on the album by Robert Cornford. It starts promisingly, with atonal, abrasive strings but soon settles into its middle-of-the-road uniform. As ever, Scott wears it well, but it's an aptly inconclusive finale, both for the album and his recording contract with Philips.

Scott did whatever promotion could be scrounged, but, as the album struggled even to flounder, executives at Philips seriously considered the merits of taking up another option on Scott's contract.

A mutual disillusionment had set in, and it is reasonable to speculate that at this point both parties were hoping for a clean break. Any consideration now given to the shared future of Scott and Philips was merely a case of going through the motions.

While the accountants did their sums, a welcome distraction surfaced for Scott when John Maus, refreshed from months of casual globetrotting, arrived for a brief stop off in London. Following a phone call to Scott and a shared drink or three, the two 'brothers' temporarily teamed up again, Scott overseeing the recording of demos in the hope of getting John a new deal.

"They were supposed to do something – an album for John – for the Green Mountain label," remembers Dave Shrimpton of Philips. "But, typically, they couldn't get it together." The meeting had been an agreeable one, however, and the two kept in touch.

Leaving Scott in London, John sought out a more famous mentor for his project. "At that time I was friendly with Bill Wyman, and he wanted to get into record production. I wrote a couple of rock songs and Bill recorded them. ... He and the Stones were living in France, so I moved to France to work with Bill. It was a big learning experience for him and me."

In the end, only a single emerged from the latest Maus venture, 'Good Days'/'Midnight Morning'. Promisingly, both were Maus originals, brooding mid-tempoed rockers, the latter boasting a particularly demonic swagger. Without proper distribution, a promotional disc was leaked out in America, circulating exclusively among selected radio stations. It failed to elicit any serious response, and Maus left France for California, leaving Engel to an MOR limbo in London.

Looking back on the previous few years, John was not so much embittered as plainly realistic. "I got very fed up. I finally got rid of that chap who was looking after me. I had decided that the management thing was all wrong. But a lot of damage had already been done. So I decided that the best thing I could do at that point was not do anything. I had lost my management, dumped the record company, dumped everything, and I almost had to decide what it was

I was going to do. If I was gonna have a solo career of any nature." On his aborted recording sessions with Engel and Wyman, he commented: "I did a lot of experimental work in the studio. And [I] spent a couple of years getting into writing songs and not particularly doing anything with them, but just going through the exercise of sitting down and trying to write original pieces and things. Re-learning to play my instrument. I got past the point of panicking and rushing into things."

As John recuperated in the Californian sunshine, Scott accepted the latest break back in rainy London. Despite a few routine television appearances, it became very quickly clear that *Any Day Now* would not be re-lighting any fires. Without ceremony, Philips and Franz let Scott go. Five years earlier, this would have been considered unthinkable, but now, in 1973 and with no more distance left to run, the parting came as a relief.

Semel was wordly enough to expect such an eventuality, and Scott's manager immediately scouted for another deal, one that would allow the singer the freedom and means in which to record his own songs.

With a manager and a family to feed, and between record deals, Scott picked up a repeat prescription for Valium and returned to the working-men's clubs of the north of England: quick cash for short, excruciating sets. During shows at Blighty's in Bolton and at Manchester's Talk Of The North that August, a well-lubricated Scott was unusually effusive and talkative, joshing with both audience and band and good-naturedly referring to his old group as "The Walker Mothers".

He opened with a disarming: "I hope you're well loaded tonight. You've got to be to watch this show!" Scott sank a champagne glass-full of Scotch and roared into 'Amsterdam'. The reaction from hardcore fans present was, as ever, ecstatic. Between numbers, a still youthful-looking Scott would request a Bogart impression of his bandleader and, depending on the audience, make a good-humoured reference to the noise of the less attentive diners. Despite occasional hints of tetchiness and the rebellious touch of wearing open-toed sandals with a denim leisure-suit in a venue that demanded a suit and tie of its clientele, Scott was on his best behaviour, delivering his middle-of-the-road balladry with charm and grace.

As for the material, if he was at all perturbed at running through a set that contained no originals, he didn't show it. Tanned and looking fitter than ever, despite his intake of Scotch, he sailed professionally through an intimate concert that included Paul McCartney's 'The Long And Winding Road', an aching 'Speak Softly Love', and a jubilantly received 'Make It Easy On Yourself'. Pausing to chat with his group members and take gifts from the audience (usually flowers or a bottle of Scotch, or both), the set continued apace: 'Help Me Make It Through The Night', 'Joanna', 'If', 'Stormy', 'If You Go Away', 'Jackie'. While by no means challenging, most of this was quality material. When Scott applied himself, it was as good as cabaret got. The show climaxed gently with his band's favourite, 'The Lady Came From Baltimore'. Encores were rare, though. Once the job was done and Semel had picked up the fee, Scott was gone.

Some fans still hogged the stage door, if only for a glimpse. Margaret Waterhouse and her husband were among the small gaggle. "We waited round the back where his orange VW Beetle car was parked. Eventually he came out with his manager, got into the driver's seat, and agreed to sign a few autographs. I remember he didn't say much at all and drove away as quickly as he could, almost running over my toes in the process."

By the time the Beetle screeched back into London, it seemed that things were on the up. Semel's negotiations had been successful, and a deal was signed with CBS Records. The personal advance (exclusive of recording costs) was for £15,000, and the deal was that Scott could once again record his own material. It must have seemed almost too good to be true. It was.

Scott: "CBS led me to believe, when I went there, that I'd be able to record my own music. So I signed with them very eagerly with this in mind. But there was nothing in the contract, unfortunately. Then they got this new guy who took over at the time, and he was gonna get a hit for everybody and change everybody around and give everybody a new look. So, when they told me this, this really got to me. Once again, I was in a contract I couldn't get out of, and I couldn't afford to get out of it, y'know? If I'd have gone and sued them, they would have kept me locked up there even longer than they did.

"The best thing for me was to make the records and wait, and get out as soon as I could, which I did. You know: just do the two records and leave. But that was the worst thing that happened to me. That really did hurt me, because I thought I was actually running into something really new."

Other promising initial rumours suggested that Philadelphia soul songwriting and production duo Kenny Gamble and Leon Huff would be producing Scott's CBS debut. The idea of a team responsible for hits by The O'Jays and Lou Rawls doing their thang on Scott Walker during this period is a seductive one but, ultimately it wasn't to be. The proposal fizzled out and the 'new Johnny Franz' in Scott's life would be up-and-coming producer and arranger Del Newman.

New man was an experienced engineer who had worked with Cat Stevens, Petula Clark, and The Faces and was now making inroads into production. He was a deeper-than-average record producer, with particular personal philosophies informing a masterful studio technique. He immediately connected with Scott, who, once again, began to work with his producer in an atmosphere of mutual respect. Newman's engineer of choice was Richard Dodd, who remembers: "Del was very much an artist producer, rather than an out-and-out going-for-the-commercial-jugular producer. He was trying to make the record that the artist would want."

Despite the recent betrayal by CBS, Scott soldiered on. Once committed to a recording, the professional in him took over and he would simply approach the job as well as he could. He kept any feelings of reticence or bitterness resolutely in check. No one who worked with him on the album encountered anything but an easygoing professionalism, and he did not bemoan the circumstances that had brought him to such a project.

Perhaps in an effort to encroach on Scott's long-neglected American market, it had been decided that the album, which would eventually be entitled *Stretch*, would lean toward outlaw country music, using songs predominately by writers who shared his Midwest roots (although Scott had left the area at age seven). The musicians included the English pedal-steel guitarist B.J. Cole. "We recorded *Stretch* and *We Had It All* at Nova studios near Marble Arch," says Cole. "He was very, very into country at that time. He was very ahead of his time, being into Billy Joe Shaver and people like that.

"I always got the feeling that he was trying to blaze a trail for that kind of music when nobody else was interested in it. To do an album of renegade country in an era when it's not popular – it'd be like him doing an album of doo-wop today. He was going against the grain back then."

According to Scott, this was not quite the case. "They wanted something for the American market," said the battle-weary singer. "I mean, everybody was recording ... they were getting Sinatra and people to do country music in those days. Everybody was having a shot at country music. It was a 70s nightmare."

Either way, Scott now found himself a walking anachronism: an unpopular pop singer. As committed as Scott was to his instrument, his voice, it seems that, understandably, he was now not nearly as interested in the production as he had been at his peak with Franz and Oliff. Coincidentally, the Philips studios were at this time just a short walk from Nova, but the distance between past and present was immeasurable.

During his time with CBS, Scott would at least be able to forfeit the cabaret ticket and could earn good money by doing the one thing that everyone seemed to want of him: sing. And so, for CBS, more than ever before, Scott Walker would be a singer and nothing else. Throughout the month it took to record his debut CBS album, Scott Walker would broach no new studio philosophy, take no new sonic risks, and advance no personal artistic boundaries. He would be little more than the lead singer of an exquisitely produced and supremely accomplished session band, singing excellent songs beautifully.

While the resources available were not as massive as they had been back in the day, they were still far from frugal, as Dodd confirms. "Del would only record string sections with 32 to 36 players, so while it was by no means a big-budget album, it was certainly not a low-budget record. This was the opposite of how Scott would have recorded at Philips. We'd record the basic tracks with the band and then overdub the orchestra and the sweeteners – you know, B.J. Cole and stuff."

Although this was the 70s, the band was a hired one, and each musician clocked in like any other nine-to-fiver in London at that time, give or take an hour. Cole: "The session would start at ten, break at one. Come back and finish from two 'til five. All the players together. Live. That was the way it was done, and an awful lot got done in that time. Scott did rough vocals while we were playing, but he re-did them afterwards. There would be chord charts. We wouldn't have heard demos. Strings were put on separately."

Scott would join in as a band member during the early stages, but ultimately his role was as interpretive vocalist only. "Scott never played on the records," confirms Dodd. "But I'd see him with a guitar ... though never the bass. We'd be outlining something and Scott would play, so we could work out harmonies or whatever. Scott didn't seem a stranger to a guitar."

For Cole, then in the earlier stages of a successful career as a session player, the Scott gig was a perfectly amiable experience. "It took us about a week to do the basic tracks. We didn't socialise after the sessions, but he was perfectly charming to talk to. He seemed quite open. He obviously had a good working relationship with Del. As far as the musicians were concerned, it was very much a boss–employee type of situation. You'd go in and do the job and leave. No booze around that I saw. It was a very organised set-up. It wasn't like the Stones would have recorded. They were the exception, they were breaking the rules. And Scott wasn't breaking the rules at that time in terms of recording sessions."

The penultimate 'instrument' to be added was Scott's final vocal takes. (Strings came last.) Finally free of the archaic Musicians Union – a new ruling had allowed overdubbing some years before – the singer could now afford to take his time over the job. Other factors had not changed, and he still preferred to work in a climate as close to solitude as possible.

Richard Dodd: "Scott would do his vocals standing up, but I would always put a stool there, because Scott would have a table, a makeshift table, for his 'voice lubricant'. The bottle of Scotch – Old Grand-Dad [actually bourbon] – was ever-present, but I don't remember him gulping it down. I think it was more of a prop and a crutch than it was an eye-opener. I think he was just subtly altering his state of mind with it, maybe.

"Scott was static when he recorded a vocal. I don't remember him doing any actions or facial expressions other than what was required just to get the sound down. I think he was very static ... all his emotion and all his intent came from his voice.

"Recording-wise, if he liked what he heard – and he left that to us – then it was fine. He'd have opinions about reverb on the vocal or not. His strongest opinion would be on ... we'd actually re-record lines, because he'd hear too much of his breathing, regardless of how well he'd sung it. He'd sing it again.

"To coin a Del Newman phrase, Scott knew about getting 'the sound of the sound'. Partly the breathing thing, partly the sibilance thing ... he actually listened to records and to recordings, not just to the music: the whole package.

"We would have subdued lighting when we did the vocals, but not dark. The songs we'd start with first were the ones that he knew suited his voice type or ones he hadn't attempted to sing, and he would use the time to warm up. He seemed pretty capable of singing whatever he wanted whenever he wanted to."

Unlike so many of his peers and fellow musicians at this time, Scott most certainly did not come to work to party. His aesthetic, albeit stabilised by the ever-present bottle of Old Grand-Dad, was more monastic than most, mixing a heavy work ethic with the indulgence of his drinking. But he was there to work, and that alone, as Dodd testifies. "The studio was a closed set to anyone not involved in the making of the record. There were no blonde dolly birds about; no friends visited. The only person I remember popping in was Scott's friend from the [London record shop] Record & Tape Exchange. Scott was a big collector of show tunes, soundtracks from theatre, and stuff like that. All on vinyl. He'd always be talking to a friend about trying to track down some rare record or something ... even then he was a big fan of vinyl."

The singer would then at least be able to appreciate his next record on a purely aesthetic level, if nothing else. CBS prepared for yet another unwanted musical offering, as far as Scott was concerned. But at the same time a far weirder mutant Walker offspring was taking its first lurching steps somewhere in the depths of rural England. Using a borrowed Berkshire mansion as a lab, John was attempting to resurrect the ghost of his recent past.

The *Reading Evening Post* reported: "Hidden away in a small room at the South Hill Park Art Centre, Bracknell, the old sound of The Walker Brothers has been brought out, dusted, and developed over the past weeks, ready to be launched again on the pop world. But although the sound may be very much the same, all but one of the faces are not."

Just as with Scott being dropped by Philips, The New Walker Brothers was something that would have been unthinkable five years previously. Backed by Steve Gilbert on drums, Dave Lingard on guitar, Mike Keeley on bass, and Jon Turner on keyboards, John's 'new Scott' was 30-year-old Irish-born singer Jimmy Wilson. Although almost a full 12 inches shorter than either John or Scott, Wilson, a regular on the northern club circuit, possessed a full, rich baritone and was cute, in a refined, Bay City Rollers kind of way.

John was, as ever, a man with a plan, and that plan was to get the group in shape with a nationwide tour before decamping to Bill Wyman's recording studio in France.

Publicly, John's reasonings behind this bold move sounded typically vapid. "I thought it would be nice if we had another band with a similar sound, and what we have now is what I believe The Walker Brothers would have developed into, only more interesting."

Compared to their lead singer, neither John nor Gary had truly used the Walker Brothers' success to build and grow from, at least musically, although John had managed beautiful moments of reaching. Until 1970, Scott had obviously made a huge progression in every sense. So perhaps what John meant by his nebulous statement was that The New Walker Brothers did indeed sound how the original Walker Brothers would have sounded by 1973, if they hadn't split. And if, that is, Scott Walker had never been a member.

The new group was a highly proficient pub band, but they couldn't possibly compare to their namesake. And that surely wasn't the point. John was an occasionally exceptional writer, and rarely sounded better than when singing his own melodies and lyrics, but from day one he had ultimately lacked focus and direction as a singer-songwriter. Perhaps aware of this inherent weakness, he had above all else chosen the path of entertainer.

With a set consisting of predictable standards like 'I Believe In You', 'You Are The Sunshine Of My Life', 'If', and 'Oh No, Not My Baby' as well as the two Walker Number Ones, The New Walker Brothers and their tour of decent, down-to-earth regional cabaret clubs (revealingly, London was not included) were true to Maus's ideal. Occasional encores included the brooding storm-in-a-brandy-glass of the Maus-penned 'Midnight Morning', but ultimately, The New Walker Brothers was less a musical concern and more a means of bringing home if not even the bacon, then at least a little Spam.

Perhaps if the group had acquired a record deal, we would today have one of the more intriguing entries in the Walkers discography. But after 18 months, with little media interest outside Scotland, the band split. Although such an uneventful 18 months is easily reduced to a few lines in a biography, to live this year and a half would have been exhausting and ultimately and emphatically disillusioning. And yet, even then, with balls seemingly cast from pig iron, a punch-drunk Maus staggered on.

Battered by indifference and coshed by kismet, he nevertheless managed to lasso members of his immediate family toward yet another venture. Sister Judy and cousin Terry would prop up brother John through three final, poorly-attended one-night stands, until, stupefied, Maus returned once again to the bosom of Los Angeles. With not even enough energy or inspiration left to prefix this last incarnation with the word 'The', John Judy & Terry allowed nature to take its merciful course and pulled the plug on the New Walker Band in late 1974.

Walkers fan Robin Edwards recalls: "I was living just outside of Birmingham, and I remember seeing an advert in the local rag that said 'The New Walker Brothers'. I thought, bloody hell, The Walker Brothers are back together. I phoned the booking office and said, 'Is this Scott Walker and John Walker?' and the girl laughed and said, 'No, it's just John with his new group.' And I didn't go."

Back in the land of the living, Scott's CBS album debut, *Stretch*, was released. The handsome-bastard offspring of a deal that had promised so much more came out in the November of 1973. It as apparently titled after one of the various nicknames that Scott was known by back in LA. The cover image, by a friend, the photographer Michael Joseph, is at distinct odds with the content. The beaming Scott, denim-clad, in aviator shades, and reaching for the sky like a soused superman, seems far removed from the bourbon-imbued songs within.

The press release that came with promotional copies quoted at length the singer's enthusiasm for the project, in particular praising the Zen touch of Del Newman. Dubiously, Scott also confessed: "This is the first album where I can listen to most of it and say I really did my best on that. That's what's so good about it."

Reviews mirrored the quality of the album: above average, but nothing to shout about. No post-Philips brave new world was due to dawn. An import single of 'A Woman Left Lonely' half-heartedly appeared in some London shops, but like the album that had spawned it, they would soon disappear.

On the opener, 'Sunshine' (Newbury), Scott harmonises flawlessly with himself, evoking the ghost of dearly-departed brother John. The band begin, cruise, and fade out, with little happening in between besides the fluid, golden loops of B.J. Cole's pedal steel. The singer sounds relaxed and fluent, betraying the side effects of any alcohol he may have consumed.

Richard Dodd: "He didn't look like a drinker ... you wouldn't have pegged him as a drinker. He looked fit to me. He was tall, blond, and good-looking."

Scott doesn't sing 'Just One Smile' so much as testify in a low, oaken croon. Most versions of this Randy Newman song concentrate on the redemptive aspects of the chorus. Scott focuses on the sadness in the verses, illuminating the melancholy grain within. The strings sigh around him as Del Newman makes sublime use of space and silence.

'A Woman Left Lonely' (Oldham–Penn) is one of the most dynamic pieces on the record, and it was released as a single. It has a soaring chorus that nevertheless fails to fly, partly dragged down by the stodgy rhythm section.

At the time, three versions of the classic 'No Easy Way Down' (Goffin–King) had already been made popular, by Carole King, Jackie DeShannon, and Dusty Springfield. Scott acquits himself superbly, but if anything he sounds almost too believable, singing such lines as "When each road you take / Is one more mistake" with the voice of a man adrift, leaving the listener disconcerted. This is blooded heartbreak in MOR clothing.

Richard Dodd: "His goal as far as covering stuff was to do a 'responsible' version. He didn't want to damage the song in any way. He was working on songs that he had chosen because he liked them. So he wanted to interpret them in such a way that he wouldn't do the song any injustice. You know: some artists have a little trick, and just by imposing that trick or their 'signature' on a song would make it theirs. I don't think that was Scott's thing. I think he was trying to find 'the other way' of doing it great."

'That's How I Got To Memphis' (T.T. Hall) is a travelogue that goes nowhere, a jaunty ditty with Scott lapsing into his countrified twang against Cole's pedal steel and dobro.

Although he was never naturally drawn to such white-bread funk, on 'Use Me' (Withers), Scott does seem to revel in the precise rhythms and risqué lyrics. It is presumably session percussionist Ray Cooper who provides the handclaps. 'Frisco Depot' (Newbury) is the prettier country cousin of 'That's How I Got To Memphis'. Although Del Newman's arrangement is as tasteful as ever, the overall effect is mawkish and the piece sounds incomplete.

One of the few true originals of the set, possibly written by

Newman specifically for Scott, 'Someone Who Cared' is the most Scott-sounding song to appear since 'Cowboy', with its tearful piano and cinematic strings billowing beneath a sad-eyed, watery vocal. An album full of such collaboration would have surely been a treasure.

The three final pieces – 'Where Does Brown Begin' (Webb), 'Where Love Has Died' (Owen), and 'I'll Be Home' (Newman) – are all quietly lovely, each with its own merits: the warm string bass on Jimmy Webb's 'Where Does Brown Begin'; the broken baritone of Scott's voice on 'Where Love Has Died'; the lush, empty space of Randy Newman's 'I'll Be Home'.

But what is ultimately missing from the record is Scott himself. His first four solo albums had all contained a wealth of differing material: originals and covers. But the records worked as a whole because they were the tangible proof of a man's quest. *Scott 1* to *Scott 4*, however flawed, were trophies.

Circumstance had conspired against Scott the writer to the extent that he was forced to absent himself from his work. Work that paid him well. As such, no amount of fine material, sympathetic arrangements, or great players could ever cover up that which was at the heart of all his recent work: a void.

In the few UK interviews Scott gave to promote the album, he complained astringently that enough material had been recorded at the time of the *Stretch* sessions to warrant a superior and more truly countrified sequel, but CBS, lacking faith, were refusing to release it. Semel did harangue label boss Maurice Oberstein, but neither party could come to an agreement on either a tracklisting for this follow up or an album of Engel originals. As for the latter, the notion of another record like *'Til The Band Comes In* was mooted, but Engel maintained that if he couldn't write the entire album, then he'd rather do just another album of covers.

Another ineffectual compromise was reached. Nova and Del Newman were booked again, and the plan was to record a batch of slightly more middle of the road country songs, to add balance to the arsenal of renegade country material already in the can. Once again, aware more than ever of his dwindling commercial stock, Scott took on the job with good humour and grace. Richard Dodd was back engineering the new sessions and was just as aware as anyone of Scott's shrunken status. "By then, Scott was a has-been as far as the music business in London was concerned. He wasn't a Walker Brother any more. He was just Scott Walker trying to do his solo thing, and he didn't seem to have much interest from the industry."

In the world outside of Nova studios, David Bowie was beginning to fulfil the role once cast to Scott almost a decade previously. The template of frail, pale boy with a manly virile voice was as effective as ever in slaying the hearts of pretty, hormone-happy teenage girls everywhere. Although he could never channel the star-crossed innocence of his forerunner, Bowie had been born just late enough to disentangle himself from the 50s undertow that had so stilted the boy Engel's growth. As such, he would enjoy and successfully utilise the kind of artistic carte blanche for which Scott had fought so painfully.

The public pandemonium once witnessed at Walker gigs had been passed down to the Walkers via Sinatra, Elvis, and The Beatles, and was now manifest at Bay City Rollers concerts. The Scott Walker of 1974, who sat in a dimmed studio supping Scotch and crooning country ballads, was 33 years old. But as far as the pop market was concerned, he may as well have been as old as Satchmo.

Despite such strange weather, Scott knew how to do his job, and he did not bring his personal problems into the workplace. While occasionally sentimental, he was not nostalgic, as Dodd noticed. "The past would only ever come up as a little respite or in conversation between [Scott] and Del. I'd never instigate any questions like that.

"He seemed to have it all, but he wasn't happy. Although he wasn't at the top of his game, he looked great, had a family, and a regular gig with good players. He would be very loose talking about show tunes and old vinyl recordings, but if it came anywhere near to personal things, or somebody else talking about themselves, he wouldn't necessarily perpetuate the conversation by talking about himself. He was very professional."

Professionals also surrounded Scott. As such, even his public mistakes (as he saw them) would retain a precise standard of musicianship, rendering them exceedingly listenable on a cosmetic level. While the album sessions motored on, some profound questions arose among his supporting cast – questions regarding the project. Although these were never voiced at the time, they now appear obvious.

"The strangest thing of all was that those songs were very much American songs ... so why didn't he do it in America?" muses Dodd. "It would have been much better. I don't know why he chose to do Americana-type country in London. Musically, to choose those songs and do them in England is just strange. The kind of player you had in the UK would have the kind of life which is ten 'til one, two 'til five, and so on. And you're asking them to play something casual, laidback, and stoned ... it doesn't work, you know? Not as well as if you've got someone who is laidback, casual, and stoned."

B.J. Cole agrees. "If he had wanted to do an authentic sounding outlaw country album, he should have gone to Nashville. British musicians are different to Nashville players."

Yet it is perhaps this very skewed approach that lends the albums some longevity. They sound slightly weird, perverse, wrong. Dodd: "If you think they sound a bit warped, well ... I can now see Scott smiling where he can hear some of the things we're talking about, and he's liking that 'warped' thing. He is warped! And I think he got off on that, in a way. By the time Del had finished producing and arranging it, it worked. The nice thing about that is that it doesn't fully work, so you get something different. So those records aren't strictly authentic country. So it's interesting and it's acceptable, I think."

Scott was aware of the paradox but was able to find relief in any situation. 'I was recording it here – recording country musicians here. It was totally absurd. But at the time I thought, well, you could be recording standards, it's not as bad as that.'

They completed backing tracks as quickly and slickly as ever. When it came to Scott's part, Dodd now knew what to expect. "Two things about Scott: one, he didn't like anyone to be able to hear him breathe on a record. If you listen to some records, you'll hear that some people use the sound of their breath for emotional effect. Scott would go to great lengths with me to not hear his breath. On the other hand, he would encourage sibilance. He loved it. It's one of those things he's attached to records that he loves and he's associated the anomaly with the reality of the medium ... whatever, he just, loved it. He'd say, 'Yeah, I want sibilance on my records. And no breath.' He was a stand-out guy and the opposite of everybody else."

Scott and Semel's tenure with CBS had been distorted from the start. Scott was quoted in the meagre press surrounding both albums, complaining that "CBS rode shotgun on my ass" throughout work on both albums. No one but the dwindling hardcore of fans had been interested in *Stretch* and even fewer were concerned with the sequel, *We Had It All*, or its lost single, 'Delta Dawn'.

We Had It All came out in August 1974 to universal indifference. The album sleeve used photographs from the original Michael Joseph sessions, and they were apt. Scott's expression of terminal disappointment spoke for all concerned.

On 'Low Down Freedom' (Shaver), Scott sings from the bottom of his bottle of Old Grand-Dad, leaning against the rail of some honky-tonk bar in his mind. The rock drums are at odds with the authentic country vibe.

'We Had It All' (Fritts–Seals) is another morose, haunting standard that would have fitted easily on *Stretch*.

'Black Rose' and 'Ride Me Down Easy' (both by Billy Joe Shaver, the latter also recorded by Waylon Jennings and David Allen Coe) are much darker than anything Scott had recorded with Del Newman thus far. By now, he sounds like an authentically broken cowpoke, crooning in a cracked and stained mumble about Satan and yesterday's wine.

'You're Young And You'll Forget' (Reed) is another paean to self-loathing, albeit set to a refreshingly original melody and line-dancing rhythm. 'The House Song' (Bannard–Stookey) and 'Whatever Happened To Saturday Night' (The Eagles) both brew on the morbid side of moribund and ache with the sound of abandoned homes and empty beds.

'Sundown' (Lightfoot) is one of the most vital songs on the record, with Scott's harmony sounding uncannily like John. Scott would have ably covered Gordon Lightfoot's classic 'If You Could Read My Mind'. The string arrangement here is luscious.

Richard Dodd: "'Sundown' was a great one. Del was responsible for all those string arrangements. Beautiful. One of his signatures was the string codas."

By the end of his tenure with CBS, Scott was inhabiting his 'outlaw country' persona utterly. He had never sounded so American. In particular, on 'Old Five And Dimers Like Me' (Shaver), the man once associated with the pinnacles of European culture was now sounding like a used-car salesman awaiting bail. The final track, 'Delta Dawn' (Harvey–Collins, a US Number One for Helen Reddy), popped and swaggered, but to little avail. The new beginning at CBS had turned out to be no more than a torturous extension of the fag-end of the Philips days.

After seven successive flop albums, Scott may have assumed the game was up. There seemed to be no particular logic attached to his successes and failures. The Walkers had mixed standards and originals. His first three solo albums had been huge, and these consisted mainly of challenging arrangements of chanson songs. Since the commercial hiccup of *Scott 4*, he had given in to overbearing circumstances and did as his paymasters asked. He had tried to sell out – but ultimately, no one was buying.

Years later he would gain some perspective on it all. "The funny thing is, whenever I've made a record that I haven't written myself – except for The Walker Brothers – I've never had any kind of success from it at all. Not critical success. Not artistic success. Not financial success. Never anything. Because you can hear ... when you hear me singing it ... it doesn't register any kind of feeling. It's just dead, you know? It's just nothing."

Even his colleagues didn't get it. B.J. Cole: "I find his attitude a little indulgent. He could sing the Yellow Pages and it would sound fantastic. How someone with such a fantastic, melodious voice can be so picky over what he chooses to sing and why it matters so much. If he'd waited another three or four years, then outlaw country was starting to become quite trendy, with Waylon Jennings and Willie

Nelson, and all those people doing it. I mean, he didn't include any Gram Parsons material on those records, because it was meant to be more obscure than that. It wasn't the most obvious music to be doing. No other reason for doing it, really, unless somebody else had that idea and was using him to do it."

Scott had been miscast. He had all the outward attributes of a legendary pop singer: the voice, the looks, the style. And yet it just wasn't working. As 1975 approached, Scott must have felt very far away from the man he was meant to be. A love of European cinema and Frankie Lymon had brought him all the way here for ... what? He obviously had something, but what it was, what it meant, and how it should be used – this he had yet to work out. Others noticed this, too.

Richard Dodd: "He was no flash in the pan or anything, or a lucky-just-to-be-there sort of person. He had a lot of talent and a lot of control, which is what makes an artist apart from others. Even though he had drinking habits and a lifestyle that I knew very little about, and was certainly not mine and not typical. Some weird things going, but ... he was just very different. Not at all what I expected from an international pop star."

CHAPTER 14

NO REGRETS

It's all down to me, basically. All those wasted years.

Scott Walker (2005)

By early 1975, as the final pre-punk year dawned, the Walkers were all washed up. The energy and impetus of their glory days – days amounting only to a year back in the mid 60s – were well and truly spent. The three very different Southern Californians had brought a strange and futuristically flashy beauty to the UK pop scene of 1966, the effects of which had been total at that time. But, nine years later, what remained of this sudden deep impact was negligible.

Eventually returning to London, Gary, Scott, and John were, professionally speaking, in something of a vacuum. The aftershock of their break-up had long ago run into silence and yet it was far too soon for the Walkers myth to take effect. By the mid 70s, their legacy was merely bleached tumbleweed, idling in the space left by a vaporised teardrop. The golden image and ornately huge sound was now down to the echo of an echo, and their flash glam registered only vaguely in the static created by Ziggy Stardust and Roxy Music.

On returning to the scene of their greatest victory, the trio initially moved in a silence and anonymity that was too total even for Scott. London had forgotten that Walker summer of '66 and moved on. Now was as good a time as ever to reform.

Dick Leahy, ex-employee of Philips, was now making his own way in an industry where the idea of a Walker Brothers reunion seemed little more than a curious novelty. "You'd always hear comments like, 'Why isn't Scott Walker making great records?'," recalls Leahy, a long-time admirer of Scott's voice. "But I think the perception was a bit quizzical as to them getting back together. Visually, it was quite a strange thing. To have Gary involved. Scott and John – yes, that looked good – but I don't think there was much of a perception other than they used to make great records."

The hip young Turks at *Melody Maker* and *NME* would greet the news of the forthcoming reformation with a deathly sneer, and while the Brothers Walker still had the respect of many in the recording industry, they were far from hot property. As solo artists, each had taken his own particular amount of time to exhaust the benefit of doubt. Up until the last signing – Gary's one-off single deal with United Artists in late 1974, an ingeniously stupid cover of The Easybeats' 'Hello! How Are You!' – each record company managing director must have had outside odds on some fluky second-wind, some chart-topping return, pop Lazarus-style. These guys after all, had been as big as The Beatles for a while.

As John would point out, this didn't always work in their favour. "The Walker Brothers tag really stuck. It stuck on Scott, it stuck on me, it stuck on ... Gary. You got stuck into the thing where, if you wanted to do something different, other than these ginormous ballads, these Phil Spector things ... . If you went to a record company and said, y'know, you were in The Walker Brothers, then that was what they wanted to produce. And you couldn't produce that without The Walker Brothers. You couldn't do it with one of 'em. You had to have the group."

Maus had had plenty of time to consider such dilemmas. Prior to their eventual return, he had been bummed out in Brentwood, West

Hollywood, on the sad side of a second marriage. John had all but given up on music, shortly after it had seemed to give up on him. His ill-fated round of the UK cabaret circuit as The New Walker Brothers looked like his last roll of the dice, and it was a losing throw. John spent most of early 1975 rising at sunset, watching the television through the bottom of a whiskey bottle, and hanging out at the local beach and bars. It was while flipping through the gameshows and reruns that fate took a hand.

"*Deadlier Than The Male* came on the TV," testified Maus. "We sang the theme for that movie. I was listening to that, and I went, 'Well, that's really very good.' I thought, 'Damn! Well, maybe I'll give Scott a call and see what he's up to.' I called him up, and he wasn't really doing a whole lot of anything, and neither was I."

As for Gary, The Rain had run its course, trickling along pop's guttering to return to the great water table of anonymity. "I had trouble with the management and all that," he explained with his usual understatement. "There was a bunch of arguments, and [Maurice King] called me this and I called him that. So I said, 'I'd rather starve,' and he said 'OK.' So I started starving. I went back to America and was doing demos for different people up in Hollywood and all ... then got out of the bands and started working on cars, painting them and fixing them up and all that stuff. And that was about it."

Much to Scott's amusement, Gary had also helped out at his friendly uncle's morgue. "It's a little different, being a mortician in America," Leeds pointed out. "You're making about £4,000 a week. So that didn't bother me at all. I didn't stuff the bodies, no – you run the fluid in and out of them, and you can do the hairstyle and the make-up and stuff like that."

Scott, like John, had also encountered marriage difficulties and was now more or less based in England. Although still managed by Ady Semel, he lacked a record label and a proper address, spending most of his time living at what is now White's Thistle Hotel on London's Edgware Road. Following Maus's transatlantic phone call, the two rendezvous'd in the neutrality of a Hampstead pub. Scott: "John was there drinking. I don't why. John never touches the stuff!

[Laughs] He was there drinking, and so we ran into each other and started to rap. We had seen each other on and off in the course of the eight years, but just briefly. He and I thought it would be interesting to make an album and see what happens. And Gary was in town and we said, 'Well, you know, what's Gary doing?' Gary had phoned me in Denmark to say hi, and I had just come back from Denmark. So we all just got together and just tried to get into a groove with something, you know?"

John: "I said, 'Well, why don't we just get back together and maybe we can try something again; who knows.' We sat down – literally, sat down – and got some guitars and started singing some songs and thought, 'Y'know, it might be kinda fun to have another go and see what happens.'"

Despite the lack of any buzz, it was indisputable that Ady Semel, still very much in the picture, was now managing what had been one of the biggest groups of the 60s. As solo artists, Scott, John, and Gary had nine flop albums between them. As The Walker Brothers, their last album had hit Number Six and sold in its millions.

Still, the sunny spring of 1967 must have felt like an awfully long time ago, especially in terms of cashflow. So, perhaps to avoid the lengthy delays and negotiations of a bidding war, Semel followed his clients' wishes and signed quickly to a new UK independent label, GTO records, founded by former Philips–Fontana employee and long-time Scott admirer, Dick Leahy. He signed the group almost immediately. "I think it was Gary who phoned me," says Leahy. "And then there was a meet, with Ady Semel. I vaguely knew him from his Philips days. Semel was a very unusual man, very hard to call. It occurred to me that Scott would always be recording from time to time, but it surprised me that they were getting back together. My conclusion was that the main reason was financial. I don't think it was creative. Why GTO and not RCA? I think Scott was seen to be difficult creatively. I don't think anyone found him difficult as a person; I didn't. Or maybe they just didn't want to go with a big company?"

They signed hastily, for a personal advance of £20,000 (cash) to be split between John, Scott, Gary, Ady, and the taxman. A further

£40,000 was budgeted for the recording, processing, manufacture, and marketing of the album. The GTO operation was a much more relaxed and informal set-up than the Walkers had been used to, with artists from the label often hanging out at the offices.

Although now their 'boss', Leahy was at heart a fan. "When they came into the office, it was great. It was The Walker Brothers! They looked a bit older, but not much. They looked great. Having worked at Philips and Bell Records, we [now] did business as the antithesis to how Philips would have done it. Musicians would drop in, managers, radio people."

Gary, always the most sociable Walker, would pop in more than most. "When I walked in there, the first one I met was [Rod [Temperton] from [GTO stablemates] Heatwave. Oh, and Billy Ocean was there. He came running up and went right past me and went straight to Scott, and was all, 'Oh, wow, you're the best singer in the world.' He really, really liked Scott and all that. Scott didn't know what to say."

Billy's heartfelt reaction was a good sign. The Walkers were loved by many. They always had been. The group and their potential audience just needed to be reminded, that's all. Leahy could sense this. "There was now a bit of a buzz, with me having come out of a pop label. There was some speculation about, 'Well, a new pop label and The Walker Brothers?' There was quite a bit of excitement about it. And I guess it must have felt a bit, for them, 'Well, we're gonna go back to how it was in the old days.' Which wasn't quite how it worked out."

The next step was to set up a Walker HQ. Their choice was hardly picked for its anonymity, as old touring buddy Dave Dee attests. "I was sat in my favourite restaurant on the King's Road, having some lasagne or whatever it was, and I look up and in walked The Walker Brothers. I couldn't believe it. They looked great: a bit older, but not much. Turns out they were all living together upstairs."

The family were reunited once more and, thanks to GTO, on a comfortable retainer of £400 a month each. Monkees-style, all three moved into a flat above Dave Dee's favourite diner, a trendy bistro at 517 New Kings Road. Gary added to the sitcom scenario by setting up

THE IMPOSSIBLE DREAM

a Lawrence Of Arabia-style tent in the living room. Like old fighters who had retired well before their peak, the legendary Walker trio, all the way from Hollywood, California, began training for their return. What followed was a strict regime – takeaways from the bistro below, heavy drinking, nightclubbing at Tramps, and sunbathing sessions.

Gary: "[Tramps] was a gay restaurant, very expensive and a popular place. Lots of atmosphere and that. A good crowd. Marc Bolan would come in there with Gloria [Jones]. Marc Bolan was brilliant. And we really wanted to meet this guy. And I thought, 'Oh, this is gonna be terrible,' because of the way Scott is, you know: he won't say boo or hello to anybody. And Bolan came over to the table and started talking and got this saucer and started singing a song.

"And we became really good friends. We went around his house [25 Holmead Road, Fulham] to play, and he had drums and everything, and we did this for an hour, two hours. I always wondered if he'd sneakily recorded this and we didn't know about it. And he was really shocked that we could play! We were playing all this blues stuff. This was a real night-and-day type of person, from the way you saw him and the way he was. And he was really funny and really great. He wanted us to do his television show, but he had that crash and that was it." Bolan died in a car crash in August 1977.

They set up a makeshift studio on the top floor of number 517, where John and Scott, facing each other with acoustic guitars, would routine potential material. As the time of recording approached, their mornings would be dominated by extended trips to the record store. These shopping sprees were part of Scott and Gary's unpretentious approach to A&R-ing their next album. They would simply buy in bulk, listen to the lot, and choose those songs they felt would best suit the Walker 'sound'. Anything that struck a personal chord would often find a home in their respective personal collections, and the remainder presumably went to Scott's buddy at the Record & Tape Exchange.

"The songs would be their choice," affirms Leahy, a relatively easygoing label manager. "Scott already had some ideas of the songs he would sing. It did strike me as odd that they would not be doing any original material, but we both wanted to move on at a pace. I couldn't wait and sit around for a couple of years. I probably did ask if he had written anything, because it's my nature, but he already had songs he wanted to sing, and [that] was what he wanted to do."

Scott, while seemingly unconcerned at using this opportunity to write and record his own material, was nevertheless as pragmatic as ever. "I just picked up tons of albums; it was the only way of doing it. I suspected that publishers wouldn't be hot-footing it to be getting The Walker Brothers material, because I knew all the cynicism that was going around. I thought, 'Fuck it; I'll get it myself.' I guess we must have bought three, four, even five-hundred LPs. And you know what? I only wanted to keep about four out of the lot."

Despite Scott's recent bad experience with one strain of country music, John was keen that they peruse the more conservative side of the genre. Gary put him straight. "John was obsessed with the country & western thing because of the Kenny Rogers thing. I said, 'That's a different thing, John, that Dolly Parton thing. You don't wanna do that. You've got to be original here, or something, y'know?' Because that's all that counts, and the rest follows, you see."

While as a whole the new deal seemed fresh and positive, for all concerned there were still occasional ghosts to be dealt with. "When we did the deal," states Leahy, "one thing which Scott made perfectly clear was that he was prepared to work, but the one thing he would never do, ever, in his life would be to sing 'The Sun Ain't Gonna Shine Anymore'. Never. He was absolutely clear in his mind that he was never going back to the old Walker Brothers, creatively. And that was a gamble I took.

"They had a terrible hang-up with that song. He would never do it on stage, no matter how much promoters offered him. He was very clear about it. And I don't think it was because they feared being seen as a 'nostalgia act'. It went deeper than that. My take on it, sitting where I am today, is that, in his mind at least, 'The Sun Ain't Gonna Shine Anymore' was the song that stopped him being the musician he could have been."

If this dismissal of one of their greatest musical moments was a bummer for Gary and John, they didn't dwell on it. Friends again, and with the future looking good, who knew? Maybe this time they'd be even bigger than they were back in 1966.

With an arsenal of sturdy if safe tunes ready to lay down, Gary, John, and Scott headed to Marquee studios to record as a unit for the first time in almost a decade, ten years that had proved much more arduous than anyone would have dared predict at the sunny outset. As they entered the Soho studios, the Brothers' relief at getting another chance, of being 'with family' again, was tangible. The new young faces they'd encounter at these new fresh studios could not help but notice the good vibe that hung above the trio like some giant communal halo.

Phil Harding, a fresh-faced assistant engineer not then out of his teens, remembers their entrance well. "The first day the guys arrived, they seemed really up, really happy to be there. I was made aware that it was kind of a 'comeback' album, and they seemed incredibly happy to be together and happy to be in London recording. The day we started the album there was a very 'up' vibe."

Harding's boss was Geoff Calver. The resident head engineer of Marquee studios, he'd been appointed co-producer of the album, with Scott's blessing. He was just as enthused by the good mood but was able to put another more practical spin on the vibe. "I think they'd realised that getting together again was a good thing – and it meant that they could eat again! Although, in this regard, I think Scott was in a slightly different situation to the other two. He'd always been the obvious frontman and had had solo albums as well. He had a reasonable back catalogue."

The artistes themselves knew they had been lucky. John spoke with the verve of someone just out of Alcatraz. "The pop business takes few prisoners, and it's even rarer that the prisoners get released to have another bash."

"It was good to be back together," stated Scott plainly. "We had a lot of laughs. ... Now that all that shit had been wiped away, right, we could talk again, and we were cool and everything was fun. We had a really good time and we really discovered each other again, like for the first time. And, of course, being a lot older we had a lot more tolerance."

Before Scott confirmed Geoff Calver as his right-hand man, he tried again to secure the services of his old mentor, Johnny Franz, as producer. It's odd to imagine the impeccably-tailored, old-school A&R man taking over the desk at the Marquee's hip, new Soho studios, a man who, even in the mid 60s, was affectionately considered to be old-fashioned by his colleagues. It's even harder to imagine the pinstriped, chain-smoking Johnny among the feast of aviator shades, clingy t-shirts, and leisure suits that would turn the inner sleeve of the eventual LP into a fiesta of denim.

At the time, Leahy wasn't aware of the full extent of this backward glance. "Scott certainly routined 'No Regrets' with Johnny. He loved Johnny and the work they had done together at Philips, but as for asking him to produce the album, I don't know."

Dave Shrimpton still held a high position at Philips and witnessed the encounter directly. "When Scott was signed to CBS, he had met up with Johnny Franz again. They got on well. In 1974–5, Scott was having difficulty with a recording. By now he was a producer, not in name but in actuality as far as his own records went, and was apparently having trouble getting the kind of sound he wanted. So there I am sat in my office, opposite Johnny Franz's office – complete with grand piano – and Scott's old PR man at Philips, Paddy, comes in and speaks to Johnny in private.

"Paddy eventually leaves, and Johnny comes into my office, says, 'You're not going to believe this, but Scott wants me to help him produce his album.' Why? 'I think he wants to re-create the old sound again.' He was so pleased."

It was not to be. Still fully employed by Philips, and enjoying 70s success with the popular Peters & Lee, Franz had to decline. As if by default, the producer's role fell solely to Scott. He had no hands-on experience of the latest developments in studio technology – his last substantial hand in production was around the time of *'Til The Band Comes In* back in 1970. So Scott needed Geoff Calver to back him up. Calver was enthused. "I'd been a big Walkers fan when I was a teenager. I'd liked them from the first time I'd seen and heard them. Those shimmering Spector-style productions were tremendous."

From 19-year-old engineer Phil Harding's perspective, the roles were blurred. "Scott coming in as producer was a bit confusing to me, cos back in those days, an engineer like Geoff, who was very good and very experienced, would do sessions where you might have a band, like The Walker Brothers, and you would also have a producer, like, say, Tony Visconti. He, in turn, would have an engineer, like Geoff, and then you'd have an assistant, like myself. And that would be the team. To be honest, it's a little confusing to me as to who the producer was on the album."

Harding's attitude also illustrated the pros and cons that (relatively young) old-timers like The Walker Brothers would face. "I had no prior expectation when I heard they were coming in," says Harding flatly. "At that time, I was into rock music – I mean heavy rock – which the Walkers weren't.

"Because I was young, it was assumed that maybe I wasn't familiar with their hits in the 60s. I think Geoff and some other people might have pre-warned me that, when these guys come in, to be particularly kind of careful as to what I might say. You know, not everyone who would come in during those days were necessarily successful people. I remember quite a particular warning that, 'These are special guys coming in, and we need to give 'em some respect. Some special treatment, Phil!'."

"They were really, really nice in return. Not at all pretentious. Certainly not John or Gary. I remember Scott being incredibly nice but incredibly confident. Gary was particularly shy and unconfident. He was still friendly and outgoing which, to the tea boy, not everyone necessarily is. I don't remember him drumming on the sessions. I remember no hassles at all. Just good vibes and all being very professional and tight."

Having made his decision in the signing, Leahy was happy now for events to take their natural course. "I'd pop into the studio occasionally to see if it was going OK. It felt fine. Scott was very much in charge of what he was doing. A very professionally-run operation."

"We had a lot of fun," adds Calver. "If we'd ever want a break, we'd just put a Lenny Bruce tape on in the studio. They all, particularly

Gary and Scott, would bounce off each other. If you're gonna spend two or three months working together, there has to be some light relief there as well."

Despite boogieing with Bolan, despite this being the rock'n'roll business of the mid 70s, despite the fairly public knowledge of John and Scott's love of booze, it seems that listening to Lenny Bruce routines was as hardcore as it got. "It was a very sober session," insists Harding. "I don't even remember any alcohol going around, let alone anything else. That was one of the differences, say, to the Elton John mixing sessions, where smoking would be going on among the musicians and the staff, quite openly. The only runs I did [for the Walkers] were for Chinese food."

Scott, Gary, and John's youthful looks and slim waistlines were not purely down to lucky genes. "Scott was very interested in a healthy lifestyle," says Calver. "He had a very strict diet and he used a lot of vitamin supplements. So was Gary, to an extent. John was not really on the same wavelength, in that respect, at all. But Gary and Scott were always coming up with some new vitamin supplement that they discovered that was supposed to be good for this, that, or the other. Very health conscious. I think John thought a drink helped his voice somewhat, but the side effects of that aren't very helpful at all."

Once the initial rush of being back in the old gang again had peaked, a mellower, less committed vibe ensued. As the initial buzz receded, Gary would soon find his attention wandering after contributing little more to the recording than some token percussion (salt shakers on the track 'Remember Me'). Although John was contributing more than ever, taking occasional lead vocals and playing acoustic rhythm guitar, he would find himself at something of a loose end once these duties were fulfilled. Rather than watch Scott's intensive labours, he would instead often drift out to the nearest pub. Although the Marquee sessions started with the entire team in attendance, the old roles began to gradually resurface, leaving the bulk of the responsibility with Scott.

As producer, Scott was able to pick and choose his musicians, and one of the first on his 'wants' list was a veteran of the CBS sessions, B.J.

Cole. "This struck me as a much more important recording," says the pedal-steel guitarist. "It was obviously a more commercial venture than the country albums had been. It was less a personal vision of doing something. John and Gary were there [and] it was very much them as a group."

"They weren't always there together," counters Harding. "They didn't all turn up together on each session. Some days only Scott was there."Leahy: "Scott was in charge in the studio. He got together with musicians he used to work with, like Alan Parker. Gary was kind of like a manager, he was sort of the hub of the triangle. He did most of the talking."

As Scott's partner in production, Calver was perhaps best placed to give the truest perspective. "The other two, John and Gary, didn't really do anything. We did try Gary on a couple of vocals, but not really much came of that. Still, John had a great voice. As to how aware they were of the dynamic between them, I think they were just doing what they did and maybe hoped to make a little money from it. I don't think there was much more to it than that, really. John was an easy-going American. Scott was much more European in outlook."

Once the selected songs had been routined and the appropriate musicians booked, the recording process followed a standard pattern. Drums and bass were put down as a foundation, followed by the secondary rhythm tracks: percussion, piano, and guitars. Over this would go the sonic sweeteners: pedal steel, lead guitar. Vocals went on penultimately, with the orchestral overdub completing the recording. The whole thing would then be painstakingly mixed, with further overdubs occasionally added when necessary.

As the recordings came to sound increasingly complete, Leahy's business sense began to reawaken. "I was certainly wondering, 'Would I get a hit out of this?'," he confesses. "It was lovely music, no question, but it was Scott Walker and The Walker Brothers rather than The Walker Brothers. Which was a concern from a marketing point of view, but this would only be addressed once the record was finished."

One song, although still far from completed, was an obvious stand-out, even at these early stages. It was the song that would ultimately provide the album with its name, Tom Rush's 'No Regrets'. Originally recorded for Rush's *The Circle Game* album a few years previously, the song had not been a hit, and most who heard it at the Walker sessions were hearing the song for the first time, among them the session musicians.

B.J. Cole: "'No Regrets' was not the most obvious song to put pedal steel on, but you hear me at the beginning and the end, so they obviously had some plan. As ever, it was all arranged stuff, charted with chord sequences. It wasn't a matter of sitting around and working it out. It was all laid out, pretty much. When it came to my solo, that was up to me. The notes of the solo wouldn't be written out. Like, at the intro and outro of 'No Regrets', Scott just said, 'Take it here!'.".

Harding recalls the birth of this ballad. "The bulk of the title track was recorded at Marquee." Further recording was done at AIR studios. "My memory of recording that track, apart from the vocals, is the guitar solo. I set it up and I heard a run-through. And I then had to run an errand to Wardour Street. Then, coming back and just hearing this amazing solo. That really seemed quite unique for the time. My memory of that solo is the sound of it was driven into the desk. It was a unique sound. Everyone was talking about that sound."

Calver: "The guitar solo was done in about five minutes flat by a session guitarist called Alan Parker. The sound was the result of a funny little quirky idea: we had a little practice amp called a Pignose, on top of a Fender Twin. The Pignose is battery-powered, you'd just use it for rehearsal usually, or quietly working something out. But we actually used both, we mic'd the two amps and got this tremendous big sound. And it has one bit right at the end, a great harmony part. Five or six notes with the orchestra."

Indeed, Parker had been on board since the earliest sessions, way back in 1965. His musical relationship to Scott was by now much more than that of just a paid session man. "By now I was less a player and more of a contributor," confirms Parker. "For that solo, I spent something like about two hours with 'em, and they'd say, 'That line there!' or 'What if we did this, can you try that?' and so on. We sewed the whole thing together.

"I think I tracked the guitar solo two or three times, and Steve Grey would then score the orchestra to my solo, as far as the outro goes. I did loads of stuff through that little Pignose amp. You know David Bowie's 'Rebel Rebel'? That's all me, through a Pignose."

The song was now hugely impressive as a backing track, but it would only truly come into being with the laying on of vocals. Harding may have been young, but he had plentiful experience in recording singers. Even so, he was taken aback at hearing Engel for the first time, even if only in playback: "I remember the impression of this huge singing voice that Scott had. His voice was unusual. It's odd that someone with such a low voice should stand out as a lead vocalist."

Neither Harding nor anyone else would be allowed in the studio when Scott actually sang live. "When it came to doing his vocals," says Calver, "Scott would want only me in the studio. I'd have to send the assistants out. If someone walked into the control room while we were doing the vocals, he would throw the headphones down and get very agitated.

"Basically, the process of recording vocals was one of handling it sensitively. He was all about feel ... everything had to be right. He had to be in the right mood, the time and the place had to be right to give the performance. Generally, the first take was often the best, and it was always worth keeping that first take.

"Scott was not the kind of guy who would sing through it a few times while you got the right microphone and the right sound; he couldn't do that. He wouldn't be able to give you much before the moment had gone. In Scott's case, you had to be ready to capture it. Add to this that he was very self-critical."

With Scott's potently restrained vocal on board, it was obvious that this was a contender for a lead single. Obvious to everyone but the singer himself. Leahy was now in full head-of-the-record-company mode, and he suggested 'No Regrets' as a single. "Scott said, 'You're mad, Leahy.' I asked them to go back in and change it. The basic track had only Scott on it, and it was obviously a very personal song to him. And it was not the record it turned out to be. So, I asked him to put a bridge in or to big-up the bridge and build it into more of a work, including John's voice. And he went back in the studio, and John's voice was added, and the guitar solo was made more of a feature ... and it was quite different to the original version, which had just continued in the vein of the bulk of the song. But I was looking for my first single. Both Scott and Gary argued that it was too long but [they agreed to give it a go]. I thought it was a fantastic record, and once I had that, I knew I had something to work with."

The reaction at the GTO office to the now completed album, while not ecstatic, was professionally positive. A fine-sounding and saleable product had been delivered, on time and within budget. Looking ahead, Leahy was almost certain at this point that there would be a follow-up. On the surface, at least, the reunion had been justified and the Walkers were, once more, part of an extended family.

As the album and seven-inch title track were launched to the public, Leahy told the boys to take a break and consider the next album. In the meantime, as the GTO machinery rolled into action, Scott would be pushed back into the public arena. If he was nervous about such a prospect, it was justified. In this respect, Calver was a first-hand witness:

"Scott had always been hassled. Even I had a problem because of it. I lived in Ladbroke Grove at the time, and I had a public phone number. I started getting all these odd phone calls from people who had got my name off the album sleeves and my number out of the phone book.

"Mainly guys, actually; people saying, 'Oh, are you the guy that did this album?' And I'd sort of say, 'Uh ... yesss?' And they'd say, 'Oh, I've got to meet Scott and I've got to talk to him, can you arrange it?' Or they'd say, 'I've got these songs he really needs to hear,' and all this type of stuff. It started to really worry me. This is not a problem I'd had previously. Eventually, I had to get an unlisted number.

"Scott was, like anyone in the public eye, very protective about his privacy. He had this special code whereby you had to ring this number two or three times and then do it again before he'd answer it. But then, having been approached by some of these weirdos myself, I could understand that."

CHAPTER 15

REGRETS

We made the mistake of trying to make a record that sounded like "The Walker Brothers".

Gary Leeds (1993)

The 'comeback' album was released to modest acclaim in the late summer of 1975. The cover, again by Michael Joseph, is one of the less typical in the Walkers' portfolio. Scott and John are shirtless, with Scott caught mid-swig from a can of beer. Mateus Rosé and Old Grand-Dad have apparently given way to Newcastle Brown Ale. The inner sleeve is a classic 70s montage of muso snapshots on one side and individual portraits on the other. Gary wears the same Boy Scouts Of America shirt he wore as a kid, and the elaborate necklace is not some garish cocaine accessory but a gift recently given to Michael Joseph by his fiancée. The magpie-like Gary had pounced on it for the duration of the shoot.

The packaging was the strangest thing about the record. The music was accomplished, slick, and professional AOR. Reviews reflected just this and, while their press presence was nowhere near what it had been at their height, much like the album itself, it was respectable and adequate.

No Regrets begins with the title track, although a substantially different mix to the seven-inch, as Geoff Calver bemoans. "The album mix of the title track is quite poor. The vocal is very strong and very loud and the backing track is quite weak. That wasn't the single mix, which was much better. But for some reason Scott insisted that the original mix went on the album, which was a shame, really, because if you listen to the single mix, it's more like [forthcoming single] 'Lines'."

John's lead vocal on 'Hold An Old Friend's Hand' (Weiss) shows that Maus had matured subtly in the last decade. The voice is more substantial, while paradoxically sounding smokier than ever. Suzanne Lynch provides harmony vocals, as does Scott, who, intriguingly enough, sings exactly the kind of part that John usually sings when accompanying Scott. The song itself is unremarkable, weighed down by heavy air and a lumpen rhythm section.

The first half of 'Boulder To Birmingham' (Harris–Danoff) has Scott singing in his deep cowboy voice accompanied by Rhodes piano and B.J. Cole's gossamer pedal steel. It sounds like a beguiling outtake from either *Stretch* or *We Had It All*. The chorus suddenly mutates into gospel. This piecemeal effect is redeemed by Steve Grey's exquisite string arrangement. It became a live favourite in the final shows.

Although John gets faux-funky with Scott's subtle vocal shading in the chorus of 'Walkin' In The Sun' (Barry), it fails to raise itself above sounding like a good-natured jam. John is on autopilot – and was actually a last-minute stand-in for Gary, as Calver states. "Scott was quite keen to get Gary to try it and to see if he could do anything with it. In the end, it wasn't successful. Or maybe it was deemed that John was probably better doing it. But certainly Scott was quite protective and keen for Gary to have a bit more profile in what they were doing."

On Janis Ian's 'Lover's Lullaby' (from Ian's *Between The Lines*), Scott sings with powerful tenderness through a small lagoon of reverb. The delicate arrangement and delivery once again recalls the work with Del Newman. It's the only song on side one that comes close to matching the title track.

Scott takes lead vocal again on Kris Kristofferson's 'I've Got To Have You', coming across like a parched and horny cowpoke. One of the more atmospheric tracks, it does seem that the backing and arrangements raise their game to meet a Scott vocal.

On Curtis Mayfield's 'He'll Break Your Heart' (originally written for Jerry Butler and The Impressions), John sings ska for the first time since 'Yesteday's Sunshine', and he wears it well. The band is enthused by the lively arrangement, and the bubbling bass of Brian Odges is particularly playful and irreverent. The strings sound synthetic, however, and are, perhaps, a mellotron.

'Everything That Touches You' (Kamen) had been a hit for The Association. Scott is as professional as ever, but the backing is pedestrian and uncommitted, sounding moribund compared to the previous number.

John, straight-faced in frayed denim, imparts a sincerity that is close to cloying on 'Lovers' (Newbury). The gloopy backing and mawkish lyrics bring to mind a musical equivalent of the sentimental television show *The Waltons*.

The album ends with 'Burn Our Bridges' (Ragavoy–Laurie) and the Walkers do disco. Almost. The intro hints at Barry White but soon descends into variety-show fodder. It's the sound of Scott and co burning bridges they had yet to cross. (Outtakes from the sessions which didn't make it to the album apparently include 'The Long And Winding Road', 'Baby Don't You Tell On Me', and 'People Get Ready'.)

Despite such a patchy and unengaging record, their previous incarnation as pop gods made it relatively easy to secure interviews. "I didn't have any problem getting them press," says Mike Peyton, their press officer at the time. "A lot of people were interested. These were The Walker Brothers!"

Leahy had no real complaints: "We used in-house promotion. I'd brought a good team with me from Bell Records. I don't know if the 'No Regrets' single would have been as big if Scott hadn't agreed to the changes, but it was, and that record put a focus on them for a while."

'No Regrets' was released as a single in November 1975. It took three months to peak at Number Five in the UK charts. Although it departs from the traditional Walker sound of the 60s, it is as much a Walker Brothers classic as any from their heyday, and a country mile from its original, by composer and singer-songwriter Tom Rush.

Rush's version is folksy and acoustic, employing a slightly different accent on the melody and rhythm. The Walkers' interpretation is much more triumphant and 'rock', and it is the definitive reading of the song, making Rush's sound more like a pencil sketch compared to the full-colour, oil-on-canvas panorama of the Engel–Calver production. It also inverts the obvious meaning of the song – an effect they had also achieved with 'The Sun Ain't Gonna Shine Anymore'). Here, they make heartbreak sound like something to be embraced.

Scott's vocal was more refined, much less dramatic in approach than usual, as if he has boiled the voice down to its essence. In this regard, it is a forerunner of the style he would use exclusively from 1984 onward. The main power of such a vocal is in its restraint, within the suggestion of what's held in reserve. Set south of the sombre side of neutral, the voice rarely raises above an impression of recitation, even at the end of each chorus, a point at which any other singer would let loose a little. The slim groove and the sweeteners – strings and B.J. Cole's steel – are sublime and unobtrusive, providing a rich seabed, above which the vocal cruises lugubriously like an iceberg.

In contrast to such subtleties, the legendary overblown lead-guitar solo is slightly obtrusive by comparison. It does, however, serve as a release for the anguish only hinted at within the lyric and vocal.

John's composition on the flipside was 'Remember Me', credited to 'A. Dayam' at its author's insistence, to avoid any royalties being automatically siphoned off by the taxman. As with the name Walker, it remains a mystery why John chose this particular alias – even to Gary. "Whenever you see that name, that's him. But why he picked that as opposed to 'Lance Gold' or something – evidently he must have owed some money. They would have paid it to this name and John got the money. He was great with money but bad with money. He was the only one conscious of money."

John's effort is a fine and sturdy country-tinged rocker that would have easily suited his beloved Dolly Parton or Kenny Rogers, if they, on encountering tax problems of their own, had to take up bar gigs. Insidiously melodic, it was re-recorded by John to greater effect five years later with his then wife, Brandy.

In its initial stages, 'No Regrets' was picking up a lot of UK regional airplay and selling mainly through word of mouth. Inexplicably, the largest radio station in the UK began by ignoring the record, much to the frustration of those who had made it. Calver: "In the context of the 70s, BBC Radio 1 was all-powerful, and they had a very rigid idea of what was suitable to be played on radio in terms of single length. This, presumably, was to accommodate prattling DJs at the time."

"It took about three months for the record to break. It was slow," remembers Leahy, weary at the memory. "It took a lot of effort, a lot of persuading. Radio 1 wouldn't play it at first: they were playing the rival version, the new Tom Rush version that Warner Bros had put out. I had to go into Radio 1 personally and convince them otherwise."

While Leahy locked horns over tea and biscuits with the heads at Radio 1, the Walkers themselves set off on a promotional jaunt of Britain. Scott, in particular, was in no rush to get back on stage, but in all other respects, he was willing to play the game.

Mike Peyton accompanied the three on their trip. "We did a two-week promo tour of the UK, starting in Scotland and working our way down. I didn't have a driving licence and neither Gary, John, nor Scott wanted to drive, so we took the train. Standard, not first class. We'd do radio and local TV and so on.

"Scott was a bit apprehensive at first, but he soon got into it. He was never recognised or hassled that I can recall. It was all pretty easy-going, except now and then John would disappear. He was drinking a lot, and he could be a bit unpredictable. I remember once he went missing in Edinburgh. I think he had some friends there. We lost him for about three days. Scott wasn't happy about it, not at all. But John turned up eventually, with no explanation, and nobody asked, so we went on as before. We used to play card games a lot on those long train journeys. They were nice guys and we got along well. They did quite a bit of promo in Europe too."

As the single was building in the UK, appearances on national television included Mike Mansfield's pop show *Supersonic*, *Top Of The Pops*, and *The Vera Lynn Show* (syndicated to *The Twiggy Show* in the USA). Gary had fond memories of that one. "We did this Vera Lynn thing, and we came out there, as I recall, and did 'No Regrets' and things – and, uh, the whole audience went absolutely wild and really clapping, and this really got us. This was a real cheer, and they were all adults, y'know? There was no kids there. And they had to stop the camera and everything else, and the cameramen were clapping their hands and everything, and it was really flattering. I mean, it was like they were really happy that we were back."

Although it appeared to be John playing live lead-guitar in these appearances, it wasn't always quite so. "I never played live with 'em," reveals Alan Parker, "but I did a lot of TV, especially on 'No Regrets'. Often I'd have to play it live, play that solo live. I'd be behind a curtain playing."

The *Top Of The Pops* appearance (since wiped) featured Scott giving in to a fit of the giggles – just as with 'The Lights Of Cincinnati' a decade earlier. Scott explained to a phone-in caller on Capital Radio that they'd had to do it live when asked if that really was a laughing fit he'd had on television the night before. "If you're outside of the Top 30, there's a union law, which I don't really understand, that means you have to do it live with the orchestra. And the sound that they shoot to you while you're trying to sing and everything else ... you can't hear yourself sing, first of all, and the balance is very bad. Once you're inside the Top 30, then you can 'track down' and sing along over the track, which is a lot nicer. The whole thing became difficult for me to hear so I just started laughing."

There was good reason for joviality, generally. 'No Regrets' was a bona fide hit. Leahy's faith had paid of. "It reached the Top Five by the end of January, I think. We didn't have a party, but what we would do with our acts was, if they appeared on *Top Of The Pops*, we'd all go out for dinner together afterward. Johnny Franz rang me when 'No Regrets' was a hit to say well done. Which was really nice. They were offered a lot of live shows and the like after the success of 'No Regrets', but Scott wouldn't do them. He would not budge on that."

Such success had already cooled on Scott. "Yeah, sure it's important to us that the record's a hit. It matters to us all because it buys you freedom, it doesn't limit anybody. I suppose I am a bit surprised about it being a hit, but then I don't know what a single is any more." The album, rejuvenated by the late-blooming single, had still stalled at Number 49. In the short term, however it did sell steadily and respectfully, becoming the first of any Walker album to recoup while they were still a functioning band.

Even so, Scott was hardly doing a jig. "There are a few nice things on it [but] I don't think anyone in the group is going around celebrating; we still drink every night, but not for that reason." Calver, too, was disappointed that the album was not all it could have been. "The No Regrets album actually ended up being quite weak because some of the best songs were not used." Summing up the whole project thus far, Leahy was astutely succinct. "The Walker Brothers was basically Scott doing songs he wanted to do in the guise of The Walker Brothers."

It does seem that with this first flush of success, The Walker Brothers were once again returning to standard mode. Whatever their plans at the outset of the re-formation, the trio were quickly becoming Scott's baby alone, if only by default. "I met Scott again in the mid 70s," recalls DJ Dave Cash. "He was doing an interview with Michael Aspel for 'No Regrets' at Capital Radio. He was very pleasant and very professional, but when I looked at him properly, I just thought, 'God, he seems so lonely, seems so on his own.'"

In the comfortable lull between the first two GTO albums, Scott spoke of grand plans, at least to the press. He declared that the next album would contain completely original material by all three Walkers and that he himself would, in addition, record a solo follow-up to *Scott 4* that June. (He presumably did not count the four solo albums he had released since that opus.)

While he did not publicly acknowledge that the motive behind the reunion was purely financial, neither did he make any claims to the purely artistic. The true reasoning for the regrouping had probably been an unspoken hybrid of both factors. At this stage, a full-on tour was planned, and, while he still hadn't quite worked out why, Scott admitted that he hated to perform live alone and that he would sooner "dig ditches" than do cabaret again. The Walkers' success meant they could do decent shows on reasonable terms, and make some good money, while sharing the spotlight (that is, the responsibility) three ways. As far as Scott was concerned, this was as ideal as any live experience could get.

Among the more perceptive fans and journalists at the time, there was a feeling, bordering on hope, that while these Walker Brothers albums were artistically somewhat mediocre, their commercial success would allow Scott a financial stepping-stone back to where he had left off in 1969. Such a fate would be unavoidable if Scott Walker were to retain his self-respect, his sense of purpose, and his sanity. But in early 1976, with a hit single as truly great as anything they had ever enjoyed, The Walker Brothers' brandname headed for the Top Five, and it still seemed to all involved that they might credibly enjoy the best of both worlds. Since late 1965, Gary, Scott, and John had been talking about using The Walker Brothers as a planet, around which each could orbit the moons of individual solo careers. All three still held on to this ideal, even now – especially now.

The voice of the 34-year-old Scott Walker in 1976 sounded heavy not only with the usual gravity of purpose but also with an obvious world-weariness. "You walk into a company and they say, 'Well, yes, Scott, we can do a few pieces of your material, but I've got this great dynamic song from the States and, when you hear it, blah blah.' And it sounds just like 'Joanna'," he sighed. "But you wanna do the whole album, man, and that's when you say, 'Fuck it! If it's not the whole thing, I'm not gonna do it.' They always want to support your songs with some schlep from the States."

No live dates materialised around the mini-phenomenon of 'No Regrets', although it was trailed by a glut of television and radio promotion, both in the UK and Europe. The television appearances, in particular, show that if there ever was any chemistry between the two singers, then it was most evident while performing on stage. John and Scott would often sing directly to each other, usually during the "Our friends have tried / To turn my nights to days" verse, accompanying the words with mutual knowing grins. At such times, one is reminded of the *Shindig* duets from a previous era. The apparent relief at being a hit act again is tangible, and all three seem in such excessive good humour, so glad to be in each other's company, that it's a shame they didn't perform a few low-key gigs as a trio. Offers from promoters were forthcoming, but it was Scott alone who refused, fearing, among other hassles, that they would be burdened with the nostalgia angle.

Leahy looked on, noting John and Gary's growing frustration. "No matter how much promoters offered them ... there were lots of offers after 'No Regrets' to work and make some money, and [Scott] would not budge on things, not on something like that. Gary and John would have done it. It would have been the best thing in the world for them. There was no question at that time that they could have done slots in summer festivals, things like that, *but* people wanted The Walker Brothers. In which case they didn't want to not hear 'The Sun'. But Scott would never sell out on those principles. He was very, very firm."

While the album headed south at a much quicker rate than its seven-inch offspring, Scott was talking to interviewers about such varied subjects as the Russian gulag survivor and writer Alexander Solzhenitsyn, the music of Miles Davis, a hatred for Nixon, how he held Howard Hughes as a role model, and why he worried about Henry Miller's health. When he said that the next album would be "stark and direct", it would seem, in retrospect, that he was referring to the album after next. The second 'comeback' album would in fact refine the AOR formula of *No Regrets*.

By the searing British summer of 1976, Leahy had happily taken up the next option and booked the Walkers' new studio time. Following a short song-hunting break, where Maus and Engel took to Nashville to scout for new tunes, the familiar posse headed home to London, clocking in at AIR Studios once again to make what would in effect be *No Regrets* part two: *Lines*.

The base of operations was now moved fully to the AIR complex near Piccadilly Circus, but the studio set-up was essentially the same as that of the previous summer. Although the comeback hadn't been quite the Second Coming some might have hoped for, it was certainly a worthy success. The modest sales of the album may even have cheered Scott, reflecting a selectivity in their audience that suited both the maturity of the group and their record-buying public. People weren't just buying it because of the pretty faces on the cover. However, such a mellow vibe was not necessarily fruitful. An overly comfortable recording scenario often results in a dull record. The Walkers had always made their best work, both as a group and individually, when they were pushing themselves to extremes. *Lines*, by comparison, was being made on Walker autopilot. No one in the Walker–GTO camp seemed particularly concerned by such factors at the time, or was even aware of them. The relationship between artist and label, producer and studio, was largely free of friction, and, in this instance, familiarity bred contentment.

The livin' was easy and the atmosphere friendly. Like Franz before him, Calver was by now essentially the fourth Walker Brother. The well-bred Englishman recalls: "Being American, they always used to refer to each other by their surnames. It would be Engel, Leeds, or Maus. That was always the case. I would always address them by their first names, but they would always address each other and me by surname. I used to say, 'What's wrong with Geoff?' They'd say 'Nothing at all, Calver.' It was a macho thing. They'd only refer to each other by their first name if they'd upset each other or something like that."

Leahy had also noticed this trait, with some amusement. "During the short time we worked together, Scott developed into calling me – the only person who's ever done it, actually, apart from Maurice Oberstein – he called me Leahy. In that slow drawl. Always referred to me by my surname."

High above Regent Street, the recording process proceeded as orderly and professionally as ever, the smoothly flowing sessions only occasionally interrupted by the similarly smooth flow from John's brandy bottle. Although his glass of Courvoisier would sometimes runneth over, often to the point of interrupting John's sessions, his colleagues were used to such scenes by now. In addition, people nevertheless respected his talent and success. No one outside the privileged inner sanctum would have felt the right to criticise John's drinking, and even then, Scott and Gary themselves were a long way from teetotal.

Ultimately, whatever state John got himself into, he did the job. And then some. Not only was John a gifted singer and writer, but also he was, apparently, an accomplished charcoal artist. As the recording wound down, it was mooted that John could draw the cover artwork. Although he was encouraged by Scott and Gary, most of his attempts ended up torn apart by John himself, and the cover would eventually rely on a treated photograph by Mike Putland. *Lines* would continue in the tradition of oddly-flawed Walker covers. Featuring a mustard-coloured line-drawing effect of all three – based on the one-sheet poster for the Brando–Nicholson western *The Missouri Breaks* – the effect is slightly tacky and, like the record it houses, ultimately unconvincing.

The cover was greeted with disdain by the staff at GTO, who were similarly unimpressed by the content. In time, the album would be somewhat lost both critically and commercially. But back in 1976, once mixed, all involved were as committed to and as hopeful of the record as anything they had ever worked on. Calver, in particular, would be utterly dedicated to each and every sonic process of the record, way beyond final mixing. He was completely involved in the final mastering. "In terms of vinyl distortion, there is something called inner-groove distortion, which meant that it was best to keep the more dynamic tracks to the outside of the disc. If you had a really heavy track as the last track on a side of an album, it was more likely to suffer from inner-groove distortion.

"So, while running order was always an artistic decision as to what went where, thinking of the flow of the songs, it was also very compartmentalised, because you were doing it within two sides of the disc, and each was a kind of mini album in itself. This was important, then. Working with vinyl, you were working within a much more defined set of parameters. An album then was supposed to be a good collection of songs that contained other potential singles. That was the whole point.

"And that's the point of 'We're All Alone', the song of choice from

Lines – it seemed like an obvious, very big hit, and we did prepare it as such and did a special single mix."

Lines begins with the Jerry Fuller-composed title track. Scott never sounded more sober than when singing about cocaine addiction. He meditates on the plight of the addict, while the arrangement around him aches and soars grandly. It opens the show perfectly, showing that the Walker–Calver relationship had matured and deepened, like the brandy in John's glass.

'Taking It All In Your Stride' (Snow) is handled by John. Backed for once by a substantial arrangement and working with a strong, bittersweet melody, he matches the opening track gracefully but is let down by the drums. As with the title track, it suffers from the same dead, boxy sound.

'Inside Of You' (Jarvis), a minor-chord and vaguely oriental-sounding ballad, occupies the same sphere as the title track. The hardly typical subject matter and tender harmonising by John and Scott combine for a spooky delight. Scott plays his role wonderfully, and the strings are sumptuous yet streamlined. It is a melancholy wet dream that shines like the world's biggest diamond compared to what follows.

John does the longhaired rocker thing on 'Have You Seen My Baby?' (Newman), which is little more than a mediocre pub ballad. Scott appears briefly on the chorus, and one is instantly taken back to the set of *Shindig* all those years ago.

'We're All Alone' (Scaggs) is the great lost single, and even now sounds like a massive hit. Scott's vocal is classically radio-friendly – it neither overpowers the magnificent backing nor is dwarfed by it. The instrumental coda is the sound of a million mid-70s cigarette lighters held aloft. And yet it is lacking something. By now, Scott was beyond such lightweight material, and no matter how hard he tried, his voice could not disguise the fact. Yet, at the time, 'We're All Alone' offered great expectations.

Geoff Calver: "There was an acetate of 'We're All Alone' pressed up. It was going to be a single but, well … . This song had not been released before. Ultimately, it was a hit for Rita Coolidge, but we had the song first and we … you know, everybody that heard it just said 'Phew!

That's massive.' And we mixed it, we did a single mix, we cut it, and it was pressed – we pressed thousands – but for some reason at the last minute they withdrew it and put out 'Lines' instead. Which, still, is a very powerful piece."

Although Scott had the psyche and vocal tools perfectly suited to songs such as 'Many Rivers To Cross' (Cliff) – songs of heartbreak, struggle, and frustration – by 1975 he had outgrown such forms. The traditional verse-chorus-bridge structure of the ballad could still work for him, but only if the instrumentation was in some way inverted, as his future compositions would prove. Thus, even when he sang a fine song with a respectable backing and production, the end result would be flawed and only superficially satisfying.

'First Day' (Dayam) is an unconvincing, mediocre rocker and a wasted opportunity by its composer, John Maus.

Scott and John hijack the Grand Ole' Opry on Jesse Winchester's 'Brand New Tennessee Waltz' – one of the few productions where Scott's breathing is apparent between his vocal phrases.

On 'Hard To Be Friends' (Murray), John sings from the bottom of his range and with a sympathetic backing, and the verses are heavy with promise. Alas, the song itself lacks something, failing John's performance. Calver: "John had a great voice, but it was nowhere near as intense as Scott. He didn't have the self-awareness that Scott had. He didn't come across as such a, shall we say, cerebral being as Scott. He was pretty much more 'what you see is what you get'.

"Scott was on a voyage of exploration, I think, that extended far beyond music, and he was interested in philosophy and literature. I think the other two were far simpler souls by comparison. But this wasn't a problem as such, because they weren't a band as such. They were two singers and a guy who used to play drums on TV. They were not like a gigging band."

Scott and John go unplugged in Nashville on 'Dreaming As One' (Palmer–Smith). Everything about this recording is unremarkable, from the performance to the song itself. It's an apt finale for an album that almost offends in its inoffensiveness.

The response to the record was muted. The public had not taken to the magnificent lead single, and the overall reaction, radio and press included, was one of indifference.

Other factors helped bring the record down, too. Behind the scenes, there was much debate over the choice of singles and to why and when they were released. This was a source of real frustration for those who had laboured so hard on the album.

"The *Lines* album is a much more cohesive album than *No Regrets*," argues Calver. "*Lines* did OK – not as good as *No Regrets*, but it was a record to be proud of. But it wasn't going to do anything for me; selfishly, in a way, I suppose I'd hoped 'We're All Alone' would have done it. I think it was Dick Leahy at GTO who decided not to go with that, and there were many reasons why that could have been so. Something to do with publishing or business, maybe. I've no idea.

"In the meantime, other versions of the song came out and were very successful. The Walkers' version was released eventually, but so what, you know? It was far too late by then to have the impact that it would have had if it had come out first. But for reasons of which I'm unsure, 'Lines' was put out first, instead. And I was pretty devastated by that, because I thought 'We're All Alone' was gonna be a huge hit."

Although Leahy would undoubtedly have made that decision, he doesn't recall now what informed it. "I'm afraid I can't remember why we didn't put it out as a first single. It wasn't a publishing thing, because I wasn't involved in publishing then. I can't remember. I suppose it was because I just wasn't convinced by it."

Once again, BBC Radio 1 wasn't convinced either. A song about coke addiction was unlikely to be A-listed, even if the radio producers were deaf to the song's true meaning. "I was very proud of the song 'Lines'," affirms Calver. "It had a fantastic dynamic to it, and it was of course a very ambiguous song, probably over the heads of your average Radio 1 listener at the time. It was a very dramatic and dynamic piece, a record to be proud of, but I don't think it had the same commercial appeal as 'We're All Alone'.

"Despite the fact that there was a lot of good music being made around that time, there was also a huge amount of rubbish. Radio 1 at the time was an incredibly eclectic mix of really powerful good stuff with some absolute blatant commercial rubbish going on. There was a lot of 'glitter' music around at the time ... and punk had made an appearance by then as well. Things were beginning to change, and, I think, in that context, 'Lines' as a single was head and shoulders above what was happening. But I don't think that had much impact one way or the other: the punk era really impacted less on artists like the Walkers and far more on some of the traditional stadium bands. You took the rough with the smooth in those days.'

Scott had almost certainly moved on by now, but he still did the promotional rounds, although he sounded weary when asked to name his favourites from the record. "The *Lines* album has about three dazzling tracks, but I think that the rest of the album doesn't come together right. We like 'Lines', 'Many Rivers To Cross', and, I think, 'Taking It All In Your Stride'."

Calver is philosophical. "It was a lot of fun to make those records. Scott didn't seem to recognise his own talent in the way that others did, but maybe that's not that uncommon, anyway, with vocalists." The promise of the reunion had already soured for Scott. "We weren't happy with [*No Regrets* and *Lines*] – not as a whole, not totally. There are some tracks that are all right. But we had a lot of hassles. Just getting back together is a lot of hassle, anyway."

From the onset, touring had seemed an obvious option, but between Scott's reticence, John's drinking, and Gary's lapsed musicianship, the subject had been ably displaced. Following the arid commercial reaction to the *Lines* album and its two singles, the money was once again drying up. Had 'No Regrets' or the bulk of either album been written by Engel–Leeds–Maus, then the publishing royalties would have come rolling in. Instead, while the Walkers watched their bank balances drop into the red, Tom Rush was no doubt able to add another wing to his Colorado compound. Scott's self-written 60s catalogue was, by now, in a state of suspended animation. Apart from any personal investments the three may have made, GTO would have been their sole source of income.

Advances on any third album would not be due until 1977, and, in the wake of the modest commercial payback of the two records so far,

Leahy had good cause to consider such a commitment. With financial concerns now paramount for the Walkers, by the autumn of 1976 they were, once again, enduring what was for Scott a living nightmare – cabaret. Their weekly residencies went reasonably well at working-men's clubs in Newcastle upon Tyne and Manchester, where the Walkers preached to a mix of the converted and cabaret regulars. The crowd reaction was more comparable to Scott's solo shows at the very same places just a few years previously than to the hysterical, frenzied mania of the 60s. They featured few obvious hits in the set. Apart from 'No Regrets', the shows mostly comprised fillers from the recent albums peppered with the occasional standard and, intriguingly, contemporary efforts from writers such as Bruce Springsteen.

The second leg of the tour, at Fagin's in Manchester, was suddenly aborted half-way through when it became obvious that John's drinking did not allow the group to function. Neither Gary nor Scott was burning up the stage each night, anyway. The mutual relief was apparent as the remainder of the tour was written off.

The venture had seemed cursed from the start. British cabaret venues of the 70s are forever associated with also-rans and has-beens, stretching their 15 minutes of fame to seemingly infinite lengths with the artificial respirator of the nostalgia act. True, Scott had refused to sing 'The Sun Ain't Gonna Shine Anymore' and the bulk of the other songs they were known for, which would have been expected by those who patronised such venues. Yet, at the same time, by including such daring material as songs by rising star Bruce Springsteen, it's obvious that Scott wanted to challenge the audience. In doing so, however, he purposefully avoided performing the most obvious and challenging material of all – his own.

To the already converted in attendance, Scott could have sung the proverbial phone book. "Fagin's nightclub in Manchester was a great night out and such a good performance," enthuses fan Margaret Waterhouse. "They did a mixture of all their old standards like 'Here Comes The Night', 'Make It Easy', and newer stuff. I remember 'Many Rivers To Cross' well – they sang it very differently from the way Jimmy Cliff does it, but so deliciously: slowly, more deliberately, with that big, moody build-up style of theirs. They carried that one off beautifully. Their music was very good and well received by the audience on that occasion." In reality, the tour was a skewed attempt at selling-out venues while adhering to principles, but the result was an unhappy compromise, dashed prematurely.

Scott had already spoken publicly about recording a true follow-up to his last real effort. How far away the days of *Scott 4* must have seemed now. If he was suffering a crisis of faith at his own nature and talent, it was a problem that he would address directly during the coming year.

Leahy was considering selling GTO to a larger company. It was doubtful the Walkers would survive such a buy-out while retaining their record contract. At Scott's suggestion, all three decided that their next move should be revolutionary. The following album, to be recorded while Leahy was still writing the cheques, would consist of all-original material, written by The Walker Brothers themselves. For their lead singer, such a seemingly obvious proposition would be anything but painless.

Scott: "It's a long haul back, man, to that dark and dark and dark. It really is. Because it's ... it's a real dark cavern."

CHAPTER 16

LONG DAY'S JOURNEY INTO NITE

Now we're writing our own material, finally, again – because we've decided to get off our asses, because we're basically very lazy, because the years have made us this way, because people would pay you a lot of money ... not to write. So, you get very spoilt.

Scott Walker (1977)

"In the purest sense of the term, Scott was an artist," says Geoff Calver. "As his subsequent solo efforts have been art for art's sake, they are in contrast with what we were doing with the Walkers, which was blatantly commercial. I think Scott, ultimately, felt he should do things for the right reasons rather than take the obvious commercial route. He kept the Walkers going as long as he did because, you know, a guy's got to eat.

"I didn't do anything with him after *Lines*. I think he found the commercial thing a bit distasteful. I think he was a serious musician who wanted to make serious music for serious people. I don't think he really was happy doing the pop star bit, or ever had been. Obviously it had been his living, but I think he'd been a very reluctant pop star, and I think that's why he wanted a change in direction, to go off and do the more esoteric stuff that he did after *Lines*."

As it had been exactly a decade before, 1977 was to be a year of unequivocal change for The Walker Brothers. Since the initial split, all three had, to varying degrees, tangoed uncomfortably with their famous past, both in their personal and public lives.

During 1977, many of those associated with that past would disappear. Johnny Franz died on January 29, at the age of 54, his early death hastened by a chain of countless cigarettes. That summer, Maurice King died, too, from a cocktail of whisky and barbiturates, in the flat above his Baker Street office.

Franz and King had helped drive The Walker Brothers toward pop immortality. As far as Scott, John, and Gary were concerned, with these men went the last nicotine-tinted vapour trails of swinging 60s London. But perhaps their passing was a liberation for The Walker Brothers. The London of early 1978 was abuzz with both the energy of the previous year's punk storm and the new wave that would follow. On a superficial level, the Walkers were set apart from such a climate – and yet, on another, unquantifiable level, they were saturated by the zeitgeist. Scott, Gary, and John were writing up a storm, with no thought of consequence other than to hell with it.

A further reminder of how the Philips years had dissipated came when the enigmatic Ady Semel retired as the Walkers' manager. Their (underworked) live agent, David Apps, took over Semel's role in a limited capacity.

By now, the trio were no longer living together. John and Gary had moved out of the King's Road bistro, leaving Scott alone to write in the oppressively noisy stillness of the flat above. All three converged regularly, and Gary and Scott in particular still socialised frequently, clubbing into the early hours at London's Tramps and Rags nightclubs.

Despite the tepid reception of everything since 'No Regrets', two years earlier, Leahy, who was about to sell GTO to CBS, was ever-supportive. Consequently, the Brothers were in a position where they had nothing to lose. This giddy freedom left them confident and energised. John in particular, who was going through one of his periodic dry spells, spoke with the conviction of a born-again.

"Yeah, I'm teetotal these days," he beamed optimistically, "I'm feeling in darned good shape too. ... Booze was my escape when I became a victim of The Walker Brothers' success. Just as 'No Regrets' was sliding down the charts again, I found myself with some time to think. I woke up one morning and felt a new man. We're going to be tremendously successful again, and there's no way success is going to almost destroy me this time round. I'm going to enjoy it. Already I'm writing some great songs and learning to play some good guitar again. We'll make it because we've got something over most of the groups right now. We can sing, and I can't think of too many others who come into that category. Lots of acts put on a good show but have nothing for the ears. We'll do both. I'm gonna love it – and I won't be looking for an escape through a whiskey bottle."

Inexorably, the urge would return, and John's drink of choice throughout the coming recording sessions would eventually return to brandy and Cognac. Meanwhile, Scott and Gary, still pursuing a strict health kick, threatened to overdose on a rainbow-coloured array of vitamin pills.

They cut further ties with the more recent past when it came to their place of work for the new album, which became *Nite Flights*. The studio of choice was now Scorpio Sound, at Euston. Although it shared basic specifications with the Marquee studio (24 tracks at a rate of £500 a day), it was virgin territory to the Walkers, and the crew manning the newly-assigned studio were all fresh faces.

Steve Parker was the mandatory teenage assistant engineer. It was obvious to him why the trio were not continuing with Calver. "Well, maybe because the first two albums they'd done with him hadn't sold that great, it was obvious to try something new," he reckons. "I think with *Nite Flights*, Scott was trying to get an 'off the wall' vibe, and Geoff Calver was very much a mainstream producer. Scott wanted a new approach, and Dennis Weinreich, partly because he was from California, had a reputation at the time for having his own unique sound."

Weinreich was an up-and-coming studio boffin whose already impressive resumé included big hits with Supertramp and Queen (including 'Bohemian Rhapsody').

"I think Geoff was probably the better engineer," says Weinreich tactfully. "I was probably slightly more 'down and dirty' than Geoff was. His stuff was magnificent, his orchestral stuff. I respected what he did. But I think maybe that what The Walker Brothers were looking for with this album was something a little edgier. Not that he couldn't do it – but my kind of records, the kind of records I used to do with Jack Bruce, Jeff Beck, had a certain atmosphere that I was known for. People liked to work with me for the atmosphere."

Scott would no doubt have gone out of his way to listen to Weinreich's work before considering him as right-hand man. But an equally important factor in choosing Weinreich as head engineer was that he should be ignorant of the Walkers' suffocating past. The young Californian was fully qualified in this respect. "I have to admit to not knowing The Walker Brothers' material beforehand. I was aware of the hits, but I wasn't a fan particularly. They were one of those bands that weren't particularly successful where I was from."

On first meeting, Weinreich was struck by Engel's presence and sincerity. Within moments of the 'job interview', arranged by manager David Apps, Weinreich was already thinking ahead, like a man who had already bagged the job. "I remember Scott arriving at the studio in his orange Volkswagen Beetle," he says. "He had a white pork-pie hat on. Real low over his eyes, all the time. He never took it off. Constantly playing with it. So he talked to me about making records and stuff, and he said to me, 'We need to work out how to record the vocal. Because the thing that pisses me off is that, when I'm ready to sing, I'm ready to sing right now. And I need to be able to perform once, and that's it'.

"So, I got this idea of [Scott's voice] sitting very, very compressed on top of the record without a huge amount of dynamic. I felt, from listening to him talk, that he had a natural dynamic, that it wasn't based on level. It was based on this intensity he had in his voice."

Scott and Weinreich hit it off immediately. "I told Scott that once we had found a vocal sound, we'd keep it for the album and when we're ready to go. And then I'd modify it for the song. I said, 'But when you're ready to go, I'll be ready to go.'"

The younger Californian had the gig. Things moved fast, and sessions were arranged for early February. Scott's attitude was one of fatalistic resignation. It was a state of mind that was, ironically, empowering. He knew before beginning that this would be the Walkers' last stand and as such was going all out to please himself for the first time since *Scott 4*.

"It had gone on too long, the reunion, all the awfulness," said Scott. "I thought, 'I've had enough.' We were told [that GTO] were gonna fold, so went back and pow-wowed and said, 'Let's do something we wanna do.' It was as simple as that."

The ever-amiable Leahy was right behind them. "Dick backed us on this and he wanted us to do it," confirms Gary. It was agreed by all three at the outset that this record would contain no cover versions. In anticipation of the early February starting date, the trio worked apart and in seclusion, honing their pieces as best they could. Even Gary was writing up a storm. By the time they had compared notes and headed for the studio, they were as ready as they would ever be.

"Back then, records came in different categories," states Weinreich. "There were those long and luxurious ones, 'let's book a month and go into the studio', where everyone arrives on the first day and you kinda get some sounds up, and it's, 'OK, what's the first song gonna be?' Ah, well, I got this little riff. And, you know, it's all very slow and mellow. *Nite Flights* was not in that category."

Steve Parker remembers the sessions as well prepared. "There wasn't much rewriting in the studio. We would have spent the first week doing the basic tracks: drums and bass. And then strings and voices et cetera. [Musical arranger] Dave McRae would have a chord sheet prepared, and we all would have worked from that."

Once again, the dynamic of the unlikely trio made a unique impression on the studio crew. Weinreich thought that Scott was "nice looking but nothing special. He was kinda like the type of guy I went to school with. John looked like a real man, you know: kinda hunky. I certainly felt that of the three of them, the one who was in the strongest financial position was Scott. But he certainly wasn't wealthy. John was living out of town, on a council estate, I think. Hard to tell with Gary. Gary was kinda like Dennis Wilson had been in The Beach Boys: he could play, as long as you didn't dissect it, but he was no Hal Blaine."

Scorpio Studios soon became base camp Walker, and although superficially everyone assumed the usual roles, this time around, John and Gary would be much more involved. For the first time, both Gary and John would submit their own material alongside Scott, who throughout the sessions sat beside Weinreich at the mixing desk, the sonic equivalent of an actor–director.

There was a buzz in the air, as usual, but this time its accent was skewed, edgier. The Walkers had never worked together like this. "I got the feeling that they all, Scott most of all, just wanted a total break from what had gone before," notes Steve Parker. "They didn't bring any demos. I mean, you didn't even have Portastudios back then. Scott would play us records he liked the sound of."

While Scorpio Studios no doubt felt like a universe within itself during the six weeks of sessions, the record they made there would ultimately correlate with the prevailing musical trends of the day: punk and disco. And then, as RCA's advertising slogan for the album *"Heroes"* went, there was old wave, there was new wave, and there was David Bowie. In an interview following the sessions, Scott would state: "David Bowie, he's a very smart guy. He comes up with the goods and makes sure of delivery right down the line. I thought, 'Shit, if he can do it, so can I.'"

Parker agrees. "Bowie's album *Heroes* was the reference album while we were making *Nite Flights*. In fact, Scott himself bought me a copy when we started." Parker also points out a major difference between the two albums. "*Nite Flights* wasn't done in the way Tony Visconti, Bowie, and Eno worked. We could have been more adventurous, maybe. If we'd had an Eno character in there, it would have been even more stunning, I think."

Weinreich, the man closest to the Eno role, explains: "It's not unusual in the studio to have a record that you refer to. You're not ripping it off or plagiarising it, you're using it as a reference point, and Bowie's *Heroes* was like that. Scott bought me a copy. He was like that. There was a classical music magazine called *Gramophone* and he bought everybody subscriptions to it. He had a thing about *Gramophone*. He insisted that you read it."

Now that the core crew was established, it was time to draft in the players. Scott worked closely with pianist and arranger David McRae and chose to employ the cream of the session circuit. This would result in the appearance of some familiar faces and some charming incongruities. "Mo Foster on bass, Peter van Hooke on drums; these guys were the top session men of their day," states Parker. "But it meant that they did a lot of different things. For all I know, the day before they did [*Nite Flight* standout track] 'The Electrician', they would have been playing on 'Disco Duck' or 'Chirpy Chirpy Cheep Cheep'."

Sixties stalwarts Big Jim Sullivan and Alan Parker were also involved. Sullivan was glad to get the call and noted that the Walkers set-up was much more bohemian than it had been when he'd first encountered them back in 1965. So much so, that he was under the impression that the Walkers were paying for the sessions themselves. "I just got the sense that they were going to do whatever it was they wanted to do," he says. "It was much more experimental than it had been back at Philips."

Weinreich remembers everyone being open to new approaches and technology. "Big Jim had a Roland guitar synth, one of the first," he grins. "It was kind of a weird thing, it looked like a Les Paul, kinda, and I remember it being delivered, taken out of the box. I'd never seen such a thing! Nobody really knew how to use it, but we had a lot of fun messing around with it."

Sullivan: "I remember I plugged the guitar into the amp and it was set up in such a way that it started feeding back, and the lead was crackling. I went to fix it, and they said, 'No! Leave it like that, it sounds great.' I didn't go mad with effects, as I can recall, maybe some phasing. When I played on 'em, there was not much else going on. No strings; not much at all. So I just tried to use my imagination. There was only a guide vocal, bass, drums, and perhaps keyboards here and there. And I don't think the drums and bass were the finished article, either. It was a bit different to working with 'em in the 60s. They were a bit looser now. Some of the things they'd ask me to do, you know? 'Improvise! Go crazy! Make something up!'"

For those musicians new to the Walkers, it was essentially just another gig. Mo Foster: "It would have just been one session among many. I would have done my parts in about five days, recording two or three songs a session. One did the job as quickly as possible but also as well as one could. There was no 'dark atmosphere', though, no. It was lights full on and staring at music stands." Foster also raised an eyebrow at the unique dynamic of the Walker trio. "Scott was the one who knew anything. The other guys weren't that ... they didn't really play. Gary seemed lost."

Weinreich, a perceptive Walker collaborator, is quick to defend the hapless Gary. "The boys only came to the UK because of Gary," he points out. "There was an incredible loyalty between the three of them. They all knew that the sum of the parts was greater than the individuals. From outside, you may question as to why Gary was even there. But without him, there was a key ingredient missing. John has a great voice but lacks focus. Step in Gary. Scott also took something ... vital from Gary."

Parker: "It seemed that Gary and Scott were mates and John was a bit outside of that. He was more 'regular'. Scott and Gary had more going on between them, I think. I could see Scott and John as a kind of Righteous Brothers thing, but I couldn't see where Gary fitted into that – although the outthere-ness of this album seemed to me to fit Scott and Gary more than it did John. Saying that, Gary was the most unlikely pop star in the world.

"John, with his denim, jeans, and hair, you could see him out on the cabaret circuit, but I couldn't see him touring on the back of this. I think this shows in his songs too. Scott was obviously into his foreign cinema and all that, but you got the impression that John's favourite actor was John Wayne."

While the studio was Scott's domain, he dominated without any untoward expression of ego. As a producer, he was less hands-on and more of a conceptualist, describing what he wanted to the engineers in sometimes slightly abstract terms. McRae backed this up ably with his sound musical training. It was a unique mix that filtered well through the self-contained climate of Scorpio.

"It was an intimate place with a family atmosphere," says Parker. "No ego stuff at all, just a nice bunch of guys." McRae, a veteran of various homegrown progressive rock and jazz-fusion groups, was the latest in a long line of foils for Scott. Throughout the recording process, Scott had always referred to an authorative presence outside of himself. This seemed to have started seriously at Stanhope Place in 1965. The lineage included Johnny Franz, Wally Stott, Reg Guest, and, to a lesser extent, Del Newman. These individuals were visionaries in their own right, but, while technically advanced compared to Scott, they were also unified in respecting his vision.

"McRae is probably not credited as luxuriously as he should have been," Weinreich suggests. "He was the interpreter of Scott's musical vision into something that the musicians could cope with. McRae was the bandleader. He'd go to the piano and say, 'Do you want this chord or that chord?' He was a great interpreter. Scott knew music, no question, but he wasn't schooled in music. His references were obscure and McRae would translate them. He was so important, I thought of him as the producer."

Once Scott had laid down the foundations of drums, bass, and guitar, he would begin to layer and experiment on top, as a painter building from a wash. For someone considered such a 'serious' artist, his methods were often playful. "Scott wanted us to go to a farm in Hayward's Heath and set fire to a piano," grins Weinreich. "He wanted to record the 'ping!' of the strings as they heated up and snapped. I wish we'd done it."

One extravagance was the recording of the Royal Albert Hall's huge organ for the track 'Fat Mama Kick'. The RAK mobile studio was hired and Weinreich, Parker, Engel, and McRae booked the Hall for the day. McRae played some thundering chords that would be flown in to the track back at Scorpio. GTO were at first hesitant at such expense but ultimately acquiesced. "Leahy was good on this project," says

Weinreich. "A lot of people would lose interest in this kind of project as it started to evolve but Leahy maintained interest all the way through." Leahy: "I let them get on with it. My only reservation was that it was more of a Scott Walker album than a Walker Brothers album."

True to form, as the songs slowly materialised it was Scott's compositions that bloomed most vividly. As with the recording of *No Regrets* almost three years before, one track began to stand out among the others. 'The Electrician' was a huge leap in Scott's writing, drawing a luminous, gossamer thread between 'Boy Child' and his brotherless future. With John's voice haloing the least romantic vocal Scott had ever recorded, this was the closest The Walker Brothers would ever get to the 80s. Steve Parker ruminates: "It's interesting that Midge Ure apparently wrote 'Vienna' after hearing this track. If we'd had the technology that was around in the 80s, 'The Electrician' would have sounded more like 'Vienna'."

Parker remembers that they recorded two versions of 'The Electrician'. "There is another version that we recorded first," confirms Weinreich. "It was identical, really. We had a metronome in the control room, and while McRae was conducting, Scott was varying the tempo for McRae's headphones – the metronome was going right into his cans. And McRae was chasing it. But Scott wasn't happy. So we'd completed it, vocals and all, and Scott asked to do it again.

"So we were recording another bunch of songs, and Scott says 'let's squeeze it in.' So we tried, and it was better, except ... we lost the great drum sound we had on the first version. I was disappointed with that aspect. But overall, Scott had been right. The second version was better."

This was not an album with an unlimited budget, by any means. GTO could not afford to have orchestras just hanging around. Scott had to seize his chance when the moment presented itself, as Parker explains: "These were the days when, if you wanted strings, you had to get in strings. You had no samples. The orchestra would be booked well in advance. And real strings always give a track a new dimension. I think once we put the strings on 'The Electrician', then you kind of hear where Scott and McRae were coming from."

Scott was probably working to a preconceived vision that everyone else would have to trust him on. As the recording progressed, it became obvious that not only did Scott know what he was doing but that he had chosen the right personnel to help him realise that vision. "The guitar solo on 'The Electrician' is just scrumptious," says Weinreich. "Big Jim Sullivan had 'been there, done that', but he still performed with energy and passion. Everybody did. Most of the time with session players, you'd struggle to extract a performance out of it. They could play it, but could they perform it? The band who played on *Nite Flights* had passion."

Of the ten compositions, four each came from John and Scott, and the remaining two from Gary. Individual contributions to each track were less democratic, with John adding harmony to all of Scott's vocals but singing half of his own songs solo. Scott would be present throughout the entire album, adding additional bass, textural keyboards, and uncredited backing vocals to 'Den Haague'. The session musicians, reading from lead sheets and chord charts, were not aware of who wrote what, and the basic tracks of the songs were recorded back to back under unified circumstances. When the time came to record vocals, each singer would complete the lead on their own compositions, in batches.

By working apart conceptually – there was still no co-writing going on – even Scott's definitive production could not impose a unified sound. The result would be more akin to a compilation album. "It wasn't a conscious decision to be three separate people on one album," allowed Scott. "John's on all my tracks, but I'm not on his. That's just the way he heard it."

Gary added: "This was three people writing in separate rooms and bringing together this bizarre thing that really worked. I don't know how that worked, cos none of us knew what the other was writing, what the sound would be, or what the thread was – and it turned out that the three different colours made it more weird than it was."

Nite Flights would be the first (and last) album to feature a serious contribution from Gary. His vocals were recorded first. True to his reputation for wackiness, he did not record vocals like anybody else.

"Gary had a nasal problem," chuckles Parker. "And we got around that by laying him on his back to do his vocals. Gary was very hunched, and one of the things we tried was laying him down flat. It opens up the tubes. Helps his breathing."

Weinreich: "Oh yeah, Gary would have enjoyed being strapped down! We had a big grand piano in the studio and we made him lay down on the piano and put sandbags on his shoulders. And that's how he sang it." A supportive Scott ably coached Gary, and the results match those of the previous Engel–Leeds collaboration on 'You Don't Love Me' all those years ago.

Next into the booth was John. Although the studio lights would be dimmed as a matter of course during vocal sessions, John still had to move within the deeper darkness of Scott's shadow. Weinreich was sympathetic. "I felt sorry for John, because by default he was bound to be compared to Scott. He had high values, he was a decent guy, and I liked him. But he had this monkey on his back called The Walker Brothers. But he had a great voice ... although John wasn't a 'one-taker' at all. Not like Scott. But he was not far from it.

"John would 'produce' Scott's vocals, and vice versa. There was a trust. Scott needed someone in the control room to tell him if something wasn't right, if there was a pitch issue ... and the only person who had that was John. No one else could say that to Scott. I mean, Scott is one of the greatest vocalists of all time! So, who can tell him to do that verse again because it wasn't good enough? John. And it worked vice versa."

When the time came for Scott to lay down his vocals, usually done last, he tried, as ever, to move fast. It was less about performing and more about attempting to capture something: a mood, a fragment of a moment. He would occasionally sing while hearing effects on his voice, but any such technicalities would have to be set up and ready to go. "Scott had no time for that shit," exclaims Weinreich. "But ... he was an incredible vocalist." Scott sang in relative seclusion, with only Weinreich and John in attendance. Parker and anyone incidental were, as usual, prohibited from the studio while he utilised the most powerful and sensitive instrument at his disposal.

By the end of February 1978, the album was complete and the mission accomplished. This was no follow-up to *No Regrets* or *Lines* – or to anything else, for that matter. The Walkers' swansong is the most unique and daring album they ever recorded. It's the sound of psyches crashing after the MOR indulgences of *No Regrets* and the aptly titled *Lines*. At its best, *Nite Flights* (working title: *Death Of Romance*) sounds like a comedown. Scott's tracks, in particular, evoke the claustrophobic worldview that the worst drug and alcohol hangovers inflict.

"I took drugs, but it was mostly cocaine in the 70s," Scott would recall in the mid 90s. "It was mainly drinking that was the issue." By his own admission, Gary stated that he "never really liked drugs. I like whiskey". As for John: "In my bad days, I was doing everything to excess, so if I'd gotten into drugs at all, it's doubtful I'd have lived to tell the tale."

Nite Flights, their most narcotic-sounding album, was thus conceived and recorded relatively clear-headed. "The sessions were 100 per cent drug free, as far as the band was concerned. Which was pretty odd for me at that time," laughs Weinreich. "The focus was on health and wellbeing. Gary was not as committed to the healthy outlook as Scott. And John was not as committed as Scott. There was a bit of wine, as I recall, but it was no drinking session."

Similarly, Parker remembers that "they seemed to be clean-living boys, in the studio at least. Scott certainly didn't smoke – I've no idea why he does so in the cover photos of the album. John liked his brandy."

Despite the influence of *"Heroes"*, Engel and Weinreich would only touch superficially on the innovative working methods employed by Bowie, Eno, and Visconti on that album. No songs were improvised in the studio and little was left to random, certainly as far as composition went. Engel was still essentially old-school and preferred to work quickly, using for the most part whatever tools were readily available. Scorpio, while new, was not specially equipped, and the unique and progressive sound of *Nite Flights* was mostly down to the Walkers' attitude and Weinreich's imagination and technical know-how.

Nite Flights begins with the four Engel tracks. On 'Shutout', death goes to the disco. Scott's lyrics are both vivid and impregnable. "There were faces bobbing in the heat / For some rising / From her zone / Moving / Hitting / Holding on." Driven by a crisp disco groove (van Hooke's hi-hat work is particularly excellent), the effect is taut, powerful, and punchy. The nightmare lyrics and ragged guitar work add a vague sensation of vertigo. John's harmony work is perfect, hovering mosquito-like above Scott's lead.

Another nightmare scenario, 'Fat Mama Kick' makes the serious business of the opening track sound more like The Village People. The arrangement verges on the unmusical: Scott and John shriek above slabs of sound. Steve Parker: "That murky 'wash' sound is the piano chords left to ring and slowed down. The only effects we had really were delay and a harmoniser."

'Nite Flights' is a perfect symbiosis of the album's first two songs. It grooves more smoothly than 'Shutout' while retaining the eerie undertow of 'Fat Mama Kick'. It still sounds fresh and modern today, signifying some future that never was. John's vocals are, as ever, impeccable, and Scott reports that the song was written with "[John] in mind [singing] above me all the time".

Dennis Weinreich: "Scott came up with basslines; musically, he came up with everything. The blending of his and John's voices was magnificent. When you double-track somebody, you record a voice, and then you say, 'OK, we'll put the other voice over now,' and it's always loose. You have to say things like, 'Don't say any S's, only say the S's on the first track,' because otherwise you just get a big 'schh', all funny-sounding with the overlap and all. But you never had to say that with John. If he was putting a harmony to Scott, or the other way around, you never had to do that. They had something really quite special in that they knew how each other sang."

'The Electrician', according to Scott, is "about the Americans sending in these people who train torturers in South America". And: "I imagine these lovers in a conversation." The lyrics are among the most explicit of Scott's on the album. This piece is an epic in itself. It starts off sounding like a painting of Hiroshima before blooming into something akin to Rodrigo's 'Concierto De Aranjuez'. It was written by Scott in his London flat "above a very noisy restaurant, late at night.

No one could hear me, so I could work". Dennis Weinreich: "Don't you love the castanets on it? We were trying to get that South American vibe."

Gary's ambiguous but sinister lyrics on 'Death Of Romance' are a revelation: he clearly has a natural gift for the poetic and sounds surprisingly natural singing them, except on the chorus. For a drummer, his timing is particularly awkward, however.

Steve Parker: "The phrasing on the chorus does sound uncomfortable. I don't think it's meant to be. It's more that he couldn't really sing." Weinreich: "Gary was either writing from his experiences or from his fantasies. Either is possible. When Gary wandered off on his adventures, I didn't go with him. So I don't know." An unreleased outtake features a three-part harmony vocal by Gary.

Gary explained that his 'Den Haague' is "about the seediness of Amsterdam. I tried to make a comedy of it". It's among the strongest tracks on the album, slithering along at exactly the right tempo, suggesting seediness, shame, and self-reproach. It was apparently born of true-life experience. Steve Parker: "I remember Gary saying at the time that he was sitting in this brothel [probably run by the notorious Madame Xavier Holland] and someone actually did come in and 'hang their coat over a statue of Christ'."

The arrangement is pure Scott: static strings, treated piano, and even some backing vocals by Scott himself. The Bowie–Eno influence is plain in the harmonised snare and the pitch-shifted tubular bell. The slightly flanged bass sound is actually two basses, with Scott playing along with Mo Foster's line. Foster wasn't impressed by Scott's bass chops. "He was more of a bass owner than a bass player," says Mo. Gary: 'We always wanted to do something a bit funnier; that's why we did the 'Den Haague' thing. That was why we had that radical change into *Nite Flights* from the romantic stuff."

Of John's four contributions to the album, 'Rhythms Of Vision' features a down-and-dirty bass-heavy groove, over which John rasps: "She knows the hard well / And making it twitch / Just waiting to open / Her sacred stitch ... / You've lost to the bitch."

Dennis Weinreich: "Regarding the lyrics: yes, there were

discussions that went, 'Just what the fuck is this about?' I think they were looking to create images with the lyrics, not necessarily narrative. Scott is very naturally narrative, so his songs do have that quality. John's lyrics were more obscure, and I recall on a number of occasions Scott turning to me while John's vocals were going down with that 'What the fuck!' look on his face. There was quite a bit of re-writing during the sessions. Scott particularly had visual links he wanted to make. John, I felt, was looking to try to shock."

John's 'Disciples Of Death' is a neutered, polyester-clad Satan boogieing at Stringfellow's: "I sing to the opening eye / Only fools live to die." 'Fury And The Fire' is more sadomasochistic MOR, with a faintly embarrassed Scott singing along gamely, almost inaudibly in the final mix, while Big Jim Sullivan and the rest provide moving, sterling performances.

The grand production on John's 'Child Of Flames' cannot disguise the vacuum at the heart of this song. At its best, it sounds like an outtake from *The Rocky Horror Picture Show* (and it's a delight to imagine the bouffant John handclapping along to a flamboyantly choreographed dance routine). To be fair, it suffers most by its close proximity to Scott and even Gary's compositions.

Dennis Weinreich: "My personal opinion: the lyrics were mostly contrived, intended to cash in on some kind of punk–rock–glam 'you can say fuck on ITV if you want to' way. The four songs John wrote are not bad songs, but he was trying to do something, create some shock. They weren't about anything. He was not comfortable in his own skin. A well brought-up, solid human being, but you got the impression that all this wonderful stuff had happened to him and he wasn't in control of it. He was looking for some control, and I got the impression that this album gave him that. Y'know: 'These are your four songs – go do what you want.' And Scott and Dave McRae helped him."

By the summer of 1978, GTO was in a state of irreversible flux and about to be sold to CBS. While Leahy had allowed the final indulgence of *Nite Flights*, the general feeling at the GTO office was that Scott should have used the opportunity to record solo. Expectations for this new record were the lowest of all three reunion LPs, and such a pressure-free environment undoubtedly allowed the album to become what it was: a quixotic, three-headed mutant, the truest Walker Brother album ever recorded. But whatever its pedigree, *Nite Flights* was still bona fide music-business product, and GTO would process it as such.

Weinreich remembers the unveiling. "We had a playback for the album, and everybody from GTO came down. It was really strange, because it was like everyone was paying lip service. And no one was really listening to the record. It was more a social occasion. We put the record on and that first side ... it's a funny side, cos the first song is a good song but it doesn't really do much. It doesn't draw the listener in. And I had this horrible feeling that we lost them all. After that, everyone was completely blown away ... until Gary's song. And when 'Death Of Romance' came on, everyone was staring at each other thinking, 'What the fuck is this all about?'"

Gary: "Rod [Temperton, from GTO stablemates Heatwave] said that my two tracks on *Nite Flights* were the best thing he'd ever heard. I liked him." GTO press man Mike Peyton was politely understated in his response. "I remember hearing it and thinking that we were going to have trouble getting airplay."

The album was released in the mid summer of 1978. Although totally ignored by television and radio, the weekly music papers, by now staffed by writers mostly too young to have properly experienced the Walkers first time around, were unusually perceptive and enthusiastic. Those who bothered to listen were duly intrigued, and one can only speculate as to what might have happened if *Nite Flights* had been the Walkers' first GTO release.

The reviews, while refreshingly positive, matched the feeling of those at GTO who felt that the album was not so much an LP by The Walker Brothers but more a Scott Walker EP with six B-sides. They weren't far wrong. *Nite Flights* was less the death of The Walker Brothers and more the reincarnation of Scott Engel.

Weinreich: "It was a fun album to make. There were no jerks in it, the record company left us alone, Scott was great, John was great, Gary was ... great. Musicians were great."

Apart from the alternative vocal version of 'Den Haague' and the alternative version of 'The Electrician' already mentioned, there were a couple of songs recorded during the sessions that never made it to the final release.

'The Ballad Of Ty And Jerome' was mistitled due to an admin error, with the title actually belonging to a quite different reggae song. But it is one of the best things John ever wrote. It was finally released on the CD compilation *If You Could Hear Me Now* in 2001, and John re-recorded it as 'The Ballad' in 2005. It is of a higher standard than anything else by John on *Nite Flights*, but this smooth AOR ballad would not have sat comfortably on the finished record.

Scott's futuristic synth-heavy instrumental 'Tokyo Rimshot' owes more to Jeff Wayne's *War Of The Worlds* than anything from *"Heroes"*. It was finally released, as an instrumental, on *If You Could Hear Me Now*. A vocal version was apparently also recorded.

The *Nite Flights* cover is an abstract gatefold designed by the trendy Hipgnosis and attempts to depict all three reborn. The trio, their hair lightly permed and darkened, sucking earnestly on full filter cigarettes, stare meaningfully into the bleak blankness of tomorrow.

John, borrowing the jacket Bowie wore on the cover of *"Heroes"*, draws on his Camel Light while leaning against some corrugated iron, a man with no particular place to go.

Scott's facial expression veers between psychotically-wounded horror and that of a distracted model in a Marlboro advert.

Gary looks like an existential icon, or at the very least like a sexed-up world chess champion. Appearing like a set of stills from a Beckett-scripted version of *Starsky And Hutch*, the cover once again fails the record.

GTO had the balls to release a single that July, 'The Electrician'/'Den Haague', but it and the album itself would go nowhere commercially. Walkers fans of old just didn't know what to make of it.

It didn't even make a release in the USA. Gary: "If it wasn't country, blues, rock'n'roll ... [America] had to have a category. And, of course, there was no category for this. They didn't know where to put something that was this extreme."

Long-time fan Margaret Waterhouse dutifully bought the record but would rarely play it. "My first reaction on eyeing up the cover as the sales assistant was wrapping it was, 'Oh my lord – have they lost the plot?' These were not the same guys as on the two previous albums, which I had actually liked a lot. I really didn't care for it on first hearing. I was disappointed, because they had changed style from a soft, well-rounded image to an altogether sharper, jagged edge. I felt this was not for the better."

Unlike *No Regrets* and *Lines*, the LP would become a sleeper, gaining a reputation of quality and influence in the coming years, way beyond the minuscule sales it reaped that year. The cooler press got it. "Hip or otherwise, this is frontline 1978 rock'n'roll," the *NME* declared. "Engel has always had similar interests to David Bowie: his European consciousness and Jacques Brel fixation predated Bowie's by several years. If there's any influence at play here, it is latter-day Bowie/Iggy Pop." *Melody Maker* said: "*Nite Flights* makes Bowie's *Low* sound 'high'."

Although there was no fast return investment, almost everyone involved in the record would ultimately be rewarded. "I got a lot of work from being involved with 'The Electrician'," says Weinreich. "It's a lot of people's favourite piece of music. As the 70s turned into the 80s, I got calls from people saying, 'I want you to work on this record I'm doing. Because you did 'The Electrician', right?'"

Steve Parker would go on to work with some of the biggest names in the business but remains unconvinced by one of the most special entries in his resumé.

"It's strange that it's seen as such a seminal album when the way it's been done is a very traditional way to make an album. You would have thought Scott would have gone for an Eno-type character or a load of new musicians. Dennis was not a particularly off-the-wall producer, but he then was the most off-the-wall guy they had probably worked with."

Weinreich is philosophical. "The fact that *Nite Flights* didn't do so well commercially at the time ... well, there was a set of goals at the time of making the record, which were either stated or implied. Whatever they were, there was a kind of honesty about the music you were gonna make. Only later did I add 'commercial success' to the stated goals. It had nothing to do with the quality of the music.

"If we conveyed energy to you as a listener, 20, 30 years after the fact, then we succeeded in doing what we set out to do," Weinreich continues. "We wanted to impact on an emotional level to the listener. This was the stated aim. We wanted to convey an emotion from the studio to the listener in their living room – whether that was a good emotion, bad emotion, real, whatever. We wanted to impact. And there are moments on that record that do that.

"I don't think it should have been a commercial success. I don't think it was good enough to embrace a mainstream audience. I think it was slightly out of time. It was kind of ... it was mature while trying to be young, youthful, and dangerous.

"I recall a conversation with Dave McRae during the making of the album. I said, I'd like to have an image of the guy who's gonna buy this record. I wanna know. Does he live in Essex, drive a Ford Escort, and have a banner across his windscreen that says 'Brian and Shelly'? Or is he a guy in a blue suit with white collar and cuffs? I wanna know who's gonna buy this album, because I've lost focus.

"And Dave turned to me and said, 'I have no idea – but it doesn't make a difference.' I said, 'Well, it kind of does, because I want to make sure that what we're doing satisfies that goal.' And I was completely dismissed. But I didn't know who was gonna connect with [this] Walker Brothers record. And nor did they. It was their last go."

Sadly, neither John nor Gary seemed to be able to capitalise on what was, in effect, their debut Walker Brothers album. "It would have been fine if it made us some money," bemoaned Gary. "The money would have given us that thing to be able to go a bit further ... and do other things. ... It would have been good for the industry too. [But] it was a good stretch, because it started Scott on the direction that he wanted, in a sense."

John also felt an unfinished future. "We kind of went out left-field, and I think it was the beginning of something that could have happened – but it didn't continue. The record company decided to sell itself to somebody else. All kinds of strange things were going on, and none of it was conducive to actually doing anything beyond that point."

One-time fan club president Chrissie McCall thinks that "Gary never got over losing it. He really enjoyed it all. It was his dream."

For Scott, The Walker Brothers was all but over. Although as a unit they still had some unfinished business together – almost unbelievably, following such a sonic rebirth, the trio still had a month of UK cabaret commitments to fulfil – in effect, the dream was dead. *Nite Flights* was their flawed and warped swansong. In this respect, it suited the nature of The Walker Brothers aptly. And it was around about now that Scott Walker began to disappear.

Steve Parker: "I used to see Scott in Chiswick a lot after the album. We lived in the same area. I'd see him queuing in the bank with his hat on, or driving up and down Chiswick High Street in that orange Volkswagen Beetle. The last time I saw him was on a bench in the park. He'd just bought a gatefold LP and was sat there looking at it."

Weinreich: "I saw him twice in the immediate aftermath. I have an image of the very last time I saw him. It was at the end of Parkway, in Camden, opposite a pub that's been closed down now for years, opposite where Regent's Park begins. He was in his car, sitting at the traffic lights, and as I drove past I honked my horn. He rolled down the window of his car and said, 'I'm gonna call you, and we'll go for dinner.' I went, 'Great, Scott.' And I haven't seen him since."

John: "It was kind of weird: we just drifted apart. We were kind of floundering around and didn't know what we were going to do. It seemed like we just drifted apart. It was really odd.

"Nobody said anything ... nobody actually said, 'Oh well, let's do something else, this isn't working out.' We just kind of said, 'OK, let's get together, and we'll find out what's going on, yeah? OK.'

"And then, about three or four months after that, I went back to America, and I didn't hear anything from Scott and Gary for a while. It just dissolved."

Finally, abruptly, The Walker Brothers story had reached its conclusion.

John: "It was a real strange thing. I still don't know what happened. We just ... disappeared."

APPENDIX I
STAGE AND TELEVISION/RADIO APPEARANCES
By SIMON PHILIPS

Entries refer to Walker Brothers' UK appearances (television shows in italics), unless specified otherwise.

1964

n.d.	Los Angeles, California, Gazzarri's (residency)
January	*9th Street A Go-G* (US TV show)
September 30	*Shindig* (US TV show)

1965

January 20, 30	*Shindig*
March 26	*Ready Steady Go!*
April 10	*Thank Your Lucky Stars*
April 18	Leicester, De Monfort Hall (with The Kinks)
April 19	Scarborough, Futurist Theatre (two shows) (with The Kinks)
May 20	Wolverhampton, Gaumont
May 21	Bolton, Odeon
May 22	Leeds, Odeon
May 23	Derby, Gaumont
May/June	*Ready Steady Go!* and *Thank Your Lucky Stars*
May 27	*Top Of The Pops*
June	Manchester, Oasis Club; Stourbridge; Blackpool; Sheffield; Birmingham; Scarborough, Futurist Theatre
June/July	Worthing, Assembly Hall
July	Great Yarmouth, ABC; Morecambe, Winter Gardens
July 10	Manchester, Oasis Club
July 16	Exeter, Odeon (supporting The Rolling Stones) two shows

July 21	Stourbridge, Town Hall
July 29	Blackpool, Showground
July 31	Sheffield, Mojo; Nelson, Imperial Ballroom
n.d.	*Discotheque* (TV Show with Simon Dee) (Gary interview + 'Make It Easy On Yourself')
August 1	London, Palladium [?]
August	Rawtenstall, Astoria
August 12	*Top Of The Pops*
August 13	*Ready Steady Go!*
August 14	Bury, Palais
August 20	Stockport, Manor Lounge
August 21	Boston, Gliderdrome; *Thank Your Lucky Stars*
August 22	Blackpool, North Pier
August 24	*Discs A Go-Go*
August 26	Reading, Olympia; *Top Of The Pops*
August 27	Harlow, Stone Cross Hall
August 28	Nelson, Imperial
August 29	Blackpool, North Pier
September 2	*Top Of The Pops*
September 3	*Ready Steady Go!*
September 4	Market Harborough, Embi Hall
September 9	Oldham, Astoria; *Top Of The Pops*
September 10	Manchester, Oasis Club
September 11	Dunstaple, California Ballroom
September 12	Great Yarmouth (two shows) (cancelled)

September 13	Wembley, Starlite
September 16	*Top Of The Pops*
September 17	Morecambe, Marine Hall
September 18	Norwich, Memorial Hall
September (n.d.)	Colchester
September 23	New Brighton, Tower;
	Top Of The Pops
September 25	Buxton, Pavilion
October 2	March, Marcam Hall
October 3	Coventry, Orchid
October 7	Neath, Empire; Llanelly, Glen
	(or Swansea, Embassy)
October 9	Bury, Palais; Keighley, Victoria
October 11	Warrington, Parr Hall
October 16	Grantham, Drill Hall
October 18	Brighton, Silver Blades
October 21	Portsmouth, Birdcage
	(cancelled)
October 23	Altrincham, Stamford Hall;
	Hindley, Morocco
October 25	Bath, Pavilion (two shows)
October 28–29	Leeds, Queens Hall (two shows)
October 30	Southport, Floral Hall
November 6	March, Marcam Hall
November 7	East Grinstead, Whitehall
November 12	Harrogate, Royal
November 13	Rawtenstall, Astoria
November 20	Buxton, Pavilion
November 21	Bristol, Colston Hall (two shows)
November 25	*Top Of The Pops*
November 26	*Ready Steady Go!*
November 28	*Scene At 6.30*; Guildford,
	Odeon (two shows)
December	London, Palladium (?)
December 3	*Ready Steady Go!*
December 4	Lincoln, ABC
December 5	Leicester, De Montfort Hall
December 7	*Ready Steady Go!*
December 8	*Here Come The Pops*
December 10	Croydon, ABC (two shows)

December 12	Romford, ABC (two shows)
December 16	*Top Of The Pops*
December 17	*Ready Steady Go!*
December 18	Gloucester, ABC (two shows)
December 19	Peterborough, Embassy
	(two shows)
December 25	*Top Of The Pops*
December 30	*Top Of The Pops*

1966

January	Oldham, Princess Ballroom
January 8	*Thank Your Lucky Stars*
January 12	*Now*
January 13	*Top Of The Pops*
January 22	Southport, Floral Hall
January 29	*Thank Your Lucky Stars*; Paris,
	Musicorama radio show
February	Stockton, Tito's Club (one week)
February 13	Portsmouth, Guildhall
February 16	Dudley, Hippodrome
	(two shows)
February 17	Kidderminster, Town Hall
	(two shows)
February 20	Liverpool, Empire (same line-up
	as Portsmouth, February 13)
February 25	*Ready Steady Go!*
February 27	Coventry, New Theatre (same
	line-up as Portsmouth,
	February 13)
March 2	Edinburgh, ABC
March 19	Harrow, Granada; *Thank Your*
	Lucky Stars
March 20	Southampton, ABC
March 25	Finsbury Park, Astoria
	(two shows)
March 26	Birmingham, Odeon
	(two shows)
March 27	Derby, Odeon (two shows)
March 28	Walthamstow, Granada
	(two shows)

THE IMPOSSIBLE DREAM

March 29	Chester, ABC (two shows)
March 30	Wigan, ABC (two shows) (cancelled)
March 31	Glasgow, Odeon (two shows)
April 1	Edinburgh, ABC (two shows)
April 2	Newcastle upon Tyne, City Hall (two shows)
April 3	Leeds, Odeon (two shows)
April 5	Wolverhampton, Gaumont (two shows)
April 6	Manchester, Odeon (two shows)
April 7	Stockton, ABC (two shows)
April 8	Bradford, Gaumont (two shows)
April 9	East Ham, Granada (two shows)
April 10	Leicester, De Monfort Hall (two shows)
April 11	Blackpool, Odeon (two shows)
April 13	*A Whole Scene Going*
April 14	Bristol, Colston Hall (two shows)
April 15	Cardiff, Capitol (two shows)
April 16	Sheffield, City Hall (two shows)
April 17	Liverpool, Empire (two shows)
April 19	Oxford, New Theatre (two shows), date added during the tour
April 20	Oxford, New Theatre (two shows)
April 21	Dublin, Ireland, Adelphi (two shows)
April 22	Belfast, ABC (two shows)
April 23	Hammersmith, Odeon (two shows)
April 24	Ipswich, Gaumont (two shows)
April 27	Tooting, Granada (two shows)
April 28	Luton, Ritz (two shows)
April 29	Portsmouth, Guildhall (two shows)
April 30	Bournemouth, Winter Gardens (two shows)
May 1	Coventry, Coventry Theatre (two shows); NME Poll Winners Concert, London, Empire Pool
May 28	Bremen, *Beat Club* (German TV) ('Land Of 1000 Dances', 'Love Minus Zero', 'The Sun Ain't Gonna Shine Anymore')
May 28/29	Hamburg, Germany, Star Club
Mary 31/June 1	Copenhagen, Denmark, Carousel Club
June 2	Sweden
June 3	Sweden (concert & TV appearance)
June 4/5	Amsterdam, the Netherlands
June 6	Zurich, Switzerland
June 7	Munich, Germany
June 12	*The London Palladium Show*
June 19	Great Yarmouth, ABC (with Dave Dee, Dozy, Beaky, Mick & Tich)
June	Paris, France, Festival de Pop Music, Palais des Sports (with The Troggs, Cream, etc.)
July 2	Berlin-Neukölln, Germany, Neue Welt, Hasenheide (two shows); *Fernsehgarten* (German TV show) (with Peter Frankenfeld)
July 3	Blackpool, North Pier (cancelled)
July 8	*Ready Steady Go!* - Walker Brothers Special
July 14	*Top Of The Pops*
July n.d.	Southend; Dover; Southampton; Morecambe; Hull
July 17	*The Billy Cotton Band Show*; Douglas, Isle Of Man, Villa Marina
July 24–30	Bradford, Lyceum
July 31	Douglas, Isle Of Man, Villa Marina
August 8	Great Yarmouth, ABC
August 11–13	Bournemouth, Gaumont (with Dave Dee [11/12] and The Kinks [13])

August 14	Torquay, Princess Hall
August 18–20	Southport, Odeon (cancelled)
August 21	Blackpool, ABC (with Dave Dee)
August 26	Southend, Odeon (two shows)
August 27	Dover, ABC (two shows)
August 28	Morecambe, Winter Gardens (two shows)
August 29	Hull, ABC (two shows) (cancelled)
September 2	Munich, Germany, Circus Krone-Bau
September 4	Blackpool, ABC (cancelled)
September	Stockholm, Swenden, Nalen Dance Hall
September 15–18	Germany
September 23	*Ready Steady Go!*
September 25	Paris, France, l'Alhambra Maurice Chevalier (with Spencer Davis)
October 1	East Ham, Granada (two shows)
October 2	Leicester, De Monfort Hall (two shows)
October 3	Chester, ABC (two shows)
October 4	Wigan, ABC (two shows)
October 5	Glasgow, Odeon (two shows)
October 6	Dundee, Caird Hall (two shows)
October 7	Edinburgh, ABC (two shows)
October 8	Stockton, ABC (two shows)
October 9	Leeds, Odeon (two shows)
October 12	Wolverhampton, Gaumont (two shows)
October 13	Manchester, Odeon (two shows)
October 14	Newcastle upon Tyne, City Hall (two shows)
October 15	Sheffield, Gaumont (two shows)
October 16	Coventry, Coventry Theatre (two shows)
October 18	Tooting, Granada (two shows)
October 19	Belfast, ABC (two shows)
October 20	Dublin, Adelphi (two shows)

October 21	Slough, Adelphi (two shows)
October 22	Bradford, Gaumont (two shows); *The Billy Cotton Band Show*
October 23	Derby, Odeon (two shows)
October 27	Gloucester, ABC (two shows)
October 28	Cardiff, Capitol (two shows)
October 29	Birmingham, Odeon (two shows)
October 30	Liverpool, Odeon (two shows)
November 2	Exeter, ABC (two shows)
November 3	Plymouth, ABC (two shows)
November 4	Bristol, Colston Hall (two shows)
November 5	Hammersmith, Odeon (two shows)
November 6	Ipswich, Gaumont (two shows)
November 9	Portsmouth, Guildhall (two shows)
November 10	Luton, Ritz (two shows) (advertised as ABC)
November 12	Bournemouth, Winter Gardens (two shows)
November 13	Finsbury Park, Astoria (two shows)
November 29	London, Palladium, Royal Gala
December	Malmo, Sweden and onward tour of Scandinavia

1967

January 11	*Dents De Lait, Dents De Loup* (French TV show)
January 17	Singapore, National Theatre
January 21– February 2	Tour of Australia and New Zealand
January 21	Sydney, Stadium or Festival Hall (two shows)
January 22	Sydney TV show
January 23	Sydney, Stadium or Festival Hall (two shows)
January 24	Adelaide Festival Hall or Centennial Hall (two shows)

January 25	Adelaide Festival Hall or Centennial Hall (two shows)	April 20	Lincoln, ABC (two shows)
January 26	Melbourne Festival Hall (two shows)	April 21	Newcastle upon Tyne, City Hall (two shows)
January 27	Melbourne Festival Hall (two shows)	April 22	Manchester, Odeon (two shows)
January 28	Brisbane Festival Hall (two shows)	April 23	Hanley, Gaumont (two shows)
January 30	Christchurch, NZ, Theatre Royal (two shows)	April 25	Bristol, Colston Hall (two shows)
January 31	Wellington, NZ, Town Hall (two shows)	April 26	Cardiff, Capitol (two shows)
February 1	Hamilton, NZ, Founders Theatre (two shows)	April 27	Aldershot, ABC (two shows)
February 2	Auckland, NZ, Town Hall (two shows)	April 28	Slough, Adelphi (two shows)
February	Promotional & TV appearances in Japan	April 29	Bournemouth, Winter Gardens (two shows)
March 31	Finsbury Park, Astoria (two shows)	April 30	Tooting, Granada (two shows)
April 1	Ipswich, Gaumont (two shows)	**May 3**	**The Walker Brothers announce they have disbanded**
April 2	Worcester, Gaumont (two shows); *The London Palladium Show*	August 6	*The Billy Cotton Band Show* (Scott, 'My Death')
April 5	Leeds, Odeon (two shows)	August 6–13	Stockton, Fiesta Club (one week) with The Ronnie Scott Band
April 6	Glasgow, Odeon (two shows)	August n.d.	Great Yarmouth; Blackpool
April 7	Carlisle, ABC (two shows)	August 26	*Beat Club* (repeat of 28 May 1966)
April 8	Chesterfield, ABC (two shows)	September 19	*It Must Be Dusty* (Scott)
April 9	Liverpool, Empire (two shows)	September 23	*Dee Time* (Scott, 'Mathilde')
April 11	Bedford, Granada (two shows)	September	Cabaret engagements
April 12	Southampton, Gaumont (was to be Hadleigh, Kingsway) (two shows)	October 15	*The Eamonn Andrews Show* (Scott, 'When Joanna Loved Me'); *Juke Box Jury*
April 13	Wolverhampton, Gaumont (two shows)	December	*Pop Inn* BBC radio show with Keith Fordyce (Scott, 'Jackie')
April 14	Bolton, Odeon (two shows)	December	Paris, France; Amsterdam, The Netherlands; Brussels, Belgium
April 15	Blackpool, Odeon (two shows)	December 22	*The Frankie Howerd Show* (Scott)
April 16	Leicester, De Monfort Hall (two shows)	December 25/26	*Down At The Old Bull And Bush* ATV show
April 19	Birmingham, Odeon (two shows)		

1968

January	**The Walker Brothers reunite for ten-date tour of Japan**
January 2	Osaka, Festival Hall (recorded)
January 3	Tokyo, Nippon Budokan (two shows, first show televised)
January 4	Osaka, Festival Hall (recorded)
January 6	Fukuoka
January 7	Nagoya
January 9	Shizuoka, Sunpu Kaikan
March 19	*Cilla* (Scott, 'Black Sheep Boy', 'Best Of Both Worlds')
April 25	*Top Of The Pops*
May 10	*It Must Be Dusty*
May 11	*Billy Cotton's Music Hall* (Scott, 'Joanna')
May 12	NME Poll Winners Concert, London, Empire Pool; *Howerd's Hour* (Scott, 'Jackie')
May 16	*Top Of The Pops* (Scott, 'Joanna')
May 18	*Dee Time* (Scott, 'Joanna')
May 25	*Esther & Abi Ofarim* TV special (Scott, 'Black Sheep Boy') *Pop Inn*
June	Bolton (cancelled)
June 6	Birmingham, Cedar Club, with The Ronnie Scott Band
June 16	Bournemouth, Pavilion Theatre (two shows), with The Ronnie Scott Band
June 21	Brighton, Dome (two shows) with The Ronnie Scott Band
August 16	*The Scott Walker Television Special*, pilot one, Golders Green Hippodrome (broadcast date, recorded August 12)
September	Wolverhampton, Club Lafayette
September 17	*The Sandie Shaw Supplement* (John, 'Homeward Bound', 'By The Time I Get To Phoenix')
September 27	*Esther & Abi Ofarim*
October 1	*Mr & Mrs Music*
October 4–20	Scott solo tour
October 4	Finsbury Park, Astoria (two shows)
October 5	Manchester, Odeon (two shows)
October 6	Bradford, Gaumont (two shows)
October 9	Edinburgh, ABC (two shows)
October 10	Newcastle upon Tyne, City Hall (two shows)
October 11	Birmingham, Odeon (two shows)
October 13	Liverpool, Empire (two shows)
Late October	Chester, ABC (two shows); Tooting, Granada (two shows)
October 20	Coventry (two shows) Last night of tour
Late 1968	Scott's northern cabaret engagements; Manchester, Gaumont (?); South Shields, Latino Club; Sheffield, Cavendish Club
Late 1968	London, Palladium 'Save Rave' charity event
December 22	*Frost On Sunday* (Scott, 'We're Alone')
December 24	*Cilla* (Scott, 'Copenhagen', 'You're All I Need To Get By' duet)
December 30	*The Scott Walker Television Special*, pilot two, Golders Green Hippodrome (broadcast date, recorded August 13)

1969

February 9–15	Birmingham, Cavendish Club, Yardley (Scott)
March 11–April 15	*Scott* weekly BBC TV show broadcast (each show recorded one week earlier) [See Appendix II]

June 21	*Set 'Em Up Joe* (Scott, 'The Lights of Cincinnati')
July 4	Brighton, Dome (two shows)
July 6	Blackpool, ABC (two shows)
July 27	Blackpool, ABC
n.d.	Wythenshawe, Golden Garter Theatre (week's booking cancelled)
n.d.	*The Derek Nimmo Show* (Scott, ''Til The Band Comes In')

1970

n.d.	Batley, Frontier Club (Variety Club), Scott 'residency'
February	Spanish TV
March 7–29	Scott and Gary And The Rain tour of Japan
March 7	Tokyo, Sankei Hall
March 8	Tokyo, Shibuya Kokaido (two shows)
March 9	Tokyo, Kosei-nenkin Hall
March 17	Tokyo, Kosei-nenkin Hall; *The World Of Music* (Japanese TV show)
March 21	Tokyo, Sankei Hall
March 22	Yokohama
March 24	Nagoya
March 29	Osaka, Osaka Furitu Taiikukan
May	*Presenting Nana Mouskouri* (Scott, ''Til The Band Comes In'?)

1971

May	Manchester, Fagin's (cabaret appearances)
September	Batley, Frontier (one week)
October	*Top Of The Pops* (Scott, 'I Still See You')
October 31	*The Golden Shot* (Scott, 'I Still See You')

1972

n.d.	Manchester, Fagin's (Scott, cabaret appearances)
July 1	*2Gs AndThe Pop People* (Scott, 'The Loss Of Love', 'We Could Be Flying'

1973

Early, and November/ December	Manchester, Fagin's (Scott, cabaret appearances)
August	Bolton, Blighty's; Manchester, Talk Of The Town (Scott)

1974

March 10–15	Manchester, Fagin's (Scott, cabaret appearances)

1975

Mid 1975	**The Walker Brothers reform**
December 22	*Music Laden* (German TV show)

1976

February ?

The Vera Lynn Show Copenhagen, Denmark; *Top Of The Pops*; *Supersonic*; Dutch TV Show; *Twiggy* (American TV Show, repeat of *Supersonic* appearance)

British TV and Radio promotional tour: Edinburgh; Newcastle upon Tyne; Leeds; Sheffield; Manchester; Birmingham

Northern clubs: Newcastle upon Tyne (one week); Manchester, Fagin's (one week)

1978

Manchester (one week); Tyneside (one week); Cleethorpes, Bunny's Club (one week); Birmingham, Night Out (one week)

Walker Brothers split for good

APPENDIX II
LADIES AND GENTLEMEN ... THIS IS SCOTT WALKER! – AN EPISODE GUIDE TO SCOTT'S BBC TELEVISION SHOWS

The Scott Walker Television Specials

Pilot show one

Recorded August 12, broadcast August 16 1968
34-piece orchestra conducted by Peter Knight
'Follow Me'
'Days of Love'
'Mathilde'
O.C. Smith – 'Work Song'
'I'll Be Around'
'Genevieve'
Kiki Dee – 'Up, Up and Away'
'Passing Strangers' (duet with Kiki Dee)
'If You Go Away'

Pilot show two

Recorded August 13, broadcast December 30 1968
33-piece orchestra conducted by Peter Knight
'Gotta Travel On'
'And We Were Lovers'
Salena Jones – 'You Stepped Out', 'A Dream', 'For Once in My Life'
'Tender is the Night'
'Montague Terrace (In Blue)'
Blossom Dearie – 'Long Daddy Green'
'Joanna'

Scott

Episode one

Broadcast March 11 1969
'In The Still of The Night'
'Someone To Light Up My Life'
'Why Did I Choose You?'
Salena Jones – 'The Moment Of Truth'
'Winter Night'
Dudley Moore Trio – 'Pop And Circumstance'
Dudley Moore Trio – 'Romantic Notion'
'We Came Through'
'The Impossible Dream'

Episode two

Broadcast March 18 1969
'There Will Never Be Another You'
'Who (Will Take My Place)'
'It's Raining Today'
Jackie Trent – 'I'll Be There'
Jackie Trent & Tony Hatch – 'Love Story'
'The Girls And The Dogs'
'We're Alone'

Episode three

Recorded March 11, broadcast March 25 1969
'Don't Rain on My Parade'
'The Look of Love'
Scott: *"Good evening and welcome to show number three – that's three! – right? [Laughs] I'm sure you all remember the gentleman who was with us on the first week. Unfortunately he couldn't be with us last week because he had flu, and this week he's given it to me.*

Nevertheless, I'm here and so is he: Johnny Franz! [Applause] Yes! Our song this evening was written by Johnny Mercer and Gerard Philippe. It's one of those songs we wish we would have written."

'When The World Was Young'

"Ladies and gentlemen, one of the greatest living musicians in the world today, the poet laureate of the classical guitar, Mr John Williams."

John Williams – Mateo Albeniz, 'Sonata For Guitar'

"This is from my new LP, and I wrote it for a spinster who's constantly haunted by the one fleeting love affair that she knew. And the frightening reality that she can never break away from her domineering mother."

'Rosemary' (accompanied by visual effects incorporating a revolving antique clock, a Victorian photograph, a tea-set, and frosted windows)

Gene Pitney – 'Maria Elena' (with Scott on backing vocals)

'Lost In The Stars'

Episode four

Recorded March 18, broadcast April 1 1969

'My Shining Hour'

'This Is All I Ask'

'The Lady's In Love With You'

Noel Harrison – 'The Windmills Of Your Mind'

'Big Louise'

Maynard Ferguson – 'Girl Talk'

'Funeral Tango'

'Country Girl'

Episode five

Recorded March 25, broadcast April 8 1969

'The Song Is You'

'I Have Dreamed'

'Only The Young'

Scott: *"Thank you. A few months ago I did a*

couple of television shows for the BBC, and on one of them, I invited along someone who I considered a sensational singer. We're not doing a duet tonight, but I had her choose one of her own tunes, and she's on anyway so … she's someone I could sing with for 24 hours a day. It'd be my great honour to sing with miss … Kiki Dee!"

Kiki Dee – 'Games People Play'

"This is a song I wrote for one of my favourite cities, in fact it is my favourite city … and someone I met there a few years ago."

'Copenhagen' (visual accompaniment of a toy carasouel)

Billy Preston – medley including 'Yesterday' and '(I Can't Get No) Satisfaction'

'Sons Of'

Episode six

Recorded April 1, broadcast April 15 1969

'Will You Still Be Mine'

Scott: *"Thank you … welcome to the last show of the series … and it's been a particularly pleasant one for me. We have two tremendous guests for you tonight and, of course, as always, someone you all know, my very, very dear friend, mister Johnny Franz … right over here … one more time."*

'If She Walked Into My Life'

Jon Hendricks – medley, 'Motherless Child' and 'Goin' Home'

'Butterfly'

Ivry Gitlis – violin solo

'If You Go Away'

APPENDIX III
SELECTED DISCOGRAPHY
By ROBERT WEBB

Entries cover UK and US releases, except where stated. Compilations and reissues are excluded. Dates refer to original vinyl releases.

THE WALKER BROTHERS

Albums

Take It Easy With The Walker Brothers (Philips, 1965)
Portrait (Philips, 1966)
Images (Philips, 1967)
No Regrets (GTO, 1975)
Lines (GTO, 1976)
Nite Flights (GTO, 1978)
The Walker Brothers In Japan (Bam Caruso, 1987, recorded 1968)

Singles and EPs

Pretty Girls Everywhere/Doin' the Jerk (Philips, 1964)
Love Her/The Seventh Dawn (Philips, 1965)
Make It Easy on Yourself/But I Do (Philips, 1965)
My Ship Is Coming In/You're All Around Me (Philips, 1965)
The Sun Ain't Gonna Shine Anymore/After The Lights Go Out (Philips, 1966)
(Baby) You Don't Have To Tell Me/My Love Is Growing (Philips, 1966)
Another Tear Falls/Saddest Night In The World (Philips, 1966)
Deadlier Than The Male/Archangel (Philips, 1966)
I Need You EP – Looking For Me/Young Man Cried/Everything's Gonna Be Alright/I Need You (Philips 1966)
Solo Scott, Solo John EP – Sunny/Come Rain Or Come Shine/The Gentle Rain/Mrs Murphy (Philips 1966)
Stay With Me Baby/Turn Out The Moon (Philips, 1967)
Walking In The Rain/Baby Make It The Last Time (Philips, 1967)
No Regrets/Remember Me (GTO, 1976)
Lines/First Day (GTO, 1976)
We're All Alone/Have You Seen My Baby (GTO, 1977)
The Electrician/Den Haague (GTO, 1978)

The Walker Brothers' complete studio recordings are gathered together in the five-CD boxed set *Everything Under The Sun* (2006). Included are 14 previously unreleased tracks.

SCOTT WALKER

Albums

Looking Back With Scott Walker (Ember, 1967, recorded 1958/9)
Let's Go With The Routers (with The Routers) (Warner Bros, 1963)
I Only Came To Dance With You (with John Stewart) (Tower, 1966, recorded 1963)
Scott (Philips, 1967)

THE IMPOSSIBLE DREAM

Scott 2 (Philips, 1968)

Scott 3 (Philips, 1969)

Scott Sings Songs From His TV Series (Philips, 1969)

Scott 4 (as Noel Scott Engel) (Philips, 1969)

'Til The Band Comes In (Philips, 1970)

The Moviegoer (Philips, 1972)

Any Day Now (Philips, 1973)

Stretch (CBS, 1973)

We Had It All (1974)

Singles and EPs

When Is A Boy A Man/Steady As A Rock (as Scotty Engel) (RKO Unique, 1957)

Livin' End/Good For Nothin' (as Scott Engel) (Orbit, 1958; Vogue Pop, 1959)

Charley Bop/All I Do Is Dream Of You (as Scott Engel) (Orbit, 1958; Vogue Pop, 1959)

Bluebell/Paper Doll (as Scott Engel) (Orbit, 1958; Vogue Pop, 1959)

Golden Rule Of Love/Sunday (as Scott Engel) (Orbit, 1959)

Comin' Home/I Don't Want To Know (as Scott Engel) (Orbit, 1959)

Take This Love/Till You Return (as Scott Engel) (Hi-Fi, 1959)

Anything Will Do/Mr Jones (as Scott Engel) (Liberty, 1961)

Anything Will Do/Forevermore (as Scott Engel) (Liberty, 1962)

Mongoon Stomp/Long Trip (with John Stewart, as The Moongooners) (Candix, 1962)

Willie And The Hand Jive/Moongoon Twist (with John Stewart, as The Moongooners) (Essar/Donna, 1962)

Jump Down/Wish You Were Here (as The Chosen Few) (Marsh, 1962)

Let's Go/Mashy (with The Routers) (Warner Bros, 1962)

Adventures In Paradise/Loose Board (with John Stewart, as The Newporters) (Scotchdown, 1962)

Devil Surfer/Your Guess (as Scott Engel) (Martay, June 1963; Challenge, 1963)

I Only Came To Dance With You/Greens (with John Stewart, as The Dalton Brothers) (Tower, 1966, recorded 1963)

Scott Engel EP – I Broke My Own Heart/What Do You Say/Are These Really Mine/Crazy In Love With You (Liberty 1966, recorded 1962)

Jacky/The Plague (Philips, 1967)

Joanna/Always Coming Back To You (Philips, 1968)

The Rope And The Colt/Concerto Pour Guitar (Philips France, 1968)

The Lights Of Cincinnati/Two Weeks Since You've Gone (Philps, 1969)

'Til The Band Comes In/Jean The Machine (Philips, 1970)

I Still See You/My Way Home (Philips, 1971)

The Me I Never Knew/This Way Mary (Philips, 1973)

A Woman Left Lonely/Where Love Has Died (CBS, 1973)

Delta Dawn/We Had It All (CBS, 1974)

The various compilations of Scott's solo recordings (such as the iconic *Fire Escape In The Sky: The Godlike Genius Of Scott Walker* and *Scott Sings Brel*, both 1981, and *Boy Child*, 1992) have been superseded by the career-spanning five-CD boxed set *Five Easy Pieces* (2003).

JOHN WALKER

Albums
If You Go Away (Philips, 1967)
This Is John Walker (Carnaby, 1969)

Singles and EPs
Bother Me Baby/Who's To Say (as John & Judy) (Aladdin, 1958)
Hideout/Love Bug (as John & Judy) (Dore, 1959)
Tell Me/You Can't Have My Love (as John & Judy) (Dore, 1960)
Tell Me/Why This Feeling (as John & Judy) (Dore, 1960)
Live It Up/Oh! No No (as John & Judy) (Orbit, 1961)
I Love You So/ Love Slave (as John & Judy) (Eldo, 1961)
What A Thrill/Beginning Of The End (as Johnny Walker (Almo, 1964)
If I Promise/I See Love In You (Philips, 1967)
Annabella/You Don't Understand Me (Philips, 1967)
Woman/A Dream (Philips, 1968)

I'll Be Your Baby Tonight/Open The Door Homer (Philips, 1968)
Kentucky Woman/I Cried All The Way Home (Philips, 1968)
Yesterday's Sunshine/Little One (Philips, 1969)
True Grit/Sun Comes Up (Carnaby, 1969)
Everywhere Under The Sun/Traces Of Tomorrow (Carnaby, 1969)
Huellas Del Manana/Quienes Somos Nosotros (Carnaby Spain, 1970)
Cottonfields/Jamie (Carnaby, 1970)
Over And Over Again/Sun Comes Up (Carnaby, 1971)
Good Days/Midnight Morning (Green Mountain, 1973)

As a performer and recording artist post-1978, John has been even quieter than Scott, instead turning his focus to studio engineering. His return to recording began in the new millennium with an album of self-penned songs, *You* (2000). This was followed by *Just For You* (2007).

GARY WALKER

Singles and EPs
Here's Gary EP – Twinkie Lee/She Makes Me Feel Better/You Don't Love Me/Get It Right (CBS, 1966)

You Don't Love Me/Get It Right (CBS, 1966)
Twinkie Lee/She Makes Me Feel Better (CBS, 1966)
Cutie Morning Moon/Gary's Theme (with The Carnabeats) (Philips Japan, 1968)
Hello! How Are You/Fran (United Artists, 1975)

GARY WALKER & THE RAIN

Albums
Gary Walker & The Rain Album No 1 (Philips, 1968)

Singles and EPs
Spooky/I Can't Stand To Lose You (Polydor, 1968

Come In You'll Get Pneumonia/Francis (Philips, 1969)
The View/Thoughts Of An Old Man (Philips Japan, 1968)
Magazine Woman/Take A Look (Philips Japan, 1968)
Best 4 EP – Magazine Woman/Take A Look/The View/Spooky (Philips 1968)

APPENDIX IV
SOURCES

Interviews

The following were interviewed especially for this book: David Boon, Billy Bremner, Gloria Bristow, Tony Calder, Geoff Calver, Dave Cash, Tamako Chang, B.J. Cole, Dave Dee, Richard Dodd, Lesley Duncan, Robin Edwards, Mo Foster, Kim Fowley, Bobby Graham, Ralph Gurnett, Phil Harding, Tony Hatch, John Howard, Laurie Jay, Jonathan King, Kiyoko Kojima, Dick Leahy, Andrew Loog Oldham, Keith Mansfield, Chrissie McCall, Angela Morley, Simon Napier-Bell, Pete O'Flaherty, Alan Parker, Steve Parker, Mike Peyton, P.J. Proby, Margaret Reynolds, Keith Roberts, Dave Shrimpton, Big Jim Sullivan, Roger Wake, Chris Walter, Ray Warleigh, Margaret Waterhouse, Dennis Weinreich.

Other quotations were drawn from a range of published and unpublished sources, including an unpublished interview with Joe Jackson and an unreleased interview with Chrysalis TV.

Books

Bogdanovich, Peter, *Pieces of Time: Peter Bogdanovich On The Movies* (George Allen & Unwin 1973)

—— *Picture Shows* (George Allen & Unwin 1975)

Brooks, Ken, *Scott Walker – Long About Now* (Agenda 2000)

Evans, Robert, *The Kid Stays In The Picture* (Hyperion 1994)

Jeremy Reed, *Scott Walker – Another Tear Falls* (Creation 1998)

Loog Oldham, Andrew *Stoned* (Vintage 2001)

McPartland, Stephen J., *All American Boys: The Walker Brothers Genesis*

Owen, Alistair, *Smoking In Bed - Conversations With Bruce Robinson* (Bloomsbury 2000)

Peellaert, Guy and Nik Cohn, *Rock Dreams* (Pan Books 1974)

Watkinson, Mike and Pete Anderson, *Scott Walker – A Deep Shade Of Blue* (Virgin 1994)

Newspapers and periodicals

American Fan Club Magazine
Beat Instrumental
Disc
The Guardian
The Independent
Interview
Melody Maker
Mojo
Q
Record Mirror
The Times
TV/Radio Mirror
Walkerpeople
The Wire

Radio

BBC Radio (national and regional)
BFFBS
Capital Radio
Radio Hilversum
Radio Saga
XFM

INDEX

y

ACKNOWLEDGEMENTS

Thank you to all those who made up my home during the researching and writing of this book –
Tramp, Cassie, Billy, Sweep, Sweet-pea, Harvey, Tweebs, Cali, Eurydice, and Anna.

Thanks also to Graeme Milton, Mark Brend, Chris Roberts, John Williams, Joe Jackson, Robin Edwards, Paul Feneron, Arnie Potts, George Cole, and Michael Pearlstein.

Thanks to Simon Philips for the stage and television timeline and to Robert Webb for the discography.

In memory of Sean Body.